The Military Revolution and Political Change

The Military Revolution and Political Change

ORIGINS OF DEMOCRACY AND
AUTOCRACY IN EARLY
MODERN EUROPE

Brian M. Downing

PRINCETON UNIVERSITY PRESS

PRINCETON, NEW JERSEY

Library of Congress Cataloging-in-Publication Data

Downing, Brian M., 1953–
The military revolution and political change : origins of democracy
and autocracy in early modern Europe / Brian M. Downing.
p.   cm.
Includes bibliographical references and index.
1. Europe—Politics and government—476-1492. 2. Democracy—
History. I. Title.
JN7.D69   1992   940.1—dc20   91-18723

ISBN 0-691-07886-6
ISBN 0-691-02475-8 (pbk.)

This book has been composed in Linotron Caledonia

Princeton University Press books are printed on acid-free paper
and meet the guidelines for permanence and durability of the
Committee on Production Guidelines for Book Longevity of the
Council on Library Resources

Printed in the United States of America

First Princeton Paperback printing, 1993

10   9   8   7   6   5   4   3   2

Standing armies in time of peace are inconsistent with the principles of republican Governments, dangerous to the liberties of a free people, and generally converted into the engines for establishing despotism.

—American Congress (1784)

If the constitutions do not allow this, then devil take the constitutions!

—The Count-Duke of Olivares,
Spanish minister during the Thirty Years' War

The mediaeval army of knights made feudal social organization inevitable; then its displacement by mercenary armies and later (beginning with Maurice of Orange) by disciplined troops led to the establishment of the modern state.

—Max Weber

A clean slate, did he say? As if the initial word of each our destiny were not graven in imperishable characters upon the face of a rock.

—Joseph Conrad

If history is something like the memory of mankind and represents the spirit of mankind brooding over man's past, we must imagine it as working not to accentuate antagonisms or to ratify old party-cries but to find the unities that underlie the differences and to see all lives as part of the one web of life. Studying the quarrels of an ancient day he can at least seek to understand both parties to the struggle and he must want to understand them better than they understood themselves; watching them entangled in the net of time and circumstance he can take pity on them—these men who perhaps had no pity for one another.

—Sir Herbert Butterfield

Contents

Tables

Preface

INFLUENCES of military organization and war are everywhere: in the layout and names of older towns, in styles of the day, on the lives of young soldiers, and in language. The expression "son of a gun," though often replaced by a less quaint expression, comes from the medieval knight's view that firearms were evil; "upping sticks" refers to archers removing defensive spikes; "hanging fire," to operating an early form of firearm, the arquebus. Accounting for all such etymologies would of course be a forlorn hope. My argument is that the military has also shaped political organization and played a formidable role in the making of the modern world. During the Middle Ages, the feudal military was a pillar of that period's rich, underappreciated constitutional order, which formed the initial word of many political destinies and which provided the most important and least arduous path to liberal democracy. But during the early modern period, the critical period of this study, the military revolution—that is, the shift from small, decentralized knight service to large standing armies—entailed, in many countries, the destruction of constitutional government and the rise of military-centered autocracies. Where war was light, or where military modernization was achieved without relying on substantial amounts of domestic resources, constitutional government persisted, and composed the foundation of modern democracy.

This study began when I was an undergraduate studying Russian history. I pondered the country's unfortunate course and wondered why it did not develop in the direction of democracy, as did many Western countries. My suspicion was that the answer lay in the absence of a strong bourgeoisie. This led me to the "bourgeois revolution" literature, and of course to Barrington Moore's study, which further stimulated my interests in the origins of dictatorship and democracy, and showed the power of comparative inquiry. Continued research into Russian and Western history suggested two related points. First, the absence of parliaments and local autonomy in Muscovite Russia set it apart from the Western experience, well prior to the rise of the bourgeoisie or the commercialization of agriculture. Put another way, the medieval West, by an extraordinary set of circumstances that no developing country could duplicate, had a head start in the direction of democracy. Second, military changes in Prussia brought on by wars of the seventeenth century, later paralleled in Russia under Peter the Great, seemed more important than economic or class-based variables in explaining the rise of autocracy. Equipped with these two ideas and a good map of the terrain, I set out some years ago on this project.

Along the way I received encouragement and comments from numerous people, including my thesis committee, Lloyd Rudolph, Theda Skocpol, and John Mearsheimer, as well as Michael Roberts, Mark Kishlansky, J. Russell Major, Reinhart Kosseleck, Bernard S. Silberman, Michael Geyer, Ben Kaplan, Richard Lachman, Charles Tilly, John A. Lynn, Duncan Snidal, Frederick D. Weil, and Robert Jervis. Harvard University's Center for International Affairs and John M. Olin Institute mobilized resources for part of the campaign (apparently without undermining any constitution). Support of a different but no less important kind came from Linda Blanchard, Russell Hardin, and Henry C. Fieldhouse. Anyone engaged in comparative history is also deeply indebted to generations of historians whose specialized works make this sort of project easier, and often fun.

Special thanks go to Barrington Moore, Jr., not only for commenting extensively on the manuscript, but also for posing an important question twenty-five years ago, and for boldly advancing an answer that cut against the grain. Professor Moore has shown that a comparative inquiry, closely investigating historical sources and keeping a salutary distance from the conventional, can lead to pay dirt. This book was written in the spirit of a companion in the search for truth, and it is dedicated to him.

Brian M. Downing
December 1990

The Military Revolution and Political Change

CHAPTER ONE

Introduction

THE DEMISE of unilinear, evolutionary models of political change triggered a great deal of interest in the rise of the state, particularly in Western Europe. Today there are numerous books and articles on state formation, much as two decades ago there were many on political development. Yet in the rush to discard modernization theory and understand the state-formation process, many seem to have forgotten a principal concern of the political development school: the origins and development of liberal democracy. Many have proceeded with their research as though trusting (or perhaps not) in an invisible hand governing academic inquiry.

I hope here to account for the origins of both liberal democracy and absolutism in Europe. This is a study of the origins—the long-run origins—of democratic and autocratic government in Europe. No attempt will be made to provide a full explanation of liberal democracy; such an undertaking would require several volumes. My concern is rather with its institutional, legal, and ideological bases, as they existed in the early eighteenth century, as they developed from the late medieval period. Owing to the blunt succinctness of their beginnings, a fuller explanation of the origins of autocracies will, however, be provided. There are three main arguments. First, late medieval Europe had numerous political characteristics that distinguished it from other major world civilizations. These characteristics, the most important of which were representative assemblies, constituted a basis for liberal democracy, which provided Europe with a predisposition toward democratic political institutions, a predisposition that can never be repeated in the modern developing world. Second, military modernization, the "military revolution" of the sixteenth and seventeenth centuries, led to the strengthening of monarchal power in countries relying on *domestic* resources to finance modern armies. In these countries, the princes did away with medieval constitutionalism and built expansive autocracies, demolishing the fortuitous predisposition. Third, in countries that avoided the military revolution, or found alternate methods of financing war than domestic resource mobilization, military modernization did not destroy constitutional government, and a liberal political outcome, though not assured, as in the first set of cases, was at least more likely.

Most recent work on democracy has understandably been devoted to the collapse of democracy, transitions from authoritarian regimes to democratic ones, and the processes of liberalization that ensue once a basically democratic regime has been installed. But these are fundamentally different processes than the more macrohistorical one considered here. The emphasis in these studies is on those countries struggling in the twentieth century to build liberal democratic institutions, and on processes that have been established in many Western European countries since before the turn of the century. My focus is on the long-run conditions favoring the rise of democracy and dictatorship. There are five macrohistorical schools of democratic development: the works of the classic German sociologists Max Weber and Otto Hintze; modernization theory as put forth by the Committee on Comparative Politics of the Social Science Research Council; the "bourgeois revolution" school as advanced by Adam Smith, Karl Marx, Ralf Dahrendorf, and others; the idealist perspective perhaps best advanced by Reinhard Bendix; and Barrington Moore, Jr.'s account stressing the role of agricultural commercialization.

In his more encyclopedic works, Weber discusses numerous characteristics of Europe that distinguish it from the rest of the world and partially answer the fundamental question inspiring Weber's life work: Why Europe?[1] Among these characteristics are the rule of law, the *Ständestaat*, autonomous towns, decentralized military organization, and citizenship rights. Though brilliant and usually supported by later historical inquiries, Weber's notes on Europe's political uniqueness are not systematically put forth, and the relationship to modern democracy is unclear. Otto Hintze, while also noting the significance of representative assemblies, places more emphasis on aspects of feudal relationships: political immunities, the free contract at the heart of the lord-vassal tie, and the right of resisting unjust authority. He also notes land (as opposed to naval) warfare's negative impact on these institutions and relations, but by focusing on the cases of Prussia and England he gives a rather misleading account of the relationship between war and constitutional government.[2] The tradition of these two classical sociologists remains extremely valuable today despite their relatively undeveloped and unsystematic accounts. They form a starting point for my project. I hope to provide a more elaborate description of medieval constitutionalism, to establish its

---

[1] Max Weber, *Economy and Society*, two volumes, Guenther Roth and Claus Wittich, eds. (Berkeley and Los Angeles: University of California Press, 1978), *General Economic History*, Frank H. Knight, trans. (New Brunswick, N.J.: Transaction Books, 1982).

[2] See Felix Gilbert, ed., *The Historical Essays of Otto Hintze* (New York: Oxford University Press, 1975). On the role of the military in liquidating these feudal patterns, see also Hans Delbrück, *History of the Art of War within the Framework of Political History*, Volume 4: *The Modern Era* (Westport, Conn.: Greenwood Press, 1985).

origins in the dynamics between a formerly independent aristocracy and resurgent monarchies of the twelfth and thirteenth centuries, and also to elaborate precise mechanisms by which warfare undermined it.

The import of European medieval institutions for the development of liberal democracy has been largely ignored by almost all modern social scientists. One suspects that this omission is attributable to the profound influence of social history, a school that has contributed much to the social sciences but that has all too often viewed the shape of the modern world as the result of forces engendered by economic modernization begun in the early modern period, if not later. Still, a few scholars have recognized the significance of medieval configurations. Working within the Weberian tradition, Randall Collins points to the collegial nature of various aspects of medieval European political life (tribal government, towns, feudal militaries), which may continue to exist into modernity despite the loss of the social conditions that gave rise to them.[3] In addition to Collins, only Samuel P. Huntington and Gianfranco Poggi seem to appreciate the political legacies of the Middle Ages. Huntington's observations on medieval institutions effectively encapsulate a major argument of this work: "Countries where the seventeenth-century tendencies toward absolute monarchy were either defeated . . . , stalemated . . . , or absent . . . , later tended to develop more viable democratic institutions. The continued vitality of medieval estates and pluralistic assemblies is associated with subsequent democratic tendencies."[4] Poggi's sketch of the development of European political institutions clearly establishes the constitutional characteristics of the medieval state.[5]

The modernization theory literature is, of course, enormous.[6] Al-

[3] Randall Collins, *Conflict Sociology* (New York: Academic Press, 1975), pp. 393–99.

[4] Samuel P. Huntington, *Political Order in Changing Societies* (New Haven, Conn.: Yale University Press, 1968), p. 127. See also pp. 93–139.

[5] Gianfranco Poggi, *The Development of the Modern State: A Sociological Introduction* (Stanford, Calif.: Stanford University Press, 1978).

[6] Some of the more seminal works include: Daniel Lerner, *The Passing of Traditional Society: Modernizing the Middle East* (New York: Free Press, 1958); Seymour Martin Lipset, "Some Social Requisites of Democracy," *American Political Science Review* 53 (1959): 69–105; Gabriel Almond and James S. Coleman, eds., *The Politics of the Developing Areas* (Princeton, N.J.: Princeton University Press, 1960); Karl Deutsch, "Social Mobilization and Political Development," *American Political Science Review* 55 (1961): 493–514; Rupert Emerson, *From Empire to Nation: The Rise to Self-Assertion of Asian and African Peoples* (Cambridge, Mass.: Harvard University Press, 1962); Gabriel Almond and Sidney Verba, *The Civic Culture* (Princeton, N.J.: Princeton University Press, 1963); Joseph LaPalombara, ed., *Bureaucracy and Political Development* (Princeton, N.J.: Princeton University Press, 1963); Talcott Parsons, "Evolutionary Universals in Society," *American Sociological Review* 29 (1964): 339–57; Lucian W. Pye and Sidney Verba, eds., *Political Culture and Political Development* (Princeton, N.J.: Princeton University Press, 1965); Edward Shils, *Political Development in the New States* (The Hague: Mouton, 1965); Lucian W. Pye,

though the term covers a wide range of scholarship, modernizationists generally posited a unilinear, evolutionary model of political development drawn from Parsonian functionalism. Traditional society, it was held, would break down in the course of the social, political, and economic change brought on by unavoidable contact with modern societies. Precise mechanisms of democratic unfolding were not clearly developed: solving the various crises (identity, legitimacy, penetration, participation, and distribution) was thought to entail increased checks on arbitrary rule and the growth of opportunity, the franchise, and equality; democratic polities alone could provide the adaptability essential to modern industrial societies; and modern societies would engender interest groups that would demand an increased voice in political matters.

The amount of criticism directed against modernization theory has been almost as enormous as the political development literature itself.[7] Modernization theorists optimistically posited their own political system as a culmination point toward which all societies were moving, just as German Historicists and English Whigs had done. Their empirical grounding was only a loose understanding of European history that exaggerated the tradition-modernity distinction. They did not appreciate specific features of the developing world: the burden of a postcolonial state predisposed to authoritarian rule; the weak bourgeoisie endemic to late developers; and the absence of an emigration option serving as a social safety valve. Many late developers perceived a trade-off between democratization and economic growth—one which political and military elites resolved in favor of the latter.

The "bourgeois revolution" thesis pervades, in varying degrees to be sure, the works of disparate thinkers from the classical political economists to Karl Marx,[8] but probably finds its most succinct voices in Adam

---

Aspects of Political Development (Boston: Little, Brown, 1966); Leonard Binder et al., *Crises and Sequences in Political Development* (Princeton, N.J.: Princeton University Press, 1971).

[7] See Karl de Schweinetz, *Industrialization and Democracy: Economic Necessities and Political Possibilities* (New York: Free Press, 1964); Lloyd I. Rudolph and Susanne Hoeber Rudolph, *The Modernity of Tradition: Political Development in India* (Chicago: University of Chicago Press, 1967); Huntington, *Political Order*; Mark Kesselman, "Order or Movement? The Literature of Political Development as Ideology," *World Politics* 22 (1973): 139–54; Charles Tilly, ed., *The Formation of the National States in Western Europe* (Princeton, N.J.: Princeton University Press, 1975); Samuel P. Huntington and Joan Nelson, *No Easy Choice: Political Participation in Developing Countries* (Cambridge, Mass.: Harvard University Press, 1976); Raymond Grew, ed., *Crises of Political Development in Europe and the United States* (Princeton, N.J.: Princeton University Press, 1978); José Casanova, "Legitimacy and the Sociology of Modernization," in Arthur J. Vidich, ed., *Conflict and Control: Challenges to Legitimacy of Modern Government* (Beverly Hills, Calif.: Sage, 1979).

[8] See especially "Contribution to the Critique of Hegel's Philosophy of Law," in Karl Marx and Frederick Engels, *Collected Works*, Volume 3 (London: International Publishers,

Smith and Ralf Dahrendorf.[9] (The theme even haunts many of Weber's essays on German politics.) This view contends that in the course of economic expansion a strong, independent middle class will engender interest groups, civil society, rational legal systems, checks on arbitrary rule, representative government, and an expanding franchise. There are several problems with this view. First of all, many recent historical studies have argued that aristocratic elites maintained political control well into the nineteenth century, even in England and France, the putative homelands of the bourgeois revolution.[10] Second, the complexities of the political ascendancy of bourgeoisies can hardly be conveyed by the simplistic notion of the rise of a unified bourgeoisie. Blackbourn and Eley observe that the rise of the English and French bourgeoisies was a complex set of political processes involving class divisions within the burghers, as well as extraclass alliances with the aristocracy, workers, and other social groups. Third, the bourgeois revolution thesis, following Tönniesian and Durkheimian dichotomies and Parsonian "pattern-variables" regarding modernity and tradition, exaggerates the break with the past and the novelty of bourgeois effects on the polity. Many of the central components of modern government—including the rule of law, representative government, property rights, checks and balances, and immunities—predate the repeal of the Corn Laws and even the enclosure movements of Tudor England. Many were hammered out by king and baronage during the medieval period, and, in the case of property rights and civil law, they are the distant legacy of the Roman Empire, revived by medieval civilization.

The culturalist or idealist view of democratic development is probably best advanced by Reinhard Bendix.[11] This view contends that ideological

---

1975), pp. 3–129, 175–87; and "The German Ideology," in Karl Marx and Frederick Engels, *Collected Works*, Volume 5 (London: International Publishers, 1976), pp. 19–539. Anticipating the numerous critics of the German bourgeoisie, Marx and Engels contrast the politically passive German burghers with their more dynamic counterparts in England and France.

[9] Adam Smith, *The Wealth of Nations* (New York: Modern Library, 1965), pp. 373–96; Ralf Dahrendorf, *Society and Democracy in Germany* (New York: W. W. Norton, 1967); John H. Hall, *Powers and Liberties: The Causes and Consequences of the Rise of the West* (Berkeley and Los Angeles: University of California Press, 1986).

[10] Arno Mayer, *The Persistence of the Old Regime: Europe to the Great War* (New York: Pantheon, 1981); David Blackbourn and Geoff Eley, *The Peculiarities of German History: Bourgeois Society and Politics in Nineteenth-Century Germany* (Oxford: Oxford University Press, 1984). See also Göran Therborn's Marxian critique, "The Rule of Capital and the Rise of Democracy," *New Left Review* 103 (1977): 3–41; William M. Reddy, *Money and Liberty in Modern Europe: A Critique of Historical Understanding* (Cambridge: Cambridge University Press, 1987).

[11] Reinhard Bendix, *Kings or People: Power and the Mandate to Rule* (Berkeley and Los Angeles: University of California Press, 1978). Bendix's idealist emphasis, in my view, sep-

approaches to monarchal legitimation, conceptions of freedom and liberty, and numerous, diffused cultural patterns are key variables in accounting for democratic and authoritarian outcomes. This approach also has its limitations. Ideas cannot be separated from their social settings; that is, they cannot be separated from the institutions and social groups that keep systems of ideas in the socialization process. In addition, constitutional ideas, such as we find in seventeenth-century England, were also found—and in relatively equal strength—in countries where autocracy triumphed. Purely idealist perspectives do not account for the variables that liquidate cultural patterns conducive to democracy. Finally, Bendix fails to put forth clear relationships between values and the institutions of democracy (parliament, civil society, objectivity of law). Hence, the relationship between democratic ideas and their development into modern democracy remains unclear.

The final viewpoint on democratic development is that of Barrington Moore, who, partly in response to modernization theory, developed a model of political development based on rural commercialization. He found three paths to the modern world: bourgeois-democratic revolution, "fascist" revolution from above, and communist peasant revolution.[12] The principal variables accounting for the rise of liberal democracy in England, France, and the United States are in the mode of agricultural commercialization. A strong commercial impulse, reliance on market forces rather than overt political repression of labor, and the absence of peasant revolution combined to provide the basis for liberal democracy. In France, however, the triadic arrangement was somewhat different: here a weaker commercial impulse was compensated for by an *early* peasant revolution that destroyed feudal privilege and cleared the path for a liberal outcome. Weak commercial classes, labor repression, and no peasant revolution contributed to fascist outcomes in Germany and Japan, while the first two conditions and *late* peasant revolution led to the communist path as taken by Russia and China. Although most commentaries on *Social Origins* emphasize, to the virtual exclusion of other conditions, the importance of this commercialization triad, Moore actually puts forth several other conditions favorable to democracy. A rough balance between crown and nobility as well as between town and country, a benign international situation, and the absence of a town-country coalition aimed against peasants and workers are all mentioned as beneficial to liberal-democratic outcomes, whereas their opposites have facilitated authoritarian ones.

---

arates him from subsumption under the Weberian approach, which contains many nonidealist themes.

[12] Barrington Moore, Jr., *Social Origins of Dictatorship and Democracy: Lord and Peasant in the Making of the Modern World* (Boston: Beacon Press, 1966).

Moore's identification of the importance of agriculture for various political developments is an extremely valuable contribution not only to the democratic literature but also to the social science literature as a whole. Yet the subordination of other variables to the three key variables of commercialization does not address the importance of constitutional predispositions and the role of the state system and modern warfare in destroying them.[13] Problems emerge when we attempt to use his analytical framework on the history of Russia. The commercialization of Russian agriculture took place quite late relative to that in the West, in many parts not until the nineteenth century—hundreds of years after early tsars placed Russia firmly on an authoritarian track by constructing a military-centered bureaucracy to defend against the Mongols and other invaders.

Furthermore, sixteenth-century Russia lacked any semblance of the numerous constitutional arrangements that flourished in the medieval West. Muscovite Russia's origin as a subaltern tributary state to the Mongol empire, ruled by princes acting as the Mongols' tax collectors and enforcers, precluded parliamentary control over taxation, vigorous, independent towns, the rule of law, and local autonomy—cornerstones of medieval polities in the West. In short, *Social Origins* does not assess the role of medieval constitutionalism in the development of democracy, or the role of a dangerous military situation in precluding or destroying constitutionalism and fostering an authoritarian, military-bureaucratic state. Inasmuch as *Social Origins* was, in part, a critique of modernization theory, Moore may have focused too narrowly on processes occurring since the beginning of modernization and exclusively within a country's borders.

I shall argue that constitutional arrangements predating modernization and military dangers in the newly forming state system were at least as important as agrarian relations in determining political outcomes in Western Europe. To put the argument in its barest form, medieval European states had numerous institutions, procedures, and arrangements that, if combined with light amounts of domestic mobilization of human and economic resources for war, provided the basis for democracy in ensuing centuries. Conversely, constitutional countries confronted by a dangerous international situation mandating extensive domestic resource mobilization suffered the destruction of constitutionalism and the rise of military-bureaucratic absolutism.

[13] Moore's neglect of the international order has been pointed out in Gabriel Almond's review in *American Political Science Review* 61 (1967): 768–70; and in Theda R. Skocpol, "A Critical Review of Barrington Moore's *Social Origins of Dictatorship and Democracy*," *Politics and Society* 4 (1973): 1–34.

Let us now define some analytical concepts. By "medieval constitutional government" I mean a system of decentralized government that obtained in most of western Europe in the late medieval period. The area of analysis here includes the lands stretching from England, Iceland, and Scandinavia in the north, to the Spanish marchlands (excluding Castile) and Italian city-states in the south, across Burgundy, the Swiss Confederation, and the Holy Roman Empire, up to but not including Muscovite Russia. This region was characterized by parliaments controlling taxation and matters of war and peace; local centers of power limiting the strength of the crown; the development of independent judiciaries and the rule of law; and certain basic freedoms and rights enjoyed by large numbers of the population. Medieval constitutionalism, where it survived, laid the foundations for liberal democracy in the eighteenth and nineteenth centuries. It was far from perfect and democratic outcomes were by no means assured; but the medieval West was at such variance with the rest of the world that a somewhat easier path to democracy was afforded.

The "military revolution" or "military modernization" refers to the process whereby small, decentralized, self-equipped feudal hosts were replaced by increasingly large, centrally financed and supplied armies that equipped themselves with ever more sophisticated and expensive weaponry.[14] The expense of the military revolution led to financial and constitutional strain, as parsimonious and parochial estates refused to approve requisite taxes. These strains and their consequences are the stuff of this study. The third chapter will analyze in some detail the military revolution itself, the specific sources of conflict, and the means by which conflicts led either to the destruction of constitutional government or to a coexistence between a modern army and constitutionalism.

Military modernization and warfare altered many European governments. The most important new governmental arrangement, military-bureaucratic absolutism, will be the main focus of attention, but two other deviations from medieval constitutionalism will also be considered: populist-militarist absolutism and the Cromwell period. I have developed the term "military-bureaucratic absolutism" not to provide the social science literature with still more jargon, but rather to distinguish this form of absolutism from other forms of government to which the term has been rightly or wrongly applied. For instance, many have called the Tudor period absolutist, despite the continued power of Parliament and the rule of law, both of which were dismantled in Hohenzollern and Bourbon ab-

---

[14] See Michael Roberts's classic piece, "The Military Revolution," in his *Essays in Swedish History* (Minneapolis: University of Minnesota Press, 1967); Geoffrey Parker, "The 'Military Revolution' 1550–1660—A Myth?" *Journal of Modern History* 46 (1976): 195–214.

solutisms. Similarly, Charles XII of Sweden has been called an absolute monarch, even though he enjoyed overwhelming popular support, something not normally associated with absolutism.

To distinguish these forms of absolutism from the main focus here, I have defined military-bureaucratic absolutism as a highly bureaucratized and militarized central state that rules without a parliament, either by destroying or circumventing it. Military-bureaucratic absolutism has effectively penetrated and assumed control over most local centers of power, and has taken on the role of managing the economy in order to maintain a large and growing army. Key social classes are subjugated, or, more commonly, placated by offices in the state and army. Military-bureaucratic absolutism is above the law; reason of state has taken precedent over strict observance of the law. Its control over the judiciary is such that political opponents can be prosecuted in the same manner as criminals. Military-bureaucratic absolutism replaced most if not all of the components of medieval constitutionalism and assumed the commanding heights of the country, from which, for centuries to come, it patterned the broad contours of the country's social, political, and economic history.

Some caution must be used with the term "absolutism," much as one now uses the term "totalitarian" only with circumspection. As centralized and hierarchical as the states of Louis XIV and Frederick the Great were, they were not well-oiled machines that followed through with their monarchs' every command. Court intrigue, acquaintances in the provinces, and the need to avoid fomenting too much local discontent limited the power of the monarch. As Poggi wryly observes, "Louis XIV probably never said ["l'Etat c'est moi"]; if he did say it, he did not mean it that way; if he did mean it that way, then he did not know what he was talking about."[15] State officials often used their positions to thwart decrees from above that, for political or purely personal reasons, they deemed inappropriate. One eighteenth-century empress's lament conveys the less than absolute nature of even the Russian monarchy: "With what sorrow, we, with our love for our subjects, must see that many laws, enacted for the happiness and well-being of the state, are not implemented due to the widespread internal enemies, who prefer their own illegal profit to their oath, duty and honor."[16] Regardless of the appearance of autocracy, there is, it seems, always room for politics, from the court of Versailles, to the Third Reich's chancery, to the bureaus of an Islamic republic. The power of military-bureaucratic absolutisms, then, was less than total, but

---

[15] Poggi, *Development of the Modern State*, p. 161n.

[16] Quoted in Richard S. Wortman, *The Development of Russian Legal Consciousness* (Chicago: University of Chicago Press, 1976), p. 8.

nonetheless far greater than that of a monarch saddled by a parliament and the rule of law.

Military-bureaucratic absolutism is the main threat to medieval constitutionalism and a liberal political outcome. But two other threats, albeit more transient ones, may also be identified. "Populist-militarist absolutism" or "caesarism" may be found in late seventeenth- and early eighteenth-century Sweden and, in inchoate forms, in the seventeenth-century Dutch Republic. This second form of absolutism may be defined as the strengthening of monarchal or military authority based on the rallying of popular support. A military leader, royal or otherwise, exploits lower-class resentment of aristocratic or oligarchic rule and emerging sentiments of nationalism, or what Weber called "power prestige." It was the socialist thinker Proudhon who, in a moment of unguarded candor, admitted, "For the masses, the real Christ is Alexander, Caesar, Charlemagne, Napoleon."[17] To this august pantheon I shall in later chapters add the names of Charles XII of Sweden and the Dutch stadholder Frederick Henry.

Parliament, the rule of law, local centers of power, and personal rights are encroached upon by caesarism, but are not destroyed as under military-bureaucratic absolutism—that would undermine the popular basis of support. In this respect, caesarism differs also from fascism, which it otherwise resembles, or adumbrates. The caesarist leader cannot burn his Reichstag. He must use every caution not to expand his power in a manner that alienates popular support, which is antioligarchic in nature, but not a reaction to failed democracy and modernity, as in fascism. Bureaucratic articulation is less than that of military-bureaucratic absolutism, and rests more on personal appeal. Caesarism's personalism and lack of institutionalization are the keys to its not being a long-term threat to a democratic political outcome. Military defeat or the leader's death lead to collapse and the reassertion of parliamentary power, which had never been completely abolished, only made a part of the general popular mobilization. By mobilizing lower orders, albeit in a base manner, caesarism can block oligarchic tendencies and expand political participation.

A third form of militarily inspired government that developed from a medieval constitutionalism was unique to Civil War England (1641–

---

[17] Quoted in Jack S. Levy, "Domestic Politics and War," in Robert I. Rotberg and Theodore K. Rabb, eds., *The Origins and Prevention of Major Wars* (Cambridge: Cambridge University Press, 1989), p. 91. For Weber's dark but insightful discussion of power prestige, see *Economy and Society*, Volume 2, pp. 910–12; also Randall Collins's commentary, "Imperialism and Legitimacy: Weber's Theory of Politics," in his *Weberian Sociological Theory* (Cambridge: Cambridge University Press, 1986), pp. 145–66. See also Joseph A. Schumpeter, *Imperialism and the Social Classes*, Heinz Norden, trans. (New York: Augustus M. Kelley, 1951).

1660). The political, social, and religious unrest of the Civil War period required a moderately repressive state to maintain political authority. The absence of a large state and the retention of parliamentary control over finance distinguish this form of government from military-bureaucratic absolutism, despite parallel, though much shallower, intrusion into localities. Nor is it caesarism, owing to the widespread public antagonism toward Cromwell's rule and to continued parliamentary control of the army. Like caesarism, however, the Cromwell period was transient. With the Lord Protector's death came the disintegration of his government and the reassertion of full constitutional government. This type of rule cannot be subsumed under the other analytic constructs; its uniqueness in the early modern period makes an abstract name pointless. We would be doing history and the Lord Protector himself the best service by calling it simply the Cromwell period.

In sum, military change and warfare in early modern Europe have led to three alternate developments from a starting point of medieval constitutional government. Military-bureaucratic absolutism is the most important because it is the only permanent development, the only one that makes a liberal democratic outcome impossible without a cataclysmic social revolution. Caesarism is a transient movement in the direction of autocracy, relying too much on the vicissitudes of popular support for any permanence. Similarly, Cromwell left no self-perpetuating institutional apparatus. His intrusions on constitutional government were only enough to instill a popular hostility toward centralization and standing armies, as well as a widespread desire to return to constitutional government.

The perspective of political and social change presented here is one that emphasizes the role of the international order on internal political systems. There has been a tendency to view social change as the consequence of purely internal dynamics, indigenous social classes, or economic development. More recently, however, international forces have become recognized as important to political and economic change. Wallerstein has argued that international economic dynamics are critical to the understanding of economic development, class formation, and state strength.[18] Using a geopolitical rather than an economic international perspective, Skocpol contends that state-system pressures played a major role in delegitimizing and paralyzing state structures prior to social revolutions, and also in patterning state formation under the new regime.[19]

[18] Immanuel Wallerstein, *The Modern World-System*, three volumes (New York: Academic Press, 1974–1989).

[19] Theda Skocpol, *States and Social Revolution: A Comparative Analysis of France, Russia and China* (New York: Cambridge University Press, 1979).

More precisely than war or geopolitics, it is a new form of military organization and the means of financing it that are critical. Having benefited from themes in Weber's works, I believe that military organization has been one of the basic building blocks of all civilizations, quite as important to political development as economic structures.[20] Indeed, as shall be argued, military structures have even shaped the fundamental contours of economic ones. Feudal military organization, as begun by the Carolingians in the eighth century, predated and shaped the formation of the medieval state as well as the manorial economy. New forms of military organization began to appear in the sixteenth century, and, as these processes played themselves out, new state structures came into being, and, in some countries, forms of state-directed capitalism emerged.

Thus far, my perspective might sound much like a structural-determinist one: the state system and military organization determine the course of state formation and constitutional change. This is generally so, but it is important to point out that there is no direct causal relationship between international danger and the rise of military-bureaucratic absolutism. As the case of Poland shows, the presence of hostile armies on the frontier does not automatically lead to political change. The destruction of medieval constitutionalism and the construction of a modern army are not achieved by the invisible hand of the state system, but by a monarch at the head of a relatively small but nonetheless independent chancery. As we shall see in later chapters, the crown, though occasionally probing the limits of constitutional propriety, worked within a constitutional framework and was committed to it. But when constitutional institutions could no longer meet the expenses of modern warfare and defense of the realm, kings used the army against the estates and other components of constitutionalism, and transformed the small constitutional state into a large absolutist one, organized to maintain and expand the army. The perspective advanced here is not a narrow technological determinism that argues that military modernization and modern warfare lead simply to a new form of state and social organization. The key to the rise of military-bureaucratic absolutism is not modernization and warfare themselves, but the mobilization of domestic resources to fund them. As we shall see, a country could engage in long periods of modern warfare—even the Thirty Years' War—without mobilizing its own resources, provided that allies, foreign resources, or commercial wealth was available.

Are we dealing with a question of "good," constitutionally loyal mon-

[20] Pertinent citations to Weber will recur throughout this work, from the epigraphs to the final page. Michael Mann has recently suggested the importance of the military in *The Sources of Social Power*, Volume 1: *A History of Power from the Beginning to A.D. 1760* (New York: Cambridge University Press, 1986).

archs and "bad," power-hungry ones? The historical evidence suggests to me that no European monarch freed himself of constitutional limitations on power for personal or dynastic reasons. Monarchs whose ambition led them to attempt to rule without the estates were exiled or executed. The Hohenzollerns and Bourbons faced an increasingly dangerous international environment in which a powerful standing army was essential to survival. No latter-day Cincinnatus could help here by assuming temporary power, defeating the foreign danger, then retiring to his farm. War became a more or less permanent state of affairs, and remained so for centuries. In many countries a permanent, extractive state had to be built, and given the circumstances, this necessarily involved the destruction of the estates and the rest of constitutional government. The choice was less between good and evil than between continued independence and loss of sovereignty.

An argument that sees European democracy developing from a distant past must answer the charge of being a resurrected Whig history. Though it traces the development of democracy, my argument conflicts with the Whig view in several important ways. First, implicit in the Whig view is that England is . . . well, different from the rest of the world. Its freedoms and institutions reach back to the Anglo-Saxon epoch and thus distinguish it from other countries. I argue that England was not appreciably different from most of Western Europe in the Middle Ages or at the outset of the early modern period. The ancient freedoms and institutions vaunted by Macaulay and others also flourished in Sweden, France, and even Prussia. It was Western Europe and not just England that differed from the rest of the world. Second, the Whig emphasis on gradual, unilinear political change in the direction of modern democracy will not find support here. As shall be seen, Parliament itself destroyed more of the ancient constitution than any Stuart king dared, and closer examination reveals coarse grains where many see smoothness. Third, I can only hope to have avoided the Whig view that historical actors somehow strived for liberalization or had in mind the telos of liberal democracy. Men like Pym and Holles abhorred the idea of democracy as we know it; they acted only to prevent the loss of their elite privileges. One suspects that if they could survey modern liberal democracies, they would view their effort to preserve a proper political order to have been a failure.

Case selection has been partially determined by part of my argument regarding the significance of European medieval political arrangements. Inasmuch as I argue that medieval constitutional government was either destroyed by military exigency and replaced by a military-centered state, or preserved as a basis for liberal democracy, I have restricted the cases to those countries with medieval constitutionalism. Accordingly, I have ruled out China, Japan, Russia, and many other countries. (I have, however, used those countries in the next chapter to establish my claim of Western Europe's unique medieval constitutionalism.) This work is Europocentric, not in the sense of claiming the superiority of Europe, but only in the sense that the dynamics I analyze are found only there. The dynamics of military modernization and state formation are doubtless to be found in Habsburg Spain, Meiji Japan, Petrine Russia, and perhaps also Stalinist Russia, but without the prior existence of constitutional government. The more or less autocratic premodern pasts of these countries made military modernization and state expansion an easier process, but also a less politically interesting one.

Case selection was not random from among constitutional European countries. Two other considerations were operative in the selection process. First, countries had to have been involved in varying levels of warfare, from the relatively light warfare of England to the extremely heavy, protracted conflicts of Prussia. Second, the cases under study had to exhibit different political outcomes: the preservation of constitutionalism, its destruction and replacement with autocracy, and the loss of sovereignty. Six cases have been drawn from European history, with a wide range of involvement in war and of political variation. I have also decided against including certain cases after determining a basic similarity between their political trajectories and those of another case already under study. For example, Venetian political history has many critical similarities with that of the Dutch Republic, and therefore discussion of it is limited to relatively brief comparative comments. I have, I believe, accounted for the major military-state dynamics operative in early modern Europe.

． ． ．

The following chapter will sketch the array of constitutional arrangements that I argue were unique to medieval Europe and that served as a basis for democracy. I will also seek to account for this political uniqueness, then contrast the European experience with that of Muscovite Russia, Japan, and China. This discussion will highlight the differences and test my account of the origins of medieval constitutionalism. Chapter 3 will look at medieval military organization, its obsolescence in later centuries, and the military revolution that followed. Sources of conflict between modern armies and the constitution will be outlined as well as means of obviating that conflict. Chapter 4 is devoted to the political history of Brandenburg-Prussia, where the military revolution caused the destruction of the constitutional order and the development of a stable military-bureaucratic absolutism that persisted in some form until the fall of the

Hohenzollerns in 1918. After that, I shall look at France, a country that follows the Prussian pattern but with the critical difference of its absolutist state's vulnerabilities, which led to collapse in 1789 and to a second chance for democracy. Chapter 6 analyzes Poland, a country that failed to modernize despite military dangers and consequently faced partition by surrounding absolutist powers. The next chapter discusses English political history, another case of an unmodernized army, but one in a country largely removed from the tremendous wars raging on the continent. Chapter 8 is devoted to Sweden, a country generally neglected in most studies, despite its overwhelming preeminence in early modern history. Sweden built a powerful modern army, but, owing to its reliance on plunder, that is, on foreign resources, it did not suffer the destruction of constitutional arrangements. Chapter 9 looks at the Dutch Republic, which also engaged in protracted, large-scale war without upsetting its constitution. This was effected not because of foreign resource mobilization, but to the benefits of alliances, geography, and the phenomenal wealth of that maritime republic. The final chapter will summarize the findings, discuss theoretical significances, and make comparisons with other major arguments on democratic development.

CHAPTER TWO

Medieval Origins of Constitutional Government

To say that European social, political, and economic history is markedly different from that of the rest of the world is to say nothing new. The West was the first to develop innovative agricultural techniques, large-scale capitalist production, and a system of states. Europe was also the first—and, unfortunately, virtually the last—to develop democratic political systems that featured institutional checks on political monopoly, varying but frequently increasing degrees of political representation, chartered rights of citizenship, and the rule of law. The roots of these systems date back to the Middle Ages.

The social, political, and economic changes that decisively patterned European and consequently world history have usually been interpreted as coterminous and interrelated. The notion that liberal democracy was the political consequence of economic changes and the rise of middle classes is deeply ingrained in many social theories. Yet the political struggles of nineteenth-century Europe, though decisive for the *growth* of liberal democracy, must not be confounded with its *origins*. When Chartists marched for citizenship rights, middle classes pressed for parliamentary reforms, subjects demanded legal guarantees, and representative assemblies sought to reduce monarchal power, they were fighting new battles, but in old wars, the earlier campaigns of which had been forgotten by the new participants, as they have been by not a few social scientists. Struggles over institutions, rights, and ideas marked much of the political history of medieval Europe and helped to shape the modern world. Towns flourished in the medieval period and provided basic citizenship rights, distinguishing town dwellers from the villeinage outside the walls. Throughout Europe's patchwork of kingdoms, duchies, and bishoprics there were elective representative assemblies (parliaments, estates, cortes) where nobles, burghers, clerics, and sometimes even peasants determined basic matters of government within a consensual framework with the prince. The principle of royal subordination to law was reasserted by the baronage at Runnymede and elsewhere. The critical institutional groundwork upon which liberal democracy was built predates the commercialization of agriculture, the general crisis, the rise of the

This chapter first appeared in *Theory and Society* 18 (1989): 213–47. It is reproduced courtesy of Kluwer Academic Publishers.

bourgeoisie, any appreciable level of per capita income, and anything that can be meaningfully called modernization. Liberal democracy's tenuous foundations were laid centuries prior to the great transformations of the modern period.

ORIGINS OF WESTERN CONSTITUTIONALISM

Before examining components of medieval constitutionalism, it will be useful to attempt an understanding of their origins. Three principal conditions in medieval Europe provided a predisposition to democracy: a rough balance between crown and nobility, decentralized military systems, and peasant property rights and reciprocal ties to the landlord. Though one or more of these may have obtained in other parts of the world, the combination of all three, as well as the strength of each, was unique to Western Europe.

The key to a rough balance between crown and nobility lies in the incomplete collapse of the Carolingian Empire in the ninth century and of the Holy Roman Empire in the thirteenth, followed by the reemergence of imperial or princely authority, then contestation between center and locality.[1] From this set of circumstances emerged compromises, power sharing, and a climate of partial trust and partial mistrust, which informed much of medieval constitutionalism before it settled into a stable system of consensual government. The Carolingian Empire was built by military conquest and held together by short-lived fealty and the centripetal effects of the threat from Islam. Beyond this, the Carolingian state was only a rudimentary household government, with only the barest functional specialization among the *vassi dominici* residing with the great warrior at Aachen. There was no communication system, as the Romans had had, to provide effective supervision from the center. No central finance developed; the Carolingians relied primarily on demesne revenue and war booty.[2] Justice, though administered by circuit judges (*scabini, Schöffen, echevin*), was based on numerous tribal customs, not on a central codification. Military levies, too, came to rely on mobilization of numerous tribes of the Empire.[3] Such an empire had more pulling it apart than holding it together. Disintegration began, even during Charlemagne's lifetime, in the marchlands, where, owing to more immediate

---

[1] Barrington Moore, Jr., observes the importance of a "rough balance" between crown and nobility; however, a systematic evaluation of this balance is not undertaken. This chapter builds on that insight. See *Social Origins of Dictatorship and Democracy: Lord and Peasant in the Making of the Modern World* (Boston: Beacon Press, 1966), pp. 417ff.

[2] François Louis Ganshof, *Frankish Institutions under Charlemagne* (Providence, R.I.: Brown University Press, 1968), p. 34.

[3] Ibid., p. 65.

external danger, margraves had been given greater authority.[4] With the emperor's death (814), the empire was torn apart by aristocratic opportunism, appanage struggles, and destructive invasions by Muslims, Vikings, and Magyars.[5] By the early ninth century the Carolingian Empire had all but disintegrated and only a modicum of central authority remained. But that was important.

The Holy Roman Empire was built in the tenth century out of the territories of the eastern Carolingian Empire. Otto the Great restored empire in Central Europe by vanquishing the Magyars, much as the Carolingians had built their empire by defeating the Muslim invasion. Otto was no more successful than Charles in maintaining aristocratic fealty or constructing a lasting imperial system. Otto and successive Salic and Hohenstauffen kings tried to build networks of local officials, *ministeriales*, to carry through policy, but vassals countered with their own ministeriales. Neither group of local officials remained loyal to its nominal lord: each "formed a fraternity that was very conscious of its position, full of demands, and loudly insistent on its rights."[6] This description is, to say the least, at variance with romantic conceptions of a medieval state and society held together by binding ties of fealty between lord and vassal, sealed by sacred vows after a prayerful, purifying vigil. Yet one recurrent theme in medieval history, and one that presents itself with dismal routine, is the unextenuated treachery of vassals.[7]

Otto's successors were nonetheless able to build a state with the assistance of the considerable economic resources of the Church, whose wealth and administrative skills were badly needed. This arrangement augured well for the empire until it ran afoul of the Church's post-Cluniac ambitions to develop its own corporate structure, independent of

[4] Heinrich Fichtenau, *The Carolingian Empire* (Toronto: University of Toronto Press, 1982), pp. 108–9.

[5] Henri Pirenne suggests that aristocratic secessions were not simply due to ambition; they were based on the assessment that the imperial military had failed to defend the region, and that defense and political authority had to be shifted onto the local scene. See *The Cambridge Medieval History,* Volume 3, pp. 97–98.

[6] Hans Delbrück, *History of the Art of Warfare within the Framework of Political History,* Volume 3: *The Middle Ages* (Westport, Conn.: Greenwood Press, 1982), p. 230. As another historian put it, "Royal officials . . . tended to become leaders of autonomous local communities rather than agents of central authority." Joseph R. Strayer, *On the Medieval Origins of the Modern State* (Princeton, N.J.: Princeton University Press, 1970), p. 14.

[7] Marc Bloch comments, "The very epics which set such great store by the 'virtue' of the vassal are nothing but one long recital of the wars launched by vassals against their lords. . . . Struggles of the great feudatories against the kings; rebellions against the former by their own vassals; dereliction of feudal duty—these features are to be read on every page of the history of feudalism. . . . [O]f all the occasions for going to war, the first that came to mind was to take up arms against one's lord." *Feudal Society,* Volume 1: *The Growth of Ties of Dependence* (Chicago: University of Chicago Press, 1961), p. 235.

secular authority. The Investiture Controversy (1075) saw a Church-aristocracy coalition poised against the state and towns. The struggle crippled the German emperors, though not as decisively as often thought; the Empire reached its zenith over a century later under the Hohenstaufens, until a similar coalition irretrievably undermined it in the early thirteenth century. Power shifted away from the center and into the hands of the electors, nobles, bishops, and town leagues. Attendant with this power shift was a swift legitimation of the new order that was not without bearing for constitutional history. What has been said of the Hohenstaufens could also be said of the Carolingians and the Angevins: "If the central authority was weak, the nobles began at once to encroach; usurpations were in a few years translated into rights, and it was difficult, if not impossible, for the king to recover what had been lost."[8] Central authority was never completely eliminated in either empire. In the Frankish lands, where weak Capetians were no threat to ecclesiastical property or corporateness, the Church bolstered the king against a centrifugal nobility.[9] Throughout Europe the crown was still able to ally with lesser nobles fearful of ducal power.[10] Finally, contumacious nobles themselves derived legitimacy from even tenuous ties to the crown, and were reluctant to do completely away with it.[11]

By the twelfth century, central authority began to reemerge in France and major principalities of the Holy Roman Empire. Louis VI and Louis VII (r. 1108–1180) consolidated their positions in the *Ile de France* through military prowess and support from lower orders seeking a more peaceful climate than that of continuous warfare.[12] In Germany the balance of power was, in effect, transferred to a lower political level: the crown-noble balance of France was paralleled by a similar balance between the nobles and imperial princes. In England the Duke of Normandy's conquest (1066) of the Anglo-Saxon confederations laid the basis for a central state. But his Plantagenet and Angevin successors faced a strong, unified baronage that formed one side of the crucial balance.[13]

There were several constitutional consequences. Foremost was the rise of representative or parliamentary bodies in which monarch, aristocracy, burghers, and clerics determined basic matters, including fundamental

---

[8] Z. N. Brooke in *The Cambridge Medieval History*, Volume 5, p. 121. See also Brian Tierney, *The Crisis of Church and State 1050–1300* (Toronto: University of Toronto Press, 1988).

[9] *The Cambridge Medieval History*, Volume 3, pp. 97–98.

[10] Bloch, *Feudal Society*, Volume 1, pp. 197–98.

[11] Max Weber, *Economy and Society*, two volumes, Guenther Roth and Claus Wittich, eds. (Berkeley and Los Angeles: University of California Press, 1978), p. 1085.

[12] *The Cambridge Medieval History*, Volume 5, pp. 592–96.

[13] Bloch, *Feudal Society*, Volume 2, pp. 51–54; Sidney Painter, *The Rise of the Feudal Monarchies* (Ithaca, N.Y.: Cornell University Press, 1975), pp. 66–70.

ones of taxation and war—issues to which we shall return throughout this study. Monarchs were, at least initially, eager to convoke assemblies; MacIlwain observes that many monarchs believed parliaments would be mechanisms for turning the bothersome estates of the realm into dutiful instruments of royal policy.[14] They were very much disappointed.

Second, towns evolved from ecclesiastical, military, and administrative centers into vital commercial centers, whose wealth and expertise did not go unnoticed by feudatories. Towns took advantage of crown-noble antagonisms, played one side against the other, and negotiated crucial freedoms. Burghers gave fixed sums of money (collected by burghers themselves, not royal bailiffs), artisanal weaponry, and administrative specialists to kings or nobles, and received in exchange fundamental rights, freedoms, and immunities, often stipulated in written charters. Considerable variation in town alliances may be noted. Southern French towns allied with nobles against the growing power of the king to the north, while Italian cities allied with nobles in order to break away from the Empire and the Church.[15] In northern regions of the Empire, following the Investiture Controversy, towns feared the increasingly independent power of the nobility and made pacts with the emperor against covetous princes. A similar town-king alliance was forged between commercial centers of northern France and Capetian kings, whose state-building activities benefited from revenue from the towns.[16]

A third consequence of the balance of power between crown and nobility comprises the modus vivendi, charters, and legal norms agreed to by both sides, usually the crown and the upper stratum of the aristocracy. The best known of these is of course Magna Carta, won by the English baronage at Runnymede. In these arrangements, the principles of magnate representation in the *curia regis*, consultation on matters of taxation, rule of law, and due process were formalized, that is, removed from the tenuous realm of amorphous agreement (precisely where the king preferred them) and solidified into a written charter that thenceforth was a

[14] *The Cambridge Medieval History*, Volume 7, p. 677.

[15] *The Cambridge Medieval History*, Volume 5, p. 640. Philip Augustus would later conquer them, however. See Fritz Rörig, *The Medieval Town* (Berkeley and Los Angeles: University of California Press, 1967), pp. 60–61; Henri Pirenne, *Medieval Cities: Their Origins and the Revival of Trade* (Princeton, N.J.: Princeton University Press, 1974), pp. 174–75; and A. B. Hibbert, "The Origins of the Medieval Town Patriciate," *Past and Present* 37 (1953): 18–21.

[16] Painter, *Feudal Monarchies*, pp. 20–21. Where there was no effective balance of power, and towns broke free of all authority, their import for constitutional development was far less than elsewhere in Europe. These city-states were typically annexed by far more powerful states in later centuries. For their constitutional nature to have historical significance, towns must continue to exist within the geographic boundaries but at least partially outside the administrative hierarchy of existing or future nation-states.

basis for crown-noble relations. We would be guilty of Whiggish, Anglo-Saxon prejudice in not noting that parallel agreements were hammered out in the Holy Roman Empire at the Diet of Worms (1225), which checked the power of the emperor and installed the electoral principle for imperial successions; in Poland with the Pact of Koszyce (1374); and in Sweden with the Land Law of 1350, a document that even today serves as a basic instrument of government.

The second source of constitutional growth was the military systems of Europe: the feudal levies and militias. The military structure and landholding patterns of Europe were established in the early eighth century by the mayor of the Merovingian palace, Charles Martel. Lacking the resources to pay and equip a centrally administered force, the hero of Tours spoliated Church land and distributed it as benefices to his cavalry.[17] Though frequently thought of as an economic system, feudalism was primarily a military system with a supportive manorial economy, the former bringing about the latter. Noble estates did not develop from combining smaller tracts, nor were they purchased. They were originally the conditional holdings of a military elite.[18] The benefice, replete with labor, afforded the knight sufficient resources upon which he could draw in order to maintain armor, horses, weaponry, and retinue—considerable expenses for a period of low economic activity. In exchange for this, the vassal owed his lord fealty and military service. But the exchange was more nuanced than simply land for knight service. As subinfeudation spread across the continent, the social structure of Europe became a network of mutual obligations predicated on feudal military exchange that Weber described as "a cosmos, and according to the circumstances, also a chaos of concrete subjective rights and duties of the lord, the officeholders and the ruled."[19] Within that cosmos was a basis for citizenship and representative institutions. The knight, as Hintze has argued, obtained jurisdictional and administrative immunities limiting the lord's control over him and his benefice. His relationship to superiors was

---

[17] Fichtenau, *Carolingian Empire*, pp. 12–14.

[18] The basic military structure of the Carolingian Empire was elaborated by the *precarium* system, whereby private estates were given to military lords in exchange for conditional ownership and, more importantly, for protection. This system had begun in late Roman times and had been the basis of Merovingian feudalism. There is widespread agreement on the military basis of feudalism. See Bloch, *Feudal Society*, Volume 1, pp. 247–48; Max Weber, *General Economic History*, Frank M. Knight, trans. (New Brunswick, N.J.: Transaction Books, 1982), p. 53, *The Agrarian Sociology of Ancient Civilizations*, R. I. Frank, trans. (London: Verso, 1988), pp. 352–53; Joseph A. Strayer and Rushton Coulborn, "The Idea of Feudalism," in Rushton Coulborn, ed., *Feudalism in History* (Hamden, Conn.: Archon, 1965), pp. 3–11; and Joseph Schumpeter, *Capitalism, Socialism and Democracy* (New York: Harper & Row, 1975), p. 13.

[19] Weber, *Economy and Society*, p. 1085.

based not on overt command but rather on a contract into which he had freely entered, and the right of resistance to unfair authority was recognized.[20] To regulate and protect these rights there emerged a corpus of legal thinking that settled disputes arising from the more chaotic aspects of feudalism.[21] Parliaments of the late medieval period evolved, in part, from the Carolingian assemblies of military vassals. Consistent with the essentially contractual nature of military service, Carolingian kings convoked assemblies of knights in which matters of general policy and impending military campaigns were discussed by all, the king first among equals.[22] This practice continued throughout the medieval period until the warrior assemblies merged with the baronial curia regis and estate representations.[23]

A second military impetus to constitutional forms came from militias, which supplemented or took the place of the more familiar feudal knight. They are found in their greatest strength where geography was unfavorable to the knight (as in Switzerland and Scandinavia), where feudalism simply had not spread, or where conflict with irregular military units (e.g., Welsh and Scottish frontier bands) mandated a more rapidly mobilized and adaptable force. Prevalent throughout England and Sweden, village levies demonstrate a close link between citizenship rights and military service. The village hundreds, themselves important to constitutional development in Scandinavia, levied infantry formations from the male population, who, in return, were given voice in popular assemblies. As if to underscore the relationship between military service and participation in local government, members of the assembly arrived with their weapons and indicated assent to a motion by raising their javelins. Furthermore, contracts were made in a ritual during which each party demonstrated free status by bearing arms.[24]

A close parallel may be drawn between rural militia participation and service defending the medieval town from royal or seigneurial threats.

[20] Otto Hintze, "Wesen und Verbreitung des Feudalismus," in *Staat und Verfassung: Gesammelte Abhandlungen zur allgemeinen Verfassungsgeschichte*, Fritz Hartung, ed. (Leipzig: Koehler & Amelang, 1941). Weber repeatedly points out endowment of citizenship rights, the franchise, political representation, and immunities, as rewards for military service, especially in decentralized military systems like those of feudal Europe. See *Economy and Society*, pp. 1071, 1261, 1352, and *General Economic History*, pp. 320–30.

[21] Harold J. Berman, *Law and Revolution: The Rise of the Western Legal Tradition* (Cambridge, Mass.: Harvard University Press, 1983), pp. 295–315.

[22] Ganshof, *Frankish Institutions*, pp. 21–23; Thomas N. Bisson, "The Military Origins of Medieval Representation," *American Historical Review* 71 (1966): 1199–1200. Bisson points out that the words used to call together these assemblies—including *convocare, congregare,* and *convenire*—have modern parliamentary usages.

[23] Ibid., pp. 1199–1212; Weber, *Economy and Society*, p. 1085.

[24] P.W.A. Immink, "Gouvernés et gouvernants dans la societé Germanique," *Gouvernés et Gouvernants* 2 (1968): 331–93; Tacitus's *Germania* is also a useful essay.

Town dwellers exchanged military service for privileges, the most important of which were voice in town assemblies, immunities, and guarantees of legal access. Weber's succinctness and directness are unsurpassed: "The basis of democratization is everywhere purely military in character; it lies in the rise of disciplined infantry, the *hoplites* of antiquity, the guild army of the middle ages. . . . Military discipline meant the triumph of democracy because the community wished and was compelled to secure the cooperation of the non-aristocratic masses and hence put arms, and along with arms political power, into their hands."[25] The military basis of citizenship and democratization has a long, neglected history stretching from the hoplites and *assidui* of antiquity to our own time. It was the shift from feudal or militia armies to centrally organized and equipped ones that broke, at least for several centuries, the soldier-citizenship nexus.[26]

The third and final wellspring of constitutionalism is peasant property rights and reciprocal ties between tiller and lord. As suggested by the discussion of the Germanic tribal organizations, medieval Europe was hardly a uniform society that conformed neatly with simplistic views of feudal civilization. Just as there was appreciable variation in military systems and municipal dynamics, so too was there variation in property ownership and agrarian relations. Though much land was held conditionally according to the system of military benefices, the oft-heard apothegm *nulle terre sans seigneur* conveys in only the most general way the agrarian patterns of Western Europe. Allodial property was found in considerable measures in even the most heavily feudalized parts of northern France. Independent aristocrats as well as a large number of free peasants held tracts of land, without conditions set by feudal authority.

Property among the peasantry provided a solid basis for solidarity in the face of aristocratic pressures: in the thirteenth century, free peasants "were able to compel the lord to join with all his dependents in forming a manorial court in which the dependent persons functioned as magistrates. Thus the lord lost the power of arbitrary control over the obliga-

[25] Weber, *General Economic History*, pp. 324–25. See also Gina Fasoli, "Gouvernés et gouvernants dans les communes Italiennes du XIe au XIIIe siècle," *Gouvernés et Gouvernants* 4 (1984): 47–86. On the soldier-citizen relationship in antiquity, see P. A. Brunt, *Italian Manpower 225 B.C.–A.D. 14* (Oxford: Clarendon Press, 1987), and *Social Conflicts in the Roman Republic* (New York: W. W. Norton, 1971), pp. 5–16. In time of crisis, such as after Hannibal's victory over the Roman legions at Cannae (216 B.C.), slaves were mobilized and, after the Second Battle of Beneventum (214 B.C.), rewarded with citizenship. See Claude Nicolet, *The World of the Citizen in Republican Rome*, P. S. Falla, trans. (Berkeley and Los Angeles: University of California Press, 1988), pp. 94–95.

[26] With the shift to mass armies relying on mass conscription during the Napoleonic Wars and afterwards, the nexus was restored, as attest the 1918 extension of the franchise to British men (though, significantly, not to conscientious objectors), the GI Bill of Rights of the 1940s, and the lowering of the voting age in the United States during the Vietnam War.

tions of his dependents and these became traditionalized."[27] Even the more paradigmatic feudal landholdings, that is, those largely uncluttered by freeholding peasants, contained patterns of reciprocal ties between lord and serf. Noting the essential reciprocity pervading the medieval world, Sir Paul Vinogradoff writes:

> The lord was a monarch on the manor, but a monarch fettered by a customary constitution and by contractual rights. He was often strong enough to break through these customs and agreements, to act in an arbitrary way, to indulge in cruelty and violence. . . . A mean line had to be struck between the claims of the rulers and the interests of the subjects, and along this mean line by-laws were framed and customs grew up which protected the tenantry even though it was forsaken by the king's judges. This unwritten constitution was safeguarded not only by the apprehension that its infringement might scatter the rustic population on whose labour the well-being of the lord and his retainers after all depended, but also by the necessity of keeping within bounds the power of the manorial staff of which the lord had to avail himself. . . . It was in the interest of the lord himself to strengthen the customary order which prevented grasping stewards and serjeants from ruining the peasantry by extortions and arbitrary rule.[28]

Between the thirteenth and fifteenth centuries, demographic shifts brought on by the Black Death, and additional revenue demands from the crown, led to increased bargaining power for peasants, resulting in dissolution of feudal ties and consolidation of protective custom into law administered by courts. This movement was only too eagerly aided by monarchs ever receptive to anything diminishing the power of unruly nobles.[29] In sum, feudal relations on the late medieval manor were far less oppressive than might initially appear. Between lord and peasant was a buffer—comprising custom, law, and the possibility of royal intervention—that protected the peasant and endowed him with specific rights and legal guarantees.

MEDIEVAL CONSTITUTIONALISM

Three principal configurations—rough balance between crown and nobility, decentralized military organization, and feudal lord-peasant rela-

---

[27] Weber, *General Economic History*, p. 68.

[28] "Feudalism," in *The Cambridge Medieval History*, Volume 3, pp. 481–82. It is interesting to note that the explanation in this classic essay brings to mind rational-choice explanations of our own day.

[29] Weber, *General Economic History*, p. 70. On the rise of manorial law, see Berman, *Law and Revolution*, pp. 316–32; and Gerald Strauss, *Law, Resistance, and the State: The Opposition to Roman Law in Reformation Germany* (Princeton, N.J.: Princeton University Press, 1986), pp. 116–17.

tions—provided the sources of most of European constitutionalism in the late medieval period. Local government (in provinces, towns, and villages), parliamentary bodies, and the rule of law grew from this soil. Western Europe took on complicated constitutional patterns that marked it off from the rest of the world.

Several significant forms of local government may be identified: towns, ancient village government, village communes, chartered frontier villages, and, most importantly, aristocratic power in the country. After Viking, Saracen, and Magyar raids had subsided in the late tenth century, great commercial towns developed from the walled administrative, military, and ecclesiastical centers of earlier centuries. They were poised at this propitious juncture to take full advantage of the crown-aristocracy balance, though most would align their fortunes with the monarchs. The charter granted Worms in 1074 by the emperor was among the first, and it is of significance that here, for the first time, town dwellers were referred to in the charter as *cives*, a word surrounded by a legal aura, whereas previously documents had used the functional terms *mercatores* or *negotiotores*.[30] Similar charters were granted by ensuing emperors to Flemish, Dutch, and Italian towns in exchange for fixed revenue, weapons, and administrative assistance.

Towns built their own governments, separate from the administrative web of kings and nobles, though not always completely. Government began with councils composed of a small number of men, but these were soon replaced as administration became increasingly complicated. Committees of three to six members came into being, representing different groups within the walls, including the local juries, guilds, and patriciate. By 1450 Frankfurt am Main had eighteen committees supervising the military, finance, and justice.[31] Royal or seigneurial influence in municipal affairs was either nonexistent or carefully proscribed. In many less wealthy towns, however, completely autocephalous administration was impossible: Philip Augustus's bailiffs and burghers codetermined policy in northern French towns. English towns were able to refuse entry to royal sheriffs and magistrates, and, though they were required to follow specified policy directives of the English kings, implementation was left to the burghers themselves, who could carry them out or drag their feet.[32]

Town governments were oligarchic, often highly so, especially in their early days, prior to the onset of pressures from below. Elites governing northern Italian towns were drawn from the merchants, military special-

[30] *The Cambridge Medieval History*, Volume 5, p. 120. The German word *Bürger* retains the double meaning of town dweller and citizen.

[31] Rörig, *Medieval Town*, pp. 161–74.

[32] *The Cambridge Medieval History*, Volume 7, pp. 274–328.

ists, and legal experts. Although they can rightly be called oligarchic, insofar as three distinct social groups with at least potentially diverging interests and outlooks are in evidence, there was some diversity in the elites.[33] Even the most oligarchic of towns nevertheless provided negative freedom for those excluded from the franchise. They were freed from feudal ties, services, and attendant vagaries; and, after residing within the town walls for a period of time, usually a year and a day, they had access to a more rational legal system. Town air, it was said, made you free.

There was considerable variation in the rights enjoyed by the lower classes. Basel, Strasbourg, and Ulm allowed substantial voice to the numerous guilds, while to the north, the imperial towns remained narrowly oligarchic. (Proximity to the popular democracy of the *Markgenossenschaften* and village hundreds in the Swiss Confederation seems to have been decisive in accounting for this variation.[34]) Two forms of social conflict served to expand the citizenship rights of the lower orders. First, seigneurial and royal authorities, eager to gain control over the lucrative islands of capitalism to which they had previously granted charters, tried to ally with lower classes to overthrow oligarchic rule. Burghers thwarted this movement by themselves extending rights to those below, thereby coopting outside entreaties.[35] Second, the free-trade patriciate and vulnerable guilds eventually came into conflict over protectionism and representation in the town council. Overt conflict was often precluded by the two parties hammering out agreements and negotiating charters extending citizenship rights. In the Low Countries, however, change was less peaceful. The late thirteenth and fourteenth centuries witnessed strikes, migrations, and even pitched battles, which led to broader government, including the craft guilds.[36]

Of obscure but certainly ancient origins, Germanic village government survived in the mountainous cantons of what would become the Swiss Confederation and also in much of Scandinavia. The key institution of government was the popular assembly, an informal gathering electing chieftains and magistrates. It was not uncommon for an entire community to decide a case while assembled at a village tavern. Procedures and values were governed by custom law, which, despite its essentially unwritten character, nevertheless was an effective guideline that generally pre-

---

[33] Fasoli, "Communes Italiennes," pp. 54–57.

[34] Thomas A. Brady, *Turning Swiss: Cities and Empire, 1450–1550* (New York: Cambridge University Press, 1985), pp. 13–38.

[35] Rörig, *Medieval Town*, pp. 90–92.

[36] Henri Pirenne, *Early Democracies in the Low Countries: Urban Society and Political Conflict in the Middle Ages and the Renaissance* (New York: Harper & Row, 1963), pp. 125–55; Rörig, *Medieval Town*, pp. 146–60.

vented arbitrary decisions.[37] As these communities came into contact with growing state structures, they were not necessarily destroyed, co-opted, or subsumed: in England the village hundred became an essential part of Common Law courts in the twelfth century;[38] in a manner comparable to the civil disobedience of our own day, Swedish local governments coordinated opposition to the king and effected mass noncompliance to his decrees, resulting in his ouster.[39]

During the thirteenth century, villages as well as towns exploited the crown-noble balance and obtained liberties and charters. Often calling themselves communes, these villages developed their own judicial and administrative organs as well as popular assemblies for determining village policies.[40] Where nobles threatened to defeat and reabsorb them, they banded together in common defense. Such clusters were most common in valley regions cut off and ably protected from outside powers.[41] Swiss communes (Markgenossenschaften) allied with the village hundreds and later the commercial centers of Berne and Basel to form a powerful tripartite basis of confederal constitutionalism.[42] Chartered villages of the frontier regions are quite similar to the village communes in constitutional relevance, but different in origins and relationship to the aristocracy. Population pressures of the late medieval period led to village settlements in the woodlands and wastelands of unsettled regions of France and the Empire, and also in the newly conquered or reconquered regions of Prussia, Poland, and Spain. In order to attract peasants to these frontiers, knights and nonnoble *locatores* offered peasants light dues, rights of mobility and property, as well as voice in local assemblies and judiciaries. The relationship to the aristocracy then was a cooperative one in which the lord played a role in defending the newly settled area, without acquiring the political predominance found elsewhere. In return, peasants provided only small, fixed payments; they were neither

[37] Immink, "Societé Germanique," pp. 350–63; Strauss, *Law, Resistance, and the State*, pp. 120–21; Karl Bosl, "Zu einer Geschichte der bäuerlichen Repräsentation in der deutschen Landgemeinde," *Studies Presented to the International Commission for the History of Representative and Parliamentary Institutions* 26 (1963): 1–17.

[38] *The Cambridge Medieval History*, Volume 5, p. 584.

[39] Fritz Kern, *Kingship and Law in the Middle Ages* (Oxford: Basil Blackwell, 1939), pp. 85–86.

[40] Susan Reynolds, *Kingdoms and Communities in Western Europe, 900–1300* (Oxford: Clarendon Press, 1986), pp. 101–54; W. P. Blockmans, "A Typology of Representative Institutions in Late Medieval Europe," *Journal of Medieval History* 4 (1978): 193–95; Jerome Blum, "The Internal Structure and Polity of the European Village Community from the Fifteenth to the Nineteenth Centuries," *Journal of Modern History* 43 (1971): 541–76.

[41] *The Cambridge Medieval History*, Volume 5, pp. 652–54. Andorra is one such cluster whose autonomy has survived to the present.

[42] *The Cambridge Medieval History*, Volume 7, pp. 85–90.

tied to the soil nor subject to the nobles' administrative or judicial power.[43]

Despite the many towns and various forms of peasant self-government, the aristocracy dominated the European countryside. By the late Middle Ages, aristocrats in most of Europe had effectively converted the conditional benefice into de facto, heritable property. Furthermore, they retained administrative control of their manor and adjacent lands, or at least had substantial control over the king's or duke's appointments in the locality. Although the Norman conquest of the eleventh century had laid the foundations for a central state, with royal officials in every county, the monarch was required to select sheriffs and magistrates in concert with and from local notables. In Brandenburg and Pomerania, nobles built local assemblies and other instruments of government (*Kreisdirektoren*) to guard against crown interference.[44] Such was the strength of the aristocrats that royal government came to be based on an increasingly cooperative relationship with them. Government was possible only within a consensual framework.

In the late thirteenth and early fourteenth centuries, representative assemblies or estates attained some degree of institutional coherence distinct from prototypical forms in the baronial curia regis, feudal military councils, and local assemblies.[45] Having enjoyed liberties and immunities since the time of Charlemagne and Otto the Great, the aristocracy and the clergy had already acquired the status and power in the feudal hierarchy to guarantee representation in the new, increasingly formal assemblies. The communal movement, the town-monarch working relationship, and the growing financial power of the towns led to the "estatization" of the burghers, who assumed places alongside nobles and clerics as an order of the realm. Peasants were not directly represented

[43] Rodney Hilton, *Bond Men Made Free: Medieval Peasant Movements and the English Rising of 1381* (London: Temple Smith, 1973), pp. 92–95; F. L. Carsten, *The Origins of Prussia* (Oxford: Clarendon Press, 1964), pp. 10–42; Jerome Blum, *Lord and Peasant in Russia: From the Ninth to the Nineteenth Century* (Princeton, N.J.: Princeton University Press, 1972), pp. 94–102; John Beeler, *Warfare in Feudal Europe, 730–1200* (Ithaca, N.Y.: Cornell University Press, 1984), pp. 166–67.

[44] *The Cambridge Medieval History*, Volume 7, pp. 446–48; Fritz Hartung, *Deutsche Verfassungsgeschichte vom 15. Jahrhundert bis zur Gegenwart*, Eighth Edition (Stuttgart: K. F. Koehler, 1950), pp. 57–126.

[45] Church synods have also been pointed to as antecedents of the estates. However, the representative nature of these religious gatherings is unclear at best, and the synods lack the direct institutional continuity with the estates that the aforementioned councils and assemblies had. For a discussion and criticism of the ecclesiastical origins hypothesis, see Antonio Marongiu, *Medieval Parliaments: A Comparative Study*, S. J. Woolf, trans. (London: Eyre & Spottiswoode, 1968), pp. 37–41.

in the estates in the regions where feudal military and economic arrangements obtained, but where tribal customs had survived, most notably in Scandinavia, peasants formed a fourth estate.

The power and functions of estates varied across region and time, but five principal functions can be identified. First, nobles, clergy, and burghers represented both regional and corporate interests in the court of the king. Second, the contemporary expression "redress before supply" conveys a defensive posture assumed by representatives: their principal mission, at least in the time before crown and estates had managed a level of trust and become cooperative parts of government, was to defend against royal expedients. Third, estates were essential to finance and consensus building; they debated matters of war, foreign policy, trade, and justice.[46] Fourth, estates often took advantage of any upper hand they might have had by enhancing their privileges and liberties, and by expanding their role in the machinery of government. In exchange for financial support, more often than not in time of war, estates assumed increasing control of lawmaking.[47] Finally, estates provided a basis of national integration that prevented the splintering into city-states that northern Italy and southern Germany had undergone. The English Parliament aided in the formation of "an interlocal, *national* bourgeoisie" whose increasing power, channeled into Parliament, "prevented the development of a strong movement for political independence in the *individual* communes."[48] Accordingly, the constitutional qualities of the towns were preserved within the protective boundaries of an emerging nation-state, where they could not be easily destroyed by foreign conquest.

Law in the West was not an instrument for implementing royal policy and punishing opponents. Late medieval Europe is distinguishable from other parts of the world by binding legal codes setting procedural and substantive boundaries for many aspects of social, economic, and political life. Law was more than a device for superstructural sanctification of existing social relationships. It was an interlocking network of procedural and substantive norms that served as an obstacle, though not an insurmountable one, to the actions of kings and other powerholders in an era before "l'Etat c'est moi" could be proclaimed.

A number of tributaries leading to the rule of law may be identified.

---

[46] Blockmans, "Representative Institutions," pp. 200–202.

[47] Dietrich Gerhard, "Assemblies of Estates and the Corporate Order," in International Commission for the History of Representative and Parliamentary Institutions, *Liber Memorialis Georges de Lagarde* (Paris: Béatrice-Nauwelaerts, 1970), p. 300; *The Cambridge Medieval History*, Volume 7, pp. 439–82.

[48] Weber, *Economy and Society*, p. 1280 (emphasis in original).

The objective nature of law was firmly rooted in Germanic society, in its customary law, as well as in Salic Law and the *Sachsenspiegel*.[49] This reflects a more general phenomenon in the sociology of law, whereby law develops out of traditions and values imbedded in society—as Maitland and Montagu expressed it, out of the "common wisdom and experiences of society."[50] A second source lies in the systems of manorial law that emerged from the customs between free peasants and landlords, and also in the parallel feudal law worked out between lord and vassal. Feudal law emerged as the formalized regulation of contractual ambiguities of military service, the transference of service into payments in cash or kind, the forfeiture of fiefs, and royal jurisdictions in the fief.[51] Both manorial and feudal law developed out of formal and informal dealings between conflictual but mutually dependent groups: lord and peasant, suzerain and vassal. They were not imposed from above by irresistible authority. This contractual nature of law, that is, its origins in negotiated settlements between parties, is crucial to the rise of law as "a kind of protective power which existed independently of any human agency, and which not only men but kings were thought powerless to change."[52]

The recrudescence of monarchal authority in the thirteenth and fourteenth centuries brought increased royal control over justice, and the reemergence of Roman Law, a second source of medieval legalism, played no small role in that process. Royal courts replaced many feudal and ecclesiastical ones, and shifted judicial authority increasingly into the crown's hands. Though Roman Law had been preserved through the early medieval period by its influence on Gothic and other tribal law, the principal impetus to its rebirth was the Investiture Controversy of the late eleventh century. The struggle between pope and emperor led both sides to scramble for legal justification for their claims, and to develop a legal codification to better secure their corporate identity and bureaucratic machinery.[53] Both Canon Law and secular law drew heavily from the rich juridical treasures of antiquity and reintroduced Roman Law to a society whose conflicts and conceptions of property were beginning to catch up to those of Rome. A legal revolution came about. Roman Law was superior to existing legal systems in several regards. Its dual struc-

---

[49] Kern, *Kingship and Law*, pp. 70–71; Immink, "Societé Germanique," pp. 360–63.

[50] Quoted in Arthur R. Hogue, *Origins of the Common Law* (Indianapolis, Ind.: Liberty Press, 1985), p. 190.

[51] On manorial and feudal law, see Berman, *Law and Revolution*, pp. 295–332.

[52] George L. Haskins, "Executive Justice and the Rule of Law," *Speculum* 30 (1955): 529–38.

[53] Sir Paul Vinogradoff, *Roman Law in Medieval Europe* (Oxford: Clarendon Press, 1929), pp. 29–30; Berman, *Law and Revolution*, pp. 86–100. For the Roman basis of Canon Law, see Weber, *Economy and Society*, pp. 829–30.

ture of *ius*, a corpus of interrelated and mutually supportive principles, and *leges*, the specific laws derived from ius, exhibited a philosophical foundation greatly surpassing the folk wisdom upon which most legal codifications had been predicated, and hence won more respect from administrators and property owners. Second, Roman Law was more relevant and useful to an increasingly complex social order by virtue of its cumulative nature, whereby decisions built upon one another and themselves became part of law. In this process, law became more refined and acquired an internal, progressive dynamic. Furthermore, it featured sharply defined concepts, objective criteria for weighing evidence, and solid procedural norms for conducting trials. Finally, by virtue of its origin in a property-conscious civilization, Roman Law included elaborate concepts, norms, and rules that would greatly aid in governing and furthering what was becoming an increasingly commercial world.[54]

Roman Law brought advantages for central authority. Coming from the imperial system of antiquity, it had an inherent bias toward central authority: concepts, procedures, and individual courts relied upon and pointed upward toward an appellate and administrative hierarchy culminating in the prince. The entire system depended on an orderly, rational bureaucracy to maintain conceptual, procedural, and substantive standards.[55] A second advantage for centralizing authority was the increased revenue sources provided by the growing royal monopoly on justice. Disputing parties preferred faster and more decisive royal courts over the patchwork of feudal, merchant, and Canon Law courts scattered across Europe. Finally, standing at the head of the new rational legal system, the monarch and his state enjoyed a decided infusion of support at a critical early stage of state formation.[56]

The reception of Roman Law led to increased central power at the expense of the nobility, whose prestige and revenue from court fees declined somewhat. This might seem to have afforded a grasping monarch the opportunity to rise above law and use the state in an arbitrary or self-serving manner. Indeed, Roman Law was a key instrument of royal centralization, but it could not be wielded in a reckless manner. It was received rather well into the constitutional order for several reasons. First, the crown lacked the power to rise above the law, as it would in many states during the wars of the following centuries; princes still relied too

---

[54] On the strengths of Roman Law, see Hans Julius Wolff, *Roman Law: An Historical Introduction* (Norman: University of Oklahoma Press, 1978), pp. 150–58; Vinogradoff, *Roman Law in Medieval Europe*, pp. 18–22; Strauss, *Law, Resistance, and the State*, pp. 59–70; and Berman, *Law and Revolution*.

[55] Wolff, *Roman Law*, p. 195; Strauss, *Law, Resistance, and the State*, pp. 74–78.

[56] David M. Trubek, "Max Weber on Law and the Rise of Capitalism," *Wisconsin Law Review* 3 (1972): 749.

heavily on towns for revenue, military equipment, and administrative expertise. Second, Roman Law was an essentially alien legal system brought into the Middle Ages in toto from a distant past. It was not an indigenously developed legal system, produced by royal ministers. It was not simply a legal device for implementing policy; its principles had been set for centuries, and tampering with them or expeditiously bending them would have the effect of undermining the many advantages Roman Law gave the crown. Third, Roman Law was protected by an administrative-academic elite whose corporate status was bound up with the protection of the law's integrity. Legal experts in the judiciary and in the medieval universities guarded the law from meddling, and guaranteed that its cumulative, internal dynamic, not royal fiat, was the principal agent of change.[57] Even the experts of English Common Law (whose roots in Roman Law were less firm than those on the continent) maintained their independence throughout the Tudor and Stuart periods: "In the sixteenth and seventeenth centuries the judiciary stood between the public and the crown. It protected the individual from the state when he required that protection."[58]

The crown itself had an interest in maintaining the rule of law. As we have seen, it benefited from the legitimacy stemming from the administration of an equitable system of law. Support from key social groups was crucial to building a nation and a coherent state out of a feudal order. Tampering with the law would perhaps help to acquire a few manors or excises, but it would also endanger the crown's state-building program. Short-term expediency would be achieved only at the cost of delaying or destroying long-term goals. To say that there was rule of law in the late medieval and early modern period is not to say that law hovered menacingly above the crown, preventing any meddling. Many opponents of the prince were imprisoned or had property seized without due process. In speaking of the rule of law in this time, it is only meant that such transgressions, if routine, entailed the probability of noble and burgher opposition, from which monarchs and emperors of the Middle East and Orient had little to fear. The edifice of law was in effect an objective, structural restraint on the crown and other powerholders.

An account of medieval political history would be incomplete without discussing the role of the Church. The Church controlled a sizeable por-

---

[57] Berman, *Law and Revolution*, pp. 120–64.

[58] Roscoe Pound, "Common Law and Legislation," *Harvard Law Review* 21 (1908): 403. Although it is frequently thought that Common Law has no relation to Roman Law, it entered the Common Law through the agency of the ecclesiastics in the chancery who used it to "round out the law of the royal courts by drawing on the more complete Roman system." Hogue, *Origins of the Common Law*, p. 22.

tion of European agricultural production and its political influence stretched across the continent. At times a Church-centered empire was not too farfetched an idea. But the constitutional significance of the institution of the Church, which we might distinguish from the clerics in the estates (who were by no means papal delegates) is mixed. As we have seen, the Church supported Capetian centralization, but vigorously opposed excessive secular power in the Holy Roman Empire and fourteenth-century France. The Church steered a middle course between a faltering monarchy with its attendant chaos and a powerful one that could, and during the Reformation would, spoliate Church property. In this regard, the Church acted as a balancer in the twelfth and thirteenth centuries, much as England did in the nineteenth-century state system, though its motives lay less in building constitutionalism than in preserving some semblance of political order, not to mention its far-flung holdings. However, in the early modern period, that is, the age of absolutism, the Church consistently supported strong, Counter-Reformation monarchies whose objectives, inter alia, were dissolution of the estates and subjugation of towns.[59]

The relationships, coalitions, and institutions that promoted or composed medieval constitutionalism engendered a supportive array of ideologies and values, which, in turn, infused the estates, charters, and local centers of power with intellectual and emotional energies. Ideas and values held by burghers, nobles, and villagers invigorated constitutionalism. In many cases they took on a life of their own, as they were abstracted from their institutional and material origins and turned into political philosophies, popular mythology, and common sense. Constitutional ideology assumed forms drawn from distant pasts, from mythic pasts, and from what we might call the legitimation or sanctification of the status quo. The ancient Roman dictum of *quod omnes tangit ab omnibus approbetur*[60] was exhumed from centuries of repose to defend and justify representative institutions and baronial charters. The ancient, ill-defined concept of natural law was utilized by layman and cleric alike to confer legitimacy upon opposition to royal decrees and positive law that, owing

[59] It is critical that the Church attained its administrative coherence and corporate identity in the period following the Investiture Controversy. This sequence of events precluded its becoming the subaltern, legitimizing institution that the Orthodox Church became in Muscovite Russia, where, after the fall of Constantinople (1453), patriarchs sought a strong secular power and forged an alliance with the tsar, exchanging legitimacy for protection. See Richard Pipes, *Russia under the Old Regime* (London: Weidenfeld & Nicolson, 1974), pp. 72–73; and the essays in Robert L. Nichols and George Stavrou, eds. *Russian Orthodoxy under the Old Regime* (Minneapolis: University of Minnesota Press, 1978).

[60] "That which touches all is to be approved by all." On the ideology of constitutionalism see Arthur P. Monahan, *Consent, Coercion, and Limit: The Medieval Origins of Parliamentary Democracy* (Kingston and Montreal: McGill-Queens University Press, 1987).

to their man-made character, were deemed inferior to the dictates of what seemed timeless reason. Although few could agree on any precise meaning of natural law, or perhaps precisely because no such definition could be found, the principle that governmental acts must conform to human reason was as effective a weapon against arbitrary rule for medieval burghers as it was for Locke and Jefferson.

Fundamental features of virtually any social system acquire, often in the course of only a generation or two, a patina of propriety, adherence to a natural order, and justice. They take on sentiments of legitimacy and even sanctity. (This holds for constitutional arrangements as well as for unequal distribution systems, and, unfortunately, it seems also to hold for many authoritarian political arrangements.) Agreements negotiated by king and subjects in the not too distant past were endowed with a quasireligious aura. Charters became concrete acknowledgments of natural rights; Magna Carta came to be revered as an almost sacred document, enshrined like a saintly relic. Distortion of fact and the use of mythological or at least sentimentalized pasts served also to defend and carry forth medieval constitutionalism. Englishmen (especially the Levellers) strengthened their rights by deriving them from an "ancient constitution" of a mythic Anglo-Saxon past, partially corrupted by the institutions of the "Norman yoke." Peasant and noble alike harked back to an idyllic past of *göttliche Gerechtigkeit to* defend the rights and liberties upon which German princes trod. Dutch regents went so far as to compare their political arrangements to the ones Providence had ordained for the nation of Israel.[61] In short, constitutionalism produced a cultural superstructure that shaped thought and strengthened pragmatic concerns over rights and institutions.

In order to avoid the charge that the present study is only one more of these sentimentalizations of remote, mythic pasts, the modern significance of medieval constitutionalism for modern liberal democracy must be looked at. Each component carried forth, and with essential continuity, one or more of the pivotal aspects of modern representative government, at least in those countries in which constitutionalism was not destroyed by kings mobilizing domestic resources for war. Among the aspects of modern liberal democracy that obtained in late medieval Europe are citizenship rights, representative institutions, the rule of law, and a decentralized institutional basis for what could later become checks and balances on central authority.

Local government, which we have encountered in village assemblies, town councils, and gentry cliques, was a form of representative govern-

---

[61] Strauss, *Law, Resistance, and the State*, p. 44; Pieter Geyl, *The Netherlands in the Seventeenth Century*, Part 1: *1609–1648* (New York: Barnes & Noble, 1961), p. 137.

ment that persisted in one form or another into the modern era. While this was by no means democracy, there were nonetheless substantial amounts of representation and participation in government, across a wide range of social levels, from peasant to duke. Although participation was not equally distributed, this should not obscure the fact that there was a measure of popular participation in local, and in some places national, politics. Citizenship found expression in participatory government and in the chartered liberties of towns, village communes, and frontier settlements. Towns provided various levels of citizenship and representation, from narrow oligarchy to representation of the guilds and plebeian classes. The benefits of negative freedom (freedom from feudal authority and obligations) enjoyed by lower classes are easily missed by focusing too narrowly on the oligarchic nature of many towns. To be rid of even loose seigneurial authority and to have access to the more rational judiciaries of the towns were, if not rights, then benefits, not lost on those streaming in from the countryside.

The representative nature of the estates is straightforward. Politics went on between king and estates, and in time a basically cooperative and increasingly harmonious form of state emerged. The estates became the central arena of politics in successive centuries, and the struggle for citizenship rights was fought here in two senses. The main battle of liberalization was fought over the franchise, the right to vote and send representatives to the national assembly. Second, politics within the representative assembly often centered on extending freedoms and liberties by acts of legislation. The rule of law was a crown ornamenting and protecting medieval constitutionalism. Law, that "brooding omnipresence in the sky" as Oliver Wendell Holmes called it, served to guarantee citizenship rights, ensure proper consultation with the estates, and provide a normative and procedural reference governing the actions of the state.

By discussing only the constitutional qualities of medieval Europe, we run the risk of leaving the impression that political and social life was all procedural correctness and fair play, a halcyon era before the ravages of war and the market were let loose. Repression, exploitation, and other abuses were neither rare nor confined to small regions. But medieval constitutionalism ensured that extensive abuses would bring about powerful opposition. The reckless, arbitrary monarch would face increasingly hostile and parsimonious estates, and growing unrest in the countryside. Overly exploitive nobles would face not only peasant flight and possible rebellion, but also opposition from a crown eager to maintain the king's peace and reduce the power of the nobility. Constitutionalism was not a solidly entrenched political arrangement that had but to await its eventual denouement in liberal democracy. A number of critical events that lie outside the scope of this inquiry (an expanding economy, the luxuries of deferent lower classes and a gradually expanding franchise, the absence of sharp internal conflicts, and the safety valve of emigration) would be necessary to permit the rise of modern democracy from its foundations in the medieval world. Nor was it clearly defined in all areas. Constitutionalism in Western Europe had more than a few gray areas. There was no precise boundary between royal prerogative and usurpation, nor any routinization of parliamentary procedure. In England, ship money and benevolences were tolerated at one point, but fiercely opposed scarcely a generation later. Estates might not convene for several years without any substantive change in government. Rulers gained and lost the upper hand in dealings with parliaments, tested the limits of the rule of law by invoking what they deemed prerogative, and tried to circumvent taxation limits, all the while probably operating within the ill-defined bounds of constitutional propriety.

A number of dualistic states based upon a rich constitutional order emerged out of the post-Carolingian chaos. It was an impressive achievement, far short of anything rightfully called democracy, but one that gave most of Western Europe a head start and an institutional basis for democracy. Constitutionalism's import might be more clearly demonstrated by contrasting it with the political orders of several other civilizations whose political outcomes were not decided by outside forces during the age of European expansion.

RUSSIA

Russia, or at least its Muscovite core, lies in Europe, but its political history has little in common with that of the West. Indeed, Russia's contact with the West was light until Peter the Great's modernization efforts in the early eighteenth century. Almost none of the sources and components of medieval constitutionalism in the West is to be found. Russia was on an autocratic trajectory from its inception as a minor tributary state of the Mongol Empire.

Owing to the complete collapse of authority at the close of the Kievan epoch, there was no rough balance between crown and nobility—a contrast to the partial collapse of western imperial systems that laid the foundation for constitutionalism. The brutal Mongol conquest of the early thirteenth century shattered princely authority in southern Russia and converted the northern principalities, including Muscovy, into subservient tributary states. Though the status of beholden subordinate might seem an inauspicious beginning for national greatness, it did afford Muscovite princes the opportunity to build a strong state and army with which to collect the exactions of the khan and mercilessly crush opposition. The khans myopically rewarded their ambitious underlings, who nonetheless delivered tribute on time, by alloting them more lands to tax, which in turn gave Muscovite princes more revenue to purchase or conquer additional territory. The upshot of this was a solid central state and army that broke Mongol suzerainty on the Kulikovo plains in 1385. During the thirteenth and fourteenth centuries, Russia was placed firmly on an autocratic track, precluding a balance between prince and social classes.[62] The decisiveness of the Mongol period was expressed in a moment of theoretic flexibility by Karl Marx: "The bloody mire of Mongolian slavery, not the rude glory of the [Kievan] epoch, forms the cradle of Muscovy, and modern Russia is but the metamorphosis of Muscovy."[63]

Whereas the aristocracy of Western Europe broke from its narrow military-administrative roles within imperial orders and assumed independent local authority, the Russian aristocracy, from the boyar magnate to the meanest *pomeshchik*, was subordinated to the Muscovite prince. Boyars filled the highest-ranking military and administrative positions and were rewarded with heritable land grants (*votchina*), which fell just short of what one might call property. Pomeshchiki obtained conditional benefices for less august service to the tsar, usually in the light cavalry, and this brings us to the more centralized military structure of Russia. The military organization of Muscovy superficially resembles that of the West. In exchange for military service, the pomeshchik was granted an estate from which to draw resources to equip himself with horses, materiel, and retinue. Begun in the late fifteenth century, *pomestie* parallels in some ways the feudal benefice system begun by Charles Martel in the eighth. Whereas the Frankish monarchy was quite weak, and hence had to bestow rights, immunities, and other contractual benefits upon military servitors, Muscovite princes dealt from strength. Having benefited from Mongol tutelage, the state was already sufficiently powerful that coercion could enter its relations with social classes, and there were none of the contractual amenities or reciprocal obligations of Western feudalism. The relationship was not between lord and vassal, but between master and servant:

> There is a connection between military service and possession of land, even though the *pomest'e* is not hereditary. It is not, however, based on a feudal contract which involves *mutual* fealty between a suzerain and a vassal. Its

[62] A. E. Presniakov, *The Formation of the Great Russian State: A Study of Russian History from the Thirteenth to the Fifteenth Centuries*, A. E. Moorhouse, trans. (Chicago: Quadrangle Books, 1970), pp. 121–64, 340–91.

[63] Quoted in Alexander Yanov, *The Origins of Autocracy: Ivan the Terrible in Russian History* (Berkeley and Los Angeles: University of California Press, 1981), p. vii. Mongol influence entered the language in telling ways: the Russian words for "treasury," "customs," and "money" are derived from Mongolian, as are those for "chains" and "slavery." See Pipes, *Russia under the Old Regime*, pp. 57, 75. Marx's flexibility is encountered too rarely in his followers, who have been inclined to focus narrowly on class-based explanations for Russia's political trajectory.

source is the absolute sovereignty of the Tsar *requiring* service from his subject and *granting* a *pomest'e* in return for service. There is compulsion in this service, first of all, in the interest of the community, and Peter Struve defines it as . . . "a kind of state feudalism, but in its legal aspect . . . in some ways the direct opposite of classical Western feudalism."[64]

Pomestie was the instrument for liquidating landholdings on Muscovy's periphery, where free ownership, independent towns, and western-style feudalism existed. Independent boyars, towns, and other princes were forced, under military threat, to surrender their property to the tsar, who might then grant the land back to them as pomestie. Some lands were simply confiscated, and the owners exiled or put to death.[65] On the relation between pomestie and surviving nonserving landowners, Pipes states: "Conditional land tenure, when it came to Russia in the 1470s, was not a feudal but an anti-feudal institution, introduced by the absolute monarch for the purpose of destroying the class of feudal princes and boyars."[66]

Reciprocal rights and duties between lord and peasant seen in the West have no counterparts on Russian soil, at least not in Muscovite Russia. Prior to Moscow's preeminence, however, nobles lived mainly in towns, and peasants were among the freest in Europe. Nobles relied for incomes not on agrarian surplus, but on booty, tribute, and commerce with the Byzantine empire.[67] It was only when the retinues of the princes became too large to be sustained by courtly revenues that the princes granted their followers land with light control over peasants, who then became tenants or hired hands, but at this point not yet serfs. Most peasants retained de facto property rights as well as the right to quit the lord's service and move to the black earth regions to the south, which were then opening up to settlement after tsarist conquest and the collapse of the khanates.[68] Migration to the south (brought on in part by the tyrannical excesses of Ivan the Terrible in the mid-sixteenth century) as well

[64] Marc Szeftel, "Aspects of Feudalism in Russian History," in Coulborn, *Feudalism in History*, p. 179 (emphasis in original). Struve's comments are taken from *The Cambridge Economic History of Europe*, Volume 1, p. 419. See also John L. H. Keep, *Soldiers of the Tsars: Army and Society in Russia 1462–1874* (Oxford: Clarendon Press, 1985), pp. 13–55. A Western parallel to this form of military organization is found only in Castile during the Reconquista, where expansion to the south gave the crown lands and revenue to place a military service class. Because of this, and the related weakness of its estates, Castile has not been considered one of the constitutional regions of Europe.

[65] Blum, *Lord and Peasant*, pp. 139–51.

[66] Pipes, *Russia under the Old Regime*, p. 52. The destruction of Novgorod's independence, the seizure of the patriciate's lands (1470), and their distribution to loyal military retainers was, in effect, the beginning of pomestie.

[67] Blum, *Lord and Peasant*, pp. 30–32.

[68] Ibid., pp. 45–48, 96–97.

as the labor requirements of the expanding pomestie lands, led to gradual restrictions on peasant mobility, and ultimately to the reduction of peasants to chattel in 1649.[69] The legal status of the serf was abysmal: "To all intents and purposes, the only rights that had been left to him were those that his lord was willing to allow him; the only recourse he had against the exactions and oppressions of his seigneur were the illegal expedients of flight and violence."[70]

This unrelentingly bleak depiction of Russian constitutional history is only slightly attenuated by forms of popular government that persisted into the early modern period, even until Stolypin's reforms of 1906. The Russian peasant commune, known variously as *obschina, mir,* and *volost,* has been idealized and praised by reactionary Slavophiles and socialists alike.[71] Communes had their own local governments elected by male heads of household. They controlled tax collection, managed communal lands, and oversaw or codetermined local police and judiciaries. The rise of pomestie reduced the political and judicial autonomy of the communes but left much of local government intact. Insofar as communal government was an efficient method of organizing labor owed the seigneur, collecting taxes, and transmitting decrees, neither tsar nor lord wanted to dismantle it. Although local government remained in the communes, its

[69] Ibid., pp. 220–45. By the mid-seventeenth century, the pomeshchiki cavalry was becoming increasingly obsolete, replaced by infantry using new gunpowder weaponry. Pomestie became an effective administrative device for controlling the peasantry during a protracted period of rural revolt. Their function shifted from dealing with external threats to handling internal ones. See Richard Hellie, *Enserfment and Military Change in Muscovy* (Chicago: University of Chicago Press, 1971), pp. 235–65. Hence, this process of enserfment arose primarily from political and military considerations, not from the economic ones that led to serfdom in Prussia and Poland. Moore notes this distinction in *Social Origins,* p. 463n.

[70] Blum, *Lord and Peasant,* p. 276. The military service-citizenship nexus offered rights for some peasants. The *odnodvortsy* were peasants settled on the vast frontier regions whose paramilitary service was rewarded with heritable property rights and sometimes emancipation. But of course as the frontier was extended, the rights were withdrawn. See ibid., pp. 481–82, 479, 518–19. Similar arrangements emerged on Castile's southern frontiers during the Reconquista.

[71] The volost was a rural commune, primarily in the black earth region, which developed in the early thirteenth century, whereas the mir or obschina (the terms are largely synonymous) is of uncertain though certainly ancient origins. See ibid., pp. 94–98, 510–25. In correspondence with Mikhailovsky, Tkachev and Zasulich, Marx and Engels themselves held that it was not impossible that the mir could provide a socialist infrastructure enabling Russia to bypass capitalism and proceed directly to a modern form of socialism. Many disparate revolutionary movements, Decembrists, Slavophiles, and Westernizing populists, saw the mir as a means of avoiding capitalism as well as a basis for the moral and political regeneration of Russia. See Andrzej Walicki, *A History of Russian Thought from the Enlightenment to Marxism* (Stanford, Calif.: Stanford University Press, 1979), pp. 62–68, 93–98, 198–200.

impact on government was nil. It had no capacity to articulate interests or demands to the state.

As we have seen, there was no balance of power between tsar and aristocracy amidst which towns could wrest autonomy from traditional authorities. The pre-Mongol history of Russian towns suggests a further obstacle to the development of independent towns. Kievan Russia's trade with Constantinople was conducted by river towns ruled by appanage princes, not by nascent middle classes growing in the interstices of feudal rule. Muscovite princes and tsars were cautious to prevent the rise of powerful economic elites. As soon as commodities became lucrative, they were declared state monopolies, thereby forcing all sales to the state at fixed prices that enriched state coffers. Throughout the fifteenth century, rulers preserved the preeminence of Moscow by forcing artisans and merchants to reside in Moscow. Many prosperous merchants were coerced into quitting their businesses and becoming managers (*gosti*) of imperial monopolies and enterprises, while most others developed a cooperative relationship with the state, which favored them with contracts, monopolies, and loans.[72] Towns, with the short-lived exception of Novgorod, remained either subservient economic centers or administrative-military outposts of tsarist officials. Novgorod was the exception to this rule, at least temporarily. Distant from the Mongols and the Muscovite heartland, Lord Novgorod developed commercial ties with the West and even entered the Hanse League. Government was in the hands of the popularly elected assembly (*veche*), which elected a princely administrator and developed a written constitution in the mid-thirteenth century. Covetous of Novgorod's wealth and irritated by its autonomy, Ivan III crushed the town's liberties and veche. Thousands of citizens were exiled or executed, their lands seized and used to begin the pomestie system.[73]

The veche was not unknown prior to the Mongols, but it never attained the formal structure and procedural rigor of the Novgorod veche. The veches were, for the most part, informal gatherings with no control over policy, taxation, or the judiciary. Most were destroyed by the Mongols or their Muscovite vassals.[74] We must face the puzzling fact that as-

[72] Paul Bushkovitch, *The Merchants of Moscow 1580–1660* (Cambridge: Cambridge University Press, 1980), pp. 151–67; Samuel H. Baron, "Entrepreneurs and Entrepreneurship in Sixteenth/Seventeenth-Century Russia," in Fred V. Carstensen and Gregory Guroff, eds., *Entrepreneurship in Imperial Russia and the Soviet Union* (Princeton, N.J.: Princeton University Press, 1983), pp. 27–58.

[73] Pipes, *Russia Under the Old Regime*, pp. 36–37, 80–82. On continuity in town-state relations see J. Michael Hittle, *The Service City: State and Townsmen in Russia 1660–1800* (Cambridge, Mass.: Harvard University Press, 1979).

[74] Marc Szeftel, "La participation des assemblées populaires dans le gouvernement central de la Russie depuis l'époque Kiévienne jusqu'à la fin du XVIIIe siècle," *Gouvernés et Gouvernants* 4 (1984): 339–45.

semblies of the land (*zemskii sobor*) were convoked in the sixteenth century at a time when the state was already highly centralized, with its own taxation system, and social groups were either extremely weak, intimidated, or tied to the state. This contrasts with the Western pattern of origin during times of royal weakness, when the crown had to negotiate support from the estates of the realm. The composition and function of the zemskii sobor solve the puzzle. The "elections" of representatives to the assemblies were directed not by local gentry or village communes, but by the central military administration (*Razriadnyi Prikaz*). Hardly an impartial body, it arranged the election of pomeshchiki, beholden merchants, and other state servants whose support was unquestioned.[75] Zemskii sobor were never intended to be the sounding board and instrument of consensus that the estates were in the West; the prince's power was such that that was not necessary. Zemskii sobor did not control taxation and matters of war and peace. Their purposes were to provide the appearance of national support for the tsar and to intimidate independent-minded boyars prior to Ivan IV's complete subjugation of the aristocracy.[76]

Needless to say, in this land of autocracy and increasing servitude, we can hardly speak of the rule of law, only the rule of tsars. The state's origin as the enforcement agency of the Mongols gave it overwhelming power in relation to social classes whose counterparts in the West negotiated binding systems of law with, or forced them on, monarchs. Even after Mongol suzerainty was broken, Russia was continuously at war, requiring further centralization and latitude of action that strict legal propriety would inhibit. There were no legal rights or guarantees for the subjects of Muscovy, only conditional extensions of privilege to subservient clients. Law, as it developed in Muscovite Russia, concerned itself with national security and antistate activity, leaving the more day-to-day aspects of civil and criminal law to the nobles.[77] Russia remained a land in which property, almost all of which was claimed at least in theory by the state, could be seized or transferred arbitrarily. The executions, exiles, and destruction of liberties of Ivan IV's reign of terror (*Oprichnina*) were but the most intense and violent expressions of the tsar's position above the law.

[75] Ibid., p. 353; Ellerd Hulbert, "Sixteenth-Century Russian Assemblies of the Land: Their Composition, Organization, and Competence," Doctoral thesis, Department of History, University of Chicago, 1970, pp. 140–46.

[76] Ibid., pp. 116–17. Zemskii sobor exerted some influence in affairs of state during and shortly after interregna, but princely power was soon reasserted. See J.L.H. Keep, "The Decline of the Zemsky Sobor," *The Slavic and East Europe Review* 36 (1957): 100–22.

[77] Pipes, *Russia Under the Old Regime*, p. 109.

JAPAN

Prior to the establishment of the Tokugawa shogunate in 1603, Japan endured cycles of short-lived ascendencies of baronial factions followed by breakdown and civil war. The Taiho, Kamakura, and Ashikaga periods (eighth to thirteenth centuries) all failed to construct enduring political institutions. The Onin War (1467–1477) and the ensuing century of war (the Age of the Country at War) were typical of the conflicts. They involved no broad national issues such as fundamental constitutional matters or religion; they only decided which competing faction would temporarily rule. It was not uncommon for competing houses to be completely destroyed.[78] During this period there was no balance of power between shogun and warlords, only short-lived suppression of feudal warfare followed by collapse and new war.[79]

The process of imposing stability and central institutionalization was begun in the mid-sixteenth century by Nobunaga. He established a number of loyal warriors and expanded his demesnes. Hideyoshi and Tokugawa Ieyasu continued these processes in the next half century, until the latter decisively defeated a confederation of *daimyo* at Sekigahara (1600). Ieyasu's state or *bakufu* was far from rationalized; it ruled in a largely ad hoc manner through the loyal *fudai daimyo*, and left most local administrative powers, including those of the judiciary, military organization, and economic policy, in the hands of the vanquished *tozama daimyo*.[80]

Despite relative tranquility during the two and a half centuries of the Tokugawa shogunate, there was no balance analogous to the situation in the West. The relationship between shogun and daimyo resembled more that between antagonistic states in which there is stability, even peace, but little in the way of coming to terms, mutual trust, or cooperation.[81] Tokugawa revenue was based on collecting rice from the family's consid-

---

[78] See John Whitney Hall, "Feudalism in Japan—A Reassessment," in John W. Hall and Marius B. Jansen, eds., *Studies in the Institutional History of Early Modern Japan* (Princeton, N.J.: Princeton University Press, 1968), pp. 40–43; and Sir George Sansom, *A History of Japan, 1334–1615*, Volume 1 (Stanford, Calif.: Stanford University Press, 1961), pp. 3–260.

[79] The emperor had been largely a figurehead at least since the Kamakura period. He did not figure in the political calculus, except as a legitimizing force for the shogun.

[80] Albert Craig, "The Central Government," in Marius B. Jansen and Gilbert Rozman, eds., *Japan in Transition: From Tokugawa to Meiji* (Princeton, N.J.: Princeton University Press, 1986), pp. 37–39.

[81] The absence of serious external threat during the Tokugawa shogunate probably contributed to the absence of cooperative, constitutional patterns between shogun and daimyo. Foreign dangers led to increased cooperation between monarch and key social groups in medieval and early modern Europe, at least prior to the military revolution, when expenses precluded cooperation and force was needed to finance modern armies.

erable demesne, not by negotiation and dialogue with fiscally indispensable burghers and landowners. Thus, a critical nexus for constitutional development leading to the rise of the estates in Europe was missing. Owing to the regime's predilection for maintaining stability and avoiding incitement of another baronial war, Tokugawa rulers left most tozama daimyo latitude in governing their lands, and hence they had little interest in (or opportunity for, for that matter) developing representative power in the bakufu. The Tokugawa shogunate was a watchdog state that sought primarily to prevent conspiracy and rebellion, and never tried to build a national system like that found in early modern Europe. The means to that static end was a network of watchful officials and spies, forcing all daimyo, fudai and tozama alike, to reside or leave hostages under the shadow of Chiyoda castle.[82] Grisly displays of brute force demonstrated the costs of resistance. It is not surprising that, when the Tokugawa shogunate was overthrown in 1868, its demise resembled not a broad social revolution or dynastic change, but a revolt from peripheral provinces.

The shogun could boast of commanding four hundred thousand troops, but this number included samurai and bannermen of the tozama daimyo, whose reliability was questionable at best. So, despite the nominal right to levy troops and marshall supplies from all the daimyo, the shogun's forces were only a fraction of that number.[83] The Tokugawa military was sizable, however, and was paid by stipends from the family demesne. The shogun's vassals did not enjoy a range of privileges and immunities. The tozama daimyo retained administrative control of their lands, but this stemmed from the reluctance of the shogun to risk further war, not from feudal contract or largesse. Some citizenship rights had been enjoyed by soldier-farmers prior to the centralization of the sixteenth century, but the Pax Tokugawa brought on obsolescence and disarmament in Hideyoshi's Sword Hunt. The daimyo's and samurai's exclusive right to bear arms entailed the general leveling of citizenship rights among the peasantry.[84]

Village self-government was quite strong in Tokugawa Japan, but it lacked the critical dimensions of independence and popular basis. The headman and elders composed the nucleus of village government. These

[82] Toshio G. Tsukahira, *Feudal Control in Tokugawa Japan: The* Sankin Kotai *System* (Cambridge, Mass.: Harvard East Asian Monographs, 1966); Sir George Sansom, *A History of Japan, 1615–1867*, Volume 2 (Stanford, Calif.: Stanford University Press, 1963), pp. 23, 47–49.

[83] Conrad T. Totman, *Politics in the Tokugawa Bakufu, 1600–1843* (Cambridge, Mass.: Harvard University Press, 1967), pp. 43–45; D. Eleanor Westney, "The Military," in Jansen and Rozman, *Japan in Transition*, p. 169.

[84] Mary Elizabeth Berry, *Hideyoshi* (Cambridge, Mass.: Harvard University Press, 1989), pp. 102–6; Sansom, *History of Japan*, Volume 2, pp. 331–32.

positions were normally heritable, though they were sometimes informally selected by the propertied persons of the village.[85] Their work entailed collecting taxes for the bakufu, organizing public works, and maintaining the ideé fixe of Tokugawa rule, law and order. Shogunate officials either ordered or closely supervised the execution of these tasks. Outside forces also made their presence felt in the policy of collective responsibility whereby village leaders, or the village as a whole, was accountable for the transgressions of individuals. Group responsibility existed at an even more microsocial level: the *Gonin-gumi* system divided villagers into five household units, collectively accountable for taxes, enforcement of contracts, and ensuring that behavior conformed with Tokugawa senses of propriety. The system was highly authoritarian in nature: "The *Gonin-gumi* was . . . an agency of self-government not arising from popular initiative but imposed upon communities by the governing class. Its chief purpose was to preserve order and to keep authorities informed of conditions in both town and village. It was in fact a police organ for spying and delation, characteristic of the official attitude towards problems of administration."[86]

Hideyoshi's cadastral survey and attendant decrees tied peasants to the soil and effectively froze their social status. His decrees were not without rationalizing effects beneficial to the peasantry: the number of persons to whom peasants owed taxes was greatly reduced; their social position was fixed, but they were conferred with heritable tenant status. In the absence of shogunate judiciaries at the village level, custom law prevailed and provided a basis for routinizing lord-peasant relations.[87] Though the peasant was not chattel, he was squeezed, often mercilessly, by his samurai lord, and, when rebellion broke out, made into a hideous example by authorities.[88] Villages were too closely controlled by state and samurai to serve as a source of constitutional development.

The early years of Nobunaga saw the extension of some corporate status and rights to the towns under his then limited control. Tax immunities were granted, town dwellers were exempted from corvée, and debt moratoriums (decreed by many warlords, to the consternation of mer-

[85] Harumi Befu, "Village Autonomy and Articulation with the State," in Hall and Jansen, *Studies in the Institutional History*, pp. 302–3; Thomas C. Smith, "The Japanese Village of the Seventeenth Century," ibid., p. 270.

[86] Sansom, *History of Japan*, Volume 3, 102.

[87] Sansom, *History of Japan*, Volume 2, pp. 317–19, Volume 3, p. 98; Dan Fenno Henderson, "The Evolution of Tokugawa Law," in Hall and Jansen, *Studies in the Institutional History*, p. 228. On the general freezing of society, see Berry, *Hideyoshi*, pp. 106ff.

[88] Stephen Vlastos, *Peasant Protests and Uprisings in Tokugawa Japan* (Berkeley and Los Angeles: University of California Press, 1986), pp. 59–72, 123–30, 142–53; Herbert P. Bix, *Peasant Protest in Japan, 1590–1884* (New Haven, Conn.: Yale University Press, 1986). I thank Barrington Moore for these references.

chants) were prohibited. But Hideyoshi and Ieyasu reversed this course and established firm control over the towns.[89] The Tokugawa constructed many castle-towns (*jokomachi*) as administrative centers and garrisons to watch the tozama daimyo and attend to shogunate interests. Merchants were lured to the new castle-towns by the presence of regularly paid officials or were coerced into residence by the more visible hand of the bakufu.[90] Daimyo and shogun alike established monopolies, took merchants as protected clients, and made some prosperous merchants into servitors. Although the merchant elite often formed a town council, government was conducted under the watchful eyes of the shogun's officials. Merchants had neither the autonomous municipal sanctuaries from which they could challenge feudal authority, nor any appreciable independence from shogun or daimyo. There was a close working relationship between bourgeoisie and shogun: "The leading merchants became, as time went on, more strongly allied with the feudal order, more dependent upon feudal privileges, and hence less inclined to oppose the dominant political order."[91]

The judicial system, limited though it was, never attained separation from administrative apparatuses. Indeed, court chambers were often the very offices of administrative functionaries.[92] Preferring to let village headmen settle most civil and even many criminal cases through informal measures ("conciliation"), the shogun never attempted to develop an extensive judiciary in the localities.[93] A student of Japanese legal history expresses well the legal system's relation to the bakufu, and the regime's reliance on village customs: "[Law] was an art of power maintenance for the expert manipulation of self-interested rulers in a society which was in the private relations of the subjects largely self-regulated. Law was an instrument to be used by rulers but not to limit their actions."[94] The law of the shogun was not a congeries of atomistic, unrelated decrees; it had a certain level of philosophical coherence derived from Confucian politi-

[89] Sansom, *History of Japan*, Volume 2, pp. 302–31; John Whitney Hall, "The Castle Towns and Japan's Modern Urbanization," in Hall and Jansen, *Studies in the Institutional History*, p. 175.

[90] Ibid., pp. 175–80.

[91] Ibid., p. 185. The author goes on to argue, however, that the merchants did undermine the feudal *economic* order by shifting the economic center of gravity from the countryside to the towns, thereby preparing the country for the swift transformations of the Meiji period (pp. 185–88). See also Gilbert Rozman, "Castle Towns in Transition," in Jansen and Rozman, *Japan in Transition*, pp. 318–46.

[92] Dan Fenno Henderson, "The Evolution of Tokugawa Law," in Hall and Jansen, *Studies in the Institutional History*, pp. 221, 229.

[93] Dan Fenno Henderson, *Conciliation and Japanese Law, Tokugawa and Modern* (Seattle: University of Washington Press, 1965), pp. 127–70.

[94] Henderson, "The Evolution of Tokugawa Law," p. 208.

cal philosophy and ethics.[95] While Confucian thought was rich in eloquence and insight, it lacked the humanistic aspects of causation, free will, responsibility, and logical inference that informed Roman Law. It was a system of thought that grew out of another sharply stratified society, and which in turn legitimized, harmonized, and ultimately helped to maintain those social cleavages: "Nothing was of more constitutional import to the Tokugawa law than the rigid, heritable hierarchy of statuses established to classify the entire Tokugawa populace. The barriers were maintained between these statuses by Edo decrees and the Confucian thought patterns."[96] It is only appropriate that we now shift our attention to Confucianism's homeland.

CHINA

The rise and fall of dynasties in the Middle Kingdom resemble in some ways the numerous shogunates of pre-Meiji Japan. Whereas the shoguns failed to build a strong central apparatus, China had had a strong state at least since the Han period (202 B.C.–A.D. 220). China was periodically conquered by alien armies such as the Mongols and Manchus, or overwhelmed by internal movements, but dynastic change entailed either swift assumption or reconstruction of a strong state. To find a situation analogous to medieval Europe, we must go back to the Chou dynasty (1122 B.C.–771 B.C.), which had over a thousand fiefs with written charters stipulating rights and obligations. But Chou feudalism was without lasting significance; it disintegrated in the eighth century B.C. into a chaos of warring city-states.[97]

The collapse of Mongol rule (Yüan dynasty, 1280–1367) was followed by the rise of the M'ings (1368–1643) and the reconstruction of the gentry civil service, which had fallen into desuetude. The Mongols, whose expertise was always more martial than administrative, had given the provincial governors a measure of independence, but the M'ings replaced

---

[95] Henderson, *Conciliation and Japanese Law*, pp. 37–38, 58.

[96] Ibid., p. 25.

[97] Wolfram Eberhard, *A History of China* (London: Routledge & Kegan Paul, 1977), pp. 23–59. It is significant that the Chou military relied mainly on self-equipped charioteers. See Herrlee G. Creel, *The Origins of Statecraft in China*, Volume 1: *The Western Chou Empire* (Chicago: University of Chicago Press, 1970), pp. 242–387. The Taipings attempted to organize self-equipped armies along Chou patterns (*Chou-li*), but were defeated by centralized and increasingly westernized imperial armies. See Franz Michael, *The Taiping Rebellion: History and Documents*, Volume 1 (Seattle: University of Washington Press, 1966), pp. 43–44, 61; and David B. Ralston, *Importing the European Army: The Introduction of European Military Techniques and Institutions into the Extra-European World, 1600–1914* (Chicago: University of Chicago Press, 1990), pp. 107–41.

that with a strong hierarchical state.[98] In the century after the Mongol defeat, the M'ings articulated their control by building powerful state organs at various levels, controlling administration, the judiciary, the police, and an elaborate system of revenue collection.[99] It is easy to exaggerate the degree of control enjoyed by M'ing and early Ch'ing rulers. Bribery, peculation, and the mandarinate's pursuit of its own interests were widespread and acted as some limit on state power, though obviously not in the direction of constitutional government. During periods of crisis (e.g., the Taiping and Boxer rebellions), provincial authorities attempted to break free from imperial control. The upshot was not the extension of a charter from a weakened state, only brief autonomy or warlordism, as in the late Ch'ing period. Nonetheless, the term "oriental despotism," tainted as it is by suspect sociology and abstruse philosophy, is not unwarranted. Challenges to state or mandarinate power from emerging commercial enterprises were met by stifling taxation, price controls, or demands for bribes, all of which combined to thwart rivals to official power.[100] Secure in their revenue sources, state officials did not have to curry favor with a nascent bourgeoisie.

Along with the construction of the M'ing state occurred the development of a central army to replace the ragtag forces that had defeated the decrepit Mongol military. The new M'ing army defeated warlordism and crystallized into a key institution of the emerging dynasty. Begun in the 1370s, the *Wei-so* system comprised a series of military garrisons strategically stationed throughout the land, primarily for purposes of repression. Garrisons were self-sufficient military colonies based on state property and manned by ethnic groups different from the ones they were guarding. It was typical for seventy percent of the troops to work the land while the rest performed garrison duties. Officers were granted heritable status, providing honor and opportunity for their sons, but this was a privilege more than a right, without any of the immunities and contractual amenities of western feudalism. Originally developed by the Han dynasty (202 B.C.–A.D. 220) for frontier defense, the Wei-so military organization became predominant in the M'ing period, supporting 1.2 million troops on approximately five percent of the arable land of China.[101]

[98] Edward L. Dreyer, *Early Ming China: A Political History 1355–1435* (Stanford, Calif.: Stanford University Press, 1982), pp. 98–102.

[99] Ibid., pp. 124–31.

[100] Etienne Balazs, *Chinese Civilization and Bureaucracy: Variations on a Theme* (New Haven: Yale University Press, 1972), pp. 41–48.

[101] Dreyer, *Early Ming China*, pp. 76–82; Philip A. Kuhn, *Rebellion and Its Enemies in Late Imperial China: Mobilization and Social Structure, 1796–1864* (Cambridge, Mass.: Harvard University Press, 1980), p. 20. The Wei-so system was reorganized into a more centralized form in the mid-fifteenth century, but the principle of self-sufficiency was retained (Dreyer, *Early Ming China*, pp. 191–92, 240–41). Indeed, to a certain extent self-

The Wei-so army was doubly detrimental to constitutional dynamics: it was highly centralized and loyal to the state, and its function was principally to suppress peasant unrest, not to defend the nation from outside enemies.

Other forms of military organization emerged during the M'ing and Ch'ing periods. The Taiping and Boxer movements triggered state crises and moves for autonomy on the part of provincial governors. Simultaneously there emerged at the local level warlord armies, whose duties were to provide for local defense in the absence of effectual imperial forces, and also to aid in the movement for autonomy. Furthermore, local militias were formed at the village level to protect the community from brigandage and from the White Lotus's guerrilla-like forces, which evaded all too well cumbersome army units. But even here, most of the militias were closely linked to the state.[102] Owing to their transitory and antistate qualities, neither warlord armies nor village militias were of constitutional import. They were ad hoc reactions to disorder brought on by transitory state weakness. These forces sought no charter from or modus vivendi with imperial authority; instead, they either tried only to protect the village or region, or to make a bold, usually unsuccessful, bid for independence from imperial control.

Village government in China closely resembles that of Japan and Russia in its elected officials and other forms of primitive democracy. But, as in those other countries, villages were greatly overshadowed by the imperial apparatus just outside the village gates. Another resemblance is the *pao-chia* organization, which parallels the Gonin-gumi of Tokugawa Japan. Both were systems of mutual responsibility linking villagers to outside authority. Though its origins are rooted in the obscure past and seem to be based on ancient Legalist thought, pao-chia solidified as early as the T'ang period (618–906). Used as a mechanism of tax collection and conscription, pao-chia, by its principle of group responsibility for individual deviance, provided a largely invisible but omnipresent device for directing behavior to acceptable, Confucian patterns.[103]

Tenantry and bonded servitude began in the Chinese countryside during the T'ang period, not out of political or military considerations, but because of crushing debts incurred by the free peasantry. By the early

---

sufficiency is retained to this day by the People's Liberation Army. For other sources of a purely military nature, see Ch'en Wen-shih, "The Creation of the Manchu *Niru*," *Chinese Studies in History* 14 (1981): 11–46; and Liu Chia-chü, "The Creation of the Banners in the Early Ch'ing," *Chinese Studies in History* 14 (1981): 47–75.

[102] See Kuhn, *Rebellion and Its Enemies*, pp. 40–55; and Dreyer, *Early Ming China*, pp. 20–25.

[103] Eberhard, *History of China*, pp. 176–78; Kuhn, *Rebellion and Its Enemies*, pp. 24–25.

thirteenth century, an estate economy prevailed.[104] Peasant unrest during the Mongol period led to a closing of ranks by the rural gentry and imperial authority, and eventually to more unrest, which undermined Mongol rule and aided in the rise of the M'ing dynasty in 1368.[105] The M'ing restoration of the civil service engendered a corrupt new bureaucratic class whose exactions and peculation led to further exploitation of the peasantry.[106] This unfortunate lord-peasant relationship persisted until the wars and famines of the early seventeenth century brought on demographic changes, shifting bargaining power into the hands of the peasantry, much as the plagues had done in fourteenth-century Europe.[107] Bondsmen took advantage of this seller's market for labor services and won tenant status; former tenants obtained more favorable lease terms and in many cases got control of their lands; hired laborers won better pay, working arrangements, and benefits such as festivals and gifts. Written charters regulated lord-peasant relations regarding terms of leases, landlord obligations to widows and orphans, and terms of quittal.[108] Though far behind his fellow tillers in much of Europe, the Chinese peasant made substantial progress in the early Ch'ing years. Although elevation from bondsman to tenant meant improved legal status, progress was primarily of a purely economic nature. Leverage gained in the years following the wars and famine did not yield state-sanctioned charters or rights of citizenship. Village government remained narrowly proscribed, and the peasant's voice in imperial affairs remained unheard.

Chinese towns were centers of imperial administration or military garrisons: administrative commanding heights from which the mandarinate dominated the surrounding countryside. So crucial were towns to the functioning of the region that, during periods of war, generals attached primacy to vanquishing towns, secure in the knowledge that the environs would necessarily come under their control.[109] Imperial control in the towns was overwhelming. Whereas European towns were divided along functional lines (bastion, market, faubourg), imperial officials imposed an artificial system of walled subdivisions (feng), greatly facilitating social control by administrators and police. Town air made no one free: "The

[104] Balazs, *Chinese Civilization and Bureaucracy*, pp. 117–19.

[105] Eberhard, *History of China*, pp. 240–49.

[106] Ibid., p. 261.

[107] Mi Chu Wiens, "Lord and Peasant: The Sixteenth to the Eighteenth Century," *Modern China* 6 (1980): 8–12. The author estimates that the rural population declined by approximately forty percent.

[108] Ibid., pp. 12–29, 34–35. The state was not a party to these charters, which were drawn up by individual estate owners and their peasants.

[109] Herbert Franke, "Siege and Defense of Towns in Medieval China," in Frank A. Kierman, Jr., and John K. Fairbank, eds., *Chinese Ways in Warfare* (Cambridge, Mass.: Harvard University Press, 1974), pp. 151–201; Dreyer, *Early Ming China*, p. 89.

town was dominated by officials who represented the imperial government, particularly insofar as judicial and fiscal matters were concerned, and since . . . it did not embody the idea of emancipation and of liberty, neither did it act as a magnet to the people of the countryside. On the contrary, all those who rebelled against the oppressive powers of the official hierarchy took refuge in the villages so as to escape from the clutches of bureaucracy."[110]

M'ing and Ch'ing courts ruled China unrestrained by estates or local government. Nor was the court subordinated to the rule of law. It was, however, at least partially limited by the civil service and by the dictates of Confucian political and judicial principles. Early M'ing emperors ruled despotically, and, though they restored the civil service system, they aimed to preclude the bureaucracy's coalescence into a coherent organization capable of thwarting court decrees.[111] By the mid-fifteenth century, however, a corps of professional officials governed China in a less arbitrary manner, largely free from the emperor's day-to-day meddling.[112] Judicial administration was in the hands of imperial magistrates who, while not specially trained in law, were neither incompetent nor arbitrary.[113] China developed comprehensive legal codifications and guidelines that remained essentially intact until the Republican era.[114]

To some extent, Confucianism provided a philosophical grounding that gave a measure of coherence to legal codifications. But once again, Confucianism's principal concern was with maintaining the social order, not with establishing procedural and substantive norms limiting authority. On the contrary, it in effect legitimized blocking the emergence of an independent legal profession, seizure or control of private property that could upset the status quo, and the application of different legal principles to officials, peasants, and soldiers. Chinese legal thought always retained a strong measure of Legalist authoritarianism, even after Legalism had been largely eclipsed by Confucianism during the Han period.[115]

[110] Balazs, *Chinese Civilization and Bureaucracy*, p. 70.

[111] Dreyer, *Early Ming China*, pp. 107ff.

[112] Ibid., pp. 215–20.

[113] Derek Bodde and Clarence Morris, *Law in Imperial China: Exemplified by 190 Ch'ing Dynasty Cases* (Philadelphia: University of Pennsylvania Press, 1967), pp. 77–143. Imperial China, like Tokugawa Japan, limited the scope of its judiciary, preferring instead to force most litigation on less formal authorities such as the village, sib, and guild.

[114] Ibid., p. 60. For imperial control over the judicary and other elements of local government, see T'ung-tsu Chü, *Local Government in China under the Ch'ing* (Cambridge, Mass.: Harvard University Press, 1988).

[115] Ibid., pp. 27–50.

. . .

Russia, Japan, and China never developed constitutional government as found in late medieval Europe. Structural configurations conducive to constitutionalism in the West, rough balance between crown and noble, contractual-feudal military organization, and lord-peasant dynamics were absent or weak. Nor has any other substantial source, such as religion or economic organization, been uncovered to compensate for these absences and foster constitutionalism. Instead we have found powerful central states, unencumbered by estates, legal necessities, or local centers of power. There were no independent towns, only what Marx called "appendages of princely courts" and Weber termed "consumer cities." Instead of rights enjoyed by many levels of society, there were only privileges.

Village government, on the other hand, has been found to be ubiquitous and vital in some non-Western regions, but always dwarfed and sometimes supervised by authoritarian state structures. Village government, in and of itself, lacked constitutional significance unless it coalesced with other, stronger constitutional institutions. The key to understanding village self-government in autocratic countries lies in its usefulness to authority: states found it advantageous to retain village government as an efficient means of collecting taxes, organizing labor teams for fortifications and roads, and communicating imperial directives to distant subjects.[116]

In Russia and Japan we encountered military organizations that seemed to parallel feudal militaries in the West. In both countries, military service was rewarded with a conditional grant of land, but without the immunities and contractual qualities of Western feudalism. What then accounts for the drastic political differences between Western military organization and that of the tsar or shogun? Both military organizations were predicated on the ruler's inability to pay for a centralized military structure with only limited revenue sources, which, in turn, might have been due to economic backwardness, a largely unmonetarized economy, or administrative incapacity to garner sufficient revenue. Rulers built militaries by awarding estates from the royal demesnes or ecclesiastical lands. The critical dimension distinguishing East from West seems to be the relative power of the state at the outset of the military benefice system. Where the state was relatively strong, as it was under Ivan III at

---

[116] For the relationship between French absolutism and village government, see Hilton R. Root, *Peasants and King in Burgundy: Agrarian Foundations of French Absolutism* (Berkeley and Los Angeles: University of California Press, 1987).

the beginnings of pomestie and under Ieyasu fresh from his victory at Sekigahara, the ruler was in a far better power position vis-à-vis the nobility than were Carolingian or Salic kings, who were little more than military chieftains. Charlemagne and Otto the Great had only weak household governments, which compare poorly with the Muscovite state built under Mongol tutelage, or with the power of Ieyasu's bakufu. In short, weak monetary resources and weak state power yield contractual military feudalism; weak monetary resources and even modest state power change the political equation and yield a more centralized system of military benefices, without contract, without immunities, and without constitutional import.

It is important to note once more that medieval constitutionalism was not democracy, nor was it sufficient cause of it. It was, however, characterized by parliaments, citizenship, decentralized power, and the rule of law, absent in other parts of the world. Thus far, perhaps too much emphasis has been placed on beginnings in tensions, opposition, and mistrust between the monarchy and key social classes, at the expense of looking at its more hospitable stability by the close of the Middle Ages. Though in existence at the origins—let us say, for example, at Runnymede—mistrust and opposition evolved after centuries of experiment into trust and cooperation. Constitutional government was not a standoff between a would-be despot and parliamentary opposition; it was a practicable form of government, combining king and estates, based on "cooperation and a mutual willingness to oblige."[117] Estates were not adjunct opposition parties, but essential and cooperative parts of the late medieval state, which supplied revenue and a sense of the country to the king, who, in turn, was obliged to redress grievances, make concessions if need be, and govern lawfully. Cooperation and custom became deeply ingrained in king and estates. Disputes and conflicts there were, but to enlarge them beyond their proper dimensions and mistake healthy disagreement for hostile opposition misrepresents the nature of the medieval state and all too easily falls into moralizing and determinism.

The constitutional achievement, then, was the product of the chaos and mistrust of imperial decline, but, after centuries of work, an impressive constitutional edifice was built. The dualistic constitutional state was a uniquely European form of government that handled well the financial, military, and religious problems of the late medieval and Renaissance periods. The product of the Middle Ages, it was naturally suited for the problems of that period, but new problems of war and finance arose in the early modern period. When military expenses greatly outstripped

[117] Conrad S. R. Russell, "Monarchies, Wars, and Estates in England, France, and Spain, c. 1580–c. 1640," *Legislative Studies Quarterly* 7 (1982): 213.

economic growth, onerous responsibilities shifted onto the state. The intensity of war and the availability of outside resources determined if the constitutional state could endure and serve as a basis for liberal democracy, or if, like too many other medieval edifices, it would be destroyed and replaced by a less decorous though eminently functional construction.

CHAPTER THREE

The Military Revolution

MEDIEVAL constitutionalism had as its main defensive carapace a decentralized form of military organization that composed one source of constitutionalism. But conflicts within the crystallizing European state system engendered competition, technological and tactical innovation, and changes in military organization, and these had important effects on the political order. The means of destruction changed from relatively small feudal levies and militias to large mercenary and standing armies, which required a new superstructural apparatus to guarantee inputs of capital and labor. A more centralized and coercive state was needed to extract these inputs from an unwilling population. The expense of military modernization conflicted with medieval constitutionalism. Kings found estates no longer willing or able to provide the revenues for modern warfare. In many parts of the continent, constitutional government became as obsolete as the heavily armored knight.

FEUDAL MILITARY ORGANIZATION IN DECLINE, 1300–1500

The era of the armored knight originated with the system of military benefices built by Charles Martel to deal with the Saracen threat. The system was more fully developed throughout Europe by Charlemagne, Otto the Great, and William the Conqueror. Otto's successors in the Holy Roman Empire spread feudal military organization across the Elbe, into Poland, Austria, and Hungary. Feudal militaries were decentralized, scattered across the land on hundreds of benefices. Coordination at the regional or territorial level was slight: there were no annual maneuvers or training programs, only occasional musters to demonstrate the serviceability of armor and weaponry. Medieval warfare was not a national or territorial matter so much as it was the temporary coalescence of individuals trained, for the most part by themselves, in the art of war. Warfare did not mobilize national resources or integrate warriors into organized formations; it relied on a levy of knights whose character, breeding, and outlook placed a premium on individual merit and personal valor.[1]

---

[1] See Hans Delbrück, *History of the Art of War within the Framework of Political History*, Volume 3: *The Middle Ages* (Westport, Conn.: Greenwood Press, 1982), pp. 289–90. As we shall see, this individualism was a critical flaw in feudal military organization.

The low level of central organization and small size of armies made medieval warfare relatively inexpensive, at least from the point of view of central authority. Charlemagne's hosts conquered much of Europe west of the Elbe, but probably never numbered more than five thousand. At the height of the Crusades, at the Battle of Ascalon (1099), all Christendom assembled fewer than ten thousand soldiers, and even that figure diminished during lulls.[2] Furthermore, the timely sack of a city, infidel or Christian, defrayed the expenses of the noble crusaders. Armor, which became heavier in the course of the Middle Ages, was quite costly, having roughly the same value as forty head of cattle. Specially bred war horses, of which each knight required two or three, were also of considerable value. But these were expenses incurred by vassals themselves and not by their overlord. The state did not yet shoulder the costs of war.[3]

Castles were originally of the old motte and bailey variety, constructed out of earthen mounds surrounding a wooden bastion, but, in the second half of the eleventh century, the towering stone castles with which we are more familiar began to replace them. These castles, such as the line of castellar fortifications built by Plantagenets in their French holdings, were often financed and built with the king's demesnes revenues. Like their architectural contemporaries, the cathedrals, they were constructed over the course of many years, and required no extraordinary fiscal measures.[4]

Everywhere in Europe, even in the most heavily feudalized parts of northern France, the knight was supported by infantry levies, essential though secondary parts of feudal military organization. In France, the Holy Roman Empire, and England, able-bodied men were levied and organized into militias (*ban, arrière ban, Heerfolge,* and fyrd).[5] Aside from these levies, infantry for most medieval battles came from three

[2] Philippe Contamine, *War in the Middle Ages,* Michael Jones, trans. (Oxford: Basil Blackwell, 1986), pp. 59–64; Delbrück, *History of the Art of War,* Volume 3, p. 219.

[3] R. Allen Brown, "The Status of the Norman Knight," in John Gillingham and J. C. Holt, eds., *War and Government in the Middle Ages: Essays in Honour of J. O. Prestwich* (Totowa, N.J.: Barnes & Noble, 1984), pp. 18–32.

[4] On castles, see *The Cambridge Medieval History,* Volume 6, pp. 776–81; John Beeler, *Warfare in Feudal Europe, 730–1200* (Ithaca, N.Y.: Cornell University Press, 1984), pp. 25–28, 98–100; and Contamine, *War in the Middle Ages,* pp. 110–13.

[5] Beeler, *Warfare in Feudal Europe,* pp. 40–41; André Corvisier, *Armies and Societies in Europe, 1494–1789,* Abigail T. Siddall, trans. (Bloomington: Indiana University Press, 1979), pp. 25–27; János M. Bak, "Politics, Society and Defense in Medieval and Early Modern Hungary," in János M. Bak and Béla K. Király, eds., *War and Society in Eastern Central Europe,* Volume 3: *From Hunyadi to Rákóczi, War and Society in Late Medieval and Early Modern Hungary* (New York: Brooklyn College Press, 1982), pp. 1–22; Delbrück, *History of the Art of War,* Volume 3, pp. 104–7.

sources: the town militias (part of the exchange between crown and burgher guaranteeing town autonomy); the knights' retinue of sergeants and lance-holders; and those members of the old Merovingian and Saxon warrior elite who, for various reasons, had not become beneficed knights.[6]

In mountainous or hilly areas, or in regions otherwise inhospitable to heavy cavalry and manorial agriculture, infantry predominated or even became the exclusive form of military organization. Such was the case in Switzerland, Scandinavia, and the unconquered Celtic parts of Britain. English forays into Wales and Scotland met with such fierce resistance (and often outright defeat) that the Angevins adopted Celtic infantry formations and weapons, especially the longbow.[7] Elsewhere, the heavy cavalry retained supremacy in the social hierarchy and preeminence on the field of battle, where it was the knights' charge, not the bow, sword, or pike, that won or lost the day.[8]

One myth that haunts military history contends that mercenaries did not appear until the epoch of the warring city-states of Renaissance Italy or the confessional wars of the sixteenth century. In fact, mercenary troops were to be found everywhere in medieval Europe, and even earlier. The armies with which Justinian retook Italy and North Africa in the fifth century were largely mercenary. William the Conqueror's army had a large mercenary contingent; indeed, the English military continued to use mercenaries, before and after their specific proscription in Magna Carta.[9] On the Iberian peninsula, both the Spanish and the Moors used hired lances during the Reconquista, the legendary Cid being the best known of them. In France Philip Augustus built an army of mercenaries to conquer contumacious vassals and to expand his kingdom. Charles VII

---

[6] Beeler, *Warfare in Feudal Europe*, pp. 40–51; Contamine, *War in the Middle Ages*, pp. 84–85; Delbrück, *History of the Art of War*, Volume 3, pp. 266–67, 293–94.

[7] Beeler, *Warfare in Feudal Europe*, p. 100; Contamine, *War in the Middle Ages*, pp. 152–53; Delbrück, *History of the Art of War*, Volume 3, pp. 385–92. These footsoldiers were decisive in the English victories over French chivalry during the Hundred Years' War.

[8] The charge was actually more of a trot, since the weight of the armor made rapid motion hazardous. The charge, as we commonly imagine it, did not emerge until Gustavus Adolphus's innovations during the Thirty Years' War, well after light cavalry had been adopted. See Contamine, *War in the Middle Ages*, p. 99; Michael Roberts, "Gustav Adolf and the Art of War," in Roberts, ed., *Essays in Swedish History* (Minneapolis: University of Minnesota Press, 1967). The tactical predominance of the knight, at least in the later Middle Ages, was probably as much the effect of his social superiority as it was the cause. As early as the battles of Civitate (1053) and Legnano (1176), the knight's vulnerability to infantry had been clearly demonstrated. Yet, as we shall see, adaptive tactical innovations did not quickly follow.

[9] Beeler, *Warfare in Feudal Europe*, p. 42; Sally Harvey, "The Knight and the Knight's Fee in England," in R. H. Hilton, ed., *Peasants, Knights and Heretics: Studies in Medieval English Social History* (Cambridge: Cambridge University Press, 1981), pp. 159–60; Delbrück, *History of the Art of War*, Volume 3, pp. 166–67, 189, 313–21.

continued this practice until their unreliability was made evident during the Hundred Years' War.[10]

Feudal military organization suffered from inherent problems, centuries before the introduction of the pike and gunpowder. Among these were the unreliability of feudal loyalty, a decline in competence, and a lack of discipline. The loyalty of the vassal was far from the picture of fealty presented by those who have sentimentalized this period, in which self-interest and treachery were commonplaces. Without loyalty, the efficacy of feudal armies suffered. Knights often refused to respond to their suzerain's call. They bickered over the numbers required, duration of service, regions in which they were required to serve (generally, service on foreign soil was not part of the feudal obligation), and commutation of service into scutage.[11] Even the more autocratic Russian service cavalry was not immune to discipline problems: "While Russian troops were investing [Smolensk] the Tatars attacked from the south. Servitors with land in the region hurried home to the region to repair the damage."[12]

Many things contributed to the decline of the competence of the feudal warrior class, even among those willing to heed their overlord's summons. Holders of benefices had long since thought of their estates as de facto personal property, and had begun to concern themselves more with managing the manor, to the benefit of the medieval economy but at the expense of the military.[13] Inflation often meant that many knights could no longer afford the expense of equipping themselves for longer and longer campaigns.[14] Problems plagued all Europe: "It was happening ev-

[10] Beeler, *Warfare in Feudal Europe*, pp. 40–42; Contamine, *War in the Middle Ages*, p. 153; Delbrück, *History of the Art of War*, Volume 3, p. 508.

[11] Contamine, *War in the Middle Ages*, pp. 80–85; *The Cambridge Medieval History*, Volume 6, pp. 216–18; Karol Górski, "La Ligue des Etats et les origines du régime representatif Prusse," *Studies Presented to the International Commission for the History of Representative and Parliamentary Institutions* 23 (1960): 177–85; Felix Gilbert, "Machiavelli: The Renaissance of the Art of War," in Peter Paret, ed., *Makers of Modern Strategy: From Machiavelli to the Nuclear Age* (Princeton, N.J.: Princeton University Press, 1986), pp. 12ff; Geoffrey Parker, *The Army of Flanders and the Spanish Road, 1567–1659: The Logistics of Spanish Victory and Defeat in the Low Countries' Wars* (Cambridge: Cambridge University Press, 1972), p. 47; Michael Prestwich, "Cavalry Service in Early Fourteenth Century England," in Gillingham and Holt, *War and Government*, pp. 147–58; Derek Hirst, *Authority and Conflict: England, 1603–1658* (Cambridge, Mass.: Harvard University Press, 1986), pp. 186–87; Davis Bitton, *The French Nobility in Crisis, 1560–1640* (Stanford, Calif: Stanford University Press, 1969), pp. 27–41.

[12] John L. H. Keep, *Soldiers of the Tsar: Army and Society in Russia 1462–1874* (Oxford: Clarendon Press, 1985), pp. 19–20.

[13] Corvisier, *Armies and Society*, pp. 37–38; Knud J. V. Jespersen, "Social Change and Military Revolution in Early Modern Europe: Some Danish Evidence," *Historical Journal* 26 (1983): 1–3; Lawrence Stone, *The Crisis of the Aristocracy, 1558–1640* (Oxford: Oxford University Press, 1965).

[14] Fritz Redlich, *The German Military Enterpriser and His Workforce: A Study in Eu-*

erywhere: in England knights who could not ride, in Spain *hidalgos* who could not shoot, in Milan and Naples *conti* whose sword-hands stank of trade."[15] The reliability of that part of medieval society that neither prayed nor labored was clearly in decline.

The most serious problem of the feudal military system was the lack of discipline. Though highly disciplined as individuals, the knights, when assembled into the hosts, lacked the coordination and regimentation we now associate with armies. There was no routine training and so battles lacked orderly tactical movements and disciplined behavior.[16] Knights often refused orders, especially when not given directly by the king: they had sworn allegiance to the king himself, not a placeholder. Discipline further eroded as roturiers, lower nobles, and commoners took positions of command. Knights were wont to break off combat before victory was assured in order to have first crack at plundering nearby towns, villages, and even the slain.[17] Discipline was better in the military orders, such as the Teutonic Knights, the Knights Templar, and the Brethren of the Sword. Such orders had a greater level of central organization: the grandmasters, their system of commanderies, and a strong religious ethos binding them together and to the hierarchy.[18] But they were hardly the norm, and the orders collapsed in the early sixteenth century. What Oman says of the French feudal military may be said of that of much of Europe: "The strength of the armies of Philip and John of Valois was composed of a fiery and undisciplined *noblesse*, which imagined itself to

---

ropean Economic and Social History, Volume 1 (Wiesbaden: Franz Steiner, 1964), pp. 6–8.

[15] J. R. Hale, *War and Society in Renaissance Europe, 1450–1620* (Baltimore, Md.: Johns Hopkins University Press, 1985), p. 94.

[16] Beeler, *Warfare in Feudal Europe*, pp. 250–51. Weber observed: "The berserk with maniac seizures of frenzy and the feudal knight who measures swords with an equal adversary in order to gain personal honor are equally alien to discipline." See "The Meaning of Discipline," in H. H. Gerth and C. Wright Mills, eds., *From Max Weber: Essays in Sociology* (New York: Oxford University Press, 1976), p. 254.

[17] Sir Charles Oman, *A History of the Art of War in the Sixteenth Century* (New York: E. P. Dutton, 1937), pp. 654–751; Christopher Allmand, *The Hundred Years War: England and France at War c. 1300–c. 1450* (Cambridge: Cambridge University Press, 1988), pp. 43–44. Discipline problems plagued Ottoman forces as well. The beneficed *timariot* bickered over terms of feudal service, refused orders, and even mutinied. This led to increased reliance on the professional infantry, the janissaries. See Oman, *Art of War in the Sixteenth Century*, pp. 758–70. Nor were problems alien to naval warfare: as late as the English victory over the Armada (1588), Drake broke off pursuit of the main body in order to seize the highly prized *Rosario*. See Paul M. Kennedy, *The Rise and Fall of British Naval Mastery* (London: Ashfield Press, 1987), p. 32.

[18] Delbrück, *History of the Art of War*, Volume 3, pp. 243–45. On discipline in the Teutonic Knights' *Ordenstaat*, see Michael Burleigh, *Prussian Society and the German Order: An Aristocratic Order in Crisis, c. 1410–1466* (Cambridge: Cambridge University Press, 1984), pp. 55–67.

be the most efficient military force in the world, but was in reality little removed from an armed mob."[19] Many of the same problems were found in infantry militias. They were poorly trained, refused to serve abroad or for extended periods, and were badly armed. Furthermore, as rural opposition to royal centralization or increased labor requirements grew, peasants were likely to use their skills and weapons against internal, seigneurial enemies, and not against their lord's external ones. As the threat of peasant rebellion loomed larger, peasant militias were disbanded or fell into disuse. Thereafter, peasant contribution to defense would be confined to paying taxes and serving as forced conscripts.[20]

Inherent problems of the feudal military were exacerbated by the development of disciplined infantry (with pike or firearms) and intermittent forays by large Turkish armies. Though not themselves part of the military revolution of the sixteenth and seventeenth centuries, these changes further undermined feudal military organization and introduced innovations that destabilized medieval Europe's conception of war, and led to the portentous revolution that transformed European military and political organization. The challenge to the aristocratic social order posed by the urban bourgeoisie was predated, by several centuries, by one posed by impertinent peasants and townsmen who, banded together into disciplined phalanxes of pikemen, proved invulnerable to the charges of heavy cavalry. The superiority of these formations only slowly became apparent to warrior elites blinded by narcissism and defensive of their military-based privileges.

The rise of the infantry began in four regions. First, in northern Italy, footsoldiers successfully turned back Frederick Barbarossa's efforts to prevent the urban centers from becoming independent city-states. At Legnano (1176), infantry repelled heavy Hohenstauffen cavalry, ensuring secession from the empire.[21] Similarly, in Flemish towns to the north, footsoldiers inflicted a serious defeat on French chivalry at Courtrai (1302). The secession of the Swiss cantons and towns from the empire initiated a number of attempts by the Burgundians and Habsburgs to restore imperial authority in that mountainous region. Repeatedly, at Morgarten (1315), Laupen (1339), Sempach (1386), and Näfels (1388), cantonal and urban footsoldiers brandished their pikes expertly, decimated haughty aristocratic intruders, and sent them fleeing for their lives

[19] Sir Charles Oman, *A History of the Art of War: The Middle Ages from the Fourth to the Fourteenth Century* (London: Methuen, 1898), p. 592.

[20] Corvisier, *Armies and Society*, pp. 29–39.

[21] Delbrück, *History of the Art of War*, Volume 3, pp. 342–43; *The Cambridge Medieval History*, Volume 6, p. 794. At this point infantry was not yet used offensively; the pikemen only repelled the cavalry charge.

from that alpine fortress.[22] By the late fifteenth century, Swiss infantry was renowned throughout Europe. Swiss pikemen became mercenaries in French and Spanish employ, and served as prototypes for developing modern national infantries elsewhere.[23]

In England, as we have noted, repeated Celtic raids and stubborn resistance to English punitive expeditions led to increased use of infantry, principally bowmen. Infantry and the superb tactical use of them were decisive in all but the latter phases of the Hundred Years' War (1337–1453). English battle plans called for the cavalry to hold the middle, while bowmen on the flanks mowed down their adversaries. At Crecy (1346), the English knights dismounted and stood in the ranks with foot-soldiers to repel the French heavy cavalry, a melding of two military organizations and social classes. At Agincourt (1415), infantry were deployed on the offensive for the first time and annihilated a much larger French force. Only after repeated costly defeats did the French decline to engage the English on the field, a decision that transformed the conflict into a war of sieges.[24] These stunning defeats led ultimately to Charles VII's liquidation of the French feudal military system and adoption of infantry phalanxes and artillery.

Economic and geographic factors were also at play in the rise of the infantry. The defeats of Hohenstauffen and Capetian chivalry came at the hands of militias from autonomous towns of northern Italy and Flanders. Here, the absence of traditional feudalization, and hostility toward surrounding feudatories, directed military structures away from the prevailing pattern. In Switzerland and the Celtic frontiers of England, rough terrain made the armored knight even more vulnerable than he was on level ground. Accordingly, the infantry of the cantons and clans had remained dominant since antiquity. This feudal military organization was under attack from the rural communes and the emerging towns, from Europe's past as well as its future.

The superiority of infantry was unmistakable by 1400. The battles of Courtai, Bannockburn, and Crecy spelled the doom of heavy cavalry; yet

---

[22] Delbrück, *History of the Art of War*, Volume 3, pp. 551–90; W. D. McCracken, *The Rise of the Swiss Republic: A History* (New York: AMS Press, 1970), pp. 158–82. The discipline of the Swiss footsoldier, it is often observed, stemmed from the cohesion found in the canton valleys and towns. But it also came from a less romantic source: breaches of discipline were punished by death.

[23] Hans Delbrück, *History of the Art of War*, Volume 4: *The Modern Era* (Westport, Conn.: Greenwood Press, 1985), pp. 13–19.

[24] Desmond Seward, *The Hundred Years War: The English in France, 1337–1453* (New York: Atheneum, 1982); John Keegan, *The Face of Battle: A Study of Agincourt, Waterloo and the Somme* (Harmondsworth, U.K.: Penguin, 1988), pp. 78–116; Delbrück, *History of the Art of War*, Volume 3, pp. 455–68, 508–16; *The Cambridge Medieval History*, Volume 7, pp. 347–87; Volume 8, pp. 646–49.

heavy cavalry endured well into the sixteenth century. This persistence can be accounted for, at least in part, by the inability of monarchs to afford anything but the relatively inexpensive feudal levies bolstered by the odd mercenary regiment. We must also take into consideration the ability of the feudal military elite—as well as the monarch, who was not far removed from the aristocracy, especially on the ideological plane—to ignore the lessons taught so well by footsoldiers. Oman's remarks on the French knight are insightful, but perhaps overly mordant:

> The French knight believed that, since he was infinitely superior to any peasant in the social scale, he must consequently excel him to the same extent in military value. He was therefore prone not only to despise all descriptions of infantry, but to regard the appearance on the field against him as a species of insult to his class-pride. A few years before, the self-confidence of the French nobility had been shaken for a moment by the result of the battle of Courtray (1302). But they had soon learned to think of that startling and perplexing event as a mere accident. . . . Comforting themselves with the reflection that it was the morass and not the Flemish infantry which won the battle, they were confirmed in their views by the event of the two bloody fights of Mons-en-Prevèle (1304) and Cassel (1328). The fate which on those days had befallen the gallant but ill-trained burghers of Flanders was believed to be only typical of that which awaited any foot-soldier who dared to match himself against the chivalry of the most warlike aristocracy in Christendom. Pride goes before a fall, and the French nobles were about to meet [in the Hundred Years' War] infantry of a quality such as they had never supposed to exist.[25]

On a less caustic note, it might be added that doing away with heavy cavalry was not a relatively simple, coldly analytic decision like that of replacing superannuated aircraft with more modern ones. Liquidating the feudal military entailed nothing short of breaking with one's entire upbringing, culture, and social system.

Gunpowder delivered a second blow to the feudal military, but not the mortal one often supposed: pike-wielding infantry did that.[26] Firearms

[25] Oman, *The Middle Ages*, pp. 592–93. Thompson echoes this view: "In Italy and the Netherlands revolt against feudal lords was accompanied by the development of infantry forces and of a professional soldiery. . . . The amour propre of the feudal knight, however, was slow to encourage a practice which confounded him with his inferiors, and its systematic employment was long delayed." A. Hamilton Thompson, "The Art of War to 1400," in *The Cambridge Medieval History*, Volume 6, p. 794.

[26] Richard Bean exaggerates the early role of gunpowder technology in the military revolution and in state building. See "War and the Birth of the Nation State," *Journal of Economic History* 33 (1973): 203–21; and Charles Tilly's criticism, "War Making and State Making as Organized Crime," in Peter B. Evans, Dietrich Rueschemeyer, and Theda Skocpol, eds., *Bringing the State Back In* (Cambridge: Cambridge University Press, 1985), pp. 177–

were first introduced in northern Italy circa 1300 but did not become standard equipment in European armies for almost two centuries. Diffusion was delayed by the poor quality of powder, slow rates of fire, and the expense of these artisanal products.[27] Owing to their notorious inaccuracy and slow rates of fire, cannon did not become important until the mid-fifteenth century. Once they were developed, however, castles were swiftly made obsolete, and new forms of fortification using thick, low walls had to be developed. An advantage was obtained by troops whose mobility and discipline shortened exposure to the increasingly deadly cannonade.[28]

Infantry and gunpowder delivered two blows; the Turks delivered a third. By the late fifteenth century, they had vanquished the Byzantine Empire and were pressing into Christendom, by land and sea. They pressed westward into the Mediterranean, taking Rhodes and Venetian territory along the Dalmatian coast. In the lower Danube, the Turks fielded an army of perhaps a hundred thousand—an enormous force for the time. Their numerical superiority as well as their mobile, light cavalry surged up the Balkans into Hungary, defeating the Hungarians and Austrians at virtually every turn. The forces of Christendom had to augment their own numbers and replace their traditional forces with light cavalry (hussars) and modern infantry.[29]

In short, feudal militaries had inherent problems that the introduction of infantry, gunpowder, and large armies badly aggravated. By 1500 feudal military organization was moribund: "Ce qui trouvait sa raison d'être à l'époque de la 'Chanson de Roland' devint une farce pathétique au siècle de don Quichotte."[30]

The Military Revolution, 1500–1650

Albrecht Dürer's woodcut of a battle-ready knight, the devil, and death stalking the countryside conveys an essential truth of early modern Eu-

---

80. On the importance of infantry over gunpowder in undermining the feudal military, see Roberts, "Gustav Adolf and the Art of War."

[27] Delbrück, *History of the Art of War*, Volume 4, pp. 28–40; *The Cambridge Medieval History*, Volume 8, pp. 650ff.

[28] Contamine, *War in the Middle Ages*, pp. 147–49, 198–200.

[29] *The Cambridge Medieval History*, Volume 8, pp. 647–48. See also Samuel E. Finer, "State- and Nation-Building in Europe: The Role of the Military," in Charles Tilly, ed., *The Formation of the National States in Western Europe* (Princeton, N.J.: Princeton University Press, 1975), pp. 84–163.

[30] "What had found its raison d'être in the epoch of the 'Song of Roland' became a pathetic farce in the century of Don Quixote." C. Gaier, "La Cavalrie Lourde en Europe Occidentale du XIIc au XVc Siècle," *Revue Internationale d'Histoire Militaire* 31 (1971): 385–96.

rope. Warfare and its attendant evils were commonplaces. The continent was at war more than it was at peace. During the sixteenth and seventeenth centuries, warfare broke out continuously, bringing developments in infantry, gunpowder, and large armies, as well as new characteristics and greater durations, to wars.

Dynasts tried to consolidate or expand their territorial sovereignty at the expense of the indigenous aristocracy or independent duchies. The latter's resistance often won the support of adjacent states fearful of the growing power of rivals, just as Habsburg attempts at dominating the Italian peninsula led to war with France.[31] Duchies relying on feudal levies or only small modern forces were easy victims for countries with modern infantries and cannon, as were regions whose administrations were paralyzed by an interregnum or a childless marriage.

A second cause of warfare in early modern Europe lay in the agrarian transformations. From England to East Elbia, peasants fought against enserfment, enclosures of commons, or seigneurial attempts at recovering rights and privileges reluctantly extended after the Black Death. Third, religious strife was breaking out everywhere as the Reformation and the Counter-Reformation swept Europe. Religion was almost always mixed with local resistance to centralization, as in the Huguenot wars in France; with breaking from an imperial system, as in the Hussite Wars and the Dutch Revolt; or with social antagonisms, as in the *Bauernkrieg*. The oft-quoted principle set forth at the Peace of Augsburg (1555), *cuius regio, eius religio*, says at least as much about power relations between emperor and prince as it does about religion. Fourth, conflicts over international trade erupted into war, though this was hardly the cause of as many wars as Marxist historians might suggest. As the three Anglo-Dutch wars of the seventeenth century and numerous Anglo-Spanish conflicts show, war became economics by other means. Finally, Turkish pressure in Hungary and in the Mediterranean persisted, even after the Spanish victory at Lepanto (1572).[32]

A consequence of new wars was the diffusion of new technology and a fundamental transformation of military structures. Armies became much larger, adopted new techniques and weaponry, and expanded central organization. Warfare became an extremely onerous and politically sensitive fiscal burden. Like the Industrial Revolution, this great transformation did not occur simultaneously in all countries. Spain, largely unencumbered by constitutional government, was the first to build a modern army for its wars against the Ottomans; Austria, facing Turkish

---

[31] See Ludwig Dehio, *The Precarious Balance: Four Centuries of the European Power Struggle* (New York: Vintage, 1962); and Geoffrey Symcox, ed., *War, Diplomacy, and Imperialism, 1618–1763* (New York: Harper & Row, 1973).

[32] See the essays in Robert I. Rotberg and Theodore K. Rabb, eds., *The Origins and Prevention of Major Wars* (Cambridge: Cambridge University Press, 1989).

pressure and trying to hold the Empire together, built a large mercenary army; France and Sweden responded in kind to Habsburg armies during the Thirty Years' War; and Prussia underwent the transformations shortly thereafter. Insular England relied primarily on local militias for a much longer period.

The technology and composition of warfare were changing in three principal ways: the preeminence of firearms, functional specialization, and new forms of fortification. Granulated powder, improvements in the casting of cannon, and the production of calibrated iron projectiles to replace ill-fitting iron and stone ones led to more reliable and faster-firing guns. Mobile cannon were introduced during the Thirty Years' War by the Swedes, who for the first time attached them to individual regiments.[33] The use of arquebuses and muskets increased steadily, and their number reached parity with that of pikes by 1600, outstripping them two-to-one twenty years later. By the end of the seventeenth century, the invention of the bayonet enabled the infantry to double as musketeers and pikemen, dooming the venerable pike, just as it had doomed heavy cavalry.[34] Pistols replaced the lance as the main weapon of the cavalry by the sixteenth century.

Armies became more and more specialized and complex. By 1550 armies had roughly equal proportions of infantry, cavalry, and artillery, each branch evolving dramatically.[35] Heavily armored cavalry was replaced by light horsemen modeled primarily after the Albanian *stradioti* of Venetian armies, the Hungarian hussars, and later the German mercenary *Schwarzreitern*. Their principal battlefield tactic was the caracole, a quick thrust toward the enemy lines followed by firing of their pistols, before retiring to the rear for another go.[36] The helter-skelter of the feu-

[33] Geoffrey Parker, *The Military Revolution: Military Innovation and the Rise of the West, 1500–1800* (Cambridge: Cambridge University Press, 1988), pp. 16–20; Michael Roberts, "Gustav Adolf and the Art of War" and "The Military Revolution," in Roberts, *Essays in Swedish History*. For an account of military modernization in eastern Europe, see Béla K. Király, "Society and War from Mounted Knights to the Standing Armies of Absolute Kings: Hungary and the West," in Bak and Király, *War and Society in Eastern Central Europe*, Volume 3, pp. 23–55.

[34] Roberts, "Gustav Adolf and the Art of War," pp. 56–59; *The New Cambridge Modern History*, Volume 4, pp. 220–21. The pikemen were essential to defend the arquebusiers and musketeers from cavalry charges after they had discharged their weapons. On this and other military changes, see Michael Howard's essay, *War in European History* (New York: Oxford University Press, 1976).

[35] Oman, *War in the Sixteenth Century*, pp. 561–68; Delbrück, *History of the Art of War*, Volume 4, pp. 148–50.

[36] The new light cavalry made its first appearance outside Italy and eastern Europe during the Schmalkaldic War of the early sixteenth century, mostly on the imperial side against the league of South German towns. See Delbrück, *History of the Art of War*, Volume 4, pp. 119–25.

dal cavalry became a carefully drilled maneuver. Dragoons, cavalry reconnaissance, and skirmishers were developed, further complicating military organization. Even the footsoldier became some sort of specialist: light infantry, fusilier, grenadier, or sapper.[37]

Armies were broken down into smaller tactical units, from the 3,000-man Spanish *tercios*, to Maurice of Orange's 550-man units, to Gustavus Adolphus's somewhat smaller units.[38] This increased mobility and firepower, but also required more training, as individual valor and discipline—attributes of the knight—were replaced by submergence of the individual into the phalanx, squadron, or battery, guided by the steady beat of the drum and the captain's shouts. Owing in part to the expense of training, armies gradually moved away from being seasonal forces, disbanded at the outset of winter; they became increasingly permanent.

Developments in gunpowder and field pieces obviously made old castellar fortifications nothing more than large, vulnerable targets easily reduced to rubble. Fixed fortifications had to evolve: advances in one set of weaponry or techniques, whether offensive or defensive, quickly led to corresponding evolution in the other. The high walls made from brittle stone were gone, but towns surrounded themselves with low walls of earth and brick, modeled after the town fortifications of Renaissance Italy, and hence called the *trace italienne*. Town enclosures were architectural wonders, drawing from the state of the art in scientific knowledge to maximize resilience, minimize exposure to fire, and allow the most outgoing firepower.[39]

Like the innovations of the late medieval period, changes in methods and technology spread throughout the continent, at least in the regions most affected by war, from central Germany to Italy, from Hungary to the Atlantic. Diffusion was accelerated by mercenary forces who moved from employer to employer, from kingdom to kingdom, teaching or learning new techniques of destruction.[40]

[37] *The New Cambridge Modern History*, Volume 2, pp. 498–500. On continued specialization into the eighteenth century, see David Chandler, *The Art of Warfare in the Age of Marlborough* (New York: Hippocrene, 1976).

[38] Roberts, "Gustav Adolf and the Art of War," pp. 60–61; Geoffrey Parker, "The 'Military Revolution,' 1560–1660—a Myth?" *Journal of Modern History* 48 (1976): 195–97, and *The Military Revolution*, pp. 6–44; and John A. Lynn, "Tactical Evolution in the French Army," *French Historical Studies* 14 (1985): 176–91.

[39] Geoffrey Parker, *The Army of Flanders*, pp. 8–10; John U. Nef, *War and Human Progress: An Essay on the Rise of Industrial Civilization* (Cambridge, Mass.: Harvard University Press, 1950), pp. 51–53; *The New Cambridge Modern History*, Volume 2, pp. 220–21; Gunther E. Rothenberg, *The Art of Warfare in the Age of Napoleon* (Bloomington: Indiana University Press, 1980), pp. 212–25. The technology of fortifications remained largely similar from the late sixteenth century to the Napoleonic Wars.

[40] *The New Cambridge Modern History*, Volume 2, pp. 41–43. Gunpowder technology,

Rapid growth in size constituted a second fundamental change in armies of the early modern period. This stemmed from the rise in population, the flourishing wealth of the period, new methods, and the proletarianization of the soldier. Quantity became more important than quality: "The eclipse of cavalry by infantry meant that victory in war after the 1470s came to depend not on the quality of the combatants nor on the excellence of their armaments, but on their numbers. A government bent on war had now to mobilize and equip every man who could be found."[41] A reciprocal relationship existed between increased size and the specialization of troops. Augmentation of one called for or greatly facilitated the other. Furthermore, the defensive prowess of the modern infantry led to compensation by weight of numbers. The seeming invulnerability of the phalanx could be overcome by attacking it from several directions.[42]

At the outset of the Thirty Years' War, imperial forces numbered some 20,000 men, Mansfeld's Protestant opposition approximately 12,000. A decade and a half later, Wallenstein commanded over 150,000, his Swedish enemy an even larger number.[43] Parker has saved us many hours of research by compiling various troop strength data, which are reproduced in Table 1.

An important source of manpower was the military contractor and his mercenary recruits. Swiss pikemen left their poor forest cantons to serve in many armies, though mainly with the French. German *Landsknechte* and Schwarzreitern were more numerous than the Swiss, but were not their equals on the battlefield. Scots, Irish, Albanians, and Italians also served in the ranks of these motley forces. Conscription, too, provided soldiers, either to supplement mercenary troops or to serve as the principal means of manpower. This was especially the case in lands where mercenary troops had proved unreliable or where contractors' defalcations had been extreme.[44]

Numerous factors conspired to make warfare of the early modern period much longer than most of the conflicts of medieval Europe. The defensive superiority of disciplined infantry often made a single decisive battle a thing of the past. Conflicts became lengthy wars of maneuver or

however, met with stubborn resistance owing to its considerable expense and relatively slow rate of fire. See Parker, *The Military Revolution*, pp. 16–20.

[41] Parker, *The Army of Flanders*, p. 5.

[42] Roberts, "The Military Revolution"; Delbrück, *History of the Art of War*, Volume 4, pp. 117–53.

[43] *The New Cambridge Modern History*, Volume 4, pp. 322–31. These huge forces were never assembled at any single battle. Many troops were utilized for guarding communication routes and garrisons, others campaigned elsewhere.

[44] See Redlich, *The German Military Enterpriser*, Volumes 1 and 2; and Howard, *War in European History*, pp. 20–74.

TABLE 1

Increase in Military Manpower, 1470–1710

Date	Spain	Holland	France	England	Sweden	Russia
1470s	20,000	—	40,000	25,000	—	—
1550s	150,000	—	50,000	20,000	—	—
1590s	200,000	20,000	80,000	30,000	15,000	—
1630s	300,000	50,000	150,000	—	45,000	35,000
1650s	100,000	—	100,000	70,000	70,000	—
1670s	70,000	110,000	120,000	—	63,000	130,000
1700s	50,000	100,000	400,000	87,000	100,000	170,000

Source: Parker, "The 'Military Revolution,' " p. 206, with permission of the publisher.

Note: In a later chapter I shall disagree with Parker's figure for Swedish miitary strength in the 1630s, which probably excludes the large number of German mercenaries. His figures nonetheless show the unmistakable trend to larger armies.

sieges of walled cities.[45] With the decline in the significance of feudal levies, the restraints on the length of war imposed by the feudal contract regarding length and place of service were gone. Inasmuch as monarchs were no longer restrained by the need to meet the expenses of war from the demesnes, they could prosecute wars much longer than previously. As long as they could obtain revenues from the estates or from constitutional gray areas, wars could go on. But that means of finance could only support small modernized forces; larger forces meant constitutional conflict.

Organization was needed to train the pikemen in synchronized thrusts and parries, arquebusiers and artillerymen in operating and maintaining their weaponry, light cavalry in the caracole and later the sabre charge, and all of them in coordinated, almost choreographed, tactical deployment in battle.[46] In the armies of the Spanish Habsburgs, training organizations and procedures were developed that sent new troops to garrison duty in Italy and North Africa before rotating them to one of the several fronts on which Spanish forces fought.[47] Furthermore, organizational sections were needed to administer justice, garner intelligence,

[45] Rothenberg, The Art of Warfare, pp. 11–16; Oman, War in the Sixteenth Century, pp. 674–76; Parker, The Military Revolution, pp. 6–16.

[46] Martin van Creveld, Command in War (Cambridge, Mass.: Harvard University Press, 1985), pp. 1–6; The New Cambridge Modern History, Volume 2, p. 488; Roberts, "The Military Revolution," pp. 196–98.

[47] Parker, "The 'Military Revolution,' " pp. 199–200.

care for the wounded and later for the invalid, and provide other indirect means of maximizing destructive power. Science was mobilized as new principles of mechanics and geometry were studied and applied to the art of war.[48] Rear echelons formed, and war became probably the first part of Europe to be bureaucratized.

One of the most important of these administrative superstructures was the adoption of supply and logistical systems, though this development did not come until the seventeenth century, and even then initially only in Spain and France. Charles XII and Napoleon operated effectively without elaborate logistical support in the eighteenth century, as did the Duke of Marlborough in at least one critical campaign of the War of the Spanish Succession. But Charles and Napoleon ultimately met with catastrophe, in large part due to the absence of reliable supply systems. A lengthy campaign without rational logistics was risky if not foolhardy, and almost all armies developed them. By the seventeenth century, armies without rational supply systems faced critical problems. First of all, soldiers, especially mercenaries, mutinied when not well supplied, thereby paralyzing armies, sometimes at pivotal junctures. Allowing soldiers to forage for themselves often led to widespread desertion. Regular logistical commands enabled armies to exert greater control over their troops by making them more reliant on army organization for food and clothing.[49]

Second, the defensive superiority of infantry and the trace italienne, as well as the costs of rebuilding an army after a large battle, also lengthened wars. Each commander hoped that the other's food and money would run out, precipitating mutiny and dissolution, giving him an easy, almost costless victory.[50] A third problem associated with the absence of a rational logistical structure was the effect on the prosecution of the war itself. If an army had to rely on plundering the local economy for sup-

[48] See Henry Guerlac, "Vauban: The Impact of Science on War," in Paret, *Makers of Modern Strategy*, pp. 64–90. Of course, many of these applications, such as the use of geometry to determine with "scientific" precision the range of an army, stemmed from an overzealous faith in science—something one senses has persisted in militaries.

[49] Richard Bonney, *Political Change in France under Richelieu and Mazarin 1624–1661* (Oxford: Oxford University Press, 1978), pp. 261–63; *The New Cambridge Modern History*, Volume 6, pp. 741–833; D. W. Jones, *War and Economy in the Age of William III and Marlborough* (Oxford: Basil Blackwell, 1988), especially pp. 28–65; Delbrück, *History of the Art of War*, Volume 4, pp. 64, 160; Walter L. Dorn, *Competition for Empire, 1740–1763* (New York: Harper & Row, 1963), pp. 80–83.

[50] Hale, *War and Society*, p. 64; R. R. Palmer, "Frederick the Great, Guibert, Bülow: From Dynastic to National War," in Paret, *Makers of Modern Strategy*, pp. 94–95; Delbrück, *History of the Art of War*, Volume 4, pp. 108–9; Martin van Creveld, *Supplying War: Logistics from Wallenstein to Patton* (New York: Cambridge University Press, 1977), pp. 7–8.

plies, its movements and strength became dependent on that means of supply, and strategy had to be subordinated to supply concerns. A decisive thrust into a region might make eminent sense from a purely military perspective, but if that region lacked resources, because of nature or another army's recent plunder, logistical considerations prevailed over strategy. So it was that, during the last stages of the Thirty Years' War,

> Ragged bands were scattered across Germany, caring nothing for the cause, knowing nothing of any planned strategy, their chief care to scratch nourishment out of the soil and to avoid serious fighting. They fought only their competitors for food, of whatever party. This phenomenon created the confused campaigns of the last decade of the war. Fighting was uncoordinated and spasmodic, the headquarters staff being unable to move the mass of the troops easily or with purpose.[51]

Furthermore, an army without sound logistics is highly vulnerable to a cautious, patient enemy, especially one willing to trade territory for time. Charles XII learned this lesson too late at Poltava in southern Russia, Napoleon, during his campaign in northern Russia.[52]

Two systems of supply emerged during the Thirty Years' War. The first, developed by the Swedes, might seem little removed from plunder but, in that it relied upon a large supply staff, it actually constituted a break from the practices of the period. Gustavus's quartermasters deployed throughout Germany, took inventory of the area's economic resources, and extracted them for the army's needs, without the pillaging, rapine, and massacre normally associated with living off the land. Inasmuch as the extractions were usually spent in the same region, the effects on the economy were not as deleterious as one might initially suspect. Indeed, this long-run concern for the sources of supply was one of the key differences between Swedish and imperial methods.[53] Although this method reduced the likelihood of mutinies and the problems of a war of maneuver, strategy was still subordinated to supply.

By the later stages of the Thirty Years' War, many parts of Germany had approached exhaustion. When France entered the war after years of watching from the sidelines and subsidizing the Habsburgs' enemies, it

[51] C. V. Wedgwood, *The Thirty Years War* (Garden City, N.Y.: Anchor, 1961), p. 420. See also J.F.C. Fuller, *A Military History of the Western World*, Volume 2: *From the Defeat of the Spanish Armada to the Battle of Waterloo* (New York: Da Capo, 1987), p. 65.

[52] Rothenberg, *The Art of Warfare*, pp. 129–30; van Creveld, *Supplying War*, pp. 8–14.

[53] Michael Roberts, *The Swedish Imperial Experience, 1560–1718* (Cambridge: Cambridge University Press, 1979), pp. 53–54; F. Redlich, "Contributions in the Thirty Years' War," *Economic History Review* 12 (1959): pp. 247–54; Myron P. Gutmann, *War and Rural Life in the Early Modern Low Countries* (Princeton, N.J.: Princeton University Press, 1980), pp. 41–53.

constructed a supply system consisting of magazines (*étapes*) and private contractors in the local regions, bringing in food and fodder from various distances—a blend of state organization and private enterprise that effectively victualed its armies abroad.[54] The Habsburgs built road systems to supply and reinforce their far-flung armies. One road stretched from Vienna to the lower Rhine, the other principal one from Habsburg possessions in northern Italy to the mouth of the Rhine.[55]

Naval development in this period has thus far been neglected. This is not because, as Hintze argued long ago, navies could not be used for internal repression or against the estates—an argument based on resource mobilization must still deal with the costs of navies—but because most naval modernization took place after that of the land forces, and after most of the political consequences of the military revolution on land had played themselves out. Colbert's naval construction came almost fifty years after the army modernization of Richelieu and Mazarin. Prussia, later Germany, was almost exclusively a land power, until Tirpitz's naval program at the close of the nineteenth century. Instead, Prussia relied on the naval resources of allies, the Netherlands and England. Prior to the mid-seventeenth century, most navies were relatively small and inexpensive. Most were based on small galleys (mainly in the Mediterranean) or on privateers, that is, on privately owned naval mercenaries whose pay came from booty, not state treasuries. State expenses were also reduced by the wartime conversion of merchantmen to fighting ships.

By the late seventeenth century, technological competition, brought on by the Anglo-Dutch wars, made privateers and converted merchantmen obsolete. They were replaced by true navies: state-owned ships of the line, built exclusively for war, with sixty or more guns. The impact of this naval revolution was less important for constitutional history than one might expect. First, the construction of navies took place after the military revolution had already placed Brandenburg-Prussia and France firmly on an absolutist track; the effects, then, were only to strengthen state extractive mechanisms. Second, the expense of maintaining a modern navy was still far less than that of an army of over a hundred thousand. Third, and related to the first point regarding timing, in England, Sweden, and the Netherlands, naval modernization took place after those countries had found constitutionally benign methods of financing land

---

[54] David Parker, *The Making of French Absolutism* (New York: St. Martin's Press, 1983), pp. 62, 124; van Creveld, *Supplying War*, pp. 17–22. Ever one to find profit in the midst of war, Wallenstein constructed his own expansive supply system, which if not for his assassination, would have been the basis of a formidable central European state. See Redlich, *The German Military Enterpriser*, Volume 1, pp. 325–27.

[55] Parker, *Army of Flanders*, pp. 50–53, 96–99.

forces. Those methods, as shall be seen, were applied to funding a navy without endangering political institutions. Naval modernization played an important role in the development of military strategy and in the economic history of the world, but its relevance to constitutional history was limited by its timing and relative expense.

War had changed enormously since the days of Charles Martel, Otto the Great, and the knights of the Crusades. It became more technologically advanced, and more complicated organizationally. It required far greater numbers than even those boastfully and dishonestly entered into the pages of medieval chronicles. My argument about the military revolution is not a pseudo-Weberian one lamenting that individual valor and leadership counted for nothing or very little, or that numbers and cold technique decided who won the day. Only those whose hearts are truly hardened or whose humanism exists only at the level of unengaged abstraction will not be struck by accounts of the courage of the Spanish footsoldier at Rocroi. The Swedish army took on opponents twice its number, without blinking, usually without losing. And somewhere men were found to serve in an exposed formation known as the forlorn hope. The seventeenth century probably produced more great military leaders than any other, including our own. In future histories the names of Maurice of Nassau and Gustavus Adolphus will, I suspect, more than hold their own against those of Guderian and Giap. Nor was everything subordinated to scientific principle and rational method. Wallenstein consulted astrologers prior to campaigns, most of which were successful. Promotions were based on favoritism and intrigue far more than on professional competence.[56] Changes in military organization led to new challenges of command and motivation, and so to the epoch of the great captain. The military revolution was a qualitative and quantitative change in military organization, but not one that obviated the roles of individual valor and leadership.

The impact of such a radical transformation could hardly be confined to the military. The dynamics of the various parts of the military revolution reverberated throughout Europe and fundamentally transformed state, society, and constitution in most countries. Students of military history might point out that there was nothing new in disciplined infantry forces numbering over a hundred thousand, that huge infantry armies had existed in the Roman Empire, albeit without the technological accoutrements. One scholar has estimated the size of the Roman legions at

[56] On the painstakingly slow professionalization of European officer corps, a process that did not really begin until the nineteenth century, see Samuel P. Huntington, *The Soldier and the State: The Theory and Politics of Civil-Military Relations* (Cambridge, Mass.: Harvard University Press, 1981), pp. 24–58.

three hundred thousand.[57] The military revolution, then, was in some respect the reemergence of large infantry armies. But the Roman state had access to the resources of the entire Mediterranean world, even beyond; and, owing to Caesar's crossing the Rubicon, emperors and legion commanders could mobilize them without the bothersome intermediary of the Senate.

THE MILITARY REVOLUTION AND CONSTITUTIONAL CONFLICT

Sophisticated armaments, growing echelons of support and administration, and the trend toward large standing armies and longer campaigns meant enormous rises in the costs of war. A single cannon cost as much as feeding 800 soldiers for a month; the lowly pikeman's corselet cost as much as feeding him for over two years.[58] Standardization of weapons brought down unit costs, but the transition entailed considerable expense. The movement away from heavily armored cavalry meant that the equipment of each cavalryman was less expensive, but cavalry were now more numerous and centrally equipped. Insofar as mercenaries were often paid in booty rather than solely by salary, they were less expensive in some respects; but there was much peculation to be considered.

The cost of modern armies was no longer spread across hundreds of feudal benefices; it shifted squarely onto the shoulders of king and parliament. It had been centuries since the revenue derived from the royal demesnes covered chancery and military expenses. Parliaments had been originally convoked in the thirteenth century to obtain revenue from the country, more often than not during times of war. Spoliated ecclesiastical property provided a temporary solution to this problem, but as soon as the last tracts were sold, the need for money returned. As the military revolution unfolded in the sixteenth and seventeenth centuries, the rising expenses of armies led to conflict with the estates. Parliaments were loath to allocate monies for new armies during an era before we may properly speak of nationalism and before there was widespread understanding of international politics, even among elites. Individual members of the estates might privately favor large revenues, yet oppose them for fear of losing support from constituents in the counties. Exacerbating problems of provincialism and tight purse strings were numerous divisions in the estates and in society as a whole. Religious passions, regionalism, and class antagonisms were prevalent in the postmedieval world, and were not easily put aside once a parliament convened. Indeed, a meeting of the estates seemed the perfect time to bring such issues to

---

[57] Michael Grant, *History of Rome* (New York: Scribner's, 1978), p. 247.
[58] Parker, *Army of Flanders*, p. 49.

the fore. Estates seemed disposed to plodding deliberations, conducted by a cumbersome group of several hundred rustics whose ability to grasp the larger, international issues was hindered by particularist and regional concerns. There were no party organizations to bring order to the process. A final exacerbation stemmed from the fact that many countries faced increased military costs amidst the Thirty Years' War, a conflict that devastated economies across Europe.

Kings sought to resolve this conflict by packing the estates with those sympathetic to the royal pleas, eliding parliamentary practice through illegal taxes or ones of at least questionable constitutionality, selling royal property, selling office, or borrowing money against future revenue; but these expedients could not suffice in a major war against a modern power. Pressures arose to dissolve the estates and collect taxes without their approval. The Spanish minister, Olivares, vented his exasperation shortly before trying to overpower one provincial estates: "We always have to look and see if a constitution says this or that. . . . We have to discover what the customary usage is even when it is a question of the supreme law, of the actual preservation and defense of the province. . . . The Catalans ought to see more of the world than Catalonia."[59] The estates, though important parts of the medieval political process, were not well integrated with the monarchy. They did not meet regularly and routine procedures between crown and estates were lacking. In a dangerous international environment, where nothing less than territorial sovereignty was at stake, a more streamlined decision-making body with its own financial resources was necessary. If these innovations violated traditional rights and procedures called for by constitutional practice, then reason of state, what Olivares called "the supreme law," could be invoked to justify rising above them. Estates were suspicious of standing armies, whose loyalty might be closer to the monarch than to constitutional government, and they were all the warier after foreign monarchs had used standing armies as the engine of autocracy. Schwartzenberg, prime minister of the Elector of Brandenburg, understood well the potential of a standing army shortly after the estates had refused taxes for one: "They would have been great fools if they had tolerated it; indeed, if the prince elector came to Prussia so strong, they would have had to fear that he would make laws for them and do whatever he wished."[60]

---

[59] Quoted in John Lynch, *Spain and the Habsburgs*, Volume 2: *Spain and America 1598–1700* (New York: Oxford University Press, 1969), pp. 103–4. See also J. H. Elliot, "England and Europe: A Common Malady?" in Conrad Russell, ed., *The Origins of the English Civil War* (London: Macmillan, 1978), pp. 246–57; and Conrad S. R. Russell, "Monarchies, Wars, and Estates in England, France, and Spain, c. 1580–c. 1640," *Legislative Studies Quarterly* 7 (1982): 205–20.

[60] Quoted in Delbrück, *History of the Art of War*, Volume 4, p. 244. The Elector, as we

Perhaps the domestic battle lines in the estates have been drawn too neatly. Within the nobility, gentry, and burghers were numerous adherents to the "national security" position, whose support came from a sober assessment of international realities: survival was indeed imperiled without military and constitutional change. Second, the growth of the state's judicial, administrative, and economic roles prior to the seventeenth century incorporated many members of the nobility and middle classes into the service of the crown. Court nobles, middle-class administrators, and placemen in the royal ministries developed rather dissimilar outlooks from those of their relations and colleagues in the country and towns. And defenders of constitutional government could be mollified or won over by grants of new office. Furthermore, clerics and independent bishoprics of Catholic regions gave support to expansionist kings of the Counter-Reformation. Although there were fissures preventing consensus on immense war subsidies, many of the same fissures prevented a consensus against the king's arrogated power.[61]

Conflict with the estates, however, was only the first phase of building military-bureaucratic absolutism. An increasingly powerful state coordinated the new, complex matters of finance, recruitment, and administration: "The transformation in the scale of war led inevitably to an increase in the authority of the state. The days when war partook of the nature of a feud were now for ever gone. . . . Only the state, now, could supply the administrative, technical and financial resources required for large-scale hostilities."[62] These changes further conflicted with constitutionalism and provided the basis of absolutism:

> The entire socio-political situation of Europe was transformed with the new military organization. The standing army was the point of contention in the struggle between the princes and their Estates of the Realm, the factor that raised kings to absolute rulers on the whole continent and in England brought first the minister Strafford and then King Charles I himself to the scaffold. . . . As a prerequisite, or perhaps we should say a side effect, of the great change in the army, there developed a new administration of the state, a bureaucracy

---

shall see, eventually got his army and followed Schwartzenberg's scenario quite closely. On conflict over standing armies elsewhere in Germany, see Peter-Christoph Storm, "*Militia Imperialis—militia circularis*: Reich und Kreis in der Wehrverfassung des deutschen Südwestens (1648–1715)," in James A. Vann and Steven W. Rowan, eds., *The Old Reich: Essays on German Political Institutions, 1495–1806* (Brussels: Les Editions de la Librarie Encyclopédique, 1974); and Gerhard Buchda, "Reichsstände und Landstände in Deutschland im 16. und 17. Jahrhundert," *Gouvernés et Gouvernants* 4 (1984): 193–226.

[61] See F. L. Carsten, "The Causes of the Decline of the German Estates," *Studies Presented to the International Commission for the History of Representative and Parliamentary Institutions* 24 (1961): 287–96.

[62] Roberts, "The Military Revolution," pp. 204–5.

whose mission it was to collect the taxes required to maintain the army and, by careful handling of the economic conditions and finally of the entire welfare and agriculture, to make the country as productive as possible.[63]

Among the developments referred to by Roberts and Delbrück was the construction of central organs in localities, charged with extracting resources and conscripting men for military service. These organs came into conflict with existing forms of local government, and typically replaced them. Elders, aldermen, and even local notables were pushed aside or transformed into royal officials; local police became agents of the crown; and election was replaced by royal appointment. Magnate councils lost their significance as the chancery assumed the role of the king's advisory council and executive.

The rule of law deteriorated with each additional power arrogated by the state and with each invocation of the principle of reason of state. Such situations called for wide discretionary power in the hands of the crown to meet the challenges of a treacherous state system, in which alliances came and went with little notice and wars erupted continuously, in which internal enemies had to be sought out and squelched, and in which loss of sovereignty might be the price of respecting what seemed the quaint privileges and niceties of a bygone era. In many cases involving reason of state, proceduralism and respect for precedent disappeared; legal institutions often became means of implementing state policy and removing obstacles to it.

Personal and property rights also suffered. Villagers and town dwellers had to quarter soldiers, whose discipline in battle was hardly matched while among the civilian populace. Though manpower needs were often met by tapping the seemingly inexhaustible supply of mercenaries and desperate poor, peasants were conscripted, without benefit of the concomitant endowment with rights and immunities of earlier (and later) forms of military organization. Besides conscription, there were threats of forced impressment as well as the devices employed by the recruiters to trick the unsuspecting lad away from his village and cast him into the maelstrom of a distant war, from which, as likely as not, he would never return. (On the Russian peasant commune, a conscripted peasant was given a ceremonial farewell, ritualistically similar to a funeral rite.) Short of that, he was effectively tied, not to the soil, as was the case with the second serfdom sweeping eastern Europe, but to his province or *Kanton*, where he was required to report regularly, instructed in military matters and duties, and subjected to a welter of intrusions.[64]

In that the ability to wage war depended heavily on the economic re-

---

[63] Delbrück, *History of the Art of War*, Volume 4, pp. 223–24.
[64] Parker, *The Military Revolution*, pp. 46–61.

sources at its disposal, the state also assumed the role of manager of the economy. Towns, burghers, and other aspects of commerce were regulated and otherwise controlled. State managerialism led to investing state money in new enterprises and further control of economic life and subjects' personal lives. Accordingly, there developed not a healthy and perhaps salutary antagonism between middle classes and state, but rather a modus vivendi that left the state politically dominant.

The relationship between modern warfare and the rise of a military-bureaucratic form of absolutism is not a direct one. Not every country followed the course of Brandenburg-Prussia. Even intense, protracted warfare and a modern army need not lead to the mobilization of domestic resources and autocracy. Human and economic resources are needed—there is no escaping that—but historical conditions offered the means of engaging in protracted periods of war without the mobilization of substantial, politically destabilizing levels of domestic resources. Four factors may intervene to break the nexus between war on the one hand and the destruction of constitutionalism and the rise of absolutism on the other:

Foreign Resource Mobilization. War may be conducted exclusively or primarily outside a country's territory. This can enable an army to mobilize, through rude plunder or systematic exploitation, the resources of a host country and recruit large numbers of mercenary forces. War revenues from home are light and may be negotiated from the estates without constitutional crisis. State building in the homeland is much weaker than in lands using domestic resources. Following this pattern, Sweden fought most of its wars of the early modern period on the European mainland, availing itself of foreign (mainly German) resources.

Alliances. Military alliances enable allies to reduce the amounts of domestic resources to be mobilized. Foreign troops and subsidies take the place of domestic resources, by mutual agreement rather than by plunder. In the long wars with Spain, the Netherlands allied with England, France, and other powers, and avoided a one-on-one war with the powerful Habsburgs, a conflict that, even with intensive domestic resource mobilization, the Dutch might not have won. Formal alliance is not necessary for a country to benefit from the military capacity of another country; the Dutch also benefited from Turkish attacks in the Mediterranean and revolts in Spain, which diverted Habsburg soldiers from northern fronts.

Advanced Economy and Commercial Wealth. Foreign sources of revenue (exclusive of subsidies from allies), such as those obtained from colonies or lucrative commercial transactions, may provide a country with far greater levels of wealth than those of its enemies. Accordingly, the proportion of domestic resources mobilized may remain small and may be provided by the estates, without too much difficulty and without constitutional crisis. Venice used the wealth from Mediterranean trade to build powerful fleets and armies to counter the might of Spain and the Turks. It is essential that control of this wealth-generating commerce be in the hands of merchants and not the crown. Where the crown is in control, it has a spectacular source of revenue that can be used to build an army, wage war, and build a state devoid of parliamentary practice. This situation gave the Spanish Habsburgs the revenue to build a war-making state without having to deal with provincial estates. The domestic economies of most European states, though generally expanding, were not as yet sufficiently well developed to provide adequate amounts of wealth to preclude coercive resource mobilization. The historical evidence suggests that, at least until the eighteenth century, sufficient levels of wealth could only come from lucrative international commerce and to a much lesser extent from colonial exploitation.

  Geography and Natural Topographical Features. Island nations and ones bound by rivers, mountains, marshlands, and the like have natural barriers to invading armies that enable a relatively small or antiquated military system to fight a larger, modern one to a standoff. In this situation, it is impossible to win an offensive victory, but a stalemate can nonetheless secure national sovereignty. The Swiss relied on mountains and forests to thwart invasions, the Dutch on the Scheldt and its marshy littoral.

It is important to note that these four buffers between military modernization and military-bureaucratic absolutism are by no means choices available to states facing modern war. Three of them are, at least at the critical moments when military modernization is confronted, givens that cannot in short order be created, built, or negotiated. A monarch could not decide to double or treble his country's economic output on short notice any more than he could create easily defended borders. Foreign resource mobilization is predicated on the availability of a lucrative, defenseless border area that can be invaded by a small force, plundered, and used as a staging ground for building a large army, without triggering a sudden and catastrophic counterstroke from a powerful nearby state. During the Thirty Years' War, the weak principalities of Germany were exactly this sort of vulnerable area; but, in time, these small states were annexed by larger ones, thereby diminishing this possibility for war finance.

  However, many alliances are in fact made by states, and often on short notice, as shifting tides of war make new coalitions intelligible. Still, specific historical situations, even specific phases of a war, can force a country to face a powerful foe, and rapid military modernization, without benefit of foreign assistance. Indeed, this was precisely the situation confronted by France and Brandenburg when these countries moved in the direction of military-bureaucratic absolutism. Geography, national wealth, and the availability of foreign plunder are givens at specific moments in history, and alliances, although to some degree made by states, can disappear as quickly as they appeared, leaving a country with no resources but its own. No metahistorical claim regarding human agency, free will, or determinism is being made here. My argument is only that at specific historical junctures—France in 1634, Brandenburg in 1655—states found themselves without any of the conditions that reduce the need to mobilize domestic resources, and had to mobilize their own or face loss of sovereignty.

A fifth intervening variable, the availability of foreign loans, might come to mind. After all, this was an important and often central method of war finance upon which Spain, England, and other countries relied. Loans by themselves were only intermediate sources of money; they had to be guaranteed in some way. Even the most powerful sovereign had to demonstrate access to future resources to repay them. Then as now, bankers were irritatingly intransigent on this point. In the thirteenth and fourteenth centuries, monarchs secured war loans from bankers by pledging revenue derived from the royal demesne, but soon found themselves so deeply in debt that subsidies from the estates were needed—a situation leading to the exchange of subsidies for expansion of parliamentary power.[65] With the growing expense of war even in the late Middle Ages, the royal demesne could never again suffice as security for loans; the estates alone could secure enough resources. Tudors and early Stuarts obtained Parliamentary guarantees based on future taxes, a process that continued constitutional practice of policy by king and Parliament. In contrast, the Spanish Habsburgs assured creditors with bullion-laden ships from the New World, a process that circumvented the estates and provided a pillar of absolutism in Castile. Wary bankers hesitated to make loans that would certainly lead to a civil war whose outcome could not be reliably calculated; and if the war's outcome could not be guaranteed, then neither could repayment. Also, by the early modern period merchant and banking networks were such that the process of negotiating these loans could not have been kept secret from burghers in the estates, and any word of such impending loans would have triggered a constitutional showdown, and possibly civil war, prior to the crown's having raised an army with the foreign money.

[65] Richard W. Kaeuper, *War, Justice and Public Order: England and France in the Later Middle Ages* (Oxford: Clarendon Press, 1988), pp. 32–62.

War and the need for resources to wage it were not the only sources of conflict between the monarchy and constitutional government. Conflicts developed almost everywhere over the shift of judicial functions into the hands of the monarch. Religion was a serious point of contention in England, where Puritanism opposed the apparent Arminian bent of the monarchy, and in the Low Countries, where the Inquisition was deployed. But everywhere war was the decisive factor that brought conflict—after all, a normal part of any constitutional government, and perhaps even a healthy sign—to the level of constitutional crisis. And everywhere in Europe it was war, not the judiciary, religion, or personal animosities, that required the circumvention or destruction of the estates, and the creation of centralized organizational systems that developed into military-bureaucratic absolutism.[66]

Despite some similarities, this phenomenon differs from the military coups and states of siege of modern authoritarianism. There was no state paralysis, domestic turmoil, or parliamentary stalemate that fostered the rise of absolutism. There was only the recognition on the part of the crown and segments of the nobility and middle classes that a more decisive, independent state was needed to deal with a dangerous, external threat. Furthermore, the process described here must be differentiated from the condottieres' seizure of power in Renaissance Italy. This was simply a case of a military contractor using his troops to oust civilian government and assume control himself. Such was the means by which Sforza and his mercenaries overthrew the government of his employers, and installed himself as Duke of Milan.

Finally, let us not succumb to the temptation to see monarchs, even those who founded military-bureaucratic absolutisms, as despots who, placing ambition and lust for power ahead of respect for constitutional practice, destroyed the estates and built powerful states in their image.[67] It is all too easy to adopt this perspective when studying the origins of

[66] On constitutional conflict during this period, see Gerald Strauss, *Law, Resistance, and the State: The Opposition to Roman Law in Reformation Germany* (Princeton, N.J.: Princeton University Press, 1986); Mary Fulbrook, *Piety and Politics: Religion and the Rise of Absolutism in England, Württemberg and Prussia* (Cambridge: Cambridge University Press, 1983), pp. 45–75; Trevor Aston, ed., *Crisis in Europe, 1560–1660* (London: Routledge & Kegan Paul, 1980); Geoffrey Parker and Lesley M. Smith, eds., *The General Crisis of the Seventeenth Century* (London: Routledge & Kegan Paul, 1985); Valentin Urfus, "Die Steuergewalt des böhmischen Landtags und der Absolutismus," *Studies Presented to the International Commission for the History of Representative and Parliamentary Institutions* 31 (1964): 179–87; and F. L. Carsten, *Princes and Parliaments in Germany: From the Fifteenth to the Eighteenth Century* (Oxford: Clarendon Press, 1959).

[67] Useful correctives to this view are Russell, "Monarchies, Wars, and Estates," and works cited therein; and Herbert Butterfield, *The Whig Interpretation of History* (New York: W. W. Norton, 1965).

democracy, which we rightfully respect, and dictatorship, which we equally rightfully disdain. If we look at monarchs entangled in the net of time and circumstance, we might still be unable to follow Sir Herbert Butterfield's counsel and take pity on them, but perhaps we can understand that kings acted to defend their realms and subjects, and, after the military revolution, found cooperation with the estates and retention of other parts of the constitution incompatible with that duty. We might observe that a country's trajectory was an unfortunate one, one we might not choose to live in, and perhaps even one that bears a contingent relationship to a horrible end in the twentieth century, but let us not vilify kings or confuse their intentions. There are doubtless numerous villains to be found in the history of Prussia, France, and most other countries for that matter, but Friedrich Wilhelm and Louis XIII are not, in my view, among them. And if one should feel tempted to idealize the king of Sweden for sparing his country the rigors of domestic resource mobilization, remember that Gustavus Adolphus was not above hanging simple German peasants for hiding a few cattle from his quartermasters. Sweden's constitutionalism was a predatory one that preserved itself by mulcting foreign lands—a virtuous end occasioned by vicious means. This should instruct us that the unfolding of democracy is not always an edifying narrative.

The possibility of being militarily vanquished was a very real one, as the histories, or lack thereof, of Livonia, Novgorod, and Burgundy attest. It is significant that Friedrich Wilhelm is known in history as the Great Elector, not as Friedrich the Terrible or Friedrich the Unready. Without a modern military constructed and led by a powerful state, sovereign territories were typically devoured. Such was the case of Poland, where the gentry thwarted attempts to build a strong state. No one sings the praises of the gentry's myopic dedication to constitutionalism, and it shall not be done here; a threnody for their irresponsibility is more in order. The Great Elector prevented his country from sharing that fate, and to judge his actions by pointing to the catastrophic trajectory German history ultimately took is dubious casuistry; to argue that he embarked upon that trajectory out of ambition or hatred for the estates is sheer fiction.

.   .   .

Feudal military organization suffered from inherent flaws that had revealed themselves by the late medieval period. The military revolution made the knight obsolete and put pressures on countries to build powerful state organizations in order to extract resources for warfare. Where advantages of foreign resources, alliances, commercial wealth, or geography were not available, military requirements conflicted with and destroyed or at least seriously undermined constitutional government. In its stead, there arose a military-bureaucratic state whose overwhelming power vis-à-vis the social classes, the economy, and the whole of civil society decisively patterned the contours of its national history. The principles presented in these chapters shall now be considered within the framework of the military and constitutional histories of Brandenburg-Prussia, France, Poland, England, Sweden, and the Netherlands.

CHAPTER FOUR

Brandenburg-Prussia

THE LANDS of Brandenburg, Pomerania, and East Prussia, which Prussia comprised in 1660, faced numerous wars in the seventeenth century. Decentralized, constitutional regimes became a single, absolutist state. The absence of effective allies, foreign subsidies, commercial wealth, or natural defenses mandated systematic and harsh extraction of domestic resources. Mobilization of resources for wars destroyed constitutionalism and set into motion the development of military-bureaucratic absolutism. The estates, local autonomy, the rule of law, and many individual rights were abolished. Dynamics were put into play that led to the fusion of key classes to the state, the state's adoption of a managerial position in regard to civil society, and the manipulation of politics by the bureaucracy. In short, the broad contours of Prussian and German history were formed by the military situation of the seventeenth century.

CONSTITUTIONALISM IN EAST ELBIA

It is convenient but inaccurate to conflate German history into a monothematic, militarist drive, from the sanguinary *Drang nach Osten* to gambits for mastery of Europe during the twentieth century. The course of Prussian and German history meanders widely, from the medieval period to the outset of the early modern period, from the rigid authority of the Teutonic Knights to the Republic of Nobles of the sixteenth century, which in critical ways resembles the Whig hegemony of England, and hardly seems a foundation for military absolutism.

As we have seen, the Holy Roman Empire diminished in political importance as its principalities, duchies, and bishoprics built autonomy at the expense of the emperor. Attempts to build a permanent imperial army, financial system, and judiciary were blocked by the strength of nominal vassals. The balance between emperor and prince shifted dramatically in the latter's favor. A new balance emerged in the lands of the Empire, between the prince on the one hand and the nobles and burghers on the other.[1] This was no less true in the "authoritarian" east, that

[1] Gerhard Buchda, "Reichsstände und Landstände in Deutschland im 16. und 17. Jahrhundert," *Gouvernés et Gouvernants* 4 (1984): 193–226; Hajo Holborn, *History of Germany*, Volume 1: *The Reformation* (Princeton, N.J.: Princeton University Press, 1982), pp. 3–55.

is, Brandenburg, Pomerania, and the duchy of East Prussia, than it was in the "democratic" west. Until the middle of the seventeenth century, the East Elbian lands had substantial constitutional arrangements, ranging from villages of peasant colonists to the halls of the estates.

The Hohenzollern state prior to the accession of the Great Elector (r. 1640–1688) was hardly an imposing structure. It had only recently begun to emerge from that collection of personal retinue and demesne managers that made up the medieval state. Until the second half of the sixteenth century, when legal specialists began to enter state service, there was little in the way of functional specialization or professional training.[2] Hohenzollern bailiffs in the localities were nominally royal appointees, but in practice they were loyal to local nobles, who helped to select them. The elector's attempts to build a privy council with which he might increase chancery power at the expense of the estates ended in failure.[3]

The Hohenzollern chancery operated within a constitutional framework, the most important part of which was the estates. The estates of Brandenburg and Pomerania were first convoked in the late thirteenth century when demesne revenue no longer sufficed to pay for even small state expenditures. Though stripped of one important *Stand* during the Reformation, by the early seventeenth century the estates had developed into able representative bodies that shaped foreign policy, supervised and audited the crown's undertakings, influenced the appointment of ministers and local administrators, and handled the collection of taxes and tolls they had approved.[4] So strong were the estates of Brandenburg and Pomerania that Carsten has noted that "the power of the Estates was thus firmly secured, more firmly than in any other German principality."[5] Another source goes further: "The Estates of Brandenburg . . . kept the development of [that] polity on the Elbe and the Oder abreast of that on

[2] Sidney B. Fay and Klaus Epstein, *The Rise of Brandenburg-Prussia to 1786* (New York: Holt Rinehart & Winston, 1964), pp. 20–26, 40–43; Heinrich Otto Meisner, "Die monarchische Regierungsform in Brandenburg-Preußen," in Richard Dietrich, ed., *Forschungen zu Staat und Verfassung: Festgabe für Fritz Hartung* (Berlin: Duncker & Humblot, 1958), pp. 219–45; Sidney Bradshaw Fay, "The Hohenzollern Household and Administration in the Sixteenth Century," *Smith College Studies in History* 2 (1916): 1–64.

[3] Meisner, "Die monarchische Regierungsform," pp. 219–30; Reinhold August Dorwart, *The Administrative Reforms of Frederick William I of Prussia* (Cambridge, Mass.: Harvard University Press, 1953), pp. 5–22; Herbert Tuttle, *History of Prussia to the Accession of Frederic the Great, 1134–1740* (Boston: Houghton Mifflin, 1884), pp. 225–28.

[4] F. L. Carsten, *The Origins of Prussia* (Oxford: Clarendon Press, 1964), pp. 165–78; Meisner, "Die monarchische Regierungsform," pp. 219–25.

[5] Ibid., p. 168. See also Peter Baumgart, "Zur Geschichte der kurmärkischen Stände im 17. und 18. Jahrhundert," in Otto Büsch and Wolfgang Neugebauer, eds., *Moderne Preußische Geschichte, 1648–1947: Eine Anthologie*, Volume 2 (Berlin: Walter de Gruyter, 1981), pp. 509–31.

the Thames, down to an epoch more recent than is commonly supposed."[6]

In East Prussia the power of the estates was as well established by the seventeenth century as that of the estates in Brandenburg and Pomerania, but its origins were more recent. Owing to their cohesiveness as brothers in a military elite, the Teutonic Knights were successful in maintaining political power exclusively in their hands and in refusing an estate. It was not until the disastrous wars with Poland in the early fifteenth century that the Order found itself facing fiscal and political crises. Funds dried up and levies refused to fight. The Order had no alternative but to convoke an estates whose rights and liberties were later guaranteed by the Polish crown.[7] By the next century, the Order had been secularized and disbanded; constitutional arrangements crystallized into what Carsten called an *Adelsrepublik*.[8]

Local government, too, was very much in evidence. In the trading centers along the Baltic coast, alderman supplanted the duke's *advocati*, built their own judiciaries, and instituted charters recognized by regional authorities. The strength of the towns was sufficient in many areas to coerce nobles into razing adjacent castles.[9] Towns frequently allied with

---

[6] Tuttle, *History of Prussia*, p. 103.

[7] Kings in adjacent territories frequently protected the estates of potential rivals for reasons not long to seek: a strong estates generally meant a militarily weaker state. The Wittelsbachs protected the Estates of Württemberg from ducal authority, and Louis XIV became the champion of the *Landtage* of western Germany. See F. L. Carsten, *Princes and Parliaments in Germany: From the Fifteenth to the Eighteenth Century* (Oxford: Clarendon Press, 1959).

[8] Franz Carsten, "Die Entstehung des Junkertums," in Otto Büsch and Peter Neugebauer, eds., *Moderne preußische Geschichte, 1648–1947: Eine Anthologie*, Volume 1 (Berlin: Walter de Gruyter, 1981), p. 278. On the power of the Teutonic Knights and development of the East Prussian estates, see Karol Górski, "La Ligue des Etats et les origines du régime représentatif en Prusse," *Studies Presented to the International Commission for the History of Representative and Parliamentary Institutions* 23 (1960): 177–85; Karol Górski, "Die Anfänge der Repräsentation der *Communitas Nobilium* in Polen, im Ordensstaat Preußen und in Ungarn im Mittelalter," *Studies Presented to the International Commission for the History of Representative and Parliamentary Institutions* 36 (1966): 19–24; W. F. Reddaway et al., eds., *The Cambridge History of Poland: From the Origins to Sobieski to 1696* (Cambridge: Cambridge University Press, 1950), pp. 141–46; Michael Burleigh, *Prussian Society and the German Order: An Aristocratic Order in Crisis, c. 1410–1466* (Cambridge: Cambridge University Press, 1984), pp. 134–70. The political conflicts between the Order and the populace were exacerbated by the Order's recruitment mainly from Austria, Switzerland, and the Netherlands—a policy that served further to alienate the Order from its subjects.

[9] Carsten, *Origins of Prussia*, pp. 47–48, 81–88; Herbert Helbig, *Gesellschaft und Wirtschaft der Mark Brandenburg im Mittelalter* (Berlin: Walter de Gruyter, 1973), pp. 18–68. Towns and villages tended to augment their independence during interregna and periods of anarchy brought on by war and plague.

one another, either into the Hanse or into regional pacts separate from the great trading league.[10] Shortly after the conquest of the indigenous Slavic populace, settlers were attracted, mostly from the free peasantry of Franconia, Saxony, and Flanders. Local government came with the village settlement. A nonnoble locator contracted with prospective colonists and normally became the village *Schulz*, a position combining mayor and justice of the peace. The founding of a village was occasioned by the enactment of a *Handfeste*, a constitutional document delineating the legal status, rights, and service requirements of peasants as well as nobles. Bylaws (*Willküren, Beliebungen, Dreidingordnungen*) elaborated basic principles. The village court (*Landding*) consisted of the Schulz and juries (*Landschöffen*) comprised of villagers owning two to six *Hufen*, a property requirement that many peasants could meet. Even nobles were subject to the justice of the Landding.[11]

Though nominally under the authority of the lord, the peasant owed him only light labor services and ground rents. The peasant could quit the lord's service upon paying a mere quarter mark; his holdings were heritable, and the lord exerted little or no administrative control over him. A contemporary phrase claimed, with some exaggeration no doubt, that the noble was the "peasant's neighbor." Both were under the administrative control of the village Schulz and bound by the settlement's Handfeste.[12] In East Prussia, the numerous free peasantry (*Kölmer*) participated in councils that debated local issues and drew up agendas for upcoming meetings of the estates. Though not eligible for actual representation as a separate estate, the Kölmer nonetheless articulated interest; deputies returning from meetings of the estates were accountable to

---

[10] Philippe Dollinger, *The German Hansa*, D. S. Ault and S. H. Steinberg, trans. (Stanford, Calif.: Stanford University Press, 1970), pp. 92–97; Tuttle, *History of Prussia*, pp. 55–56.

[11] Carsten, *Origins of Prussia*, pp. 29–40, 81–88; Heide Wunder, "Peasant Organization and Class Conflict in Eastern and Western Germany," in T. H. Aston and C.H.E. Philpin, eds., *The Brenner Debate: Agrarian Class Structure and Economic Development in Pre-Industrial Europe* (Cambridge: Cambridge University Press, 1985), pp. 92–94; Helbig, *Gesellschaft und Wirtschaft*, pp. 10–12. More traditional Slavic village governments, predating the Order's conquest, survived in East Prussia. See Wunder, "Peasant Organization and Class Conflict," pp. 93–94. Brenner and Wunder conflict sharply over the independence of the Schulzen, the former seeing them as agents of the nobility or the Order, the latter as true spokesmen for the peasant village. Burleigh's impressive archival research (*Prussian Society and the German Order*, pp. 13–25) tends to support Wunder. The village Schulz seems to have been somewhere between Quisling and William Tell; nonetheless his local constitutional import as mayor, justice of the peace, and peasant representative to outside authority is unmistakable, hence placing him closer to Schiller's hero.

[12] Carsten, *Origins of Prussia*, pp. 29–68, and "Die Entstehung des Junkertums," pp. 267–69; Burleigh, *Prussian Society and the German Order*, pp. 25–34.

them.[13] The peasants of medieval East Elbia, with their legal status and codified guarantees, were among the freest and most privileged in all Europe.

Law has already been alluded to in reference to the charters, Handfesten, and village bylaws. The potential for arbitrary use of law was further restrained by the absence of a unified system of law until the mid-sixteenth century. Prior to that, law had been based on local customs brought by colonists, though the venerable Saxon customary law (Sachsenspiegel) seems to have served as a basis for most law.[14] The Elector Joachim II (r. 1535–1571) introduced a standardized legal system based on Roman Law, but implementation and interpretation lay in the hands of local judiciaries independent of the Elector. Though procedural and interpretive guidelines had been laid down, constitutional government was strong; finance, foreign policy, and important domestic matters were still under the purview of the estates.

It should be evident that at the outset of the early modern period the lands that became Prussia were not a basis for a Sparta of the North. A careful reading of the medieval history of East Elbia admits no evidence of a militaristic, absolutist outcome. In fact, the region resembles much of western Europe, including England: "The rights of the people were as clearly understood, and perhaps as securely guarded, as anywhere in Europe; and it follows that only ignorance or servility can attempt to divine the absolute Prussian kings of later times legitimately and organically from their ancestors."[15] The origins of the Prussian military state are to be found in a more recent epoch.

THE END OF CONSTITUTIONALISM AND THE RISE OF ABSOLUTISM, 1640–1740

The eastern marks of the Holy Roman Empire were founded through conquest of indigenous Slavic tribes. Though threats continued from the frontiers to the east, border defenses were not heavy; warfare was intermittent at most, and conducted by traditional feudal levies. The rise of Muscovy, the collapse of the Livonian Knight territories in Courland, and the outbreak of the Thirty Years' War (1618–1648) shattered the relative tranquility of the Baltic littoral. Brandenburg was occupied by foreign troops and systematically exploited; the government fled to the safety of Königsberg. Wallenstein's army extracted tons of gold from the treasury, only to retreat before an onslaught of Swedish mulcters. The

---

[13] Carsten, *Origins of Prussia*, pp. 10–42, 204.

[14] Eberhardt Schmidt, *Rechtsentwicklung in Preussen* (Darmstadt: Wissenschaftliche Buchgesellschaft, 1961), pp. 1–5; Tuttle, *History of Prussia*, pp. 47–51, 78–93.

[15] Tuttle, *History of Prussia*, p. 42.

Elector found himself forced to cooperate with whichever army was currently the occupying power.[16] Even after the Peace of Westphalia (1648), tensions between Sweden and Poland placed Brandenburg in a dangerous geopolitical position between two hostile states (a position Poland would know after Prussia had modernized).

The military of Brandenburg was based on town militias and an antediluvian levy. Town militias were ill-equipped, if at all; training was ludicrously poor. The levy could call up a thousand or so cavalry—a small, backward force that would have been cut to pieces by the modern cavalry of Gustavus Adolphus or Pappenheim.[17] Yet even this levy was unreliable: vassals had sworn allegiance to both the Elector and the Holy Roman Emperor and used this excuse to shirk all military duty.[18] If the region was to remain sovereign and not become a province or tributary state, its sparse resources would have to be mobilized and a modern military built, against protestations from the estates. There was no choice but to mobilize domestic resources. Brandenburg could not wage war abroad availing itself of the resources of Saxony or some other adjoining land: that would have swiftly entailed facing the armies of Austria or the Empire, with only the small forces then at its disposal. Geography had not been kind to the small principality on the east European plains. Its only natural defenses, the Oder and the Elbe, need not have been crossed by an invader from the south, and the Swedes had already established a glacis on the south coast of the Baltic.

It might well be asked why, amidst the chaotic warfare of the period, Brandenburg was not able to build alliances that would have reduced the military danger and provided subsidies, thus reducing the need to extract domestic resources. From the perspective of the great powers (Sweden, Spain, France, Austria), what would be the worth of such an alliance? Brandenburg had no army or navy to aid one's cause; it had no great wealth, as did Venice and the Dutch Republic, to subsidize an ally's army. An alliance with a small, poor territory would only have further strained one's military resources at a time when countries were locked in a life-and-death struggle.[19] Brandenburg had no great domestic wealth

[16] Ferdinand Schevill, *The Great Elector* (Chicago: University of Chicago Press, 1947), pp. 39–52; Hans Delbrück, *History of the Art of War within the Framework of Political History*, Volume 4: *The Modern Era* (Westport, Conn.: Greenwood Press, 1985), p. 243.

[17] Ibid., pp. 242–44.

[18] Gustav Schmoller, "Die Entstehung des preußischen Heeres von 1640 bis 1740," in Büsch and Neugebauer, *Moderne preußische Geschichte*, Volume 2, pp. 749–53.

[19] Timing of subsidies is crucial. Had subsidies flowed in prior to the dissolution of the estates, constitutionalism might have survived. Once Brandenburg-Prussia had established itself as a military power in wars against the Turks, Swedes, and French, subsidies and alliances were forthcoming. In the Seven Years' War (1756–1763), Frederick the Great received over 270 million talers in subsidies from England. But, inasmuch as these subsidies

from which to obtain revenues and resources for its military. The export of grain to the west was lucrative, but did not make the wealth of the Junkers rival that of the English gentry. The region's soil was rather poor, and much of the profit from the grain trade was reaped by Dutch and English merchants, who had dominated the Baltic routes for over a century. In fact, export agriculture had led to the deterioration of many commercial centers of East Elbia. Exports went through only a few ports, at the expense of the guild-dominated ones, whose labor costs made them unattractive.[20]

The wraith of Brandenburg-Prussian constitutionalism appeared during the Thirty Years' War, portending its death several decades hence. The great war and ensuing chaos offered the Elector of Brandenburg and Pomerania the opportunity to enact extraordinary policies and arrogate authority from the estates. The Elector's council, later dubbed the *Kriegsrat*, levied taxes and raised a small army without estate approval. Objections by estate members led to their arrest and trial for treason. In the face of foreign invasion, reason of state replaced centuries-old proceduralism. But the close of the war breathed new life into constitutionalism. The war council was disbanded, and the estates regained most of their power. A short peace having broken out, absolutism was postponed. The Northern War (1655–1660), in which Brandenburg fought Poland and then Sweden, proved to be the decisive turning point in Prussian political history. With war imminent, the Great Elector obtained from the estates of Brandenburg and Pomerania sufficient funding for a small standing army, in exchange for the confirmation of privileges, and exemptions, the sanctioning of enserfment (*Leibeigenschaft*). What had seemed to the estates to be an equitable quid pro quo shifted the domestic balance of power to the Elector, who now had the ultimate arbiter of future constitutional conflicts, a standing army.

The army would cast the deciding vote in 1657 when the estates refused further funding. In the midst of the Northern War and reeling from an atavistic and devastating Tatar raid, the Great Elector proclaimed his right to levy taxes without the approval of the estates, and used the army to collect them. Protest became markedly more timid and even these

came only after the destruction of constitutionalism, their significance for constitutional history is negligible. Foreign subsidies in the years after the destruction of the estates went into Frederick's war chest and only strengthened absolutism in Prussia. On subsidies, see Delbrück, *History of the Art of War*, Volume 4, pp. 246–47; and Hubert C. Johnson, *Frederick the Great and His Officials* (New Haven, Conn.: Yale University Press, 1975), pp. 134–87.

[20] See Carsten, *Origins of Prussia*, pp. 117–35; Carsten, "Entstehung des Junkertums," pp. 269–77.

were answered with terse references to the need for expedients.[21] The power of the estates became negligible; their deliberations when they gathered together were quiet and meaningless. When the close of the Northern War placed the Duchy of Prussia under Brandenburg sovereignty, parliamentary conflict began anew, this time in Königsberg rather than Berlin, and without the farcical qualities of many historical repetitions. A decade of dispute ended with the outbreak of war with France in 1672. The need for additional infusions into the Elector's army led to the deployment of troops against the Königsberg opposition. Neither the great issues of the day, nor even the small ones, would any longer be decided by parliamentary speeches and majority decisions. The union of Brandenburg-Prussia was forged in an epoch of iron and blood centuries before Bismarck.[22]

The Great Elector's defeat of the estates is a familiar story, recounting only part of military exigency's destruction of constitutionalism. The decline of the estates was accompanied by the rise of the cornerstone of Prussian military-bureaucratic absolutism, the *Generalkriegskommissariat*. In the middle of the seventeenth century, it controlled the administration, supply, and recruitment of the army, and, at least until the peace with Poland, it collected taxes and controlled its own budget. But with war against France in 1672, it regained these functions, and began to penetrate local government and virtually every part of civil society.

The Generalkriegskommissariat established a three-tier administrative apparatus with its central command in Berlin, the *Oberkriegskommissarien* in the provinces, and a network of officials (*Kriegskommissarien* and *Steuerkommissarien*) at the local levels.[23] Its original duties of collecting taxes soon expanded into administrative and judicial areas. The *commissarii loci* (as the commissions were called in the towns) assumed control of the judiciary, attained control over the mayoralties and police, and otherwise managed town affairs.[24] The instruments of local government

[21] See Fritz Hartung, *Deutsche Verfassungsgeschichte vom 15. Jahrhundert bis zur Gegenwart*, Eighth Edition (Stuttgart: K. F. Koehler, 1950), pp. 92–112; Schmoller, "Entstehung des preußischen Heeres," pp. 751–58; Delbrück, *History of the Art of War*, Volume 4, pp. 242–45.

[22] The pivotal nature of war in the defeat of the estates is noted by Carsten: "The war [against France in 1672] decisively affected the relations between Frederick William and the Prussian Estates . . . exactly as the Estates of Brandenburg . . . were deprived of their power by the war of 1655–1660." *Origins of Prussia*, pp. 218–19.

[23] Hintze, "Der Commissarius und seine Bedeutung in der allgemeinen Verwaltungsgeschichte," in *Staat und Verfassung: Gesammelte Abhandlungen zur allgemeinen Verfassungsgeschichte*, Fritz Hartung, ed. (Leipzig: Koehler & Amelang, 1941), pp. 233–35.

[24] Ibid., p. 233; Carsten, *Origins of Prussia*, p. 197; Hartung, *Deutsche Verfassungsgeschichte*, p. 68.

in the countryside fared a little better. Whereas the estates had formerly managed local affairs through the Kreisdirektoren, the directors were absorbed by state commissars into the *Landräte*. The Landrat was intended to be Berlin's overseer in the provinces, managing the police, maintaining bridges and roadways, and surveiling local nobles, but in practice it afforded the nobles a measure of politicking. The Landrat provided a forum for the articulation and protection of local interests, especially during times of state weakness. It is necessary to bear this in mind to prevent conceptualizing the rise of the Prussian state as a seventeenth-century *Gleichschaltung* (a point to which we shall return in discussing parlements and assemblies in France). Despite the preponderance of state power, a measure of politics went on, especially at the local level. The state relied heavily on the nobility and allowed a measure of local control as long as control over taxation and the army remained in its hands. Absolutism was never absolute.[25]

The extension and intrusion of the Generalkriegskommissariat must be distinguished from the growth and differentiation of social-based political development. The growth of the state came not from public demand for services or from anyone's class interest; it was a consequence of war and the need to prepare for it. The rise of the Generalkriegskommissariat stemmed from the imperative of mobilizing, by the most expeditious means, Prussia's sparse resources. This was essential in the face of a dangerous military situation in which the country's sovereignty was threatened from the north by Sweden, from the east by Poland and Russia, from the south by Austria and the Tatars, and in the distant west by France, which eyed the Hohenzollern western enclaves of Cleves and Jülich. Precedent and procedure suffered, but that was the price of continued independence.

The rise of a military-centered state made itself felt on aspects of constitutionalism other than the estates. The first steps in the transformation of law were taken with the destruction of the estates and the intimidation of its leadership. The prince was no longer first among equals; he could now act above the law, wielding the state, including the law, for reasons of state.[26] Elements of new princely authority manifested themselves in

---

[25] Robert M. Berdahl, "The *Stände* and the Origins of Conservatism in Prussia," *Eighteenth Century Studies* 6 (1973): 298–321, and *The Politics of the Prussian Nobility: The Development of a Conservative Ideology 1770–1848* (Princeton, N.J.: Princeton University Press, 1988). Hartung, *Deutsche Verfassungsgeschichte*, pp. 107–116. Though providing a measure of representation, the Junker Landräte were no carriers of constitutionalism. They strongly opposed the liberal Stein-Hardenberg Reforms and had to be replaced by civil servants. They were obstacles to democracy stemming from a labor-repressive agrarian system, as Moore's argument suggests.

[26] The Hohenzollerns made themselves officially and "legally" above the law but elected to keep their bureaucracies subject to it as a means of controlling the bureaucrats. See Hans

the legal system. The crown could order the death penalty for virtually any offense; cases could be arrogated from provincial courts to those of the crown. In many cases punishments were out of proportion to the offense (e.g., those for burglary, importing wool, and desertion during peacetime). A consequentialist logic entered the judicial process: punishments served not only to punish offenders, but also to demonstrate overwhelming power, to intimidate and regiment the country. There was no autonomy of the judiciary from the rest of the state; judge and advocate were trained in state universities. All served. The old rights of appeal to the courts of the Holy Roman Emperor and (in East Prussia) to the Polish crown were curtailed. This transition in itself is hardly evidence of an authoritarian trend; it was a common part of state building and establishing sovereignty. But now the highest court of appeal was the crown's privy council, in which law was an instrument of implementing the policies of the state. In Hintze's words: "Justice was the stepchild of the military and police state."[27]

Arrogating cases and draconian punishments conflict with Roman Law's concern with proceduralism, just punishments, and cautious weighing of evidence, and hence do not derive from that quarter. The transformation of law stemmed from the new power the crown derived from its army and bureaucratic apparatus. The crown heeded the jurisprudence of Pufendorf, who argued that, when a country is in danger, as Prussia would be until at least 1815, rights and liberties of the estates and subjects cease.[28] In a dangerous military situation, the crown could not be paralyzed by pettifogging mandates of procedural correctness and respect for tradition. It is important not to exaggerate the authoritarian nature of the Prussian judicial system. The Hohenzollern state was able to construct a highly efficient legal system staffed by trained professionals in which a fair trial could be obtained. Most criminal and civil cases were ably handled by a professional legal corps. But with the monarch effectively above the law, directing the judiciary, potential for manipulation and arbitrariness inhered in the system. Interference and arrogation were hardly the rule, but we cannot dismiss them as isolated exceptions without relation to a changed constitution. Institutional checks on pre-

Rosenberg, *Bureaucracy, Aristocracy and Autocracy: The Prussian Experience, 1660–1815* (Boston: Beacon Press, 1966), pp. 45–56.

[27] Quoted in Dorwart, *Administrative Reforms*, p. 73. Cf. Montesquieu: "Mr Law, through ignorance of both a republican and monarchical constitution, was one of the greatest promoters of absolute power in Europe." *The Spirit of the Laws* (Cincinatti, Ohio: Robert Clarke, 1873), p. 19.

[28] See Hartung, *Deutsche Verfassungsgeschichte*, p. 105; Schmoller, "Entstehung des preußischen Heeres," p. 751; and Franz L. Neumann, *The Rule of Law: Political Theory and the Legal System in Modern Society* (Leamington Spa, U.K.: Berg, 1986), pp. 92–99.

rogative were gone, but only the most myopic ruler risks legitimacy and stability by repeated, egregious violations of substantive and procedural norms. To do so might trigger a rebellion of the peasantry or aristocracy. The Hohenzollerns were not despots. Short of this, however, the new political equation between state and society afforded the Hohenzollerns the opportunity to exercise far greater discretion in legal matters than their predecessors had enjoyed.

The revolution in government made itself felt in the daily life of the peasantry. The decline of the estates of course meant little to them, but militarization of the country made itself felt everywhere, and, when it was combined with the erosion of individual rights and liberties entailed in the manorial reaction of previous centuries, the peasant of East Elbia became little more than chattel.[29] Peasants were impressed into the army or into labor crews charged with the construction of fortifications and the maintenance of roads. Delbrück deftly segues from normative to practical concerns: "[T]hese actions undermined all legal concepts and caused the most serious damage to the country. . . . The peasants were no longer willing to bring their produce into town because they feared they would be seized there and turned over to the recruiters. Younger men crossed over the border in droves in order to escape service."[30] This hurt the economy as well as the army, and led to the introduction of the *Kantonsystem* in 1733. The peasant was tied to his Kanton, trained in military skills, then sent home to maintain agricultural output at optimal levels. He had to quarter troops of the standing army; marriage and travel had to be approved by his regimental commander. When this system was combined with the results of the manorial reaction (legal ties to the soil, the destruction of peasant government, and sharply increased service requirements), the rights of the peasantry were all but destroyed. The peasants were trapped "between the manor and the regiment" (*zwischen Gut und Regiment*). Even the children of the Junkers were forcibly enrolled in cadet schools—something, one suspects, to which they soon became more receptive.[31]

---

[29] A fuller treatment of the impact of the manorial reaction on constitutional government will be undertaken in the final chapter.

[30] Delbrück, *History of the Art of War*, Volume 4, p. 247.

[31] Schmoller, "Entstehung des preußischen Heeres," pp. 758–66; Martin A. Kitchen, *Military History of Germany from the Eighteenth Century to the Present* (Bloomington: Indiana University Press, 1975), pp. 6–26; Otto Büsch, *Militärsystem und Sozialleben im alten Preussen, 1713–1807: Die Anfänge der sozialen Militarisierung der preußisch-deutschen Gesellschaft* (Berlin: Walter de Gruyter, 1962), pp. 1–163; Gerhard Oestreich, *Friedrich Wilhelm I.: Preußischer Absolutismus, Merkantilismus, Militarismus* (Göttingen: Musterschmidt, 1977), pp. 71–81; Walter L. Dorn, *Competition for Empire, 1740–1763* (New York: Harper & Row, 1963), pp. 90–99; Delbrück, *History of the Art of War*, Volume 4, pp. 257–58;

The Kantonsystem militarized the whole of Prussia, and a residue of it is our inability to think of it without associations with the army and warfare: "The whole country was a training school for soldiers. The rattle of muskets, the tramp of armed men was heard summer and winter from the Memel to the Rhine. . . ."[32] In 1760 one out of every fourteen Prussians was serving in the military, whereas in another military-bureaucratic absolutism, France, the figure was only one in eighty-six.[33] The impact of the military system on society is bluntly expressed in the opening words of a classic study:

> Das soziale System des preußischen Staates in der Epoche seiner Geschichte von den Reformen des . . . Friedrich William I., seit 1713 bis zur Zeit der Erneuerung durch . . . Stein und . . . Hardenberg nach 1807 ist im übereinstimmenden Urteil von zeitgenössischer Kritik und späterer Geschichtsschreibung in hohem Maße ein Ergebnis der altpreußischen Heeresverfassung des 18. Jahrhunderts gewesen. Die preußische Armee war Anlaß, Mittel und Basis zugleich für die Errichtung, Ausbildung und Aufrechterhaltung dieses sozialen Systems.[34]

By the early eighteenth century, virtually every aspect of constitutional government had been destroyed, replaced by a bureaucratic state charged with extracting men and material for the growing army.[35]

THE ARTICULATION OF MILITARY-BUREAUCRATIC ABSOLUTISM

The need to mobilize national resources had long-run consequences that patterned much of Prussian and German history. As absolutism became more fully developed, it shaped social, economic, and political developments, including a fusion of nobility and state, high rates of taxation and

---

[32] Tuttle, *History of Prussia*, p. 381. Cf. the Japanese army's militarization of society in Richard J. Smethurst, *A Social Basis for Prewar Japanese Militarism: The Army and the Rural Community* (Berkeley and Los Angeles: University of California Press, 1974).

[33] See André Corvisier, *Armies and Societies in Europe 1494–1789*, Abigail T. Siddall, trans. (Bloomington: Indiana University Press, 1979), p. 113.

[34] "The social system of the Prussian state in the period of its history from the innovations of Friedrich Wilhelm I of 1713 to the time of the Stein-Hardenberg Reforms after 1807 was, in the unanimous view of contemporary critic and later historiography alike, largely the result of the old Prussian military system of the eighteenth century. The Prussian army was at the same time occasion, means, and basis for the establishment, development, and maintenance of this social system." Büsch, *Militärsystem und Sozialleben*, p. 1.

[35] Owing to their poverty and lack of institutionalized power following the Reformation, the Prussian clergy became subordinated to the state. See Mary Fulbrook, *Piety and Politics: Religion and the Rise of Absolutism in England, Württemberg and Prussia* (Cambridge: Cambridge University Press, 1983), pp. 84–88, 153–73.

low rates of economic growth, the state's managerial relationship to civil society, and a supportive cultural-ideological configuration.

The first consequence of military-bureaucratic absolutism is the fusion of the nobility and the state. Barrington Moore views this as the result of commercialization of agriculture relying on overt labor repression (tying formerly free peasants to the soil), as opposed to relying on wage incentives to ensure the labor force (as in England and the American Midwest). But for Moore the fusion takes place at a much later stage in the modernization process—in the Prussian/German case, near the close of the nineteenth century, when the Junkers sought help to shore up their declining economic position.[36] Initial fusion took place much earlier, beginning with the very inception of absolutism. From its inception to its collapse, with only a brief interlude of reform during the Napoleonic Wars, the Prussian state reserved high offices for the noble caste. Prussian electors and kings generally preferred the character of men of high birth to the suspect qualities of commoners. Although the Great Elector's father and Friedrich Wilhelm I (r. 1710–1740) had a definite preference for beholden non-Junkers in the civil service, a preference shared by neither the Great Elector nor Frederick the Great, the officer corps was overwhelmingly Junker, and remained so until the National Socialist period.[37] It was this early fusion with the military-bureaucratic state, and not the petty tyranny of the Prussian latifundia, that accounts for the survival into modern times of the ideology of a natural elite and a warrior-caste ethos.[38]

There are three reasons for the fusion of the nobility to the state. First, the rise of the state had destroyed the estates and the nobility's provincial Kreisdirektoren but did not threaten the Junkers' economic position as heads of their manors. In fact, the growth of the Prussian monarchal state was occasioned by two quid pro quo with the Junkers, which solidified their economic basis. The Recess of 1653 gave the Great Elector tax revenue and an army in exchange for recognition of serfdom, administrative control of their peasants, and the right to import and export most commodities free of the excise. When the expenses of the War of the Spanish Succession necessitated the abolition of Junker tax immunities, Friedrich

---

[36] Barrington Moore, Jr., *Social Origins of Dictatorship and Democracy: Lord and Peasant in the Making of the Modern World* (Boston: Beacon Press, 1966), pp. 435–37.

[37] See Karl Demeter, "Die Herkunft des preußischen Offizierkorps," in Büsch and Neugebauer, *Moderne preußische Geschichte*, Volume 2, pp. 879–907; Walter L. Dorn, "The Prussian Bureaucracy in the Eighteenth Century, III," *Political Science Quarterly* 47 (1932): 262–69; Rosenberg, *Bureaucracy, Aristocracy and Autocracy*, p. 70; and Carsten, *Origins of Prussia*, pp. 258–59.

[38] Military service and estate ownership were closely related; together, they preserved such ideological configurations. See Büsch, *Militärsystem und Sozialleben*.

Wilhelm I mollified them and solidified their loyalty by embellishing their privileges: Junker estates were formally allodialized (the threat of archaic feudal claims of domain was removed); only nobles could purchase the land of fellow noblemen, thereby making the walls of a Stand less permeable; and local land-credit offices were set up under Junker control to help impecunious brethren.[39] Hence, a mutually beneficial modus vivendi developed quite early between state and nobleman: the latter obtained legal guarantees and privileges, the former a loyal officer corps and civil service.

Politically and socially powerful though they were, few Junkers attained the wealth of the English gentry. Most estates were relatively small tracts upon which only a barely comfortable life could be eked out. For many Junkers, state service was not just a source of more power and status, it was an economic necessity.[40] The final impetus toward fusion was the absence of the ecclesiastical offices in which nobles had traditionally ensconced their sons prior to the Reformation. Without this traditional outlet for younger sons, only careers in the state and the army could provide them with the positions of status and honor their birth required: "Die Entstehung des stehenden Heeres löste für viele Adelsfamilien die Frage, wie sie ihre jüngeren Söhne versorgen konnten: eine Frage, die seit der Einführung der Reformation besonders dringend war." [41]

High rates of taxation are mandated (at least in the absence of extraordinary means of revenue, such as massive foreign sources) by the need to recruit and outfit the army, to supply troops with efficient weaponry, to research and develop the next generation of armaments, and to fund the central organizations managing these operations. Prussia was not a wealthy land and, what is more, its population base was low. Building a first-rate army required an immense tax burden on the region, the extent of which is conveyed by comparison to France. In 1688 the Prussian state

[39] See Rudolf Braun, "Taxation, Sociopolitical Structure, and State-Building: Great Britain and Brandenburg-Prussia," in Charles Tilly, ed., *The Formation of the National States in Western Europe* (Princeton, N.J.: Princeton University Press, 1975), pp. 274–77; and Berdahl, *Politics of the Prussian Nobility*, pp. 77–80. Note that this was not a case of the nobility's use of the state to shore up its economic position—that came only much later. It was, rather, a mutually beneficial arrangement between state and important social group.

[40] Dorn shows that, in 1767, of 1,700 nobles in Brandenburg and Pomerania, only 400 could afford to live without supplementing their estate income with state service. See "Prussian Bureaucracy, III," p. 263. On the comparable poverty and fusion of much of the Russian nobility, see Robert E. Jones, *The Emancipation of the Russian Nobility, 1762–1785* (Princeton, N.J.: Princeton University Press, 1973).

[41] "The rise of the standing army solved for many noble families the question of how they could provide for their younger sons, a question that from the introduction of the Reformation was especially urgent." Carsten, "Entstehung des Junkertums," p. 280.

extracted from its population of about one million just under 3.4 million talers, while Louis XIV extracted from some twenty million subjects in his economically advanced domain the equivalent of 36.6 million talers—on a per-capita basis approximately half as much as their counterparts east of the Rhine.[42]

All this was a burden on economic development: capital formation and private investment were low, peasants fled or at least attempted to do so, and certain absolute economic declines took place as peasants slaughtered livestock to reduce taxable property. Taxation was hardly the lone factor accounting for backwardness. Most of Prussia (save East Prussia) had very poor soil. The promising growth of Hanse towns had been stifled by the loss of much of the Baltic trade to the Dutch in the fifteenth century. The Prussian economy, which had seemed so promising a century prior to the Thirty Years' War, was retarded in no small part by high and, in some cases, literally confiscatory taxation. Peasants relinquished exorbitant percentages of their income to tax collectors.[43] Two political consequences follow from the economic situation. First, the development of an independent bourgeoisie was less likely. Prussia was hardly an auspicious place to invest capital, not only because of high taxes, but also because of the state's extension to the nobility of the privileges of importing and reselling without paying the excise. There would be no economically vital burgher class pressuring for charters of rights and a share in government. Second, domestic conflict took place in a tight, constrained context in which the rise of one group imperiled the position of other groups. A disposition on the part of the state and social groups to compromise and accommodation, crucial to liberal democracy, was less likely than in a dynamically expanding economy.

The continuous perception of the threat of war, the ubiquity of the uniformed Kantonists, and the pervasiveness of the military administrators contributed to the formation of a cultural and ideological system supportive of the preeminence of the military. Military systems as well as economic ones engender ideologies that justify privations and social inequities. War and preparation for it became accepted parts of life. What other nations saw as crushing burdens on productive forces and an aberration of human behavior were widely admired. The standing army, argued one defender,

---

[42] Carsten, *Origins of Prussia*, p. 266. However, the peculation inhering in French tax-farming and the efficiency of Prussian *Steuerräte* meant that a greater proportion of extractions reached Berlin. See also Kitchen, *Military History of Germany*, p. 10.

[43] Poor soil and high taxes for war might go a long way in explaining different levels of economic growth in England and Prussia. Cf. Robert Brenner, "Agrarian Class Structure and Economic Development in Pre-Industrial Europe," in Aston and Philpin, *The Brenner Debate*, pp. 10–63.

creates many employment opportunities, and becomes a stimulus to agriculture and industry alike. . . . Even the peace-time standing army provides an opportunity to exercise certain qualities, and to develop certain capacities, which would atrophy but for the existence of standing armies, though they are important and beneficial to mankind. I reckon among these not only the refinement of the sense of honor, the training of the intellect, and the sharp eye for reality which differentiate officers from other members of the upper class; but the common soldier also benefits from military service through the improvement of his physique in strength and endurance; a better appreciation of the value of discipline, precision, activity, and subordination; and an enlargement of his intellectual horizons. The peasant who has spent several years with the colors is usually a better peasant for that very reason.

And war itself served the ends of not only the king, but also Providence. Were it not for war, one pious author wondered,

How degenerate would the human race become! The Creator . . . sporadically requires the scourge of war in order to prevent serious outbreaks of immorality in the world. War shakes up the entire constitution of men; when the paroxysm is over they feel their weakness and moderate their sensuous drives. The long-prevalent spirit of frivolity is broken; there arises, at least for a time, a more serious way of looking at the world; there is a revival of the feeling for religion and for virtue; and men resume the search for the Unknown God.[44]

The Prussian state fostered respect for the martial virtues by expenditures on parks with military symbolism, heroic statues of generals, and depiction of battles on the facades of public buildings. Military success, from Hermann's defeat of the Roman legions in the Teutoberger forest to Moltke's victory at Sedan, became centerpieces of a state semiotics, impressed onto the consciousness and identity of Prussians and Germans. In time, military monuments were built by popular initiative. Each facade, statue, and newly minted coin reminded the Prussian that his homeland was safe only by virtue of constant military readiness and the privations upon which the army was based.[45]

[44] Quotes from Klaus Epstein, *The Genesis of German Conservatism* (Princeton, N.J.: Princeton University Press, 1975), pp. 290–92. In my view, these sentiments fall short, in scope and intensity, of the glorification of war and death during the National Socialist period. Nazi ideology drew at least as much from Volkish antimodernism, in any case. See George L. Mosse, *The Crisis of German Ideology: Intellectual Origins of the Third Reich* (New York: Universal, 1964).

[45] See George L. Mosse, *The Nationalization of the Masses: Political Symbolism and Mass Movements in Germany from the Napoleonic Wars through the Third Reich* (New York: Meridian, 1977). Military symbols pervade English and American cities, too, so the distinction is one of degree; but in contrast, Dutch art frequently depicted soldiers in a rather unflattering way. See Simon Schama, *The Embarrassment of Riches: An Interpre-*

Military victory became the basic edifice of legitimacy for the state. Victory justified heavy taxation and loss of personal freedom, transforming them from mundane burdens into transcendent national duties. Military success also served as the foundation of emerging sentiments of nationalism: as old loyalties to Prussia's constitutive duchies and provinces dissolved, Hohenzollern successes on the field of battle, where peasants, town dwellers, and nobles of various provinces had fought, helped to develop common affective ties. As the army became the centerpiece of Prussian state, society, and nationalism, the military profession took on enhanced social prestige. "The great social importance of the reserve officer was the penetration of military thinking and values into the civilian life. In this way we can speak of a militarization of the German educated middle class."[46] By the nineteenth century, military service, in the standing army or at least in the huge reserve corps, was an essential part of the career pattern of the average member of the middle class.[47] From popular consciousness to the educated bourgeoisie (*Bildungsbürgertum*), from prevalent values we might call common sense to treatises from the faculties of philosophy at Berlin and Königsberg, a neo-stoicist view held that true freedom was an inner matter, independent of external political institutions, lying not in the miasma of the individual, but in obedience to the state, which field marshall and *Privatdozent* alike imbued with metaphysical sanctity and teleological legitimation.[48] While Whig historians in England interpreted history as unilinear progress toward parliamentary democracy and individual freedom, German historicism saw and approved the culmination of German history in the Prussian state. The Unification of 1871 had the same sacred teleology as the Glorious Revolution of 1688.[49]

---

tation of Dutch Culture in the Golden Ages (Berkeley and Los Angeles: University of California Press, 1988), pp. 221–57.

[46] Karl Erich Born, "Structural Changes in German Social and Economic Development at the End of the Nineteenth Century," in James J. Sheehan, ed., *Imperial Germany* (New York: New Viewpoints, 1976), p. 26.

[47] See James J. Sheehan, "Conflict and Cohesion Among German Elites in the Nineteenth Century," in Sheehan, ed., *Imperial Germany*, p. 77; Hans Ulrich Wehler, *Der deutsche Kaiserreich 1871–1918* (Göttingen: Vandenhoeck & Ruprecht, 1988), pp. 122–31; Gerhard Ritter, *The Sword and the Scepter: The Problem of Militarism in Germany*, Volume 1: *The Prussian Tradition, 1740–1890* (Miami, Fla.: University of Miami Press, 1969); and Emilio Willems, *A Way of Life and Death: Three Centuries of Prussian-German Militarism—An Anthropological Approach* (Nashville, Tenn.: Vanderbilt University Press, 1986), pp. 72–98.

[48] See Leonard Krieger, *The German Idea of Freedom: History of a Political Tradition* (Chicago: University of Chicago Press, 1957), pp. 46–80. Nicholas Karamzin, the great historian of the Russian state, held that "freedom is where there is regulation." Quoted in James H. Billington, *The Icon and the Axe: An Interpretive History of Russian Culture* (New York: Vintage, 1970), p. 263.

[49] See Georg Iggers, *The German Conception of History: The National Tradition of His-*

The mobilization of the population and economic resources begun by the Great Elector was but the first phase of the state's assumption of a managerial position vis-à-vis civil society. The dearth of resources in Prussia required the scope and intensity of this managerialism to be quite extensive. Accordingly, the state began to squeeze out scarce resources, to determine more efficient methods of extraction, and also to develop or seize additional resources (commercial enterprises or adjacent territories) that would add to state coffers.

The central institution charged with this managerial duty was, not surprisingly, the Generalkriegskommissariat, or the General Directory as it was called in the eighteenth century. Rosenberg summarizes the managerial stance:

> From the outset, the Prussian war commissars and their like . . . did not confine their work to military administration. They also . . . subjected social and economic life to steadily growing regimentation. In this blending of the management of military and civil affairs and in the methodical subordination of civil government to military considerations lies the distinctively militaristic character of Prussian public administration.[50]

And Hintze adds:

> Dieselben Behörden, die für die Unterhaltung des Heeres, für das Aufkommen der Steuern zu sorgen haben, werden auch für die Erhaltung und Entwicklung des Wohlstandes und der Steuerkraft der Bevölkerung, vor allem für die Aufnahme der städtischen Nahrungen und des Verkehrs verantwortlich gemacht.[51]

The principal reason for this management of the national economy lies in war and preparing for it, but doubly so. After the destruction of the wars of the eighteenth century, the state assumed the task of promoting economic recovery, a role that reinforced its position vis-à-vis the economy and led to the increased size of the state. After the Seven Years' War (1756–1763), Frederick the Great built ministries for the management of the nation's forest and mineralogical resources, as well as one for the su-

---

torical Thought from Herder to the Present (Middletown, Conn.: Wesleyan University Press, 1983).

[50] Rosenberg, *Bureaucracy, Aristocracy and Autocracy*, pp. 37–38.

[51] "The same authorities that had responsibility for the maintenance of the army and for the collection of taxes also were made responsible for the maintenance and development of the prosperity and taxability of the population, above all for the nourishment of the towns and for the care of commerce." Hintze, "Der Commissarius und seine Bedeutung," pp. 233–34. As late as 1914, one German historian characterized his country as an "heroic-aristocratic warrior state in which everything—taxation, officialdom, economy, society—revolved around the army, was determined by the needs of the army." Quoted in Fritz Fischer, *From Kaiserreich to Third Reich: Elements of Continuity in German History 1871–1945*, Roger Fletcher, trans. (London: Allen & Unwin, 1986), p. 39.

pervision and encouragement of overseas commerce.[52] Engineers, architects, and scientists were organized into a state academy through which the state could better control the economy.[53] Roads, bridges, and canals, what one might today call the economy's infrastructure, were built to facilitate communication and troop movements. It is a telling point that the German discipline *Verwaltungsgeschichte* (administrative history) has no counterpart in American or English historiography.

English agricultural technique (*verbesserte Englische Wirtschaft*) was studied by the appropriate ministry and practiced on the crown's demesne before being introduced onto Junker estates. This led to the agricultural sector's emulation of the English, but hardly to a gentry-dominated polity, only to more statism.[54] Protection of nascent textile and metallurgical industries began as early as 1684 and continued throughout the next centuries, as new industries critical to military power emerged.[55] State ownership of industry and investment in new factories, banks, and mines was routine. Armament and munitions plants were owned by the state, but daily operation was conducted by the state's partner and consultant in the private sector, Splitgerber und Daum, a firm that also benefited enormously from dealings with the economics ministry, which gave them numerous lucrative trade monopolies.[56] Large-scale

---

[52] Carsten, *Origins of Prussia*, pp. 260–65; Oestreich, *Friedrich Wilhelm I.*, pp. 62–70; W. O. Henderson, *Studies in the Economic Policy of Frederick the Great* (London: Frank Cass, 1963), pp. 38–84, 157–59; Johnson, *Frederick the Great and His Officials*, pp. 188–242; C.B.A. Behrens, *Society, Government, and the Enlightenment: The Experiences of Eighteenth-Century France and Prussia* (New York: Harper & Row, 1985), pp. 116–51.

[53] Johnson, *Frederick the Great and His Officials*, pp. 232–37. The author entitles this section, "Science: Captive of the State."

[54] Hans-Heinrich Müller, "Domänen und Domänenpächter in Brandenburg-Preussen im 18. Jahrhundert," in Büsch and Neugebauer, *Moderne preußische Geschichte*, Volume 1, pp. 316–59; Johnson, *Frederick the Great and His Officials*, pp. 237–41.

[55] See Hugo Rachel, "Merkantilismus in Brandenburg-Preußen," in Büsch and Neugebauer, *Moderne preußische Geschichte*, Volume 2, pp. 951–93; for the nineteenth century, see Ulrich Peter Ritter, "Preußische Gewerbeförderung in früh-industrieller Zeit," in Büsch and Neugebauer, *Moderne Preußische Geschichte*, Volume 2, pp. 1031–87; Theodore S. Hamerow, *Restoration, Revolution, Reaction: Economics and Politics in Germany, 1815–1871* (Princeton, N.J.: Princeton University Press, 1967), pp. 3–20; and W. O. Henderson, *The State and the Industrial Revolution in Prussia, 1740–1870* (Liverpool: Liverpool University Press, 1967). A curious law aimed at protecting the textile industry limited the mourning period, during which drab attire was normally worn for several weeks. See Reinhold August Dorwart, *The Prussian Welfare State before 1740* (Cambridge, Mass.: Harvard University Press, 1971), pp. 41–48.

[56] See Henderson, *Economic Policy of Frederick the Great*, pp. 2–7, 17–37, 157–59; Geoffrey Parker, *The Military Revolution: Military Innovation and the Rise of the West, 1500–1800* (Cambridge: Cambridge University Press, 1988), pp. 148–49. The role of the military in the economy declined with the liberalization of the economy in the nineteenth century but continued in some form into the twentieth century, especially during World

investment in the national economy there was, but the Hohenzollerns always retained huge monetary reserves. From a purely economic viewpoint, these would have been better used as injections into the circular flow, but monetary reserves were critical in case of war.[57]

Prussia faced a dearth of human as well as economic resources. Accordingly, foreign immigrants from Bohemia, the Swiss Confederation, and other German territories, as well as religious refugees, especially Huguenots and Jews, were encouraged to settle in Prussia, often in war-ravaged regions. They provided valuable entrepreneurial and commercial skills relatively lacking in the indigenous populace. They composed an "imported artificial bourgeoisie" (*importiertes Ersatzbürgertum*). By 1786 the state had settled over three hundred thousand émigrés (a sizeable portion of the total population) on Prussian soil in the hope that their labor would yield surplus to the state.[58]

Managerialism on the part of the Prussian state is not without parallels in the political and economic histories of countries that became liberal democracies, most notably England. In fact, most European states went through a period of mercantilism during which state policy sought to develop the economy and state revenue. The Prussian case is distinguishable from English mercantilism in three regards. First, the scope and intensity of the Prussian state's control of the economy exceeded those of Tudor and early Stuart England, the peak of mercantilism there. The English crown exerted no control over agriculture; international commerce was affected but hardly dominated by royal monopolies; and royal industry remained only in shipbuilding and a few other sectors. Second, the institutional apparatus for managing the economy wielded by the eighteenth-century Prussian state greatly dwarfed that of England. English monarchs had neither the local nor the central organs to implement a policy as ambitious as that embarked upon in Prussia. Furthermore,

War I and the Rationalization movement of the interwar period. Its end came only with the complete destruction of the German state in 1945 and the allied powers' policy of breaking the state's commanding heights over the economy. See Gerald D. Feldman, *Army, Industry, and Labor in Germany 1914–1918* (Princeton, N.J.: Princeton University Press, 1966); Robert A. Brady, *The Rationalization Movement in German Industry* (Berkeley and Los Angeles: University of California Press, 1933); and Andrew Shonfeld, *Modern Capitalism: The Changing Balance of Public and Private Power* (New York: Oxford University Press, 1980), pp. 239–64.

[57] See Henderson, *Economic Policy of Frederick the Great*, pp. 74–75, 160.

[58] Walter L. Dorn, "The Prussian Bureaucracy in the Eighteenth Century, I," *Political Science Quarterly* 46 (1931): 404. On the settlement programs, see Stefi Jersch-Wenzel, "Minderheiten in der preußischen Gesellschaft," in Büsch and Neugebauer, *Moderne preußische Geschichte*, Volume 1, pp. 486–506; Gustav Schmoller, "Die ländliche Kolonisation des 17. und 18. Jahrhunderts," in Büsch and Neugebauer, *Moderne preußische Geschichte*, Volume 2, pp. 911–50; and Behrens, *Society, Government, and the Enlightenment*, pp. 123–25.

English mercantilism was decided in conjunction with or at least subject to the approval of Parliament. Finally, the matter of timing is important. Whereas mercantilism had declined or even vanished in much of Western Europe by the eighteenth century, in Prussia it was still spreading into newly acquired territories and more deeply into old ones. Common to all these factors is the economy's role of supporting the army: "Die Wirtschaft blieb ihm immer Mittel zu dem Zweck, den Staat stark in Militärmacht und Finanzen zu machen."[59] This placed the polity and economy of Prussia and Germany more firmly and irreversibly on their special path.

State managerialism was not without beneficial aspects. Beginning in the early eighteenth century, and continuing into the next, the state enacted numerous laws and regulations aimed at preserving the social position of the peasantry. *Bauernschutz* laws tried to protect the peasant from increased labor demands of his lord and from attempts to expand manors at the expense of peasants who had retained some property. The aim of these laws was not ultimately the protection of the peasantry, or even preventing the aggrandizement of the nobility; rather they aimed to preserve the orderly extraction of revenues upon which the army depended.[60] The Great Elector and his successors (most notably Friedrich Wilhelm I and Frederick the Great) directed the resources of the state to matters of public sanitation, to the suppression of quackery, and even to efforts at public education that preceded similar efforts elsewhere in Europe by a full century.[61] Torture was abolished in civilian criminal proceedings. Owing to its huge stockpiles of grain against the event of war, the state was able to regulate food prices, the vicissitudes of which fomented riots elsewhere in Europe, including England.[62]

There is some controversy over the motivation for these welfare programs. Some argue that the king's paternal concern (*väterliche Sorgen*) with the welfare of his subjects was critical. This is not as farfetched as it might seem. Absolutist states, at least when ruled by an autocrat and not by soulless bureaucracy, are capable of enlightened policies, providing the appropriate values are firmly rooted in the autocrat presiding over the state, as they surely were in Frederick the Great. Still, Hintze's explanation seems more important: "The cultural purpose and the welfare

[59] "The economy remained to him [the king] always a means to an end: the strengthening of the military and financial power of the state." Rachel, "Merkantilismus," p. 961.

[60] See Büsch, *Militärsystem und Sozialleben*, pp. 72–73; and Kitchen, *Military History of Germany*, pp. 12–13. The Junkers were able to limit implementation of these laws at the local level, however.

[61] Dorwart, *The Prussian Welfare State*, pp. 77–90.

[62] Gerhard Ritter, *Frederick the Great* (Berkeley and Los Angeles: University of California Press, 1968), pp. 178–79.

purpose receded before the power purpose . . . Raison d'état dominated in all areas."[63] The state established public education in the eighteenth century in order to inculcate respect for authority and to improve the productivity of the docile peasantry. Pietism was used to inculcate deference to authority, divine and secular, as this excerpt from a school catechism shows:

Q: From whence comes the power held by the ruler?
A: This power comes from God.
Q: Whom does God ordain?
A: Everyone who holds authority. Because all who exercise authority are ordained by God, subjects must be submissive, loyal, and obedient. . . .
Q: What does it mean to resist authority?
A: To resist authority is to rebel against the divine order.
Q: What happens to those who do not submit to authority?
A: They will suffer eternal damnation.[64]

Welfare policies served to expand state control and, by keeping the public in optimal economic and medical health, to make administration and tax collection smoother and more predictable. The state intruded on the lives of its subjects in numerous ways that hardly helped their social welfare. Laws regulated wedding festivities, dress styles, the hours of drinking establishments, and social mores. The object of this sumptuary legislation was to restrict frivolous expenditures in order to ensure tax revenues, and also to channel the public's energies into more regimented and manageable behavior.[65]

Managerialism contained a logic favorable to imperialist expansion. A powerful organization charged with obtaining resources for national defense looked to weak neighbors as potential sources of revenue and material. When succession troubles weakened the Habsburgs in 1740, Prussia boldly annexed the geopolitically attractive and economically rich region of Silesia. Other annexations continued until the Unification. This move effectively closed a circle in the logic of the European state system:

[63] Quoted in Dorwart, *The Prussian Welfare State*, p. 17. See also Frederick's essay on the humanistic responsibilities of the crown, *Anti-Machiavel* (Athens: Ohio University Press, 1981); G. P. Gooch, *Frederick the Great: The Ruler, the Writer, the Man* (New York: Alfred A. Knopf, 1947); and Dorn, *Competition for Empire*, pp. 137–41. Weber argues that the Hohenzollerns, like the Roman emperors of antiquity, protected the peasantry in order to maintain a supply of able soldiers. See *The Agrarian Sociology of Ancient Civilizations*, R. I. Frank, trans. (London: Verso, 1988), pp. 405–6.

[64] From James Van Horn Melton, *Absolutism and the Eighteenth-Century Origins of Compulsory Schooling in Prussia and Austria* (Cambridge: Cambridge University Press, 1988), p. 186. See also Willems, *Prussian-German Militarism*, pp. 85–87.

[65] See Dorwart, *The Prussian Welfare State*, pp. 1–50; and Tuttle, *History of Prussia*, pp. 465–68.

Prussian policies of defense from foreign conquest led to the ruthless mobilization of domestic resources, and then to the seizure of foreign ones, which entailed Prussia itself becoming a threat to other European states.[66]

THE STATE AND POLITICS

The destruction of constitutional government and the rise of powerful state structures shaped the pattern of politics in ensuing centuries. Party politics, the potential for democratic development, and the rise of legitimate opposition were all stifled, often as a conscious policy of the state. Furthermore, the state was able to avoid or emerge largely intact from the crises that destroyed absolutism elsewhere in Europe. Though managerialism declined and some concessions to liberalism were made, the state maintained its position at the helm of society.

Prussia entered the nineteenth century without local or national elections, except for those in the provinces it annexed and over which it predominated. Corrupt as the most rotten borough in England was, it still provided a measure of representation, limits on monarchal power, as well as an object for which social groups and their political parties could compete. There was something for parties to grab on to. so to speak; with which to establish themselves as popular voices, political blocs, and obstacles to royal power. In Prussia, however, the absence of national representative government, at least until the mid-nineteenth century, decisively retarded the development of party politics. There was little reason to devote one's time and money to political activity that had no office to win and little if any bargaining power with a powerful state bureaucracy. Even after the introduction of a feckless parliament and some municipal autonomy in the nineteenth century, the state rode roughshod over them.[67] Parties remained weak but interest groups were much stronger. A state-society dialogue took place not in a constitutionally guaranteed parliamentary body, but in a less institutionalized yet politically significant setting. The state, as we have seen, needed the support of the nobility for the army and civil service, and formed pacts with it. By the mid-nineteenth century, a mutual dependence came into being between state and industry. Industrialists needed legal innovations to manage growing industrial corporations more effectively, and the state knew well that military might rested increasingly on a modern industrial base, on iron as well as blood. Accordingly, the state gave its ear to more and more in-

[66] See Dorn, *Competition for Empire*, pp. 137–41; Johnson, *Frederick the Great and His Officials*, pp. 167–83; and Christopher Duffy, *Frederick the Great: A Military Life* (London: Routledge, 1988).

[67] Wehler, *Deutsche Kaiserreich*, pp. 78–90.

dustrial groups. Much of what the English middle classes accomplished in Parliament, their German counterparts accomplished through interest groups.[68]

The state was not the passive instrument of the monarch, obsequiously implementing his orders. Owing to common educational experiences, co-operation on day-to-day matters of policy and routine, and concentration in Berlin, a corporate identity emerged among officials, which trans-formed them from the fearful, atomized functionaries that Frederick had hoped to maintain, into a consciously autonomous set of actors with inter-ests of their own and considerable resources: a *Staat für sich*. Officials were at first able to affect monarchal policy by fighting rearguard actions:

> By using mainly indirect methods, the managers of the administrative and ju-dicial apparatus were able to circumvent and counteract royal decisions and orders and to paralyze the execution of policy. They were equipped with the very real power to obstruct and to divert. They practiced passive resistance through inertia, chicanery, and sophistry. They influenced policy making and steered policy enforcement into channels more desirable to themselves by withholding facts or by supplying colored information to their employer. . . . [T]hey . . . carried out unauthorized policies of their own by amending, un-dermining, or altogether emasculating royal directives.[69]

The upshot of these intrigues, when combined with a monarch lacking in the personal strength of Frederick, was the bureaucracy's wresting power from the crown in the years following Frederick's death in 1786. There was at this juncture no one to guard the guardians. From this position, the state was able consciously to pattern basic political processes.

The power of the state, the fusion of key social classes to it, and the absence of elective offices combined to bring about a client-patron rela-tionship between social groups and the state. The apparatus was not an object that could be won through consensus building in the Reichstag,

[68] Ibid., pp. 90–95; David Blackbourn and Geoff Eley, *The Peculiarities of German His-tory: Bourgeois Society and Politics in Nineteenth-Century Germany* (Oxford: Oxford Uni-versity Press, 1984); Jeffry M. Diefendorf, *Businessmen and Politics in the Rhineland, 1789–1834* (Princeton, N.J.: Princeton University Press, 1980); Hans-Jürgen Puhle, *Agrar-ische Interessenpolitik und preußischer Konservatismus im wilhelminischen Reich (1893–1914): Ein Beitrag zur Analyse des Nationalismus in Deutschland am Beispiel des Bundes der Landwirte und der Deutsch-Konservativen Partei* (Bonn: Neue Gesellschaft, 1975).

[69] Rosenberg, *Bureaucracy, Aristocracy and Autocracy*, p. 193. It is interesting to note that these actions took place during the reign of Frederick the Great (r. 1740–1786), a time thought by many to have been the peak of personal autocracy. Frederick's tragic dilemma was that he needed a larger state, but, the larger it got, the more difficult it was to control. See Johnson, *Frederick the Great and His Officials*. On continuity into the next century, see John R. Gillis, *The Prussian Bureaucracy in Crisis, 1840–1860: Origins of an Admin-istrative Ethos* (Stanford, Calif.: Stanford University Press, 1971).

but client groups could negotiate and obtain favors. The state exploited this relationship in two related ways. It disarmed increasingly powerful groups by granting them desired programs. This was a curious dynamic that in a sense demonstrated a measure of power; however, inasmuch as the groups typically receded from further challenges, they obtained no institutional political power, and left the state's preeminence intact. Such was the case with the famous battleship construction that, insofar as the fleet could never challenge England's, made little sense from a strategic point of view, and in fact was a waste of resources; nevertheless, it did serve to placate key social groups and diffuse growing political challenge.[70] Second, the state could play upon divisions within oppositional coalitions. The events of 1848 illustrate a divide-and-conquer stratagem. The state faced a serious challenge from diverse social groups, united, at least for a while, by common opposition to the government. Owing to the state's playing for time and negotiating separate arrangements with artisans, peasants, and other factions, the opposition lost unity and dissolved without realizing its goals.

The enormous power prestige the state acquired through military success, especially after 1871, made it the central, most cognitively important image in Prussian nationalism. Though the nationalist pantheon of Prussia and Germany contained exhibits of Goethe and Schiller, the most popular and prominent ones were those of Frederick, Moltke, and other military leaders. This virtual coincidence of nationalist imagery with the state was an effective weapon against domestic opposition. International tensions, it has been argued, were intentionally exacerbated to ease social and political tensions, diverting attention from present internal conflicts to a potential nation-threatening one. Opposition was delegitimized and discredited by being projected as agents or dupes of the enemy.[71]

Working-class organizations also encountered obstacles posed by na-

[70] See Eckart Kehr, *Battleship Building and Party Politics in Germany, 1894–1901*, Pauline R. Anderson and Eugene N. Anderson, trans. (Chicago: University of Chicago Press, 1975); Hans-Ulrich Wehler, "Bismarck's Imperialism, 1862–1890," in Sheehan, *Imperial Germany*, pp. 180–222; Otto Hintze, "Military Organization and the Organization of the State," in Felix Gilbert, ed., *The Historical Essays of Otto Hintze* (New York: Oxford University Press, 1975), pp. 180–215. Hintze writes (p. 183), "Conflict between nations . . . has even often suppressed internal strife or forced it into compromise."

[71] See Wehler, *Deutsche Kaiserreich*, p. 108; and Geoff Eley, "State Formation, Nationalism, and Political Culture: Some Thoughts on the Unification of Germany," in his *From Unification to Nazism: Reinterpreting the German Past* (Boston: Allen & Unwin, 1986), pp. 61–84. It is useful to note the difference between German social imperialism, in which Bismarck and the state were very much in control, and the Russian example, in which the state was delegitimized after defeat and propelled by domestic considerations to engage in new foreign adventures, for which it was ill-prepared and that had disastrous consequences. See Dietrich Geyer, *Russian Imperialism* (New Haven, Conn.: Yale University Press, 1977).

tionalism. Party organizers attempted to build a counterculture separate from the dominant, militarist one, but found many leaders as well as the rank and file breaking away from much-repeated but weakly held values of internationalism. Leaders and workers overwhelmingly supported the war in 1914. The speech of a social democrat leader conveys the problem of building a coherent oppositional party within the context of German nationalism, as well as the guilt attendant on affiliation with a party opposed to the state:

> I shall never forget the day and hour—the terrible tension was resolved; until one dared to be what one was; until—despite all principles and wooden theories—one could, for the first time in almost a quarter century, join with a full heart, a clean conscience and without a sense of treason in the sweeping stormy song: "Deutschland, Deutschland über alles". . . .[72]
>
> [W]e have learned anew what we had almost completely forgotten: that apart from the class conflicts within a nation there is something common *to all classes of the nation*. We German Social Democrats have learned to consider ourselves in this war as part . . . of the German nation. We do not want to be robbed again by anyone, from the right or the left, of this feeling of belonging to the German people.[73]

Their loyalties stronger to the Reich than to the SPD, workers charged headlong into the catastrophe in 1914, shattering another grand illusion.

The military-centered state, then, was a sprawling giant that was not substantially changed by domestic forces and had no internal impetus toward liberal reform. Peaceful, gradual change was taken off the agenda by the bureaucracy's strength and ability to control domestic opposition. The historical evidence indicates that military-centered states have considerable momentum, and are decisively altered only by the alienation of elites, peasant revolution, fiscal crisis, or complete military defeat—and normally by a conjuncture of more than one of these. Elite alienation was unlikely owing to the nobility's fusion with the military and bureaucracy, as well as its growing dependency on various forms of economic protectionism during the nineteenth century. The middle classes, too, had no great conflict with the institutions that had erected tariff barriers, directly invested in many firms, and were principal purchasers of industrial out-

---

[72] Quoted in Carl Schorske, *German Social Democracy, 1905–1917* (New York: Russell & Russell, 1970), p. 290.

[73] Quoted in Gunther Roth, *The Social Democrats in Imperial Germany: A Study in Working-Class Isolation and National Integration* (Totowa, N.J.: Bedminster Press, 1963), p. 289 (emphasis in original). See also Barrington Moore, Jr., *Injustice: The Social Bases of Obedience and Revolt* (Armonk, N.Y.: M. E. Sharpe, 1978), pp. 221–26.

put. Their protests of 1848 were weak, short-lived, and almost inconsequential for constitutional history.

Peasant revolution might seem to be more likely owing to extreme oppression and the absence of a social escape valve through emigration. However, local peasant organization that might have served as a means of organizing revolt (which could have become revolution if timed with the events of 1806 or 1848) had been shattered by the manorial reaction of the fifteenth and sixteenth centuries. Junkers exercised close administrative control over their field workers, thereby posing a serious though not necessarily insurmountable problem for organization. Oppression on the manors was reinforced by the presence of nearby garrisons and by the peasant's integration into the Kantonsystem. Though we might conceive of the Prussian peasantry as a relatively undifferentiated social class suppressed by Junker landlords, there was actually a significant degree of stratification, precluding solidarity. Gradations ranged from the serfs (*Instleute*) tied to the lord's estate, to the sharecroppers and tenant farmers (*Zinsleute*) who were free of labor service to the lord, to the prosperous, free farmers (Kölmer) of East Prussia.[74] And this is to say nothing of the gradations in the regions annexed by Prussia in the eighteenth and nineteenth centuries.

Prussia was able to maintain fiscal solvency and avoid state paralysis and collapse principally by means of the harsh extraction of revenue from the country. Revenue came into the *Kriegskasse* without passing through the greedy hands of venal officeholders, a problem of paramount importance in the Bourbon revenue system. Revenue was enhanced over the years by the addition or conquest of adjacent lands. Prussia also benefited from subsidies from allies, most notably England and the Netherlands, who were pleased to purchase or rent another army to hold the French in check. It is critical that Prussia did not overextend its financial resources in dubious alliances, by bankrolling far-flung conflicts, or by acquiring remote, indefensible colonies. The Hohenzollerns wisely limited their attention to Central Europe and left the Mediterranean and the Americas to others. In so doing, they consolidated a powerful region in

---

[74] On stratification within the Prussian peasantry, see Marion W. Gray, "Prussia in Transition: Society and Politics under the Stein Reform Ministry of 1808," *Transactions of the American Philosophical Society* 76, part 1 (1986): 19–21; Berdahl, *Politics of the Prussian Nobility*, pp. 28–43; and Behrens, *Society, Government, and the Enlightenment*, pp. 140–42. My views on peasant politics have obviously benefited greatly from the works of Barrington Moore, Jr., *Social Origins*; James C. Scott, *The Moral Economy of the Peasant: Rebellion and Subsistence in Southeast Asia* (New Haven, Conn.: Yale University Press, 1976); and Theda Skocpol, *States and Social Revolution: A Comparative Analysis of France, Russia and China* (New York: Cambridge University Press, 1979).

the heart of Europe and avoided the sort of costly, dangerous adventures that led in part to the demise of French absolutism.

Prussia avoided military defeat throughout the seventeenth and eighteenth centuries—although during the Seven Years' War complete defeat seemed inevitable, even to Frederick, who it is said came close to suicide. Prussia was saved from defeat and dismemberment only by the last-minute collapse of the enemy coalition. Napoleon's devastating victory over the Prussians at Jena and Auerstädt (1806) led to the occupation of the western parts of the country, the government's evacuation of Berlin, and a political crisis that fortunately did not coincide with popular unrest or elite disaffection. Complete occupation was avoided owing to the existence of sufficient tension between France and Russia—a fortuitous circumstance that gave the state time and room to maneuver.[75]

The state introduced substantial political, economic, and military reforms that, if fully implemented, would have altered basic political relationships. The army came under pressure to adopt reforms modeled after the seemingly invincible troops of Napoleon: a mobilization of the nation in exchange for basic political rights. Gneisenau (as von Bülow had even before the French Revolution) called for a free constitution, independent town governments, and civil rights. "It is both fair and shrewd," he argued, "for the people to be given a Fatherland if they are to defend a Fatherland."[76] The army introduced reforms affording greater opportunities for advancement by middle-class officers, and built decentralized military formations (*Landsturm, Landwehr,* and *Jäger*) outside the normal army command structures, which had the radical innovation of elected officers.

Although the reform period has been the object of numerous studies, most of the reforms, such as those that introduced laissez-faire and freed the peasantry, either were never fully implemented or were reversed after the crisis ended with Waterloo. The state remained preeminent. Conservative elements entrenched in the bureaucracy reasserted themselves and disbanded newly created units or gradually merged them with the regular army. One lasting effect of what the army saw as interloping in its sacred traditions was its mistrust of popular pressures and reform

---

[75] On the reform period, see Peter Paret, *Yorck and the Era of Prussian Reform 1807–15* (Princeton, N.J.: Princeton University Press, 1966); Gunther E. Rothenberg, *The Art of Warfare in the Age of Napoleon* (Bloomington: Indiana University Press, 1980), pp. 187–96; Geoffrey Best, *War and Society in Revolutionary Europe, 1770–1870* (New York: Oxford University Press, 1982), pp. 150–67; Kitchen, *Military History of Germany,* pp. 53–101; and Gray, "Prussia in Transition."

[76] Quoted in Krieger, *German Idea of Freedom,* p. 200. Clausewitz was more cautious, favoring a *levée en masse* but no constitution; that is, military but not political-constitutional change.

in general: "The effect of these changes was again to cut the army off from the rest of society, and in an age which was relatively peaceful the main concern of military policy became the 'enemy within.' The army became consciously an instrument of domestic oppression."[77] The state withstood the political crisis of the Napoleonic era without radically altering its political trajectory. The only lasting change was the overthrow of an *autocratic* absolutism and its replacement by a *bureaucratic* one, a change with more interest for administrative than constitutional history; the military-bureaucratic core emerged essentially intact from the Napoleonic Wars.[78]

. . .

Mobilization of domestic resources for the wars of the seventeenth century destroyed Prussian constitutionalism and set into motion the development of a military-bureaucratic absolutism whose contacts with society were mainly administration and machicolation. The Prussian state attained a high level of autonomy from the society beneath it. Fundamental political change in military-bureaucratic absolutisms comes only from massive peasant revolution, complete military defeat, fiscal collapse, and deep alienation of elite social classes—situations that Prussia (but, as will be seen, not France) was able to avoid. It was the state's good fortune and Germany's fate that none of these would arise until the twentieth century.

[77] Kitchen, *Military History of Germany*, p. 69. On Landsturm, Landwehr, and Jäger units, see also Paret, *Prussian Reform*, pp. 154–255; Best, *War and Society*, pp. 161–67; and Hans Kohn, *Prelude to Nation-States: The French and German Experience, 1789–1815* (Princeton, N.J.: D. Van Nostrand, 1967), pp. 212–88.

[78] On the failures of the Prussian reform movement following the Napoleonic Wars, see Rosenberg, *Bureaucracy, Aristocracy and Autocracy*, p. 208; and Best, *War and Society*, pp. 207–22.

CHAPTER FIVE

France

MEDIEVAL FRANCE shared many of the constitutional features of other European countries, with the notable but not paramount absence of a strong national estates. The Hundred Years' War led to a somewhat modern but rather small military organization that was realized without destroying the consensual framework of king and estates. The new army of the later fifteenth century still being small, there was no showdown. France's entry into the Thirty Years' War, however, required immense revenues for a modern army equal to those of Spain and the Holy Roman Empire. Domestic resource mobilization precipitated circumvention but not complete destruction of parlements and provincial estates. By 1700 France and Brandenburg-Prussia resembled each other in critical ways: each had centralized state structures that forcibly levied and collected taxes without the approval of the estates; each state decisively patterned its country's economic, political, and social histories.

Yet French political history does not parallel that of Prussia and Germany in the nineteenth and early twentieth centuries. There was halting movement in the direction of democracy. The resolution to this apparent paradox of a military-bureaucratic absolutism and a liberal democratic outcome lies in the collapse of the Bourbon state in the late eighteenth century. Similar themes and movements in the two countries' history ended with the cacophonous coda of the Revolution. French absolutism, unlike that of Prussia, was brought down by structural and fiscal problems. The Revolution of 1789 provided the possibility of breaking from the Prussian trajectory and making progress in the direction of a liberal political outcome.

FRENCH CONSTITUTIONALISM

The steady expansion of French kings from the Ile de France is a remarkable process that need not be recapitulated here. Capetian and Valois territorial acquisitions, made at the expense of independent duchies and counties, suggest for present purposes that the French state was more powerful than contemporary Prussian or English ones. Doubtless so, but it would be unwarranted to conclude there was no comparable pattern of constitutional government in the medieval and early modern periods.

Philip Augustus and his successors built formidable central institutions, but alongside royal institutions developed local, constitutional ones. Relations between king and estates are not always best envisioned as a seesaw, with one side rising at the expense of the other: "The paradox of the Renaissance monarchy was that as its own power had grown, the various other loci of authority . . . had themselves become institutionalized."[1]

Early monarchs performed the initial state-making tasks of suppressing brigandage and private war, and installing a modicum of central officials (baillis and seneschals) in the localities. Philip Augustus (1180–1223) built a regular governing council paid mainly from royal demesne revenue, occasionally bolstered by sanguinary extortions from merchants and knightly orders.[2] Philip Augustus even constructed a royal army of approximately 2,500 knights and sergeants, paid from the crown's coffers.[3] Though attention might be rightly drawn to this nonfeudal army, it must be borne in mind that these numbers were not sufficient to enforce the crown's will and impose monarchal absolutism upon a reluctant realm, had Philip been so inclined. The thousands of armed men of the town militias and the bulk of the *noblesse d'épée*, whose martial skills had not yet atrophied, composed a powerful counterpoise to any ambitious monarch.

A national estates has been the most common bulwark of constitutional government, but we will look in vain for a powerful one in France. The Estates-General failed to become a meaningful political institution, at least until 1789, and then only briefly. Begun in the early fourteenth century as Philip the Fair prepared for a protracted struggle with the papacy, the Estates-General convened only at the crown's bidding or during periods of national crisis. It did control the feudal levy, but taxation remained in the hands of local estates and councils.[4] This weakness

[1] David Parker, *The Making of French Absolutism* (New York: St. Martin's Press, 1983), p. 27.

[2] John W. Baldwin, *The Government of Philip Augustus: Foundations of French Royal Power in the Middle Ages* (Berkeley and Los Angeles: University of California Press, 1986), pp. 101–9; J. B. Henneman, *Royal Taxation in Fourteenth Century France: The Development of War Financing 1322–1356* (Princeton, N.J.: Princeton University Press, 1971), pp. 8–12; *The Cambridge Medieval History*, Volume 6, pp. 327–30, and Volume 7, pp. 318–25. The nature and significance of these extortions shall be addressed shortly.

[3] Baldwin, *Philip Augustus*, pp. 166–68, 279–89. The author further notes that such forces were not uncommon in medieval Europe: remember the scutage forces of Angevin kings in England.

[4] Sidney Painter, *The Rise of the Feudal Monarchies* (Ithaca, N.Y.: Cornell University Press, 1975), pp. 40–42; J. Russell Major, *Representative Government in Early Modern France* (New Haven, Conn.: Yale University Press, 1980), pp. 12–19, and, "The Loss of Royal Initiative and the Decay of the Estates General in France, 1421–1615," *Studies Presented to the International Commission for the History of Representative and Parliamentary Institutions* 24 (1961): 245–59; Joseph R. Strayer and Charles H. Taylor, *Studies in*

might lead to the conclusion that nothing more is needed to account for the demise of constitutional government and the rise of absolutism, that, irrespective of warfare and military modernization, the triumph of monarchal authority during the Thirty Years' War was assured by the failure of the Estates-General in the late Middle Ages. Significant though this failure was, a little digging into its explanation is in order. Most accounts for the shortcomings of the Estates-General stress powerful regionalist sentiment and linguistic obstacles, as well as the strength of provincial estates. It was, after all, these provincial assemblies that, beginning in the late fifteenth century, sent delegates with strict voting instructions to the Estates-General.[5] The work of the Estates-General was the mediated program of powerful provincial estates. By the mid-fifteenth century, the monarchy had built numerous and widely differing constitutional arrangements with regional estates, rather than a unitary one with a national assembly. Regional estates thwarted the Estates-General and became themselves firm constituents of consensual government—a constitutional situation that allowed for adamant local opposition, but also, when conflict over money erupted, lent itself to royal bullying, piecemeal destruction, or circumvention. It is a tribute to the strength of the provincial estates that they were able to survive, in some form or another, a century and a half of absolutism, and finally succumb only during the Revolution.

Towns along the northern and Mediterranean coasts prospered during the Middle Ages and achieved sovereignty during the communal movement of the thirteenth and fourteenth centuries. Towns elected their own officials (*Prud'hommes*), obtained charters, and established judiciaries apart from the local noblesse. In time they contracted with the crown for other critical rights in exchange for monetary payments and militia levies.[6] Although the fifteenth century witnessed growing monarchal influ-

---

Early French Taxation (Cambridge, Mass.: Harvard University Press, 1939); *The Cambridge Medieval History*, Volume 7, pp. 318–27, 683–95.

[5] P. S. Lewis, "The Failure of the French Medieval Estates," *Past and Present* 23 (1962): 3–24; Claude Soule, "Les pouvoirs des députés aux Etats Généraux de France," *Studies Presented to the International Commission for the History of Representative and Parliamentary Institutions* 27 (1963): 61–82; *The New Cambridge Modern History*, Volume 3, p. 138. One English historian, whose guild is not known for underestimating the power of Parliament, has argued that, by virtue of their control over meetings and presiding officers, French provincial estates were more powerful than Parliament. See Conrad S. R. Russell, "Monarchies, Wars, and Estates in England, France, and Spain, c. 1580–c. 1640," *Legislative Studies Quarterly* 7 (1982): 205–20.

[6] Parker, *The Making of French Absolutism*, pp. 16–18; *The Cambridge Medieval History*, Volume 5, pp. 59–64; Baldwin, *Philip Augustus*, pp. 59–64; John Beeler, *Warfare in Feudal Europe, 730–1200* (Ithaca, N.Y.: Cornell University Press, 1984), pp. 41–42.

ence in municipalities, the chaos of the religious wars in the next century undid most of it.[7]

Autonomous village government and peasant rights were well established in the French countryside by the outset of the early modern period. The same communal movement that led to independent town governments also led to the coalescence of peasants, and often several village clusters, into rural communes, many with royal charters. Peasants migrated into wilderness areas and established chartered villages, just as the East Elbian settlers had done. Radical demographic shifts effected by visitations of the plague in the fourteenth century enabled survivors to obtain favorable rental agreements and freedom from labor-poor seigneurs. Village government comprised elected syndics, tax assessors, and tax collectors. Communal management of the village pastures, fisheries, and woodlands was collective, as was agreement on the details of planting and harvesting.[8] In a few fortunate villages, peasants had voice in the election of the region's representatives to the Estates-General.[9]

The foundations of a central judicial system had been laid by Philip Augustus in his efforts to wrest power subtly from a stubborn noblesse. But no attempt was made then to devise a central, common law; judicial principles derived from local custom. Roman Law only slowly and incompletely filtered in, primarily through contract law, as one might suspect in a region where commerce was reemerging.[10] As part of the crown-peasantry interest in preventing an overly powerful aristocracy, commoners were allowed to sit on the juries of the royal courts, which by most accounts were largely free of monarchal tampering.[11]

Even a cursory review of the rule of law in medieval France cannot ignore Philip Augustus's and Philip the Fair's forcible extraction of money from Jews, the Knights Templar, and foreign merchants. These

[7] J. H. Shennan, *The Parlement of Paris* (Ithaca, N.Y.: Cornell University Press, 1968), pp. 188–215. A contemporary authority said of this ebb of royal authority, "In time there will not be a single village left in France that does not claim sovereignty for itself." Quoted ibid., p. 228.

[8] Emmanuel Le Roy Ladurie, *The Peasants of Languedoc*, John Day, trans. (Urbana: University of Illinois Press, 1976), pp. 11–50; Hilton R. Root, *Peasants and King in Burgundy: Agrarian Foundations of French Absolutism* (Berkeley and Los Angeles: University of California Press, 1987), pp. 69–107; Roland Mousnier, *The Institutions of France under the Absolute Monarchy 1598–1789: Society and the State* (Chicago: University of Chicago Press, 1979), pp. 551–61; Albert Soboul, "The French Rural Community in the Eighteenth and Nineteenth Centuries," *Past and Present* 10 (1956): 78–95; Pierre Goubert, *The French Peasantry in the Seventeenth Century* (Cambridge: Cambridge University Press, 1987), pp. 178–83.

[9] Major, *Representative Government*, pp. 174–75.

[10] Joseph R. Strayer, *On the Medieval Origins of the Modern State* (Princeton, N.J.: Princeton University Press, 1970), pp. 50–51; Shennan, *The Parlement of Paris*, pp. 54–56.

[11] Baldwin, *Philip Augustus*, pp. 220–30; Shennan, *The Parlement of Paris*, pp. 151–54.

actions cannot be dismissed as exceptions that prove a rule, but one can question their long-term constitutional significance. Brutal transgressions of customs and liberties they were; agents of the lasting destruction of constitutional order they were not. Despite the unmistakable arbitrariness of the extortions and the disturbingly modern qualities of the extermination of the Knights Templar, neither systematically undermined constitutionalism or provided the crown with substantial revenue. Once seized, Templar assets were soon expended, much as the Church's were in Tudor England. Stung by royal confiscations, Jews and foreign merchants reduced their transactions in that unfavorable business climate, leading to the diminution of other royal revenues. Despite these outrages, constitutionalism and the rule of law were still generally in evidence. Extortions, in any event, fell off dramatically in the late fourteenth century, as the monarchy faced a desperate crisis of finances and legitimacy brought on by foreign armies ransacking its kingdom.

In the late medieval period, judicial institutions (parlements) begun by the crown freed themselves from the control of the king and became independent political actors, not unlike some later judiciaries. During the Hundred Years' War, English armies roamed at will across much of France, burning and looting while a helpless monarch looked on.[12] Weakened by defeat and jacqueries, the crown lost control of the judiciary. Parlements assumed control of their personnel and to a lesser extent those of the king's chancery. They gave counsel to the crown, enjoyed the right of consultation on basic constitutional matters, and at times even approved or rejected treaties. Their most important power, however, was to register royal laws and policies, a power that waxed and waned over the centuries, inversely with the crown's fortunes. Inasmuch as they had police as well as other regional authorities under their administrative control, parlements possessed certain features of local government that provided a formidable, institutional check on the monarchy.[13]

Further institutional autonomy was ensured by the introduction of the

[12] On the English armies, see Desmond Seward, *The Hundred Years War: The English in France, 1337–1453* (New York: Atheneum, 1982).

[13] On parlements, see Shennan, *The Parlement of Paris*, pp. 112–16; Roland Mousnier, "Pourquoi Etats-Généraux et Etats-provinciaux ont-ils joué un si faible rôle pendant la Fronde?" *Parliaments, Estates and Representation* 1 (1981): 139–45; John A. Carey, *Judicial Reform in France before the Revolution of 1789* (Cambridge, Mass.: Harvard University Press, 1980), pp. 8–12; Franklin L. Ford, *Robe and Sword: The Regrouping of the French Aristocracy after Louis XIV* (New York: Harper & Row, 1965), pp. 79–84; Sarah Hanley, *The* Lit de Justice *of the Kings of France: Constitutional Ideology in Legend, Ritual, and Discourse* (Princeton, N.J.: Princeton University Press, 1983); Bailey Stone, *The French Parlements and the Crisis of the Old Regime* (Chapel Hill: University of North Carolina Press, 1986), pp. 16–28; and John J. Hurt, "The Parlement of Brittany and the Crown: 1665–1675," *French Historical Studies* 4 (1966): 411–33.

venality of office during the wars in Italy of the early sixteenth century. Eager to obtain revenues for wars with Spain, Francis I sold offices in the parlements (and elsewhere in the state apparatus), which, with the introduction of the Paulette in the early seventeenth century, became the property of the growing *noblesse de robe*. Many if not most officeholders were not civil servants in the strict sense of salaried functionaries in a hierarchical structure; they were far closer to independent powers contracting with the monarch on more or less equal terms.[14] Their incomplete integration into the French state and capacity for independent action were critical to the collapse of military-bureaucratic absolutism in the eighteenth century.

Owing primarily to the early power of regional estates, France failed to develop a strong national estates like that of England. The absence of a national parliament, though by no means guaranteeing a military-bureaucratic state, probably made the destruction of constitutionalism easier by preventing the development of a central forum for the defense of constitutionalism, as the English Parliament was in the 1640s. Local estates were individually bullied and sometimes completely but temporarily ignored during the Hundred Years' War, and later during the civil wars.[15] But it is important to note that, irrespective of the strength of French medieval constitutionalism, it was ultimately destroyed by the same causal mechanisms, those of military modernization in the early modern era, that undid Prussian constitutionalism.[16] Though flawed in this regard, French constitutionalism at the outset of the sixteenth century was nonetheless a vigorous multicentered system of consensual government that maintained the principles of representation, rule of law, and, for many, a measure of personal liberty. Its demise lay not simply in early fragmentation, but in rapid military modernization during the Thirty Years' War.

WAR AND POLITICAL CONFLICT

From the fourteenth to the early seventeenth century, France engaged in numerous wars and underwent military reforms short of what can be

[14] Roland Mousnier, *La vénalité des offices sous Henri IV et Louis XIII*, Second Edition (Paris: Presses Universitaires de France, 1971), pp. 36–92, 232–308; Shennan, *The Parlement of Paris*, pp. 185–87.

[15] Major, *Representative Government*, pp. 10–305.

[16] Cf. Charles T. Wood, *Joan of Arc and Richard III: Sex, Saints, and Government in the Middle Ages* (New York: Oxford University Press, 1988). The book builds on arguments in Strayer and Taylor, *Early French Taxation* (pp. 93–94) and suggests that the absence of a unified estates foredoomed France to absolutism. I contend that absolutism makes little sense without the need to build a vast war-making capacity, and that single estates were overwhelmed in Brandenburg, Bavaria, and numerous other principalities.

called full military modernization. At the close of the Hundred Years' War (1453), French armies were neither large nor centralized. Growth of state power and occasional constitutional trespass were in evidence, but constitutionalism persisted into the seventeenth century. Military modernization and constitutional crisis came during the latter stages of the Thirty Years' War and undermined the patterns of constitutionalism of earlier centuries, though without the more or less complete deracination as in the Prussian case.

France's medieval might was based on the feudal levy of knights, secondary and tertiary levies of peasants, and a small group of mercenaries begun by Philip Augustus. Despite stunning losses to disciplined Flemish infantry, French chivalry failed to see the superiority of the new military formations, as the English had after the Scots defeated them at Bannockburn (1314). While other parts of Europe began to adopt pike and bow, the mounted knight remained the center of the French military. Consequently, France suffered catastrophic losses during the Hundred Years' War. The lessons of that protracted but essentially premodern war were not learned quickly. French chivalry was cut down by inferior numbers of English forces at Crecy (1346), again at Poitiers (1356), and once more at Agincourt (1415), where twenty-five thousand Frenchmen were crushed by only six thousand Englishmen.[17] Only after this last defeat was it evident, at least to survivors, that, if France was not to become a Plantagenet fief, military reform was necessary.

Beginning in 1439, the monarchy issued numerous ordinances aimed at restructuring the army. Unruly mercenary units, which supplemented the feudal levies and plundered as ruthlessly as the English enemy, were disbanded or integrated into *Compagnies d'Ordonnance* (1445), which were centrally organized but locally garrisoned and supplied. Another ordinance of 1448 instituted the short-lived *Francs-Archers*. They were initially organized by royal baillis, but later supplied their own weapons (as did the English bowmen after whom they were modeled), and were remunerated not by central treasurers, but by the antiquary method of tax exemption. A critical innovation, however, was the royal artillery, which systematically reduced English fortresses and expelled English armies from the continent.[18]

---

[17] John Keegan, *The Face of Battle: A Study of Agincourt, Waterloo and the Somme* (Harmondsworth, U.K.: Penguin, 1988), pp. 78–116; Hans Delbrück, *History of the Art of War within the Framework of Political History*, Volume 3: *The Middle Ages* (Westport, Conn.: Greenwood Press, 1982), pp. 455–68; Seward, *The Hundred Years War*, pp. 77–188; *The Cambridge Medieval History*, Volume 7, pp. 346–87.

[18] Christopher Allmand, *The Hundred Years War: England and France at War c. 1300–c. 1450* (Cambridge: Cambridge University Press, 1988), pp. 91–119; Delbrück, *History of*

Was this a military revolution requiring a new, more powerful state? Though, as we shall see, some political changes occurred, the French army that eventually emerged victorious from the Hundred Years' War differed from the truly modern ones of the Thirty Years' War. With the exception of some artillery, the army was not widely equipped with gunpowder technology or any of the other instruments of the early modern arsenals. Central organization was in evidence with the artillery and with the initial organization of the Compagnies d'Ordonnance and Francs-Archers, but garrisoning and supply were, again, local matters.[19] These were innovative forces, but not a modern standing army. The French army was also much smaller than the hundred-thousand-strong behemoths of the seventeenth century. Finally, the discipline and training of modern armies were utterly lacking. In fact, the Francs-Archers were rather useless, and were disbanded or converted into pikemen in the late fifteenth century.[20]

Still, there were political changes arising from the war and military reform. At the outset of the Hundred Years' War, the king attempted to levy a tax without the approval of the provincial estates. The ensuing uproar led to retreat from this internal front, and to negotiation of complicated tax systems based on agreements between either the crown and the provincial estates (*pays d'états*), or the crown and elected or venal officials (*pays d'élections*).[21] Taxation without approval of the estates was not unknown during the changing fortunes of the war, but there was no destruction of the estates. The crown knew there were limits to these transgressions and was careful not to try the provinces' patience: "At times the kings had violated their privileges by taxing without consent, creating offices for revenue purposes, and instituting other measures designed to improve their financial position, but at no point did any of them seek to weaken or destroy the estates, which emerged in 1560 in a stronger position than before."[22] The crown's institutional structures were augmented by the innovations of the Hundred Years' War, but so too were those of the provincial estates, which negotiated with the crown and collected its taxes.

Armed with the knowledge of France's political trajectory, one is

---

the Art of War, Volume 3, pp. 508–16; *The Cambridge Medieval History*, Volume 8, pp. 254–59.

[19] Delbrück strongly maintains that the French military during the Hundred Years' War was neither a standing nor a modern army. See *History of the Art of War*, Volume 4: *The Modern Era* (Westport, Conn.: Greenwood Press, 1985), p. 227.

[20] Ibid., p. 13.

[21] Major, *Representative Government*, pp. 39ff. While the crown enjoyed the upper hand in the pays d'élections, it could not tax at will without precipitating unmanageable protests from the estates.

[22] Major, *Representative Government*, p. 96.

tempted to see these new tax offices of the Hundred Years' War as at least a first step toward absolutism. A system of royal agents throughout the countryside and in the towns, sometimes collecting taxes illegally, would seem a propitious beginning for absolutism. But it was not these royal officials who brought absolutism, rather it was the Bourbon intendants, who were sent into the provinces over a century later to replace the old *élections* and *trésoriers*, who had settled in and become far too respectful of local privileges and liberties for the desperate needs of the Thirty Years' War.[23] Conflicts in Italy and internal wars of religion plagued France in the century and a half between the close of the Hundred Years' War and the outbreak of the Thirty Years' War. Venality of office and ennoblement became routine means of war finance, but war needs were also met through subsidies from provincial estates, though often now with some measure of monarchal pressure exerted upon individual assemblies. The civil wars led to the introduction of royal *commissaires* into the localities; however, their task was keeping the peace, not resource mobilization.[24] Forced collections occurred sporadically throughout the religious conflicts, yet the estates and élections, despite occasional trespass, entered the seventeenth century with their constitutional powers intact.[25]

The Thirty Years' War began as a dispute between the estates of Bohemia and the Habsburgs, but swiftly escalated into a hegemonic war raging across Europe. France avoided direct involvement during the first half of the war, which saw Bohemia, Denmark, and the Palatinate fall to Habsburg and Catholic League armies. When the latter armies seemed on the verge of conquering most of the continent, France delivered subsidies to the Swedes, whose timely intervention (1630) rolled back Wallenstein and Tilly, stalemated the Habsburg forces, and temporarily secured French national interests. Constitutional government was maintained during this period despite Richelieu's gradual troop build-ups and extension of the élections into the pays d'états. A small army was fielded by ordinary revenues, augmented by unsystematic intrusions into illegal or quasi-legal revenue collection. But when a Spanish army soundly defeated the Swedes at Nördlingen (1634), France was gravely imperiled. Nothing stood between the Spanish army and the frontier. Though the army had grown during the 1620s, it was still inferior to those that had

---

[23] Richard J. Bonney, *Political Change in France under Richelieu and Mazarin 1624–1661* (Oxford: Oxford University Press, 1978), pp. 163–90. The estates also bribed local officials to limit royal influence. See Major, *Representative Government*, p. 67.

[24] Robert R. Harding, *Anatomy of a Power Elite: The Provincial Governors of Early Modern France* (New Haven, Conn.: Yale University Press, 1976), pp. 193–99.

[25] Major, *Representative Government*, pp. 205–449.

been active combatants; training and equipment had not at all kept pace with the changes adopted by enemy forces encamped in the Spanish Netherlands, Germany, and Spain.[26] To match the seasoned Habsburg tercios, rapid army mobilization was needed, and theretofore unheard-of revenues were necessary to pay, train, and supply a new army. Military expenditures went up by two-thirds in the year after Nördlingen,[27] and circumstances dictated that the resources for these expenditures be extracted mainly from France.

Inasmuch as the Habsburgs had either annihilated, intimidated, or allied with most other powers, only alliances with the Dutch Republic and Sweden were open. Russia was preoccupied with internal troubles and expelling, with Swedish help, a Polish army. After recent conflicts over disastrous forays onto the continent, Parliament was loath to allow another expedition, and by 1640 England was embroiled in internal conflicts leading to civil war. Sweden and the Netherlands were indeed powerful allies, probably the strongest European land and naval powers, respectively. But the embattled Netherlands was unwilling to provide much support, and Sweden, already benefiting from French subsidies, in any case was licking its wounds following Nördlingen.

Why then not a war à la Suédoise? That is, why not adopt the Swedish method of striking swiftly into foreign territory to build and supply an army from another country's resources? First, the presence of a strong Spanish army just to the east made such a gamble too dangerous; a modern army had to be built in France itself, and that meant with French resources. Second, after more than a decade and a half of occupation, plunder, and battle, much of Germany could no longer sustain the confiscations of large armies. A rational system of supply was required, otherwise the French army would have to eschew decisive engagements in order to wander about Germany searching for supply, subordinating military strategy to logistics.[28] Finally, in recent military engagements in

[26] On the perhaps counterintuitive backwardness and smallness of the French army prior to entry into the Thirty Years' War, see Geoffrey Parker, *The Thirty Years' War* (London: Routledge & Kegan Paul, 1987), pp. 148–49; Delbrück, *History of the Art of War*, Volume 4, pp. 228–30; Geoffrey Symcox, ed., *War, Diplomacy, and Imperialism, 1618–1763* (New York: Harper & Row, 1973), p. 8; and *The New Cambridge Modern History*, Volume 4, pp. 346–48. On numbers, see John A. Lynn, "The Growth of the French Army during the Seventeenth Century," *Armed Forces and Society* 6 (1980): 568–85.

[27] Bonney, *Political Change*, pp. 42ff; Symcox, *War, Diplomacy, and Imperialism*, pp. 19–24, 117–25; R. J. Bonney, *The King's Debts: Finance and Politics in France, 1589–1661* (Oxford: Clarendon Press, 1981), pp. 172–73; Parker, *The Thirty Years' War*, p. 150.

[28] Martin van Creveld, *Supplying War: Logistics from Wallenstein to Patton* (New York: Cambridge University Press, 1977), pp. 7–17. This is not to say that French supplies came exclusively from France itself; many perishables had to be obtained locally in Germany. Domestic resources had to be used for building a large army *before* deploying it abroad,

Italy, the French had experienced severe discipline problems and en-countered fierce local resistance while relying on foraging and local con-tributions.[29]

Existing capital markets had been stung by several recent Bourbon bankruptcies, one as recent as 1634, and would not extend royal credit without guarantees from the estates, a process that would take time, of-fered an unsure outcome, and would handcuff the state in time of crisis.[30] Nor would geography provide a break from the onus of domestic resource mobilization. Although the Pyrenees to a certain extent hindered Span-ish troops to the south, other Spanish armies were camped just to the north and east in the Spanish Netherlands and Germany, and little stood between the victorious Spanish army and French soil. The situation left the French ministers of state only one alternative to defeat: rapid mobi-lization of French resources. This, they knew, meant constitutional crisis and political change.

New taxes and political institutions came into direct and fierce conflict with the parlements, estates, and towns:

> Ever larger armies and fleets made imperious demands for more, better, and more costly armament. Taxes had to be raised beyond what the king's subjects deemed legitimate limits, and fairly often beyond what the taxpayers really could afford to pay. The difficulties of levying taxes, contributions, and forced loans, of one sort or another, and the opposition to such levies, frequently in-volving armed conflict, forced the royal government, more often than not against its will, to accomplish its ends either by turning to new institutions or by changing the way in which old institutions functioned, and to circumvent freedoms, exemptions, and privileges of many kinds, whether of corporations, provinces, fiefs, seigneuries, cities, or communities, even though these were well-established customs, consecrated by tradition.[31]

The mechanism for realizing this policy of extraction was the corps of intendants, who had begun to appear in the provinces in the late six-teenth century to oversee other officials, but whose numbers, functions,

---

where it could rely on plunder for some foodstuffs, but on rational logistical systems for many other supplies.

[29] Bonney, *Political Change*, pp. 260–63. The Habsburg generalissimo, Wallenstein, sup-plied his army mainly by plunder, and this afforded him a great deal of autonomy vis-à-vis his nominal Habsburg master, who, alarmed by the independence of action afforded by his autonomously supplied army, eventually had him assassinated. One suspects that the les-sons learned by the Habsburgs might also have figured in French planning.

[30] See James B. Collins, *Fiscal Limits of Absolutism: Direct Taxation in Early Seven-teenth-Century France* (Berkeley and Los Angeles: University of California Press, 1988).

[31] Roland Mousnier, *The Institutions of France under the Absolute Monarchy 1598–1789*, Volume 2: *The Organs of State and Society* (Chicago: University of Chicago Press, 1979), pp. xv–xvi.

and unpopularity shot up dramatically with the turn of events at Nördlingen. In 1636 the intendants used the military to collect forced loans in the pays d'élections. Two years later, new taxes earmarked for the army were forcibly levied and collected in the pays d'états as well as in the pays d'élections. In 1641 the state levied a sales tax throughout France, narrowing the constitutional distinctions between the two *pays*.[32] The efficiency of the intendants is attested to by the increase in French military expenditures, which rose from 41 million livres in 1630 to 108 million in 1636.[33]

Protests against the state's breach of custom and privilege were met by Séguier's justification based on the principle of reason of state. The intendants, he said in blunt contemporary French, "exécutent dans les provinces des eedictz qui n'ont point esté enregistrée au Parlement, eedictz que la nécessité publique de l'estat rend nécessaire."[34] The parlements' judicial duties were partially arrogated by the intendants, as cases stemming from laws against treason and tax evasion came under the intendants' growing purview. Like his counterparts in the Prussian Generalkriegskommissariat, the intendant also served as informant, keeping the crown aware of the activities of his province's notables.[35] Town guilds, banks, tax collectors, and other administrators came under the eyes of the intendant, who was also acquiring considerable influence in the outcomes of municipal elections.[36]

[32] On the rise of the intendants during France's direct involvement in the Thirty Years' War, see Bonney, *Political Change*, pp. 42–46; Harding, *Provincial Governors*, pp. 205–11; Mousnier, *France under the Absolute Monarchy*, Volume 2, pp. 502–27; Delbrück, *History of the Art of War*, Volume 4, pp. 227–35; William Beik, *Absolutism and Society in Seventeenth-Century France: State Power and Provincial Aristocracy in Languedoc* (Cambridge: Cambridge University Press, 1985), pp. 131–46; and *The New Cambridge Modern History*, Volume 5, pp. 222–47.

[33] Bonney, *Political Change*, p. 42. The use of soldiers to collect taxes was normally avoided; the expense made it not particularly cost effective, and their depredations hurt future revenues. See Collins, *Fiscal Limits of Absolutism*, pp. 101–2.

[34] The intendants "execute in the provinces edicts that have never been registered by Parlement, edicts that public necessity of state makes necessary." Quoted in Bonney, *Political Change*, p. 246. See also Hanley, The Lit de Justice, pp. 281–328. In what one might today call a propaganda campaign, a state pamphlet campaign diffused reason-of-state ideology. See William F. Church, *Richelieu and Reason of State* (Princeton, N.J.: Princeton University Press, 1972).

[35] Douglas Clark Baxter, *Servants of the Sword: French Intendants of the Army 1630–70* (Urbana: University of Illinois Press, 1976), pp. 68–71; Mousnier, *France under the Absolute Monarchy*, Volume 2, pp. 512–22; Bonney, *Political Change*, pp. 244–58; Albert N. Hamscher, *The Parlement of Paris after the Fronde 1653–1673* (Pittsburgh, Pa.: University of Pittsburgh Press, 1976), pp. 82–154; Sharon Kettering, *Judicial Politics and Urban Revolt in Seventeenth-Century France: The Parlement of Aix, 1629–1659* (Princeton, N.J.: Princeton University Press, 1978), pp. 81–109.

[36] Bonney, *Political Change*, pp. 318–43; Mousnier, *France under the Absolute Monar-*

When peace prospects collapsed in 1647, new extractions were implemented, precipitating a violent, widespread reaction from the parlements, estates, and provincial nobility—the upheaval known as the
Fronde. Lacking leadership and the unity a national estates might have
provided, the revolt was crushed by 1653, clearing the way for further
state expansion at the expense of constitutionalism.[37] Many elected officials became ceremonial figures under the intendants' regime. The failure of the Fronde also signaled the further reduction of the influence of
regional estates and judiciaries in what had been a cumbersome political
process.[38] Intendants assumed control of the feudal levies (ban and arrière ban) as well as a new, more modern militia that conscripted peasants and attached them to regular army units deployed far from the unfortunate conscripts' villages. Royal agents were responsible for
quartering troops, as well as for supplying them upon return from foreign
campaigns. In times of need, they were empowered to appropriate
means of transport as well as the labor of their owners.[39]

---

chy, Volume 1, pp. 429–75; P. Deyon, "Manufacturing Industries in Seventeenth-Century
France," in Ragnhild Hatton, ed., Louis XIV and Absolutism (Columbus: Ohio University
Press, 1976), pp. 226–42.

[37] See Paul Rice Doolin, The Fronde (Cambridge, Mass.: Harvard University Press,
1935); Ernst H. Kossmann, La Fronde (Leiden: Universitaire Pers Leiden, 1954); Richard
Bonney, "The French Civil War, 1649–53," European Studies Review 8 (1978): 71–100,
"The English and French Civil Wars," History 65 (1980): 365–82; Sharon Kettering, "Pa-
tronage and Politics during the Fronde," French Historical Studies 14 (1986): 409–41; and
A. Lloyd Moote, "The Parliamentary Fronde and Seventeenth-Century Robe Solidarity,"
French Historical Studies 2 (1962): 330–54.

[38] Bonney, Political Change, pp. 57–75; Mousnier, France under the Absolute Monarchy,
Volume 1, pp. 563–605, Volume 2, pp. 611–33; Nora Temple, "The Control and Exploitation of French Towns During the Ancien Régime," in Raymond F. Kierstead, ed., State
and Society in Sixteenth-Century France (New York: New Viewpoints, 1975), pp. 67–93;
Jean-Dominique Lassaigne, "Les revendications de la noblesse pendant la Fronde," Studies
Presented to the International Commission for the History of Representative and Parliamentary Institutions 23 (1960): 269–75. Beik's study of Languedoc, which argues that the
estates there remained obstacles to state penetration, has forced a rethinking of the scope
of Bourbon absolutism. He does note, however, that during critical times, such as entry
into the Thirty Years' War and Louis XIV's wars against coalitions, the crown's demands for
large new revenues could not be refused or even moderated. Estates continued to exist in
several provinces, but increasingly relinquished control over taxation and major policy matters in the face of Bourbon threats and bribes (Absolutism and Society, pp. 132–35). His
emphasis on bargains between crown and local notables seems to me to shift attention un-
duly away from the essentially coercive and military nature of the French state after 1635.
Bargains abounded, and nobles benefited from privileges and offices, as they did in the
Great Elector's state—absolutism was never absolute. But in neither state were such bargains defining characteristics or critical parts of the state's origins. Both states were, in
origin and essence, war machines. Cf. Major's discussion of state and society in Languedoc,
Representative Government, pp. 642–45.

[39] Baxter, Servants of the Sword, pp. 72–76; Mousnier, France under the Absolute Mon-

Reason of state affected law and the judiciary. All Gaul was divided into two parts:

> There [is] a great difference between public and private justice, between the government of the state and the distribution of justice to individuals. . . . [I]n the conduct and administration of the state . . . it should be in the discretion of sovereigns to arrest those on whom suspicion falls. . . . [I]n the government of states it is more expedient that a hundred innocent persons suffer than that the state perish by the fault of an individual.[40]

Parlements' traditional right to remonstrate was proscribed until after the royal laws had been officially registered. Violation of this proscription led to arrest and exile. Traditional courts could no longer interfere in matters of state, and appellate functions shifted to intendants.[41] Cases of national import were removed from the dockets of parlements, leaving them with only the more mundane cases whose decisions could not affect state policies. Louis XIII's remarks at a *lit de justice* of the troublesome Paris parlement set the tone for the judiciary of his successors: "You are here solely to judge between Master Peter and Master John, and I intend to put you in your place; and if you continue your undertakings, I will cut your nails to the quick."[42]

Provincial estates, too, were intimidated or pushed outside the process of government. Of the changed relationship between the crown and the provincial estates, John Locke, somewhat sensitive to such matters, wrote, "One of the States told me that he was at an assembly twenty years ago when, the king asking for 7 or 800,000 *livres tournois*, they thought it too much and gave him nothing at all, but that they dare not do so now."[43] Many estates did not meet for over a century, others could not be convoked owing to opposition of the intendant, while still others were paralyzed by bribes and strategic manipulation of antagonisms between the nobility and middle classes. At best, a parlement could fight a

archy, Volume 2, pp. 512–38; Root, *Peasants and King*, pp. 23–26; André Corvisier, *l'Armée Française de la fin du XVIIe siècle au ministère de Choiseul, Le Soldat*, Volume 1 (Paris: Presses Universitaires de France, 1964), pp. 109–28, 222–31; Alexis de Tocqueville, *The Old Régime and the French Revolution*, Part 2 (Garden City, N.Y.: Doubleday Anchor, 1955), pp. 32–41, 120–37; Goubert, *French Peasantry*, pp. 183–87. Though considerable, the intendants' power was not unlimited. Local notables had to be consulted and often mollified to prevent the coalescence of local opposition into overt rebellion. Some intendants, despite routine changes of locale, became defensive of local interests. See Beik, *Absolutism and Society*, pp. 98–116; and A. Lloyd Moote, *The Revolt of the Judges: The Parlement of Paris and the Fronde 1643–1652* (Princeton, N.J.: Princeton University Press, 1971), p. 367.

[40] Quoted in Shennan, *Parlement of Paris*, pp. 272–73.

[41] Shennan, *Parlement of Paris*, pp. 275–78; Ford, *Robe and Sword*, pp. 79–97; Bonney, *Political Change*, pp. 24–28, 246; Hurt, "Parlement of Brittany," pp. 411–33.

[42] Major, *Representative Government*, p. 583.

[43] Quoted in *The New Cambridge Modern History*, Volume 5, p. 238.

rear-guard action against royal demands. As one minister put it, "Le secret pour réussir dans les Etats consiste à réunir Messieurs les Evesques et les barons en un mesme sentiment."[44]

Prior to the Thirty Years' War, substantial but nonmodern military changes brought on with the Hundred Years' War did not lead to the destruction of constitutional government. In fact, provincial estates and parlements emerged from that war strengthened by routine and institutionalized tax negotiations with the crown. It was not until the military modernization of the Thirty Years' War that French constitutionalism came to an end. The war mandated the construction of a large modern army, and led to the circumvention but not the complete destruction of constitutional government.[45] In its place emerged a network of intendants with extensive power predicated on a hierarchical bureaucratic command structure. The essential nature of Louis XIV's state is best conveyed by Church's words: "In Louis's hands, his nationwide administrative system became a vast instrument for making available the human and material resources of the realm, directing it toward feats of greatness and implementing the doctrine of reason of state."[46]

THE ARTICULATION OF FRENCH ABSOLUTISM

The military-bureaucratic state patterned the development of the economy and class dynamics in ways resembling those in Prussia. The economy and key components of civil society came increasingly under the direction of the state. But in other, highly portentous ways, France did not resemble its eastern neighbor, and these differences were the keys to France's second chance for liberal democracy.

The French economy of the early seventeenth century was much more vigorous and diverse than that of Prussia. Textiles, viniculture, as well as

[44] "The secret of success in the estates consists of uniting the clergy and the baronage in the same sentiment." Quoted in Bonney, *Political Change*, p. 376. On the role of the estates after the Fronde, see also Mousnier, *France under the Absolute Monarchy*, Volume 1, pp. 609–27; and Major, *Representative Government*, pp. 630–52. The rights, liberties, and corporations that had been granted to the Huguenots at the close of the Wars of Religion were also abolished in the extension of central power in the second half of the seventeenth century. See Mousnier, *France under the Absolute Monarchy*, Volume 1, pp. 383–410; Beik, *Absolutism and Society*, especially pp. 133–34; Hamscher, *Parlement of Paris after the Fronde*, pp. 82–154; and Kettering, *Judicial Politics*, pp. 182–250.

[45] The reasons for this incomplete destruction of constitutional institutions such as the parlements and provincial estates figured in the state's collapse in the late eighteenth century, and shall be addressed in a later section.

[46] William F. Church, "Louis XIV and Reason of State," in John C. Rule, ed., *Louis XIV and the Craft of Kingship* (Columbus: Ohio State University Press, 1969), p. 380.

agrarian production were all key sectors of the economy, whereas Prussia, at least before the Generalkriegskommissariat began development policies, was primarily an agrarian region, its towns having declined with the concentration of export ports and the failing fortunes of the Hanse. Commerce in the northern and Mediterranean towns of France was more vital than that in the Prussian towns. Nonetheless, the need for resources led the state to embark on a systematic program of economic development, directed by one of Louis XIV's many brilliant ministers. What Vauban and Le Tellier had been for the military, Jean Baptiste Colbert tried to be for the economy.

Prior to Colbert's appointment in 1661, the state had only a few programs of economic protection and regulation, though they increased somewhat during the Thirty Years' War.[47] With new expenses from France's involvement in the conflict, as well as further engagements in the War of Devolution (1667–1668), the Dutch War (1672–1679), and the War of the League of Augsburg (1689–1697), the state stimulated the economy to support an army numbering 290,000 during the War of the Spanish Succession (1701–1714). Colbert's ministry subsidized industry, gave tax exemptions to others (especially those in backward provinces), and imported Dutch and Swedish engineers to boost domestic mineralogical production. Skilled foreign workers were lured to add to France's human capital, and colonies were used as closed markets. (But religious hatred led many industrious Huguenots to flee abroad, many to Brandenburg-Prussia.) Anticipating by three centuries the policies of the Japanese trade ministry, Colbert's ministry regulated the quality of national output.[48]

The French state pursued ambitious legal and economic programs that have often been thought to be the achievements of middle classes or the Revolution. Colbert restructured civil law, giving France national laws on contract, trade policies, bankruptcy, and even bookkeeping.[49] It was also Colbert's policy to construct an integrated, national market by means

---

[47] Charles Woolsey Cole, *Colbert and a Century of French Mercantilism*, Volume 1 (Morningside Heights, N.Y.: Columbia University Press, 1939), pp. 102–64.

[48] Cole, *French Mercantilism*, Volume 1, pp. 325–55, Volume 2, pp. 363–463; C.B.A. Behrens, *Society, Government, and the Enlightenment: The Experiences of Eighteenth-Century France and Prussia* (New York: Harper & Row, 1985), pp. 116–51; Deyon, "Manufacturing Industries," pp. 226–42. The French state's managerialism, like that of Prussia, was not without beneficial programs for the population. Colbert's concern with economic vitality led to concern with the health and welfare of the general public. Accordingly, programs originally dealing with wounded soldiers and invalids were expanded to form a modicum of public health care. The state also regulated the price of grain by marketing vast quantities from its granaries to maintain public peace. See Cole, *French Mercantilism*, Volume 2, pp. 508–26.

[49] Cole, *French Mercantilism*, Volume 1, pp. 360–61, 312–14.

of a system of roads, bridges, and canals linking various parts of the nation together, especially those recently acquired through war. It is important to emphasize that this was not an intended or unintended consequence of a congeries of economic programs and laws advocated by middle classes; rather it was the result of the purposeful action of the state, which sought to develop the economy in order to support and expand the army.[50] The centerpiece of French mercantilism was the stimulation of international trade. Growth in commerce would benefit domestic industries, the state's revenues, and of course its war-making capacity—the ultimate end, never far from the mind of the ministry's helmsman. The relationship is probably best expressed by Colbert himself: "Trade is the source of finance and finance is the vital nerve of war."[51] Subsidies and state shipping insurance followed, but interdiction of French merchantmen by foreign navies, pirates, and privateers was widespread.[52]

In order to defend commerce, Colbert increased naval expenditures from 300,000 livres in 1660, to 7,600,000 two years later, and to 13,400,000 by 1670.[53] The state built major naval bases in Toulon, Brest, Rochefort, and Dunkirk, as well as its own shipbuilding yards and cannon foundries. New intendants were installed in these regions, charged with mobilizing skilled laborers and administering the facilities. When naval recruitment began to cut into the merchant marine's supply of sailors, Colbert built a national conscription program for the navy, which supplied much of the personnel for France's hundred-thousand-man navy of

[50] Cole, *French Mercantilism*, Volume 1, pp. 368–83. Cf. Perry Anderson's account of the Western absolutist state's relation to legal and economic integration in *Lineages of the Absolutist State* (London: Verso, 1980), pp. 1–42. For parallel developments in Russia, see Vasili Klyuchevsky, *Peter the Great*, Liliana Archibald, trans. (Boston: Beacon Press, 1984), pp. 112–56.

[51] Quoted in Edward Mead Earle, "Adam Smith, Alexander Hamilton, Friedrich List: The Economic Foundations of Military Power," in Peter Paret, ed., *Makers of Modern Strategy: From Machiavelli to the Nuclear Age* (Princeton, N.J.: Princeton University Press, 1986), p. 217.

[52] Cole, *French Mercantilism*, Volume 1, pp. 164–208. The effort to stimulate commerce also led to the development of local advisory councils elected by a town's prominent magistrates and merchants. Hence, Colbert's policies led to the establishment of a small amount of representation within autocratic government. But there is no evidence of these councils having any substantive input outside the confines of local commercial programs. Like the Prussian Landräte, these councils carried on a measure of the constitutional principles of representation and local autonomy, but their effects on the whole of absolutist government must be judged to be rather minuscule. See Thomas J. Schaeper, *The French Council of Commerce 1700–1715: A Study of Mercantilism after Colbert* (Columbus: Ohio State University Press, 1983), pp. 73–104.

[53] Cole, *French Mercantilism*, Volume 1, p. 45. See also Peter Padfield, *The Tide of Empires: Decisive Naval Campaigns in the Rise of the West*, Volume 2: *1654–1763* (London: Routledge & Kegan Paul, 1982), pp. 64–79.

1690.[54] Just as Vauban had mobilized the nation's scientific community to rationalize land war, Colbert founded the Académie Royale des Sciences (1666) to engage the disciplines of cartography, chemistry, and engineering in the ends of naval warfare.[55]

Emphasis on commerce as a means for stimulating the economy was not without significant antagonistic and imperialist ramifications. Colbert's tariffs and preferential treatment of French shipping led to hostility from other commercial powers, this at a time when peace was easily shattered and commercial advantages were as good as any reason for war. A protectionist policy could bring on, if not open war, then at least retaliation in the form of sanctioned privateering. When backed up by the power of a fully developed army and navy, French commercial policy and security concerns made the invasion and annexation of economically thriving regions seem like the unfriendly business takeovers of our own day: there are some initial unpleasantness and losses, but in the long run one's resources are expanded and interests assured. This was one of the main reasons for Louis XIV's ill-starred invasion of the Dutch Republic, whose fabulous wealth and huge battle fleets, even against the combined opposition of other European powers, could have made France a hegemonic power.

Another consequence of managing the economy was the development of middle classes neither politically independent nor active, at least not until the second half of the eighteenth century. Though they had by no means been created ex nihilo by Colbert, most middle classes had little quarrel with French absolutism; there was, in fact, a strong community of interest. The state protected them, forged a national market, and, though many aristocratic privileges and immunities remained until the Revolution, made substantial headway in the construction of a legal system conducive to capitalist development. The wine merchant or textile manufacturer who purchased state office and entered the noblesse de robe was in some respects the counterpart of the English businessman who bought an estate and, if possible, a title. But the political significances of these actions are quite dissimilar in that the English parvenu's purchase did not tie or ally him with the state or service in it. With the Paulette of the early seventeenth century, a now heritable office was not

[54] Symcox, *War, Diplomacy, and Imperialism*, pp. 8–26, *The Crisis of French Seapower 1688–1697: From the* Guerre d'Escadre *to the* Guerre de Course (The Hague: Martinus Nijhoff, 1974); Armel de Wismes, "The French Navy under Louis XIV," in Hatton, *Louis XIV and Absolutism*, pp. 343–62.

[55] Henry Guerlac, "The Impact of Science on War," in Paret, ed. *Makers of Modern Strategy*, pp. 64–90. In Russia, the word *nauka*, originally designating military skill, came to mean science and learning. See James H. Billington, *The Icon and the Axe: An Interpretive History of Russian Culture* (New York: Vintage, 1970), p. 113.

only prestigious, but also a sound business investment, with comfortable, even lucrative, returns. Other burghers were tied to the state by its expenditures on military and luxury goods. The community of interest began to deteriorate only well into the eighteenth century, as commerce began to emerge from government tutelage, as public debt shook the confidence of the financial sector, and as new, unbeholden professional middle classes came on the scene.

The fusion of the Prussian aristocracy to the state was, as we have seen, predicated in part on the relative poverty of all but a small proportion of Junkers. Supplementing one's income with service to the state or in the military was essential for most Prussian aristocrats. The French rural economy was more vigorous and enjoyed successful harvests throughout most of the eighteenth century. Viniculture, tax farming, and simply capitalizing on feudal privileges that squeezed surplus from peasants assured the basis of an economically independent aristocracy. While many had entered state service, they had done so through the spacious and accommodating portals of venality, which afforded the officeholder personal and political independence based on contract. In exchange for cash payment, the purchaser acquired the right to income derived from a heritable office, whereas the Prussian bureaucrat or the Russian service noble was dependent on the salary or benefice he earned solely by satisfactory execution of duty. He had no comparable legal basis to claim his office as property. Herein lies a critical difference in the allegiances of key social groups in France and Prussia. While both countries' bourgeoisies were closely associated with the state, French aristocrats, whether of old military heritage or of relatively recent ascendence through venality, were not only more independent, but also quite influential in the state machinery; and this influence they used to deflect disadvantageous royal policies aimed at abolishing venal offices and tax exemptions. As long as these two main privileges remained intact, as they did until the fiscal crises following the Seven Years' War (1763), the aristocracy remained, if not loyal, then at least complacent.[56]

The independence of the aristocracy, then, was a critical shortcoming in the articulation of the French absolutist state, which set it off from the

---

[56] Ford, *Robe and Sword*, pp. 124–70. As soon will be apparent, this section on the Revolution has benefited enormously from Barrington Moore, Jr., *Social Origins of Dictatorship and Democracy: Lord and Peasant in the Making of the Modern World* (Boston: Beacon Press, 1966); Theda Skocpol, *States and Social Revolution: A Comparative Analysis of France, Russia and China* (New York: Cambridge University Press, 1979); and William Doyle, *Origins of the French Revolution*, Second Edition (New York: Oxford University Press, 1988). It must be noted that Moore sees the aristocracy largely as reactionary obstacles to democratic outcomes, whereas this study sees them as reactionaries, but nonetheless defenders of principles of representation and constitutional balances. We share the view, however, that their independence helped to topple the monarchy in 1789.

Prussian state and afforded it an oportunity to take another political trajectory. We would now do well to consider other fissures and weaknesses in French military-bureaucratic absolutism.

WEAKNESS AND COLLAPSE

Further comparison between French and Prussian political history reveals differences in the ability to remain fiscally solvent, the preservation of independent political institutions, and the capacity for peasant revolution. Individually, each variation from the Prussian case was probably unable to bring down Bourbon absolutism, but a fortuitous conjuncture of all of them could. There certainly will be no attempt here to provide a full account of the causes, key events, or outcomes of the French Revolution; present concerns are with constitutionalism and absolutism. A more manageable agenda will be undertaken: that of describing key structural fissures that provided France the opportunity for another chance for liberal democracy. Let us begin with fiscal insolvency.

The numerous wars of Louis XIV were costly, largely unsuccessful, and often foolhardy. It is wry commentary on Louis's ambitions that, after a century of bitter, continuous warfare, Spain and the Dutch Republic settled their differences and allied against France during the War of the Spanish Succession. Paths of glory led but to a diplomatic legacy for France of having almost all the European powers aligned against it; but its fiscal system, the sinews of war as the expression went, was serviceable at the time of Louis's death in 1715.[57] Despite Louis's deathbed lament of having waged war too much, his successors were only a little less bellicose: the national budget of 1752, a period of relative calm between the War of the Austrian Succession and the Seven Years' War, devoted forty-two percent of expenditures to the military, and, ominously, another twenty-one percent to debt servicing.[58] But it was the Seven Years' War that led to the loss of colonial revenue and the penultimate debt crisis, soon followed by another from financing the American War of Independence—revenge for England's seizure of much of the French colonial empire. Its sinews diminishing, the French state rapidly atrophied,

---

[57] This was not always due to the Sun King's or Colbert's budgetary skill or restraint in the international arena. After the Thirty Years' War and the War of the Spanish Succession, public debts were simply repudiated—a stratagem no longer open in the late eighteenth century owing to the increased power of the French financial sector. See James C. Riley, *The Seven Years War and the Old Regime in France: The Economic and Financial Toll* (Princeton, N.J.: Princeton University Press, 1986), pp. 132–33; Doyle, *Origins of the French Revolution*, pp. 43–52.

[58] Riley, *Seven Years War*, p. 57.

struggled desperately to find new sources of revenue, but found itself challenged by social classes and long-dormant institutions emboldened by seeing the state in crisis.

First among these opponents was the aristocracy, whose political acquiescence came at the price of continuing an arcane system of privileges—tax immunities the most salient of them. When new fiscal needs led to royal challenges of traditional immunities, the noblesse used its considerable presence in the state to block them, leading to further paralysis.[59] Using political institutions within the central state itself was followed by contestation from the old parlements and provincial estates—the return of the suppressed. Thus, the French aristocracy was an order with considerable influence in numerous, independent political institutions throughout France. Kept well in check while the monarchy's power was high, surviving components of the old constitutional government found new courage with Bourbon repressive capacity in decline.

The question naturally arises as to why the parlements and provincial estates survived the Thirty Years' War and entered the eighteenth century. Why didn't the Sun King simply order a detachment of soldiers to close them once and for all, as the Great Elector had done to his? True, the Prussian monarch had fewer constitutional institutions to crush in his smaller domain, but certainly Louis had more intendants and regiments sprawling across his lands with which to do the job. Consider the potential costs and benefits of such a move. By the late seventeenth century, parlements and estates seemed quite innocuous from the viewpoint of Versailles: despite occasional protests, which effected only minor concessions, the state generally collected its taxes and otherwise enforced its will. The collapse of central power, a prerequisite to any revival of estate and parlement, simply did not seem on the horizon. Second, allocation of military resources toward an internal clean-up operation was unlikely during time of war, and doing so during a breathing space between wars might encourage a quick attack from Spain or Austria. Also, complete repression might rekindle the flames of the not so distant religious wars, sources of division absent in Protestant Brandenburg-Prussia.[60] Foreign dangers, then, led to the rise of French absolutism, but ironically also prevented the development of fuller monarchal power by providing a potential ally for constitutional elements. Decisive internal suppression was not without considerable international risks. Venal offices in parlements

[59] Doyle, *Origins of the French Revolution*, pp. 96–138; Georges Lefebvre, *The Coming of the French Revolution* (Princeton, N.J.: Princeton University Press, 1967), pp. 21–37.

[60] See Bonney, *The King's Debts*, p. 16. The crown's tolerance of parlements might well have been born during the Fronde, when ministers and intendants became accommodating in loyal provinces in order to contain the rebellion. See Beik, *Absolutism and Society*, pp. 134–35; and Moote, *The Revolt of the Judges*, pp. 374–76.

were a small revenue source for the crown and there was no point in tampering with a steady, if now and then bothersome, fiscal asset. Finally, estates and parlements had been cowed and to varying degrees integrated with absolutism: parlements were components of the judiciary and the estates had become part of local administration.[61] In short, the potential costs of full repression exceeded any gains that might seem to come from that quarter.

Just as there was a calculus of repression, there was also a calculus in the parlements' and estates' opposition to the crown. Soon after the defeat of the Fronde in 1653, they conducted rearguard actions against the crown, the intensity of which varied with the political climate, but generally increased during the eighteenth century. With Louis's death in 1715, the perception of the accession of a weaker monarch led to more and more remonstrances aimed at winning popular support for the parlementary effort. Efforts by the crown to abolish venality were blocked, usually by parlements. With the loss of legitimacy and the debt crisis following the Seven Years' War, parlements voiced opposition to management of the provinces, refused to bow to lits de justice, and even began to challenge the extravagances of Versailles.[62] By 1789 opposition from the estates and parlements had become increasingly aggressive, thereby deepening the crisis.[63]

Another front against the *ancien régime* was opened by the peasantry, which had kept a rather low profile in French political history, at least since the days of the Fronde. The capacity for large-scale peasant rebellion constituted a third major difference between France and Prussia. This capacity was quite low in the the Prussian case owing to the destruction of autonomous village government in the course of commercialization, close administrative control by seigneurs and agents of the Kanton-system, and internal stratifications that divided the peasantry and prevented collective action. But neither intendants nor seigneurs undermined village government in the French countryside. Landed elites gave peasants leeway in local affairs, preferring instead to squeeze out rents and dues. The crown and its intendants found that peasant communal institutions were efficient units of taxation: village defaults could be compensated by suing wealthy peasants, and the formidable costs of determining tax obligations and prosecuting cheaters shifted into village

---

[61] On the integration of old constitutional organs within the absolutist state, see Beik, *Absolutism and Society*.

[62] On these running battles with the king, see Ford, *Robe and Sword*, pp. 96–104; Hurt, "Parlement of Brittany," pp. 53–62; Mousnier, *France under the Absolute Monarchy*, Volume 2, p. 634; and Riley, *Seven Years War*, pp. 192–222.

[63] Stone, *French Parlements*, especially pp. 3–15; Doyle, *Origins of the French Revolution*, pp. 115–77; Lefebvre, *Coming of the French Revolution*, pp. 62–75.

elders.[64] The French peasantry, like that of Prussia, was under the watchful control of state officials, but, with the dissolution of the state's capacity to maintain control in 1789, this means of administrative control disappeared. In short, autonomous peasant organizations and a relative absence of outside administrative control contrasted with the situation of the East Elbian peasantry. Revolutionary capacity was furthered by the relatively unstratified nature of the French peasantry. When combined with the common experience of increasing seigneurial exploitation, a hostile, unified class was in evidence: "Social differences within the community were much less important than the antagonism between the peasantry as a whole and the landed aristocracy which benefited from the seigneurial régime."[65] As the state's repressive capacity decreased, peasant rebellions spread throughout France, shattering what remained of the state's institutional coherence in the provinces.

Unlike its Prussian counterpart, French military-bureaucratic absolutism lacked the capacity for maintaining itself into the nineteenth century and beyond. Owing to fiscal overextension from the injudicious use of military resources, the survival of the political institutions of an independent noblesse, and the peasantry's capacity for widespread revolt, the old regime fell and constitutional institutions reemerged. But this did not assure France an easy way back to the liberal democratic path.

THE LEGACY OF INSTABILITY

Revitalized local assemblies and the convocation of the first Estates-General since the early seventeenth century were unable to provide a stable political system upon which democracy could be built. None of these institutions had participated meaningfully in the eighteenth-century Bourbon state; they had no clear procedures, guidelines, or delineations of powers to provide coherent rule. They were probably incapable of governing France in the best times without some sort of institutionalized executive, and in the turbulent years after 1789, the worst of times, they were as dismally incapable of governing as they had been during the Fronde. The promise of democracy was followed by chaos, terror, and Napoleon. Instability and disorder continued to plague France through-

[64] See Mousnier, *France under the Absolute Monarchy*, Volume 1, pp. 559–61; Root, *Peasants and King*, pp. 28–33, 45–65.

[65] Soboul, "French Rural Community," p. 84. Soboul notes the irony in that the land grabs of the revolutionary period led to the breakdown of peasant solidarity and communal government, which, in turn, paved the way for the French peasantry's becoming "sacks of potatoes," as Marx called them in his day. See also Skocpol, *States and Social Revolution*, pp. 126–28.

out the nineteenth century, as the nation failed to establish a stable polity until at least 1871. The instability of that period was, in part, patterned by the politicizing and divisive events attendant on the collapse of the military-bureaucratic state.

The events of the revolutionary period led to new or exacerbated old social, religious, and regional antagonisms. Peasant revolts entailed the seizure of noble lands, the destruction of châteaux, and not a few ghastly murders. Regional revolts like those in the west and the Midi were repressed by military force, leaving enduring hatred for central power, irrespective of whether the tricolor or fleur-de-lis flew on regimental guidons. Thousands of nobles were executed on the orders of the Committee for Public Safety, leaving enmity between the aristocracy and the middle classes whose members composed the leadership of the Terror. Anticlericalism erupted as well. Church lands were seized, the feudal privileges of the ecclesiastical estate were abolished, and peasants vented long-suppressed hatred on clerical but nonetheless exploitive seigneurs.[66] Animosities were assuaged only briefly and partially by Napoleon's intoxicating victories, but, with his defeat in 1815, they resurfaced and became lasting parts of French political life, blocking fundamental trust, broad-based parties, and viable coalitions. French politics lurched from constitutions aimed at excluding social groups to those requiring coalitions between two or more social groups. Both in and out of the national assembly, consensus and trust were elusive.

Related to these social divisions was the rapid politicization of virtually every segment of society during the Revolution. During the early phases of the Revolution, parlements and the Estates-General mobilized popular support to strengthen their hand against the state. The humblest sansculotte became Monsieur le Citoyen. In the heady days of 1789, when old processes of government had fallen and new ones had yet to take form, popular assemblies reemerged, even below the provincial level, in the bailiwicks and villages.[67] In order to sustain the Revolution's more

---

[66] See Jacques Godechot, *The Counter-Revolution: Doctrine and Action 1789–1804*, Salvator Attanasio, trans. (Princeton, N.J.: Princeton University Press, 1981); and Charles Tilly, *The Vendée* (Cambridge, Mass.: Harvard University Press, 1964). Many of these hostilities resurfaced as recently as the Revolution's bicentennial celebration, or should I say commemoration.

[67] John A. Lynn, *Bayonets of the Republic: Motivation and Tactics in the Army of Revolutionary France, 1791–94* (Urbana: University of Illinois Press, 1984); Lynn Hunt, *Politics, Culture, and Class in the French Revolution* (Berkeley and Los Angeles: University of California Press, 1984); Richard Cobb, *The People's Armies: The Armées Révolutionnaires: Instrument of the Terror in the Departments April 1793 to Floréal Year II*, Marianne Elliott, trans. (New Haven, Conn.: Yale University Press, 1987); Jean-Paul Bertaud, *The Army of*

radical phases, the leadership mobilized antiaristocratic and egalitarian sentiments in the lower classes to intimidate conservative elements favoring a more limited agenda. Napoleon himself contributed to this widespread politicization of the masses by using newspapers, architecture, and the arts to impress political and military goals on the public.[68]

A further agent of mass politicization of the period was the army. The new army of late-eighteenth-century France was the product of no less profound a military revolution than the one that had brought about the modernized armies of the sixteenth and seventeenth centuries. The first military revolution replaced feudal hosts with large standing armies; a second military revolution now replaced them with still larger mass armies that mobilized the entire nation's energies. The army of the Revolution, numbering some seven hundred thousand strong in 1794, could not be drilled as methodically as Martinet would have insisted. Instead, the army relied on political indoctrination in the hope that raising the soldier's political consciousness and convincing him that he, a citizen of the new Republic, had a stake in the war's outcome would compensate for lack of drill. Efficacy in battle would be based on an inner sense of patriotic and moral duty, rather than on rote.[69]

Popular politicization in the early phases of the Revolution made the Coalitional Wars more than abstract, dynastic wars whose outcomes mattered little to the public. The days of kings contracting with mercenaries or leading standing armies of only a few hundred thousand were numbered. War could no longer leave the majority of the population unaffected. The approaching armies of the European autocracies led to the involvement of the French people in the war, not only in the service of armies, but also in the production of war materiel; the coalescence of a national will; and commitment to the preservation of the goals and achievements of the Revolution. Military service was no longer restricted to dregs, criminals, and mercenaries; it became once more what it had been for the ancient hoplite and feudal knight: an aspect of commitment

---

the French Revolution: From Citizen-Soldiers to Instruments of Power, R. R. Palmer, trans. (Princeton, N.J.: Princeton University Press, 1988).

[68] Alfred Cobban, A History of Modern France, Volume 2: From the First Empire to the Second Empire 1799–1871 (Harmondsworth, U.K.: Penguin, 1986), pp. 36–38; Maurice Agulhon, Marianne into Battle: Republican Imagery and Symbolism in France, 1789–1880, Janet Lloyd, trans. (Cambridge: Cambridge University Press, 1979), pp. 1–37.

[69] See Gunther E. Rothenberg, The Art of Warfare in the Age of Napoleon (Bloomington: Indiana University Press, 1980), pp. 94–114. A contemporary writer observed, "Suddenly war again became the business of the people—a people of thirty millions, all of whom considered themselves to be citizens. . . . The people became a participant in war; instead of governments and armies as heretofore, the full weight of the nation was thrown into the balance." Quoted in Geoffrey Best, War and Society in Revolutionary Europe, 1770–1870 (New York: Oxford University Press, 1982), p. 63.

between government and governed, implying reciprocal obligations, rights, and freedoms.

The mobilization tactics of the revolutionaries as well as the mass army and national war effort of the Napoleonic era led to the elevation of the political consciousness of most of the French nation. These events and processes had transformed Frenchmen from passive subjects and taxpayers into citizens with rights and political expectations with which they would not part easily. When settlements in 1815 and 1830 sought to impose a political system based on an extremely narrow franchise favoring the landed aristocracy, virtually ignoring the middle classes, and completely ignoring others, social antagonisms and popular restiveness could be held in check only temporarily until these governments collapsed when confronted by popular insurrection. The 1848 attempt at government based on universal suffrage led only to the inability to find a stable consensus, military intervention, and a form of authoritarian government that shrewdly discharged popular passions by means of military adventurism and plebiscitary spectacles.

.   .   .

The French case, when seen in the light of other European cases to be discussed, suggests that the optimal, but by no means only, path to liberal democracy lies in direct institutional continuity of medieval constitutional government; avoiding sudden, mass participation in government; and a social context free of deep antagonisms and mistrust. All of these characteristics stand out in English, Swedish, and to a lesser extent Dutch political development; all of them are tragically absent in the French case. Circumvention of medieval parlements and estates by seventeenth-century statesmen combined with the divisive and politicizing aspects of absolutism's collapse to make the path to liberal democracy far more tortuous and sanguinary than it was in England, Sweden, and the Netherlands, where medieval constitutionalism entered the modern period intact, and expansion of participation occurred in a social context of popular political deference or even indifference, free of sharp divisions brought on by civil war or social revolution.

The Revolution's significance for political developments was twofold. It engendered popular mobilizations and hostilities that plagued French politics for generations to come, but, perhaps more importantly, it also destroyed military and bureaucratic organs that dominated politics and much of the economy. In that Bourbon absolutism's fall at least made an eventual liberal outcome a possibility, the Revolution's legacy, stripped of the mythology and sentimentality surrounding it, was a mixed one that entailed opportunities as well as millstones. Its significance for constitutional development, though, cannot be overemphasized: military-bureaucratic absolutism was gone, replaced by a state that, although intrusive and rather authoritarian or at least "administrative,"[70] was nonetheless one unable to restore the monolithic edifice of Louis. France had to make do with stumbling along with its vociferous, unmanageable populace until a viable polity embracing principles of constitutionalism could be made.

[70] See Ezra N. Suleiman's historical background in *Politics, Power, and Bureaucracy in France: The Administrative Elite* (Princeton, N.J.: Princeton University Press, 1974), pp. 13–37. Suleiman attaches more importance to Napoleon for the construction of the state than the present analysis which, following de Tocqueville, sees the ancien régime as the modern state's major founder.

CHAPTER SIX

Poland

BRANDENBURG-PRUSSIA and France responded to the military revolution by building autocratic state structures to mobilize domestic resources and field a large modern army. Other countries in this study either faced relatively light military threats or avoided harsh domestic resource mobilization by various specific means: mobilization of foreign resources, the benefit of geographical advantages, international alliances, or the wealth of an advanced commercial economy. The history of Poland demonstrates the tragic consequences of failing to build an effective response to modernized enemy armies. Polish constitutionalism was the privilege of a large, lesser nobility whose number, paralyzing institutions, and diverse loyalties prevented any measure of state centralization and military reform, until it was too late. The price was loss of sovereignty.

Though aided for the better part of the seventeenth century by alliances and subsidies, Poland entered the following century without them, and stood alone against a unified alliance of absolutisms, whose capacity for cooperation lay only in partitioning a helpless neighbor. Without natural defenses, alliances, or the ability to mobilize foreign resources, or without domestic resource mobilization and a modern army, constitutional government in Poland had little, if any, opportunity for survival. Independence was lost and the land was divided among the great powers of the region. It should be no surprise that Poland was partitioned by powers that had learned the lessons of the military revolution. Prussia, Russia, and Austria overwhelmed the backward military of Poland, and removed it from contemporary maps of Europe.

GENTRY CONSTITUTIONALISM

In the fourteenth century, the Piast dynasty imposed a weak monarchal order over the Slavic tribes of Eastern Europe. Although it was able to avoid substantive ties of fealty to either the Holy Roman Empire or the Papacy, it failed to construct any measure of central control parallel to that of Angevin England or Augustan France.[1] A constitutional balance, however, was in evidence between the crown on the one hand and the

---

[1] *The Cambridge Medieval History*, Volume 6, p. 447, Volume 8, p. 562.

magnates and gentry (*szlachta*), whose assistance in governing the expansive region was vital.[2]

It is the szlachta who figure so highly in the unfolding of Polish history, and it should be noted that, even at this early point, their power relative to the throne was considerable. Their role in thwarting centralization and military reform in ensuing centuries was predicated on their beginnings as a strong, cohesive knightly class, whose military functions had not waned, as had those of many counterparts to the west. The knights were organized not as individual families, but rather as clans. Such was the import of this system that a knight assumed as his last name a part of his clan's battle cry. Though widely dispersed throughout the sprawling realm, clans had considerable contact with their members and constituted formidable political entities with which the crown had to reckon.[3]

A classic medieval constitutional pact, reminiscent of Magna Carta or the Swedish Land Law of 1350, was negotiated in 1374. The Pact of Koszyce won for the crown the succession of the king's daughter in exchange for limiting noble taxes to a mere two groschen per year, no other taxes without szlachta approval, gentry control of the judiciary and mint, and, critically, future accessions to the throne only by means of election.[4] The inequity of this exchange is indicative of existing power relations between crown and nobility, which continued throughout the nation's history, and in no small way determined its ultimate demise.

The Pact of Koszyce's provision that new taxes had to be approved by the gentry naturally called for a diet (*Seym*) to discuss such matters. By 1520 the diet's procedures and structures had been established: diets met every four years, each member of the gentry was entitled to vote in the Seym, and a single negative vote could veto not only the bill under discussion, but also all acts of legislation adopted at that session of the Seym.[5] These last two provisions, the sheer numbers of the legislators and the so-called *Liberum Veto*, made the governmental machinery the

[2] *The Cambridge Medieval History*, Volume 6, pp. 451–52.

[3] Ibid., 462; W. F. Reddaway et al., eds., *The Cambridge History of Poland*, Volume 1 (Cambridge: Cambridge University Press, 1950), pp. 105–6. As we shall see, foreign sovereigns, too, reckoned with, and often manipulated, the szlachta.

[4] *The Cambridge Medieval History*, Volume 8, pp. 566–67; *The Cambridge History of Poland*, Volume 1, p. 193; Karol Górski, "Les chartes de la noblesse en Pologne aux XIVe et XVe siècles," *Studies Presented to the International Commission for the History of Representative and Parliamentary Institutions* 56 (1979): 247–72.

[5] *The Cambridge History of Poland*, Volume 1, pp. 320–21, 421–23; Volume 2, pp. 54–56; Norman Davies, *God's Playground: A History of Poland in Two Volumes*, Volume 1: *The Origins to 1795* (New York: Columbia University Press, 1982), pp. 344–48. Seyms, like the French Estates-General, were preceded by smaller assemblies (*seymiks*) at the district and provincial levels.

most unwieldy in all Europe. In addition to routinized diets, an ad hoc diet, or *rokosz*, was frequently convoked on the occasion of calling up the feudal levy, thereby forcing concessions at critical moments. Pacts and concessions were worked out, including periodic reaffirmations of noble rights, gentry control of the judiciary, and supervision of the royal mint.[6] The szlachta built a substantial, but extremely cumbersome, constitutional order that firmly guaranteed their rights and liberties, at least from internal dangers. But it had tragic consequences for the country, as a weak, subordinate monarchy and unwieldy diets proved unable to respond adequately to external threats.

In 1572 the Jagiellonian dynasty died out, and with its passing came reassertion of the principle of elective monarchy, which had fallen into disuse. Though kings were often from the same families, the gentry maintained the upper hand, and rewarded an unobtrusive family with a dynastic facade. Each accession entailed solemn reaffirmation of traditional constitutional arrangements. Constitutional government took a decisive turn with the conjuncture of the demise of the Jagiellonians—the country's last chance for a strong monarchy—and the further rise of an independent social class, the gentry, now enriched by the Baltic grain trade.[7] The gentry had subordinated the monarchy, just as many histories say the English gentry had subordinated its monarchy in 1688. But celebration was not in order. Instead of signaling the triumph of the constitution, szlachta ascendancy was a death knell. England benefited from the Channel barrier, great commercial wealth, and plentiful foreign aid, but when Poland faced foreign threats in the eighteenth century, it was unprotected by nature, far from wealthy, and hopelessly alone. Perhaps most importantly, its diet-centered government lacked executive coherence. But that gets ahead of the narrative.

The peasantry and burghers of the late Middle Ages enjoyed most of the rights and privileges of their Prussian neighbors prior to the Great Elector's reforms. It could hardly be any other way, since both regions' towns and villages were founded during the same migration to the east. Peasants were attracted to Poland in the thirteenth century by the prospect of light services and dues. The village *solti*, like the etymologically related German Schulz, settled peasants, administered justice, and took

---

[6] *The Cambridge History of Poland*, Volume 1, pp. 313–14, 320–21, 419–21, Volume 2, pp. 57–68; Catherine S. Leach, ed., *Memoirs of the Polish Baroque: The Writings of Jan Chryzostom Pasek, A Squire of the Commonwealth of Poland and Lithuania* (Berkeley and Los Angeles: University of California Press, 1976).

[7] "The Szlachta . . . now anointed themselves with the majesty that once belonged to the crown and looked upon their king as a chosen representative with strictly limited authority." *The Cambridge History of Poland*, Volume 1, p. 369.

up the cause of the villagers in disputes with the lord or crown.[8] Towns, meanwhile, were settled by merchants from the West, especially Jewish ones fleeing intolerance fueled by the fervor of the Crusades. Charters were obtained; aldermanic government and guild democracies flourished.[9]

GEOGRAPHIC DETERMINISM, POLITICAL STRUCTURE, AND POLAND'S DESTRUCTION

There is perhaps no more common and intuitively appealing explanation for Poland's dismemberment than the geographic-determinist one. According to this line of reasoning, fate, in the intransigent form of geography, placed Poland in an unviable position amidst three expansionist empires. To worsen matters, Poland was without the benefit of mountains or other natural barriers to invaders. Hence, physical realities foredoomed the republic of nobles to partition and extinction. The argument seems to have merit. As one surveys Polish history and sees absolutist armies partition the land, the scenario unfolds, and it seems ineluctably so. But one soon suspects an element of wounded national pride in this argument, and the suspicion is strengthened if one considers the poor geographic hands dealt to two other players in the game of European geopolitics.

Brandenburg, it will be remembered, was once a frail constitutional territory surrounded and exploited by Sweden, Austria, and Poland itself, whose military might prior to the military revolution was, as we shall see, sufficient to fight against other unmodernized armies. During the Thirty Years' War, foreign armies traversed Brandenburg and availed themselves of its resources with impunity. But from little Brandenburg emerged mighty Prussia, no longer a victim—quite the opposite. A powerful military state developed from a similar geographic disadvantage. Similarly, Austria was far from blessed by geography. It faced Ottoman invasions from the south, and French and Russian ones from the west and east.[10] Nor can one amend the determinist argument by claiming that Poland lacked the resources to defend itself. In the early seventeenth century, Poland was one of the largest countries in Europe, with a pop-

[8] *The Cambridge History of Poland*, Volume 1, pp. 104–5, 130–38. A further parallel with the Prussian peasantry is in the subjugation of both in the manorial reaction of the fifteenth and sixteenth centuries.

[9] Davies, *God's Playground*, Volume 1, pp. 293–320; *The Cambridge History of Poland*, Volume 1, p. 105.

[10] On successful outcomes for countries starting with marked geopolitical disadvantages, see Paul Kennedy, *The Rise and Fall of the Great Powers: Economic Change and Military Conflict from 1500 to 2000* (New York: Random House, 1987), pp. 88–92.

ulation of between eight and nine million, controlling a fertile agricultural region of 375,000 square miles from the Baltic to the Black Sea.[11] And its soil was far richer than that of Brandenburg, which was known as the sandbox of the Holy Roman Empire. Poland's geographic position, then, was no worse than that of Prussia and Austria, and probably no worse than those of most other continental states. Furthermore, its economic and human resources were far greater than those of Prussia; the nation's wealth, though never exorbitant, grew rapidly from grain trade with the West. One must look elsewhere for the answer to the question of why Poland lost its sovereignty.

The answer, I contend, lies in Prussia's and Austria's abilities, and Poland's failure, to build state structures capable of developing and fielding large modern armies. To put this in terms of the dynamics presented in this study, the crown in some countries was able to obtain a preponderance of organizational and military resources, abolish or circumvent the estates, and pursue policies of state centralization and militarization. Alternately, following the Dutch example, the estates themselves, or a portion thereof, assumed control of modern military structures and, with the assistance of international alliances, geographic alliances, and extraordinary commercial wealth, were able to form a viable executive and pass through periods of protracted warfare, without the onus of autocratic organizations.

Poland was unable to follow the military-bureaucratic pattern of France and Prussia for two principal reasons that stand out from the outlines of its constitutional history. First, the demise of the Jagiellonian dynasty combined with the rise of a wealthy, independent, and politically powerful gentry effectively took a military-bureaucratic outcome off the agenda. The constitutional balance had been upset, but in the opposite direction from the Prussian and French examples. The gentry had taken virtually complete control of government, and by the late sixteenth century the Polish king was little more than a subordinate steward of szlachta interests—an executive for managing the common affairs of the gentry, one might say, thus making monarchal absolutism highly improbable: "In the Age of Louis XIV and Peter I, a radical and total negation of Absolutism was born on the banks of the Vistula."[12] There was no royal chancery independent of the diet, to recognize foreign danger and engineer the deals, threats, and maneuvers needed to rise above consensual rule with

[11] *The New Cambridge Modern History*, Volume 1, p. 585.

[12] Perry Anderson, *Lineages of the Absolutist State* (London: Verso, 1974), p. 293. See also Jacek Kochanowicz, "The Polish Economy and the Evolution of Dependency," in Daniel Chirot, ed., *The Origins of Backwardness in Eastern Europe: Economics and Politics from the Middle Ages until the Early Twentieth Century* (Berkeley and Los Angeles: University of California Press, 1989), pp. 92–130.

the estates and build military-bureaucratic absolutism. There was only a parsimonious, parochial, and incoherent estates with its elected king.

The second model, parliamentary control as exemplified by the Dutch regents and States-General, was not to be followed owing to the unwieldy numbers of the Polish Seym, the paralyzing effects of the Liberum Veto, and the absence of unity and coherence among the gentry elite. First of all, although most European estates consisted of several hundred members, owing to the principle of representation of each member of the szlachta, the Seym was far larger than any other European estates. The mass of the diets made effective decision making extremely difficult. Debates were interminable, directionless, and inconclusive. Second, the Liberum Veto was a serious obstacle to coherent and controversial policies such as those necessitated by protracted war, military reform, and centralization. The work of an entire diet could be undone by a single unexplained shout of *"Nie pozwalam"* ("I do not allow it"). The Liberum Veto limited the actions of crown and Seym alike. Reform aimed at streamlining this absurd form of constitutional government could itself be thwarted by a single veto. Indeed, belated eighteenth-century reforms replacing the Liberum Veto with the reasonable and constitutional principle of majority rule had to be forced through by illegal means.[13] A Russian minister ominously observed: "Poland is constantly plunged into disorder; as long as she keeps her present constitution, she does not deserve to be considered among the European powers."[14]

In regard to the dearth of coherence in the szlachta, we might cite as evidence the numerous factions that ignored national interests in favor of conspiring with foreign powers to prevent a strong state and to place sympathetic monarchs on the throne. These are recurrent themes in Poland's early modern history.[15] But accounting for widespread irresponsibility is more difficult than illustrating it. Perhaps comparison to the Dutch Republic will prove illuminating. Three forces may be identified that gave Dutch elites a coherence conducive to effective wartime leadership. First, the burghers of the northern provinces of Burgundy and the Low Countries that became the Dutch Republic were men whose livelihood and wealth were based on trade. A substantial amount

---

[13] See Daniel Stone, *Polish Politics and National Reform 1775–1788* (New York: Eastern European Quarterly, 1976).

[14] Quoted in Davies, *God's Playground*, Volume 1, p. 511.

[15] Stone, *Polish Politics*, pp. 44–46; *The New Cambridge Modern History*, Volume 5, pp. 562–64; *The New Cambridge Modern History*, Volume 6, pp. 686–97. On foreign manipulation of internal politics, Stone states: "The *Liberum Veto*, which was supposed to check the absolutist designs of the Polish monarchy, was made to serve the purposes of the Russian Empire."

of cooperation among shippers, bankers, insurers, and merchants led to a community of interest, concentrated in a few seaports, that to a certain extent complemented, but perhaps more importantly sharply conflicted with, similar communities in rival commercial centers. There was a political economy of centripetal interests distinguishing them from other areas' merchants, which, when embellished with certain types of historiography and sentimental semiotics, became nationalism, or at least a sound basis for it.

Second, the Dutch Revolt itself furthered nationalism and elite responsibility by pitting the community against an intrusive foreign power with administrative control over the Netherlands. Habsburg ministers threatened the economic, political, and religious bases of the community when they attempted to strengthen control over the Low Countries. Wars with Spain furthered the sense of community and forced the burghers to arrive at some measure of responsible government, or face becoming a subordinate tributary of the Spanish empire. Comparisons to the Polish elite reveal no parallel community of interest. The unity of the numerous clans served well to check Piast and Jagiellonian dynasts, but, with the latter family's demise and the boom in grain production, the clans were no longer a unitary warrior caste, carriers of prototypical nationalism. The szlachta became individual landlords who left the vagaries of transporting and marketing grain to foreign (coincidentally, Dutch) merchants, and so did not develop cohesive ties that might form the basis for a coherent elite. They were little more than gentry sacks of potatoes, whose main concern outside their manors became the protection of their liberties and incomes from the crown, and the surest method of ensuring that seemed to be the maintenance of a narrowly proscribed state. Nor was there the centripetal force of overt foreign government, at least not until the late eighteenth century, when it was too late. But by then, the patriotic revolution led by Kosciuszko was, as we shall see, easily overwhelmed by the modern armies of surrounding powers.

Third, the problem of the numbers of the gentry reasserts itself. The szlachta comprised a large number of landowners, sprawled across central Europe, without adequate means of communication. In the Netherlands, merchant elites were highly concentrated in the coastal provinces of Holland and Zeeland, with a powerful group of regents centered in Amsterdam, facilitating executive capacity. The large number of the Polish gentry contrasts with the cliquish Dutch regents, who, tied together by business communities and fear of Spanish authority, formed a competent executive to manage the country, even in the desperate hours of war. The szlachta, in contrast, allied with foreign powers to prevent political change. In their amateurish attempts to play the game of international intrigue, they succeeded only in becoming the dupes of calculating foreign autocrats. The Polish gentry exchanged the privilege of national sovereignty for the right to make money.

Geographic-determinist explanations for Poland's dismemberment are vitiated by the examples of Prussia and Austria, which were hardly blessed by position in the state system, yet nonetheless survived by building modern states and armies. Poland entered the early modern period with a state—the term seems only barely appropriate—far weaker than that of other European territories, thereby making the prospects for military-bureaucratic mobilization, at the very best, unlikely. Nor was the Polish diet's assumption of effective rule any likelier. Unwieldy numbers, the Liberum Veto, and the absence of unity of purpose in the szlachta prevented the evolution of the diet into a coherent decision-making body. The problems of Polish constitutional government cannot be expressed more clearly or eloquently than here: "Few can now doubt that the 'golden freedom' of the Polish squires was chaos thinly gilded, or that their pride in a constitution which as they held drew the best from monarchy, aristocracy and democracy, sprang from failure to comprehend any of the three."[16]

MILITARY SUCCESS AND MILITARY STAGNATION

Szlachta control of the polity meant control of the military. The gentry consistently rejected military reform along the lines undertaken by Prussian and Russian heads of state. Poland entered the seventeenth and even the eighteenth century without a modern military structure. It had no large infantry formations, rational supply systems, or substantial numbers of cannon; its more modern, though less constitutional, neighbors did not allow it to enter the nineteenth century. Yet between the rise of the szlachta republic and the partitions in the late eighteenth century, Poland had a string of notable military successes. Indeed, even in the seventeenth century there were impressive victories over Russia and the Turks at the very gates of Vienna. It is to this paradox that we must now turn.

From the earliest struggles in the medieval period until the eighteenth century, the Polish military was based on the levy of gentry knights. To be sure, these hosts were augmented, as were Western feudal armies, by occasional mercenary units and a levy of peasant foot soldiers, but the knights were the mainstay, performing quite well in the Middle Ages, subjugating indigenous tribes and repulsing invaders. Such were their victories over Cossack and Tatar raiding parties, as well as the German

[16] *The Cambridge History of Poland*, Volume 2, p. xiii.

Order's drive to the east, that medieval Poland attained the reputation of a considerable regional military power. Victory over the Teutonic Knights at Tannenberg (1410) gave the seemingly invincible knights of the German Order their most stunning defeat since the days of Alexander Nevsky, and made the once-proud knights the humble vassals of the Polish crown.[17] But in the decades after Tannenberg, the feudal hosts fared poorly against the resurgent Order, and also against the Hussites. The latter's tactical innovations and increased use of disciplined infantry made as little impression on the Polish military as the victories of Flemish and English infantry had on French chivalry.[18] While Poland's neighbors modernized their forces, problems with the feudal levy increased: it was notoriously slow to gather; law prevented its deployment outside the country; it could not be tactically divided; and, in a display of medieval sensibility, it refused to fight at harvest time. Judging by a contemporary journal, campaigns were somewhat of a lark, filled with frivolity and hobnobbing between infrequent engagements.[19]

The szlachta obstinately opposed raising a modern infantry. When infantry began to make some inroads, it was not used in battle, and was disbanded at the earliest opportunity.[20] During wars with Sweden and the Ottoman Empire in the early seventeenth century, the infantry made up over half of the military, but the szlachta adamantly refused to maintain a standing army, despite danger throughout Eastern Europe.[21] Opposition stemmed from three main sources. First, the gentry saw its preeminence in the military as a basis for its cherished privileges and rights, so they were naturally reluctant to endanger that basis by restructuring the military in a manner that made commoners of such social, and possibly later political, importance. Opposition to modern infantry is, of course, a familiar story in European history, but the political strength of the szlachta was far greater than that of its counterparts. Thus, the weak Polish crown, despite clear external threats, was unable to pursue modernization over diet objections. Second, the gentry refused to pay the expenses of a standing army. Instead, the parsimonious nobles held fast to the principle, long since obsolete in the West, that the king must fi-

---

[17] See Sven Ekdahl, *Die Schlacht bei Tannenberg 1410: Quellenkritische Untersuchungen*, Volume 1: *Einführung und Quellenlage* (Berlin: Duncker & Humblot, 1982); Michael Burleigh, *Prussian Society and the German Order: An Aristocratic Order in Crisis, c. 1410–1466* (Cambridge: Cambridge University Press, 1984), pp. 70–72.

[18] *The Cambridge History of Poland*, Volume 1, pp. 247–72.

[19] Ibid., p. 519; Leach, *Polish Baroque*. As noted earlier, the levies were also occasions for a destabilizing rokosz.

[20] Jan Wimmer, "l'Infanterie dans l'armée polonaise aux XV–XVIIIe siècles," in Witold Bieganski, Piotr Stawecki, and Janusz Wojtasik, eds., *Histoire militaire de Pologne: Problèmes choisis* (Warsaw: Edition du Ministère de la Défense Nationale, 1970).

[21] Wimmer, "l'Infanterie dans l'armée polonaise," pp. 88–92.

nance state and army from his personal demesne, a burden not even the latifundia of the Radziwills could assume.[22] Even during the disastrous Northern War (1655–1660), which came close to extinguishing national independence at an earlier date, the crown's triumph in obtaining an infantry conscription system was negated by the gentry's refusal to allocate sufficient money for equipment.[23] Finally, opposition to military reform came from the gentry's reluctance to share entrenched estate labor with the army, and the idea of arming serfs raised decidedly unsettling possibilities.[24]

Aside from these worries, two other factors help to account for Poland's retention of feudal levies as the basis for the army. First, a substantial external threat was presented, not by modern armies, but by Cossack and Tatar raiding parties, and the light cavalry of the Polish gentry was about as useful as centrally directed standing armies in irregular frontier warfare. It was effective in reconnaissance and pursuit along Poland's lengthy, ill-defined, and exposed frontiers to the southeast.[25] Second, in the seventeenth century, the Polish military was nonetheless able to win impressive victories over large modern armies, despite increasing obsolescence. It is not possible to recount each conflict in which Poland found itself during this century, but important reasons for these initially puzzling successes may be elucidated by focusing on three principal ones: the defeat of Russia in the early part of the century, the Northern War, and the legendary defeat of the Turks at century's close.

Poland won great victories over Russia, had a protégé temporarily installed as tsar, and expanded far to the east. But this was during a time

[22] *The New Cambridge Modern History,* Volume 3, p. 397; *The Cambridge History of Poland,* Volume 1, pp. 318–19; Davies, *God's Playground,* Volume 1, p. 478.

[23] Wimmer, "l'Infanterie dans l'armée polonaise," pp. 89–92.

[24] Stanislaw Herbst, "l'Armée polonaise et l'art militaire au XVIIIe siècle," *Acta Poloniae Historica* 3 (1960): 33–48. While the fear of an armed, trained peasantry may indeed have motivated the gentry, the existence of the Kantonsystem in nearby Prussia ably belied the incompatibility of peasant infantry with servile labor. Furthermore, mercenary units were readily available.

[25] Jerzy Teodorczyk, "L'armée polonaise aux XVe–XVIIIe siècles," in Biegnaski, Stawecki, and Wojtasik, *Histoire Militaire de Pologne,* pp. 102–3; Geoffrey Parker, *The Military Revolution: Military Innovation and the Rise of the West, 1500–1800* (Cambridge: Cambridge University Press, 1988), p. 37. These raiding parties, one of which, as we have seen, razed Berlin, were particularly bold in the period from 1630 to 1660, a period of rapid military modernization in Europe. See *The New Cambridge Modern History,* Volume 4, p. 598. In the early seventeenth century, the Polish cavalry also fared well against small Swedish contingents, who were initially bewildered, as the English had been by their Celtic adversaries, by their foe's unusual, outdated army. See Michael Roberts, *The Early Vasas: A History of Sweden, 1523–1611* (Cambridge: Cambridge University Press, 1986), pp. 400–404, and *Gustavus Adolphus: A History of Sweden 1611–1632,* Volume 2: *1626–1632* (London: Longmans, Green, 1958), pp. 189–337.

of internal chaos in Russia, the so-called Time of Troubles or *Smuta*, during which it was wracked by civil wars, boyar treachery and intrigue, and jarring peasant rebellions. There was no coherence in the Muscovite state, only an operatic succession of usurpers and pretenders. Poland undertook this war with Russia with little fear of encountering strong military opposition, modern or feudal.[26] It would be quite another matter after the military reforms of Peter the Great.

In the 1650s, Poland warred with Russia, Sweden, and Brandenburg. Battles with the latter two foes were unmitigated disasters for Poland. The levies performed miserably, and many provinces, as well as Warsaw itself, capitulated to invaders. When sizeable annexations seemed inescapable, state-system dynamics came to Poland's aid. Fearing a disadvantageous shift of power to its Scandinavian nemesis, Austria prevailed upon the Romanovs to cease hostilities, thereby freeing Poland's eastern forces. Diplomacy triumphed where its army had failed when Poland ceded East Prussia to the Great Elector in exchange for his volte-face. Fortuitous but short-lived international dynamics, not military might, won this round in the struggle for sovereignty. But it is important to note that the respite granted by international dynamics did not stem from long-term diplomacy—the chaotic Polish state was incapable of that. Its reprieve came mainly from external actors, in Vienna and Berlin, who feared a more powerful predator in the region.

In the late seventeenth century, Poland engaged in wars against Austria and Prussia, and later allied with Austria against the Ottoman Empire. This, of course, was the period of Poland's greatest military hero, Jan Sobieski, who fought lengthy wars against large modern armies, including that of the Porte. But again, alliances and foreign subsidies, not internal military modernization, account for the successes of this period. It will not, it is hoped, tarnish the great king's military reputation to note that he commanded scarcely twenty-five thousand Polish soldiers, or that he received two hundred thousand livres a year from Louis XIV to wage war on his Prussian and Austrian enemies, or that his legendary relief of Vienna (1683) was undertaken by the same number of Polish troops augmented by thirty-one thousand imperial and mercenary troops, recruited, paid, and supplied by Austrian money.[27]

---

[26] *The New Cambridge Modern History*, Volume 4, pp. 593–95; V. O. Kluchevsky, *A History of Russia*, Volume 3, C. J. Hogarth, trans. (New York: Russell & Russell, 1960), pp. 1–90. Meanwhile, Sweden began to carve out an empire on the Baltic, largely at Poland's expense, and helped Russia to expel Polish troops and collaborators. See *The Cambridge History of Poland*, Volume 1, pp. 475–87.

[27] Ibid., pp. 547–48. Sobieski was unable to parlay his military successes into a stronger state or military reform. See Ibid., pp. 555–56.

Foreign subsidies and alliances, not modern military structures, were the keys to Polish success on the battlefields of the seventeenth century. Subsidies and alliances served, it is true, to preserve Polish constitutionalism, but, by fostering the illusion that the levies could still more than hold their own against the modern armies of the region, they justified deferment of badly needed military reforms. Military prowess was a domestic illusion and an external facade: "Poland emerged from war nominally among the victors, in reality a ruined and a second-rate power."[28]

THINGS FALL APART

By the outset of the eighteenth century, the constellation of protective factors upon which Polish sovereignty depended had disappeared, and new ones did not emerge. The facade was falling away, revealing a weak state and an antediluvian army. Political turmoil in Russia settled with the accession of the Romanov dynasty (1613), and, though peasant rebellions continued to erupt periodically, the tsars and the gentry forged a strong repressive apparatus, and the Russian state became ever more powerful. Peter the Great's state and military reforms in the early eighteenth century made the Russian army among the best in Europe.[29] Poland's other neighbors also modernized. Brandenburg-Prussia's military developed from the Great Elector's small force into the vaunted armies of Frederick the Great. Austria, too, had modernized in the course of protracted wars with the Turks and Bourbons, especially after the Thirty Years' War.[30]

Surrounded by such might, Poland could not rely on foreign resource mobilization, as had the Swedes in most of their wars. Even an initial penetration of foreign soil would have resulted in a swift, crushing counteroffensive from one or more of the major powers in eastern Europe, the likes of which the weak German principalities or the distant and partially demobilized Catholic armies could not have delivered against the small Swedish force that availed itself of German resources to build a powerful army. Nor was sufficient revenue forthcoming from interna-

[28] *The New Cambridge Modern History*, Volume 6, p. 715. In the decades following the defeat of the Armada in 1588, England too suffered from an exaggerated sense of military might that helped delay military modernization, but with a less unfortunate outcome. See Conrad Russell, *Parliaments and English Politics 1621–1629* (Oxford: Clarendon Press, 1983), pp. 70–84.

[29] J.L.H. Keep, *Soldiers of the Tsars: Army and Society in Russia 1462–1874* (Oxford: Clarendon Press, 1985), pp. 95–174.

[30] See Robert A. Kann, *A History of the Habsburg Empire, 1526–1918* (Berkeley and Los Angeles: University of California Press, 1974), pp. 125–33; and Eugen Heischmann, *Die Anfänge des stehenden Heeres in Österreich* (Vienna: Österreichischer Bundesverlag, 1925), pp. 181–224.

tional trade to provide sufficient wealth to modernize without onerous
domestic mobilization. Grain trade with the West was lucrative enough
to build impressive manors, but it hardly brought in wealth rivaling that
of the Amsterdam regents or the Venetian oligarchs.[31] Once-thriving Polish towns declined rapidly when the fall of Constantinople (1453) sev-
ered trade with the Levant, and when grain exited only a few Baltic
ports, principally Danzig.[32] Even after winning suzerainty over East
Prussia in the early fifteenth century, Poland failed to gain meaningful
control over the Baltic ports, and in any case ceded the region to Brandenburg in 1660.[33] Nor could commercial wealth be fostered by means of
state-directed activities as Colbert had done in France. This strategy
would have required shifting considerable power and responsibility to
the state, a move antithetical to szlachta interests, as they saw them.[34]
Alliances provided the basis for the survival of the country in the seventeenth century, but became the basis for its demise in the eighteenth.
Although state-system dynamics frequently bring the protection of a major power, this foreign help cannot always be relied upon, and, although
to a certain extent alliances stem from the logic of the international order,
they nonetheless must be made, continued, and remade when need be.
But Poland had no coherent state to pursue a sustained diplomatic policy
aimed at preventing an irresistible alliance of surrounding countries.

The Great Northern War (1700–1721) shattered Poland's illusions as
well as its security. Following the Treaty of Warsaw, Poland came under
Russian hegemony: its army could not exceed twenty-four thousand men;
foreign armies could avail themselves of Polish resources; and, as though
to ensure that there would be no military reform, Prussians were barred
from state service.[35] The next half century was one of foreign manipulation of szlachta cliques, which prevented state and military reforms and
maintained a weak neighbor.[36] Hegemonized and manipulated by foreign

---

[31] Owing to the greater profitability of transporting and distributing grain, much of the
wealth generated by the Baltic grain trade went to the shippers and merchants, not the
growers. It is perhaps ironic that these services were dominated by the Dutch.

[32] *The Cambridge Medieval History*, Volume 8, pp. 582–83.

[33] Perry Anderson asserts that the szlachta did not pursue maritime empire because of
opportunities for easy expansion to the south and east, where land and servile labor
abounded. See *Lineages of the Absolutist State*, pp. 288–89. Similarly, it has been argued
that China failed to expand overseas because of the relative ease with which it could expand
inwardly toward central Asia. See Immanuel Wallerstein, *The Modern World-System 1:
Capitalist Agriculture and the Origins of the European World-Economy in the Sixteenth
Century* (New York: Academic Press, 1974), p. 57.

[34] *The New Cambridge Modern History*, Volume 6, p. 682.

[35] Davies, *God's Playground*, Volume 1, pp. 496–510; *The Cambridge History of Poland*,
Volume 2, pp. 65–66; *The New Cambridge Modern History*, Volume 6, pp. 776–77.

[36] Michael G. Müller, *Polen zwischen Preussen und Russland: Souveränitätskrise und
Reformpolitik 1736–1752* (Berlin: Colloquium Verlag, 1983); Jerzy T. Lukowski, "Towards

powers, Poland was unable to mount effective reform. This preserved a measure of sovereignty, but only until the surrounding powers could agree on dividing the estate and arranging the death of the eastern European sick man. But perhaps Frederick the Great, his gift for metaphor heightened by proximity to the situation and appreciation for its potential, expressed it better: Poland, he observed was "an artichoke, ready to be consumed leaf by leaf."[37] The First Partition (1772) was made possible by a Hohenzollern-Romanov alliance based on Frederick's desire to secure his annexations from Austria in the Seven Years' War (1756–1763). Austrian acquiescence to the partition and accompanying change in its region's power order was won by allowing the Habsburgs a share of the spoils, a diplomatic formula repeated successfully in 1793 and 1795.

Encircled by neighboring powers, Poland could expect no help from distant powers. The French position, as constructed by the crown's minister, was resigned, but unalarmed:

> The condition of Poland was abject and anarchic. Continued French involvement in Polish affairs could only mean immense expenditure with no results. Choiseul recommended that Poland be abandoned to her natural fate, that France not interfere. . . . He had no faith that Poland could be reformed and no fear of her dismemberment. . . . Even if Poland's neighbors jointly agreed to dismember her, France still had nothing to fear, because within a short time the despoilers would fall into disagreement among themselves and the balance of power in eastern Europe would be readjusted.[38]

Nor would Great Britain come to Poland's defense. Alluding to its distance from the reach of British military might, Edmund Burke said on the floor of Parliament, "Poland must be regarded as being situated on the moon."[39]

The Polish diet was unable to mount an effective response to the First Partition. Divisions, unwieldiness, and intrigues prevented an already weak, elected monarchy from embarking upon the regrettable but necessary path of military-bureaucratic absolutism. Even with its enemies partitioning its country, the diet could agree upon authorizing only a fifty-five-thousand-man army. It is lamentable, but predictable, that the

---

Partition: Polish Magnates and Russian Intervention in Poland during the Early Reign of Stanislaw August Poniotowski," *Historical Journal* 28 (1985): 557–74; Stone, *Polish Politics*, pp. 44–46; *The New Cambridge Modern History*, Volume 5, pp. 562–64, Volume 6, pp. 686–97, Volume 8, pp. 365–95; Davies, *God's Playground*, Volume 1, pp. 347–48.

[37] Quoted in Ibid., p. 515.

[38] Herbert H. Kaplan, *The First Partition of Poland* (New York: Columbia University Press, 1962), p. 18. France gave diplomatic aid for a brief period, but withheld military and financial support prior to abandoning Poland to its "natural fate." See Kaplan, pp. 18–31.

[39] Quoted in Davies, *God's Playground*, Volume 1, p. 524.

feudal cavalry remained in the forefront of this force, whose task it was to engage the modern infantry, cavalry, and artillery of the great powers—a mismatch almost as great as one pitting cavalry against panzers.[40] Renewed efforts at governmental centralization had limited success but were ultimately thwarted by internal gentry opposition, and by Prussian and Russian pressure.[41] Increased opposition to foreign domination proved to be too little, too late. With most of Europe preoccupied with the events of the French Revolution, Prussia and Russia crushed opposition and divided the rest of Poland in 1793 and 1795.[42] Austria received its douceurs. The last vestiges of Polish sovereignty, and constitutionalism, vanished beneath the armies of absolutist powers.

In the interlude between the Second and Third Partitions, a valiant and desperate effort to mobilize the nation was undertaken by Thaddeus Kosciuszko. Inspired by the victories of the French *levée en masse*, this great patriot and student of modern warfare rapidly mobilized a peasant infantry, linked command and promotions to merit rather than birth, and introduced modern artillery and infantry tactics.[43] Slapdash to be sure, yet similar desperate measures in revolutionary France had fielded a highly nationalistic mass army that soundly defeated Austrian and Prussian armies, and formed the basis of Bonaparte's armies. But the successes of the French mass mobilization were not repeated in Poland, and for reasons that call for investigation.

First, though damaged in the early years of the Revolution, the French military, unlike that of Kosciuszko, nonetheless had a solid infrastructure upon which the levée en masse could be built. Thanks to the military priorities of French absolutism, supply systems, conscription networks, and modern artillery were already in existence. The largely aristocratic officer corps had been decimated by purges and emigration, but the

[40] Herbst, "l'Armée polonaise," p. 35. Recognizing their potential for helping to achieve Prussian foreign policy objectives, Frederick the Great had insisted on the retention of the Seym as well as the Liberum Veto. He munificently allowed, however, one exception to the veto right of each squire: there could be no veto of the ratification of the partition treaty. See Kaplan, *The First Partition*, pp. 170–75.

[41] Stone, *Polish Politics*, pp. 10–75.

[42] Davies, *God's Playground*, Volume 1, pp. 526–43.

[43] Zdzislaw Sulek, "Tadeusz Kosciuszko—Chef et Réformateur Social," in Biegnaski, Stawecki, and Wojtasik, *Histoire Militaire de Pologne*, pp. 114–32; Leonard Ratajczyk, "La défense territoriale pendant l'insurrection de Kosciuszko," in Biegnaski, Stawecki, and Wojtasik, *Histoire Militaire de Pologne*, pp. 133–48; Herbst, "l'Armée polonaise," pp. 36–48; Wimmer, "l'Infanterie dans l'armée polonaise," pp. 93–94; *The New Cambridge Modern History*, Volume 8, pp. 345–55. Inasmuch as Kosciuszko's military reforms were accompanied by governmental and social ones that freed the state as well as the peasantry from gentry abuse, one senses that success on the battlefield, unlikely as that was, might have ushered in an interesting new epoch in Polish history.

ranks were filled by capable middle-class officers—Bonaparte among them—who had been languishing in the less prestigious branches of the service, such as the engineers and artillery. Kosciuszko, on the other hand, faced the burden of building a mass army without the logistics, personnel, and equipment of a modern army. Second, again thanks in large measure to the preceding military-bureaucratic period, France entered the wars of coalition with a formidable economic system with which it could support its armies.[44] The contrast with the Polish nationalist army of 1794 is tragic. Kosciuszko's infantry could not be outfitted with muskets and integrated with existing regimental cadres. Most went into battle with nothing more than the scythes they carried with them from the fields; a romantic and inspiring image, worthy of a David or a Delacroix, but the peasants were mercilessly hewn by the volleys of Russian foot soldiers, and that is an image more worthy of a Goya. Third, numbers were against Poland. Kosciuszko's brave effort to mobilize the nation enabled him to field a force of a hundred and fifty thousand. A sizeable increase over the feudal host, but still woefully inadequate against the forces at the disposal of its enemies. The tsar could field four hundred thousand troops, Austria another three hundred thousand, and Prussia two hundred thousand.[45]

. . .

Kosciuszko's exploits were an heroic last stand that could not make up for a century and a half of neglecting military reform. Poland entered the post-Westphalian world with a military structure ably suited for frontier skirmishes, but hopelessly incapable of ensuring territorial sovereignty in a time of continuous military growth. Though it was hardly favored by natural barriers, Poland's demise must be attributed to failure to modernize, as did surrounding powers. One might speculate that, had it done so, Russia, Prussia, or Austria might have found Poland a desirable alliance partner against the others, possibly precluding the partitioning alliance. As it was, Poland was only a weak and tempting target for surrounding states, a source of regional instability and tension that the major powers only too willingly removed.

Poland did not modernize army and state, and blame for this can be placed at the dragging feet of the Polish gentry, whose intransigence delivered the nation into foreign domination from which it has never recov-

[44] Though availing himself of France's considerable economic output for equipping the army, Napoleon, it will be remembered, preferred to obtain his armies' food through mobile plunder.

[45] For the troop strengths of Poland's enemies at the time of Kosciuszko, see Ratajczyk, "La défense territoriale," p. 136.

ered for more than a couple of decades. Only now, after the horrific defeat of German and Austrian military power, and the apparent dissolution of Russian might, is Poland regaining control of its national destiny—happily, in an increasingly peaceful European order. The gentry's guilt is the verdict reached in a considerable portion of the historiographical literature, much of it seething with only thinly veiled contempt for them. It is difficult to survey Poland's history without concluding that the szlachta was perhaps the most irresponsible elite in all European history.

CHAPTER SEVEN

England

THE CONSTITUTIONAL NATURE of English government, as is well known, dates back at least to the signing of Magna Carta, but wars left their mark, and any notion of its unilinear development into liberal democracy surely needs closer examination. Neither the Tudor nor the Stuart period was one of sustained, protracted war against a modern army. Despite conflicts with the Stuarts, as well as a moderately coercive Parliament during the Civil War period, constitutionalism carried through into the eighteenth century largely unscathed. The most damaging attacks on the constitution came not from the Houses of Tudor or Stuart, but from the House of Commons. Another period of history, starting in the late seventeenth century, will be examined. With the rise of French expansionism, England could no longer stay aloof from continental wars. Beginning its role as balancer of power, it increased the size of its armies, though even here not to the extent of France or Prussia. In the wars against Louis XIV, England found methods of exerting military power without mobilizing constitutionally debilitating amounts of its own resources.

MEDIEVAL CONSTITUTIONALISM

The Norman Conquest made England a more centralized state than any other in Europe. William and his successors stood at the head of a taxation and administrative system exceeding anything in Western Europe. The Domesday Book, judges, and reeves afforded the monarch more control over his domain than that wielded by early Capetians or Hohenstauffens. But a highly centralized state in the eleventh century did not contain an inherent mechanism for continuing its lead in centralization, nor did it undermine or preclude the cooperation between center and locality that was at the heart of constitutional government. Local agents of the crown were never tightly tied to an administrative apparatus by means of training, promotion, or salary. They were unpaid amateurs, at least as closely linked to local notables and MPs as to the king. This linkage became increasingly close, and provided a serious obstacle to Stuart and Cromwellian centralizing efforts, well intended or not: "[Q]ualified lawyers, the members of the House of Commons, and the J.P.s in Elizabethan and Stuart England were so closely intertwined that they were essentially different embodiments of a single social entity."[1]

Controlling an area only the size of a large German principality or Capetian fief, Plantagenet and Angevin kings stood at the head of a small state that was essentially an undifferentiated household government. Though English kings were too powerful to be considered firsts among equals, they were nonetheless unable to use William's early state as a basis from which to expand their power at the expense of the baronage, lesser nobles, and burgesses. Attempts by John to do just that led to a coalescence of opposition and the crown's embarrassed recognition of fundamental rights at Runnymede. Royal courts did, however, begin to replace manorial ones during the twelfth and thirteenth centuries, but this transition reflected the preference of noble and commoner alike for the swifter and fairer Common Law courts. The crown's income and prestige were insufficient to upset the constitutional balance, and could not, at least at this point, be risked on an uncertain bid for greater royal authority.[2] By the close of the medieval period, Common Law courts had developed institutional autonomy, spread throughout England, and elaborated basic principles and precedents into a body of jurisprudence governing English civil society from the king to the lowly tiller.[3] The sanctity of the Common Law and the sovereign's subordination to it were such that the mightiest Tudor and Stuart could not attempt to place himself or herself above it without suffering consequences ranging from a vociferous Parliament to a march to the scaffold.

The origins and fates of parliaments, as we have seen, are closely linked to the military and warfare. Edward I convoked the first English general assembly, the so-called Model Parliament of 1295, to obtain funding and support for wars against the Scots and Welsh.[4] Further wars with contentious Celtic neighbors led to a series of negotiations in which Parliament exchanged tax grants for extension or confirmation of basic privileges and rights, a process that led to the institutionalization and

---

[1] J. H. Gleason, *The Justices of the Peace in England 1558 to 1640: A Later* Eirenarcha (Oxford: Clarendon Press, 1969), p. 122.

[2] *The Cambridge Medieval History*, Volume 5, pp. 528–9, 584–90; Arthur R. Hogue, *Origins of the Common Law* (Indianapolis, Ind.: Liberty Press, 1985), pp. 5–18; Theodore F. T. Plucknett, *A Concise History of the Common Law*, Fifth Edition (London: Butterworth, 1956).

[3] Hogue, *Common Law*, pp. 145–81. On the machinery of the royal courts, see Robert C. Palmer, *The County Courts of Medieval England 1150–1350* (Princeton, N.J.: Princeton University Press, 1982).

[4] Sidney Painter, *The Rise of the Feudal Monarchies* (Ithaca, N.Y.: Cornell University Press, 1975), pp. 80–83; *The Cambridge Medieval History*, Volume 7, pp. 404–8, 677ff. It was Edward's amusing miscalculation that this assembly would provide the means of gaining the upper hand in dealings with his subjects.

expansion of parliamentary power.[5] This constitutionally significant process of quid pro quo continued throughout the Hundred Years' War, as Parliament granted customs taxes (tunnage and poundage) in exchange for a measure of routinization of Parliamentary meetings, sovereignty over law, control over royal ministers, and even boards of inquiry to investigate expenditures.[6]

Military organization in medieval England deviated somewhat from the classic medieval pattern in two regards: a higher proportion of infantry and a larger complement of mercenaries. Of course, neither foot soldiers nor mercenaries were unknown to other contemporary armies, but the proportion of armored knights was even lower in English forces. Owing to the painful lessons of Bannockburn (1314), where Scottish clans had defeated English chivalry, to continued border skirmishes with Scots and Welsh, and to the successes in the Hundred Years' War, English military organization used foot soldiers armed with bows and bills to a greater extent than did most of the armies of Europe. Every able-bodied Englishman served in decentralized militias (fyrds). The militia was no modern infantry: it was under local control, deployment outside the county (let alone outside the country) was not subject to royal decree; it was smaller than the modern infantries of later centuries; and its reliance on the bow and bill separated it from arquebus- and pike-wielding modern infantry.[7] The constitutional significance of the militia was threefold: military service endowed tenants and villeins with certain rights and immunities; local control gave notables the resources with which to negoti-

---

[5] *The Cambridge Medieval History*, Volume 7, pp. 404–9; F. Miller, "War, Taxation and the English Economy in the Late Thirteenth and Early Fourteenth Centuries," in J. M. Winter, ed., *War and Economic Development: Essays in Memory of David Joslin* (New York: Cambridge University Press, 1975), pp. 11–31.

[6] Richard W. Kaeuper, *War, Justice and Public Order: England and France in the Later Middle Ages* (Oxford: Clarendon Press, 1988), pp. 119–20, 388; *The Cambridge Medieval History*, Volume 7, pp. 456–81; Volume 8, pp. 366–72; Michael Powicke, *Military Obligation in Medieval England: A Study in Liberty and Duty* (Oxford: Clarendon Press, 1967), pp. 232–41; F. Miller, "War, Taxation and the English Economy," pp. 20–22. Throughout English history, Parliamentary oversight waxed and waned with the degree of trust between crown and Parliament. Even the vaunted oversight committees built after the Glorious Revolution (1688) fell into disuse. See Conrad Russell, "Parliament and the King's Finances," in Conrad Russell, ed., *The Origins of the English Civil War* (London: Macmillan, 1978), pp. 91–116.

[7] John Beeler, *Warfare in Medieval Europe* (Ithaca, N.Y.: Cornell University Press, 1971), pp. 91–100; Christopher Allmand, *The Hundred Years War: England and France at War c. 1300–c. 1450* (Cambridge: Cambridge University Press, 1988), pp. 64–65; Lindsay Boynton, *The Elizabethan Militia, 1558–1658* (Toronto: University of Toronto Press, 1967), pp. 7–17; Hans Delbrück, *History of the Art of War within the Framework of Political History*, Volume 3: *The Middle Ages* (Westport, Conn.: Greenwood Press, 1982), pp. 385–92.

ate with the crown; and the militias were substantial military resources that could have prevented the small mercenary forces of the crown from obtaining predominance, had a monarch attempted such a move.

Mercenaries were a major part of royal campaigns, at least since the Conquest, and remained so due to the transmutation of many knights' military obligations into payment (scutage), and to the general unreliability of the feudal levy and the fyrd. But the possibility of using mercenaries to expand royal power was limited because of the presence of superior numbers of chivalry and militiamen, and because of the necessity of Parliamentary subsidies to bolster scutage payments for paying hired lances. Such was the case during the campaigns of the Hundred Years' War, though plunder too figured highly as a major source of revenue for English armies.[8] In summary, then, the military was not the tool of the crown; the crown was dependent on Parliament, the nobility, and even the rude commonalty for military resources. Contract, written and unwritten, abounded. These three bases of dependence served also as bases of constitutionalism.

The Middle Ages saw considerable commercial growth in England, most notably in the wool trade with the Low Countries. The accompanying rise of the towns was enhanced by charter grants extended by the king. The early strength of the state prevented English towns from gaining the autonomy enjoyed by the great commercial centers of southern Germany or northern Italy, but they were certainly not appendages of princely rule, as in Muscovy and the East. The thirteenth century was one in which towns and boroughs obtained charters limiting royal control. Aldermen and mayors managed local affairs and sent representatives to Parliament, much as the local gentry and nobility did outside the city walls. Towns and boroughs were able to exclude the king's reeves, implement or finesse royal directives, and maintain their own judiciaries.[9]

There is an array of recent as well as classic historical studies arguing that traditional, oppressive patterns of feudal authority diminished substantially during the late medieval period, even before the demographic changes brought on by the Black Death (mid-fourteenth century) shifted bargaining power, and liberties, to the peasantry. During the twelfth century, labor dues for most of the English villeinage declined a great

---

[8] Allmand, *Hundred Years War*, pp. 15–22, 54–56. Loot from the continent built many a noble manor.

[9] Susan Reynolds, *Introduction to the Study of English Medieval Towns* (Oxford: Clarendon Press, 1977), pp. 70–72, 91–117. Reynolds cautions us that liberties stipulated in royal charters were not realized in all cases, but does not dispute the constitutional significance of these charters. See also *The Cambridge Medieval History*, Volume 5, pp. 274–78; and Frederic William Maitland, *Domesday Book and Beyond: Three Essays in the Early History of England* (Cambridge: Cambridge University Press, 1987 [1897]), pp. 185–87.

deal. Tiller rights increased and seigneurial authority declined.[10] Rents, labor services, and other landlord-tenant matters were not arbitrary. They became closely tied to custom, which in time became admissible in Common Law courts, and later, inasmuch as custom is a principal basis of law, these customs became cornerstones of jurisprudence.[11] Peasant access to justice was on the rise: "By the early thirteenth century, Englishmen of quite low rank were becoming accustomed to availing themselves of common-law protection. . . . [T]he conception of peasants as chattels was, it is true, quite artificial and most inappropriate to the actual circumstances of the English countryside. Nor would English rural custom submit easily to coercion by men armed with logical theories."[12] In further regard to peasant legal status, one might note that the legal rights of heritable property, horizontal mobility, and jury service were commonplaces in the medieval countryside—again, well prior to the Black Death.[13]

THE TUDOR STATE AND THE CONSTITUTION

The Tudor period (1485–1609) saw many radical changes that figure highly in English history. The Reformation, governmental reform, dynastic turmoil, economic growth, and occasional wars all stand out. The increased power and activity of Henry VIII and Elizabeth have led many to call them despots or absolute monarchs. We might agree that the Tudors wielded greater power than did Yorkist or Lancastrian predecessors, yet consistently maintain that constitutional patterns more than persisted. It is only natural to feel somewhat uncomfortable with the designation of absolute monarchy. Henrician ascendancy in political, ecclesiastical, and commercial matters was accompanied by a close working relationship with the House of Commons and other constitutional centers, especially the Justices of the Peace (JPs). If this corresponds with some understandings of absolutism, a decided amorphousness of the term must be admitted. In any regard, it certainly does not correspond

[10] P. R. Hyams, *King, Lords and Peasants in Medieval England* (Oxford: Oxford University Press, 1980), p. 185; Rodney Hilton, *Bond Men Made Free: Medieval Peasant Movements and the English Rising of 1381* (London: Temple Smith, 1973), pp. 9–62.

[11] M. M. Postan, *The Medieval Economy and Society: An Economic History of Britain in the Middle Ages* (Harmondsworth, U.K.: Penguin, 1984), pp. 161–64. Common Law, however, did not always support custom in every locality. See F. W. Maitland, *The Constitutional History of England* (Cambridge: Cambridge University Press, 1950 [1908]), pp. 22ff.

[12] Hyams, *King, Lords and Peasants*, p. 1.

[13] Postan, *Medieval Economy*, pp. 131ff; Maitland, *Domesday Book*, especially pp. 26–107; Alan Macfarlane, *The Origins of English Individualism: The Family, Property and Social Transition* (New York: Cambridge University Press, 1979), pp. 80–101; P.D.A. Harvey, *The Peasant Land Market in Medieval England* (Oxford: Clarendon Press, 1984).

to what I have called military-bureaucratic absolutism. It shall be argued here that the Tudors did not build extensive, intrusive state structures, did not undermine or destroy Parliamentary power, and did not build a large modern army.

There are, one might say, three towering figures in Tudor history: Henry VIII, Elizabeth, and G. R. Elton. Professor Elton has argued that Henry VIII's chief minister, Thomas Cromwell, effected a momentous modernization of the English state, a revolution in government. His reforms are said to have swept away the ill-defined and all too ineffectual household government, and introduced rationalized bureaus for administering fiscal, judicial, and other matters.[14] Over the years his arguments have been countered by contentions that household government prevailed in Henrician times, and that the growth of power in the Privy Council was more evolution than revolution.[15] It is essential to point out that neither side (nor apparently any other) contends that these changes paralleled those in Brandenburg-Prussia or France in the next century. Tudor reforms did not damage local centers of power, undermine Parliament, or abolish the rule of law. Though chancery power did rise, one must not fall prey to a seesaw metaphor in which increased royal power necessarily means a weakened Parliament. The key to the rise of the Tudor state was a coalition of the crown and, through the House of Commons, the gentry. It came at the expense not of the constitution, but of the peerage and the Roman bishops, both of which were closed elites in the upper House. In this respect, Tudor state making actually diffused political power into a social class ranging from the lower nobility to the upper yeomanry. The Tudor state grew in power within a growing consensual framework. The gentry became the Tudors' working partner in Parliament, and, in the JPs then replacing the Norman sheriffs, their administrative agents, further linking the chancery to the local gentry.[16] Even Star Chamber, the

[14] G. R. Elton, *The Tudor Revolution in Government: Administrative Change in the Age of Henry VIII* (Cambridge: Cambridge University Press, 1979), *Policy and Police: The Enforcement of the Reformation in the Age of Thomas Cromwell* (Cambridge: Cambridge University Press, 1985).

[15] Christopher Coleman and David Starkey, eds., *Revolution Reassessed: Revisions in the History of Tudor Administration and Government* (Oxford: Oxford University Press, 1986); Penry Williams, "Dr. Elton's Interpretation of the Age," *Past and Present* 25 (1963): 3–8, "The Tudor State," *Past and Present* 25 (1963): 39–58; J. P. Cooper, "A Revolution in Tudor History?" *Past and Present* 26 (1963): 110–12; G. L. Harriss, "Medieval Government and Statecraft," *Past and Present* 25 (1963): 8–39.

[16] See Wallace T. MacCaffrey, *Queen Elizabeth and the Making of Policy, 1572–1588* (Princeton, N.J.: Princeton University Press, 1981), pp. 466–99; Conrad Russell, *The Crisis of the Parliaments: English History 1509–1660* (Oxford: Oxford University Press, 1971), pp. 48–49; and G. R. Elton, *The Parliament of England 1559–1581* (Cambridge: Cambridge University Press, 1986).

harbinger of despotism in many venerable histories, consistently upheld Common Law principles; and the gentry found it a fair arbiter of disputed Parliamentary elections.[17] Within the context of the European trend toward increased state power, Elton assesses Tudor constitutionalism in this way: "On the face of it, the power of the Crown was more evident in England, too; but the discerning eye can surely see beyond to the essential constitutionalism of the Tudor monarchy."[18]

The Tudor state compares unfavorably with the Generalkriegskommissariat or the Bourbon ministries. The reforms may be best seen as necessary adaptations to an increasingly complex nation, which did not pose a threat to the ancient constitution. One can but conclude that this controversy is one of those interminable and frequently caustic debates occasionally found in English historiography, a few more of which we are bound to encounter. It is contended in this work that modern warfare requiring large quantities of resources has undermined constitutional government, so it will be useful to keep our attention on the broad constitutional concerns, and investigate the effects Tudor war making and fiscal innovations had on Parliament, local autonomy, and personal rights. Whatever the scope of Henrician and Elizabethan state building, the Tudor period experienced no military revolution or military-centered bureaucracy.

Sixteenth-century Europe was ablaze with wars stemming from religion, dynastic instabilities, commercial antagonisms, and a general sorting out of the international order. Protected somewhat by the Channel, England nonetheless took part in a few, if not always by choice. War, or disputes just short of it, took place with France over the Huguenot conflicts, and with Spain as it sought to reassert control over the Netherlands. Most of these wars were, at least for England, rather brief and did not require high levels of domestic resource mobilization. Henry VIII led armies onto the continent on several occasions: in 1513 he stood at the head of thirty-one thousand soldiers, and in the campaigns of 1544–1546 his force was fifty-two thousand. These are a bit larger than feudal levies,

[17] J. A. Guy, *The Cardinal's Court: The Impact of Thomas Wolsey in Star Chamber* (Hassocks, U.K.: Harvester Press, 1977), pp. 31–35; Mark A. Kishlansky, *Parliamentary Selection: Social and Political Choice in Early Modern England* (Cambridge: Cambridge University Press, 1986), p. 17. The view of Star Chamber as agent of despotism might stem from its use by Charles I and Archbishop Laud to punish religious opponents. But this was not until the 1630s. Only then does Maitland's observation of Star Chamber really hold true: "It was a court of politicians enforcing a policy, not a court of judges administering the law." *Constitutional History of England*, p. 263.

[18] *The New Cambridge Modern History*, Volume 2, p. 458. See also G. R. Elton, "The Rule of Law in Sixteenth-Century England," in Arthur J. Slavin, ed., *Tudor Men and Institutions: Studies in English Law and Government* (Baton Rouge: Louisiana State University Press, 1972), pp. 265–94; Plucknett, *History of the Common Law*, pp. 39–47.

but only a fraction of the armies Spain was beginning to field. Nor were they professional soldiers as in the Spanish tercios, or even knights and militiamen: the Wars of the Roses in the late fifteenth century had decimated English chivalry, and Henry VII's suppression of private war as well as the lure of agricultural enterprise had further eroded the martial skills of the nobility. Problems with deploying the militias outside their counties have already been mentioned. Henry's force was little more than a rapidly put together collection of freebooters and dregs, augmented by a few thousand Landsknechte.[19] Neither gunpowder nor even the pike made serious inroads into English armories. Instead, as if to support the saying that armies prepare to fight previous wars, bow and bill predominated, as they had a century earlier during the Hundred Years' War.

Elizabeth's wars with France and Spain had only slightly more political significance. Modern cavalry and infantry (pikemen) were introduced but again failed to become the standard.[20] Expeditionary forces, including those fighting Spain in the Netherlands, were rapidly assembled as war clouds loomed, then equally rapidly disbanded as threats diminished. War was still on the cheap, paid for by Parliamentary subsidies and ad hoc measures to which we shall turn shortly. In regard to the source of manpower, Parker states, "There is no doubt that a substantial number of the 40,000 English troops raised for service abroad between 1588 and 1595 . . . were 'undesirables' recruited against their will by magistrates who were compelled by government order to supply a fixed quota of men."[21] Although state coercion is in evidence, it was largely displaced onto criminals whose liberties were to be curtailed in any event, through legal means. However, inasmuch as Elizabethan law defined the unemployed as criminals, the magistrates' actions had some measure of coercion, though legally and constitutionally sanctioned.[22]

There were neither quantitative changes nor substantive centralization. Elizabeth, it is true, had placed Lords-Lieutenant in the counties to supervise the militias, but, as in the case of the JPs, they were appointed only after consultation with local notables.[23] Other than this, the

[19] Gilbert John Millar, *Tudor Mercenaries and Auxiliaries 1485–1547* (Charlottesville: University of Virginia Press, 1980), pp. 44–48; Sir Charles Oman, *A History of the Art of War in the Sixteenth Century* (New York: E. P. Dutton, 1937), pp. 320–48; Helen Miller, *Henry VIII and the English Nobility* (Oxford: Basil Blackwell, 1986), pp. 133–61.

[20] Corelli Barnett, *Britain and Her Army 1509–1970: A Military, Political and Social Survey* (London: Allen Lane, 1970), pp. 21–37.

[21] Geoffrey Parker, *The Military Revolution: Military Innovation and the Rise of the West, 1500–1800* (Cambridge: Cambridge University Press, 1988), p. 52.

[22] The practice of allowing petty criminals to enlist in the military rather than face confinement was not unknown in the United States during the 1960s.

[23] Barnett, *Britain and Her Army*, pp. 32–35.

"Catholic threat" led only to the construction of a beacon system and placing batteries in some coastal communities.[24] At a time when the military revolution began to sweep Europe, Parliament enacted laws aimed at encouraging Englishmen to hone their martial skills by practicing with the longbow. Some militia units, the trained bands, received a measure of modern training and weaponry, but military reform was only half-hearted, and remained so for quite some time.[25]

It is well known to anyone familiar with swashbuckling novels and films that much of English warfare was fought on the high seas. Again, however, there was no large-scale state expenditure or centralized control. The Elizabethan fleets that defeated the Armada and interdicted Spain's colonial commerce were not composed of state-financed ships of the line. Most of the ships were independent privateers, whose governmental letters of mark afforded a modicum of legality for an undertaking many might readily brand piracy. (One suspects Philip II did.) During almost two decades of naval warfare with Spain (1585–1603), England spent on average only £55,000 per year on naval forces, and with it crippled Philip's fleet and made his supplies of American bullion, Spain's sinews of war, anything but secure.[26] By way of comparison, £55,000 per year would furnish approximately eighteen thousand foot soldiers with pikes and corselets, but not with food, clothing, and other necessities. Spain spent approximately ten million ducats (4 ducats = £1) on the Armada alone, and over two million ducats per year fighting the rebellion in the Netherlands, a war that raged intermittently for eighty years.[27] Privateers proved quite successful in preventing French or Spanish land forces (whose superiority was above question) from quickly demonstrating the backwardness of the English military.[28]

---

[24] Boynton, *The Elizabethan Militia*, pp. 145ff.

[25] Stanford F. Lehmberg, *The Later Parliaments of Henry VIII, 1536–1547* (Cambridge: Cambridge University Press, 1977), p. 150; Russell, *Crisis of the Parliaments*, pp. 163–64. See also Michael Barraclough Pulman, *The Elizabethan Privy Council in the Fifteen-Seventies* (Berkeley and Los Angeles: University of California Press, 1971), pp. 188–201. For Elizabethan diplomacy and military expeditions on the continent, see R. B. Wernham, *After the Armada: Elizabethan England and the Struggle for Western Europe 1588–1595* (Oxford: Clarendon Press, 1984).

[26] H. W. Richmond, *Statesmen and Sea Power* (Oxford: Oxford University Press, 1946), cited in Paul M. Kennedy, *The Rise and Fall of British Naval Mastery* (London: Ashfield Press, 1987), p. 26.

[27] See Geoffrey Parker, *Philip II* (Boston: Little, Brown, 1978), p. 178, and *The Army of Flanders and the Spanish Road, 1567–1659: The Logistics of Spanish Victory and Defeat in the Low Countries' Wars* (Cambridge: Cambridge University Press, 1972), pp. 48–49.

[28] See Kenneth R. Andrews, *Elizabethan Privateering: English Privateering during the Spanish War, 1585–1603* (Cambridge: Cambridge University Press, 1964), *Trade Plunder and Settlement: Maritime Enterprise and the Genesis of the British Empire, 1480–1630* (Cambridge: Cambridge University Press, 1984), pp. 223–55; Kennedy, *British Naval Mas-*

Although we find neither a military revolution nor a protracted land war, the state nonetheless incurred costs greater than could possibly be covered by the traditional feudal method, the royal demesnes. Henry's second campaign in France (1544–1546) cost £1.3 million; Elizabeth spent £750,000 from 1558 to 1563 and £5.5 million from 1585 to 1603.[29] The sums were substantial, but the money was obtained by routine Parliamentary subsidies, augmented occasionally by ad hoc measures, none of which by itself or in combination secured a lasting independent source of royal revenue. Parliament remained an important source of revenue, the only sustained and reliable one. Tunnage and poundage, as well as other taxes, were granted only after haggling with a parsimonious Commons,[30] but these revenues were insufficient, and had to be enhanced by the sale of royal lands (including recently seized Church property) and precious metals of the royal family. Other measures included securing foreign loans guaranteed by Parliament (some negotiated by Gresham himself) and granting royal monopolies. The sale of royal land and plate was obviously a nonreplenishable source, foreign loans could not be made without Parliament's assent, and the monopolies yielded no lasting and formidable incomes.[31] Of Tudor finances, Stone observes:

[B]etween 1536 and 1552 the Crown laid hands on the vast property of monasteries and chantries, usually reckoned . . . to amount to at least a quarter of the country. Had this property been retained and exploited, both for the wealth it could provide and for the political and religious patronage it carried with it, it could have provided the state with overwhelming resources, which could have made it virtually independent of Parliamentary taxation. But before it had even been assimilated and absorbed, the bulk of the property was sold off to pay for war, so that by 1562 the Crown was left with an independent income which with a tight rein on expenditure was just sufficient, but no more

---

tery, pp. 24–35; Wernham, *After the Armada,* pp. 235–61; and Oman, *History of the Art of War,* p. 372. By the mid-seventeenth century, however, England indeed had a navy composed of modern fighting vessels, ships of the line as they were called. It is an irony of history that many of these ships were paid for by Charles I's controversial, though legal, ship money, the collection of which led to conflict with Parliament and, in part, to the Civil War.

[29] Millar, *Tudor Mercenaries,* p. 156; Frederick C. Dietz, *English Public Finance, 1558–1641* (New York: Barnes & Noble, 1964), pp. 16–21.

[30] Dietz, *English Public Finance,* pp. 16–75; Lehmberg, *Parliaments of Henry VIII,* pp. 40ff; Barnett, *Britain and Her Army,* pp. 48–50; Millar, *Tudor Mercenaries,* p. 156.

[31] Dietz, *English Public Finance,* pp. 16–21; Pulman, *Elizabethan Privy Council,* pp. 182–87; Wernham, *After the Armada,* pp. 80–82; Andrews, *Trade Plunder and Settlement,* especially pp. 41–100. It is critical that at this juncture the exploitation of colonial assets was granted to private enterprise in exchange for relatively small fees. The Spanish crown, it will be remembered, itself exploited colonial wealth and thereby obtained the revenue for absolutism.

than sufficient, for peace-time purposes. At the first hint of war, the Crown
was obliged to go cap in hand to Parliament for funds.[32]

The crown had to maintain support from the gentry, upon whom it relied
not only for local administration, but also for support against the magnates and sporadic anti-Reformation rebellions such as the Pilgrimage of
Grace. The gentry received no small share in the spoliated wealth, and
were in considerable control of the local disposition of seized lands. The
gentry emerged from the Reformation strengthened.[33] Elizabeth successfully pleaded with Commons for further aids in the form of grants and
loan guarantees, a situation that made her successors increasingly dependent on Parliament and a conservative money market. Elizabethan war
finance, then, began to merge state finance with both Parliament and the
merchant-dominated capital markets, a move that moderately strengthened Parliament.

Many have nonetheless come to think of the Tudor period as one of
increasing royal prerogative and seizure of person and property.[34] Tempting as it is to excuse Henry and Elizabeth, and dismiss these privations
as exceptions, more investigation is in order. As arbitrary and unfair as
such actions might seem to twentieth-century sensibilities, a strong case
can be made for their constitutionality. Parliament recognized the need
for wide discretionary powers during dangerous times, and enacted laws
that sometimes augmented, sometimes diminished, royal prerogative
powers—wartime responses that are not without analogues in twentieth-
century democracies.[35] The rule of law was intact throughout the Tudor
years: "[E]ven the queen was bound by the laws of the land—that is, was
herself subject to certain specific restrictions. . . . [A]lthough she and her
council could vary the enforcement and influence the interpretation of
law, they could go clean against it only when doing so was sufficiently
uncontroversial as to be unlikely to arouse widespread opposition."[36]

The view of the essential constitutionality of the Tudor monarchs certainly goes against the arguments of many traditional historians who have

[32] Lawrence Stone, *The Causes of the English Revolution, 1529–1642* (New York: Harper
& Row, 1972), p. 61. The author also mentions that attempts to obtain royal control of the
country's mineralogical wealth also failed to secure an independent revenue base.

[33] See Richard Lachmann, *From Manor to Market: Structural Change in England, 1536–
1640* (Madison: University of Wisconsin Press, 1987), pp. 66–99.

[34] See Sir David Lindsay Keir, *The Constitutional History of Modern Britain since 1485*,
Ninth Edition (New York: W. W. Norton, 1969), pp. 98–99.

[35] Elton, *The Parliament of England 1559–1581*, pp. 37–39. The thrust of this work is
that, *pace* Marxist and Whig historians, no deep conflict existed between crown and Parliament, and that scholars who see such conflict are distorting events to find long-term fissures
causing the Civil War in the 1640s. See also Lehmberg, *Parliaments of Henry VIII*; and
MacCaffrey, *Queen Elizabeth*, pp. 366–99.

[36] Pulman, *Elizabethan Privy Council*, p. 227.

interpreted the period as one of increasing acrimony between crown and Parliament, culminating in the Civil War of the next century. As well entrenched as this interpretation is and as aesthetically pleasing as it might be to those who equate the distant past with tradition, servility, and despotism, many recent studies, more disposed to close examination of parliamentary records and other sources, have uncovered no such increasing acrimony: the Tudor period was, as Elton put it, no high road to the Civil War.[37] Throughout the Tudor period, indeed until well into the 1630s, monarchal relations with Parliament reveal senses of mutual obligation and cooperation, not an irreversible slide to civil war. Such was the degree of trust that the medieval principle of "redress before supply" was no longer part of sessions, and, should consensual agreement elude them, monarch and Parliament alike felt disgraced.[38] Parliament granted the subsidies for the small wars in which England occasionally found itself, perhaps at times grudgingly, but that stemmed not from mistrust, but from the parsimony characteristic of all contemporary estates. Tudor and early Stuart warmaking was conducted within a consensual, constitutional framework.

THE SEVENTEENTH CENTURY: CIVIL WAR AND THE ANTINOMIES OF PARLIAMENTARY RULE

Wars figure highly in English history to 1688, but none required high levels of domestic resource mobilization. Though England was able to remain relatively uninvolved in the Thirty Years' War, constitutional conflicts nonetheless developed, foreshadowing those of the Civil War (1642–1648). The crisis and breakdown of government (1640–1642) led to open warfare between king and Parliament, and, perversely, to centralizing intrusions on the part of the Whig heroes, the Long Parliament, a turn of events that facilitated the Stuart Restoration in 1660. A final conflict with the Stuarts led to the Glorious Revolution, after which state constitutional government returned.

England was only tangentially involved in the Thirty Years' War (1618–1648). The king's relations in the Palatinate were endangered by the armies of the Counter-Reformation, and a Parliamentary consensus supported a small effort for the Protestant cause. The disbanding of Eliza-

---

[37] See G. R. Elton, "A High Road to Civil War?" in his *Studies in Tudor and Stuart Politics and Government* (Cambridge: Cambridge University Press, 1974).

[38] Conrad Russell, *Parliaments and English Politics 1621–1629* (Oxford: Clarendon Press, 1983), pp. 1–84; J.C.D. Clark, *Revolution and Rebellion: State and Society in England in the Seventeenth and Eighteenth Centuries* (Cambridge: Cambridge University Press, 1986), pp. 1–91.

beth's expeditionary forces, however, left England with no troops, save for guard units and small garrisons; the only operative militia act dated back to the time of Edward I, though Parliament allowed militias and trained bands to drill under expired Elizabethan acts. Charles was able to deploy a few thousand soldiers and raid a few coastal towns, including, in the finest traditions of the English navy, a raid on Cadiz. Unlike Drake's raid a generation earlier, however, this one was unsuccessful. Other efforts were dismal failures, and by 1625 war weariness had set in and alloyed with tensions over constitutionally ambiguous taxation. Ship money, benevolences, a forced loan, the quartering of unruly troops, and imprisonment of opponents made many feel that fundamental issues were at stake.[39] Concern was expressed by MPs and also in the country, where taxation took on less a constitutional hue than a more practical one. Pockets were emptying and local officials found that their duties incurred the wrath of neighbors, who, after all, had placed them in office: "[A] successful war could not be readily combined with the local self-government which was the tradition of the English counties. Deputy Lieutenants, like Justices of the Peace, depended for their claim to obedience on retaining trust among those they governed: in the cause of sending their countrymen into battle, those who did the king adequate service risked forfeiting their countrymen's trust."[40] The Petition of Right (1628) that followed was a classic quid pro quo between king and estates, like those of the Celtic border wars and the Hundred Years' War, and a return of the principle of "redress before supply" that had disappeared during the previous decades of close cooperation. Subsidies were granted in exchange for Charles's recognition of the illegality of certain taxation and enforcement measures—in effect, official recognition of an important parliamentary role in war making.[41] The Petition of Right also clarified many gray areas that monarchs had taken advantage of in the face of resistance from Parliament, and thereby brought about a less flexible crown-Parliament relationship, a result that makes more intelligible the breakdown thirteen years later between an intransigent Charles and the equally determined leadership of the Long Parliament.

[39] Russell, *Parliaments and English Politics*, pp. 204–59, 330–47; Derek Hirst, *Authority and Conflict: England, 1603–1658* (Cambridge, Mass.: Harvard University Press, 1986), pp. 146ff.

[40] Russell, *Parliaments and English Politics*, p. 324.

[41] Ibid., pp. 343–96; Perez Zagorin, *The Court and the Country: The Beginning of the English Revolution* (New York: Atheneum, 1971), pp. 109–12; Richard Cust, *The Forced Loan and English Politics 1626–1628* (Oxford: Oxford University Press, 1987); Lois Schwoerer, *"No Standing Armies!" The Anti-Army Ideology in Seventeenth-Century England* (Baltimore, Md.: Johns Hopkins University Press, 1974), pp. 19–32.

This of course leads us to the English Civil War, where the historiographical battles have seen almost as many casualties and atrocities as Marston
Moor and Drogheda, and where erring colleagues are, like Amalekites,
smitten boot and hip. It is, then, with considerable trepidation that the
nonspecialist sets foot on the terrain where Generals Tawney, Trevor-
Roper, Hill, and Stone fought bravely, at times savagely, but ultimately
inconclusively. Though more interested in the results of the Civil War
than in its causes, we may do well to note that whether causes lay in
class, religious, cultural, or purely political antagonisms, each interpretation contains, clearly or implicitly, issues of a fundamentally constitutional nature. The political power of a rising gentry and declining peerage, toleration of recusants and dissenters, and country opposition to a
sybaritic court all directly address issues regarding the proper distribution of power and the sanctity of individual rights.

Yet these venerable generals, looking as they did for social causes of
the war, might have fought in vain. The causes of the breakdown of consensual government and ensuing civil war, according to many recent explorations, lay more in proximate conflicts between king and Parliament,
not in the long-run, economic causes that social historians of the interwar
period sought out. The breakdown that plunged a bewildered country
into an unexpected civil war stemmed from Parliamentary opposition to
royal expedients such as ship money, and to the spread of doctrines and
bishops deemed inimitable to Puritanism. Things came to a head when
an army was needed to suppress troubles in Ireland and Scotland. Mistrust fed upon itself, no compromise could be reached, and the two
halves of constitutional government reluctantly and sadly went to war.
Let us not, then, treat the Civil War as the culmination of long-standing
grievances over Tudor policy or the exclusion of the gentry from its
proper share in political power; nor as a battle between a grasping,
would-be despot and a virtuous Parliament looking beyond the storm
clouds to a new, democratic day; but simply as a war that required some
degree of resource mobilization.[42] It is important to consider the size,
revenue sources, and political consequences of both royal and parliamentary armies.

Charles's army was naturally cut off from traditional sources of revenue
granted by Parliament. He arranged a daughter's marriage to the Prince

---

[42] For the causes of the war, see Russell, *Crisis of the Parliaments*, pp. 313–43; G. E.
Aylmer, *Rebellion or Revolution? England, 1640–1660* (New York: Oxford University Press,
1986), pp. 1–12; J. P. Kenyon, *The Civil Wars of England* (New York: Knopf, 1988), pp. 1–
47; and Clark, *Revolution and Rebellion*, pp. 1–91. Cf. the social historians' interpretations:
R. H. Tawney, "The Rise of the Gentry," *Economic History Review* 11 (1941): 1–38; Hugh
R. Trevor-Roper, "The Gentry 1540–1640," *Economic History Review* Supplement 1 (1953):
1–55; and Stone, *The Causes of the English Revolution*.

of Orange's son in the hope that he could draw upon the Netherlands' considerable resources, but in this he was disappointed: the Dutch regents would not risk disrupting commerce.[43] The king fielded an army funded by taxes levied in occupied counties, by donations from wealthy sympathizers, and by the sale of sequestered estates of Parliamentarians. Despite this, the royalist army remained small, poorly equipped, and infrequently paid; only unity of purpose and initial command superiority prevented a shorter war.[44] Parliament's forces were not large either. Owing to the nature of the war, king against Parliament, there were no constitutional disputes between the two over resource mobilization, but how would Parliament, unaccustomed to the executive side of things, handle the onus of resource mobilization, even if light? And what of conducting day-to-day government?

Despite four years of war with the king, Parliamentary forces underwent no military revolution as experienced by continental armies. Early failures led to the creation of the New Model Army, whose principal reforms were the dearistocratization of most military commands and the creation of well-organized tactical units patterned after Oliver Cromwell's Ironsides regiment of the Eastern Association. The New Model, however, never reached the twenty-one thousand men authorized by Parliament, and its finances and logistics never attained any level of regularity or coherence. No extraparliamentary source of income or central command structure developed during the Civil War. Indeed, there were serious impediments to the development of a powerful structure like the Generalkriegskommissariat. First, along with dearistocratization came Parliamentary politicking over commissions in the New Model. Various constituencies and religious groups had to be mollified by awarding them high posts. Owing to the nature of the war, forces were geographically dispersed and tactically independent, hindering development of command structures at higher levels. The Council of War (staffed by senior military persons) experienced only minor organizational growth in the course of the war. In any event, it was always beholden to Parliament,

---

[43] Pieter Geyl, *The Netherlands in the Seventeenth Century*, Part 1: *1609–1648* (New York: Barnes & Noble, 1961), p. 136. The marriage was not without future significance for the two countries, as it produced William and Mary, who returned to rule England in 1689 after the final ouster of the Stuarts.

[44] Ronald Hutton, *The Royalist War Effort 1642–1646* (London: Longman, 1982), pp. 86–94; Peter Young, *The Cavalier Army: Its Organization and Everyday Life* (London: George Allen & Unwin, 1974); David Underdown, *Revel, Riot, and Rebellion: Popular Politics and Culture in England 1603–1660* (Oxford: Oxford University Press, 1987), pp. 208–38; Parker, *The Military Revolution*, p. 59. For a general military history of the conflict, see Kenyon, *The Civil Wars of England*, pp. 48–157; and J.F.C. Fuller, *A Military History of the Western World*, Volume 2: *From the Defeat of the Spanish Armada to the Battle of Waterloo* (New York: Da Capo, 1987), pp. 85–117.

which maintained not only power of the purse, but also control of strategy.[45]

It is one of the twists of the war, and one Whig historians have ignored, that Parliament itself adopted some rather unseemly, authoritarian measures to finance the war, measures easily lost in gradualist, unilinear sweeps of English history. Parliamentary revenue was initially predicated on control of commercial centers in the south, including the customs collection offices, the traditional sources of revenue. But as the Civil War dragged on, commerce and revenue declined, requiring new sources of revenue, a development that surely must have puzzled many who viewed the war in manichean terms.[46] In 1642, quite early in the war, both Houses authorized the confiscation and sale of royalist property, as well as taxes, to be collected forcibly if need be. They were. County Committees were set up in the country, where they interfered with elections, quartered troops, and otherwise meddled in local affairs, disaffecting local notables and the populace as a whole.[47] The problem is captured best by Morrill:

> In order to win the civil war, Parliament had to trample on those very susceptibilities and conventional political wisdoms which it went to war to protect. The parliamentarian propaganda of 1642 is drenched in the language of civil liberties: of freedom from arbitrary taxation; from arbitrary imprisonment; from misguided paternalism; and from the centralizing tendencies of early Stuart monarchy. The dream-world of many Parliamentarians, particularly in the provinces, was of a well-ordered state comprising semi-autonomous local communities meeting common problems, and seeking powers to answer local needs, through free parliaments under the general regulation of a monarch whose role was that of chief justiciar and arbiter. Instead, . . . Parliament was forced to break with all the cherished nostrums conjured up by their propaganda. They fought to protect a herd of sacred cows each of which was slaughtered to propitiate the god of war. . . . Indeed, every article of the Petition of Right, the most cherished statement of the rights of the subject drawn up in the early seventeenth century, was broken by Parliament in the course of the war.[48]

[45] Mark A. Kishlansky, *The Rise of the New Model Army* (Cambridge: Cambridge University Press, 1983), pp. 41–69.

[46] J. H. Hexter, *The Reign of King Pym* (Cambridge, Mass.: Harvard University Press, 1941), pp. 13–30.

[47] Hutton, *Royalist War Effort*, pp. 105–8; Hexter, *King Pym*, pp. 17–30; Underdown, *Revel, Riot, and Rebellion*, pp. 208–38.

[48] J. S. Morrill, "The Army Revolt of 1647," in A. C. Duke and C. A. Tamse, eds., *Britain and the Netherlands*, Volume 6: *War and Society* (The Hague: Martinus Nijhoff, 1977), p. 54. See also Morrill's *The Revolt of the Provinces: Conservatives and Radicals in the English Civil War, 1603–1650* (London: Longmans, 1980), especially p. 52. Those taken by

We have an agonizingly convoluted situation that recalls the words of an American major in a different but no less convoluted war: in order to preserve the constitution, it was necessary to destroy it, or at least certain parts of it.

It would be mistaken, however, to argue that English constitutionalism was demolished at this point, and that military-bureaucratic absolutism was in the offing. Even during the 1650s, when England fought small wars with Scotland, the Dutch Republic, and Spain, and when the army swelled to perhaps as many as seventy thousand men, we find on the Parliamentary side neither an autocrat reigning above the law nor an extractive state independent of Parliament. Local autonomy was not completely or even substantially done away with. The rationale for these authoritarian measures lay not in a sustained external threat—Scotland was swiftly defeated by the New Model, and the other wars were naval duels—but in a transient internal one and attendant social unrest. Finally and most importantly, Parliament was still a major part of government. Seizures and privations were carried out in its name, through constitutional means (save of course for royal approval), by men elected by the country.

With war's end came loss of Parliamentary unity; dissension and factionalism erupted. Collapse and an effortless royal victory were avoided by Pride's Purge (1648), which dismissed many MPs and ushered in the rule of Cromwell in conjunction with the purged Parliament (or Rump) and later nominated or monitored Parliaments.[49] Conflict between Parliament and the country was aggravated as the Rump, whose linkage to the counties and towns was weaker following the purge, sought to return order to a land wracked by depression, unemployment, inflation, and near famine, but no longer by war.[50] The answer seemed to lie in central control:

> To some extent they could rely on the common acquiescence in even an unpopular government as a shield against anarchy; but for the positive implementation of policy they were bound to insist on greater direction from Whitehall. The Commonwealth was far from being the paradise of local independence of which the country gentry had dreamed in 1640. As in other areas of policy, the Rump's attitude to the local communities was the product of circumstances; and circumstances dictated centralization.[51]

---

allegories might savor the story of the naval vessel *Charles*, which was renamed *Liberty*, but which foundered shortly thereafter.

[49] Kishlansky, *New Model Army*, pp. 105–38; David Underdown, *Pride's Purge: Politics in the Puritan Revolution* (London: George Allen & Unwin, 1985), pp. 7–172.

[50] Morrill, *Revolt of the Provinces*, p. 30; Underdown, *Pride's Purge*, p. 298.

[51] Underdown, *Pride's Purge*, p. 298.

Recalcitrant sheriffs, JPs, and even County Committees were replaced at the orders of the Independents (radical Puritans) who dominated the Rump. Local militias as well as other parts of traditional local life came under the watch of Cromwell's Major Generals, who the normally egalitarian Christopher Hill says were "low-born upstarts, [who] came from outside the county: all had troops of horse behind them to make their commands effective."[52]

Was *this*, then, military-bureaucratic absolutism? Again, the intrusions and institutionalizations of Cromwell and the purged Parliaments fall short. Four differences stand out. The Rump, Barebones (1653), and later Protectorate Parliaments (1653–1660) introduced unpopular measures into the countryside, but were nonetheless elected representative assemblies. Purged or sometimes nominated, they were not ideally representative bodies—what early modern estates was?—but neither were they autocratically commanded bureaucracies, rubber stamps, or dour sanhedrins. And Cromwell himself was always committed to Parliament and gentry constitutionalism. Interest articulation and regional voice were still proffered. The intrusiveness of the Major Generals (exaggerated in many accounts anyway) was reined in after Parliament expressed opposition.[53] Perhaps the clearest evidence of the independence of Protectorate Parliaments is the fact that Cromwell had alternately to dissolve and convoke so many. The political history of the Protectorate is one of continuous conflict between Lord Protector and Parliament over a constitutional settlement, with Cromwell relenting on many points.[54] War needs were met by Parliamentary subsidy, loans, and naval booty, as well as a fair amount of arm-twisting by Whitehall, but Cromwell never resorted to or even contemplated abolishing representative government and local autonomy. The Protectorate may be seen as an anguished, largely unsuccessful, but basically constitutional effort to return England to stable government following the turmoil of the Civil War.

A second difference between the Protectorate and military-bureaucratic absolutism is the retention of much of local autonomy. While many local officials had been replaced by Whitehall, many more remained in place, either silently acquiescing or dragging their feet. Local autonomy was damaged in some areas and compromised in others, but on the whole

[52] *God's Englishman: Oliver Cromwell and the English Revolution* (New York: Harper & Row, 1972), p. 175. See also Underdown, *Pride's Purge*, pp. 292–303; and Hirst, *Authority and Conflict*, pp. 337–39.

[53] Ibid., pp. 343–56; G. E. Aylmer, *The State's Servants: The Civil Service of the English Republic 1649–1660* (London: Routledge & Kegan Paul, 1973), pp. 48–49, 305–17. Both works criticize overdrawn accounts of the rule of the Major Generals.

[54] Russell, *Crisis of the Parliaments*, pp. 390–96; Aylmer states that the 1654 elections were as free as any in the century. See *Rebellion or Revolution*, pp. 161–89.

it survived the intrusions and upheavals of the 1640s and 1650s. The extent of penetration does not compare with that of Brandenburg-Prussia or Bourbon France.[55] Third, it is important to remember that state intrusions stemmed less from the needs of a protracted war that required a permanent local presence, than from the need for law and order after a decade of upheaval, and from a reformist zeal that soon withered and fomented opposition, in Whitehall and the country. In this respect, it is important to note that constitutionalism may be damaged in ways other than the irreversible one of military-bureaucratic absolutism. Deadlock in the estates, like that of the Long Parliament prior to Pride's Purge or the Swedish *riksdag* of the next century, may also lead to a coup that damages constitutional patterns, without destroying them and replacing them with autocracy. Finally, the government of the 1650s never built self-generating bureaucratic machinery. Nor did it have a stable autocratic center to provide an element of continuity. The Lord Protector's death in 1658 led to a succession of directionless Parliaments (including the reconvened Rump and Long Parliament) and, owing to the absence of a solid *Staat für sich*, ultimately to a Stuart Restoration two years later.

The Civil War period was filled with colorful figures, turmoil, and religious fervor, but not with high levels of domestic resource mobilization. The army was certainly better equipped than Tudor armies, but not much larger, and less than half the size of the principal armies in the Thirty Years' War. Cromwell's fleets were quite large, over two hundred ships and twenty thousand men, but more than half of the ships were prizes seized on the high seas, while many others had been built years earlier with Charles's ship money.[56] Military expenditures peaked at about £1.7 million in 1655, high by English standards, but per-capita taxation in England was only one-fourth that of Prussia in 1688, and England's wealth greatly exceeded that of backward Prussia, a circumstance that greatly attenuated the strain of Protectorate fiscal demands.[57] So domestic resource mobilization was far less extensive than in Prussia but still sufficient to cause one to question how an early modern parliament, chaotic in normal times, could govern without a monarch and executive

[55] "If we consider the basic tasks of those engaged in local government, notably of the JPs and those working under them, the changes are often hard to seek; such as there were cannot always be directly related to the political changes at the national level." Aylmer, *The State's Servants*, p. 305. See also Underdown, *Pride's Purge*, pp. 309–18.

[56] Bernard Capp, *Cromwell's Navy: The Fleet and the English Revolution 1648–1660* (Oxford: Clarendon Press, 1989), pp. 4–7, 212.

[57] Russell, *Crisis of the Parliaments*, pp. 394–96; F. L. Carsten, *The Origins of Prussia* (Oxford: Clarendon Press, 1964), p. 266.

chancery. Why wasn't it like a Polish diet or the Parisian parlement during the Fronde?

The Long Parliament, which went to war with Charles, changed in composition over the next few years. At the outset of the war, royalists "seceded" from Parliament and joined their sovereign at Oxford, unwittingly aiding unity in Parliament. Shortly thereafter, Parliament expelled holders of royal monopolies. A consensus emerged of radicals militantly opposed to the Stuarts and the half-hearted who opposed Charles's policies in the 1630s, but hoped that a battle or two would lead to reconciliation.[58] With the king's defeat and capture (1648), consensus broke down and coherent government came only after the expulsion of a large number of MPs (Pride's Purge) and the abolition of the House of Lords.[59] From 1648 to 1660, government was in the hands of purged, nominated, or monitored Parliaments and a council of state composed of MPs and army officers, with Cromwell, a member of both groups, as the balancer.

An army in government must surely raise an eyebrow, for this sounds a bit like the Great Elector's move or a military coup of our own day. But generalizations about armies and politics cannot substitute for cautious analysis. Consider the composition of the New Model, especially the leadership. It was no army of freebooters or mercenaries loyal only to their paymasters or an adventurous legion commander.[60] The New Model was an army built and paid by Parliament, its officers as fiercely dedicated to gentry constitutionalism as any MP. Indeed, they came from the same local gentry cliques as did most MPs. Many officers had sacrificed much in the war against Charles, and were ill disposed to tyranny in any form. The army's intervention in government came not to extract enormous revenues to fight foreign wars, but to put an end to the drift in Parliament, which might have lead to a new royalist uprising and the undoing of the Parliamentary cause.[61] Had it been necessary to mobilize high levels of domestic resources for war, the officers might have formed the nucleus of a military-bureaucratic state, and only then might one properly speak of Cromwellian autocracy and the demise of constitutional government. But as it was, no such mobilization was needed; its presence in the state throughout the 1650s provided a measure of executive coher-

[58] Underdown, *Pride's Purge*, pp. 7–8.

[59] Kishlansky, *New Model Army*, pp. 179ff; Underdown, *Pride's Purge*, pp. 143ff.

[60] The New Model proclaimed that it was "not a mere mercenary army, hired to serve any arbitrary power of a state, but called forth . . . to the defence of our own and the people's just rights and liberties." Quoted, approvingly, in Austin Woolrych, *Soldiers and Statesmen: The General Council of the Army and Its Debates 1647–48* (Oxford: Oxford University Press, 1987), p. 14.

[61] See Austin Woolrych, *Commonwealth to Protectorate* (Oxford: Clarendon Press, 1982) and Russell, *Crisis of the Parliaments*, pp. 386–96. "If this was a military dictatorship, it was a reluctant and exceptionally legalistic one." Aylmer, *Rebellion or Revolution*, p. 173.

ence that prevented anarchy, a Stuart resurgence, and possible foreign conquest.

Is there a contradiction in a military purging Parliament and preserving constitutionalism; in an authoritarian measure preserving constitutional government and a democratic trajectory? The apparent contradiction perhaps comes from deeply ingrained assumptions, themselves products of pat unilinear histories and modern democratic socialization, that insist that good things come only from good actions, that democracy is the denouement of past generations' brave and honorable deeds. As we have seen, however, constitutionalism was begun in part by the treachery of vassals who demanded concessions from weakened suzerains to whom they once vowed fealty; it was preserved by men who selfishly feared loss of privilege and who opposed losing power to the people at least as much as losing it to a monarch; and it is continued in our own day by processes few if any, should they care to inquire, would find edifying, processes that have been likened to sausage making. The actions of the New Model are best seen, not as contradictions, but as ironies that help better to appreciate the complexities of political development, then and now.

The rule of Cromwell and the Protectorate Parliaments did not overwhelm constitutionalism. It was just intrusive enough to increase and focus hostility to the state at many levels of society, and convince them that the best course was a return to the old constitution, with, it was hoped, a monarchy made tame by fortune's blows. The Restoration was greeted with cheers, and, in a priceless bit of charivari, with roasted rumps. But it was not intended to be a return to the status quo ante bellum: that benevolences and forced loans were unconstitutional was now clear, as the Long Parliament had insisted they were twenty years earlier; and royal prerogative courts were not to be reinstituted—Common Law courts were the rule. The New Model was, to everyone's relief, rapidly demobilized, leaving only a small standing army better suited to ceremony and guarding bullion movements than to modern war. There was little change in equipment or tactics from 1660 to 1688. Although some internal operations were conducted against tobacco growers and brigands, in such cases administrative control was temporarily transferred to local magistrates.[62]

Warfare during the Restoration consisted of only small deployments to Tangiers and onto the continent, and two brief wars with the Dutch Republic (1665–1667 and 1672–1674). During these, a new executive body

[62] John Childs, *The Army of Charles II* (London: Routledge & Kegan Paul, 1976), pp. 63–69.

developed, ominously named the Cabal. Its exotic name notwithstanding, it was merely an administrative streamlining of the privy council,
which had grown to the unwieldy size of fifty. Still, there was conflict
between monarchy and Parliament over military failures and increasing
debt. Parliament forced the country out of the last Dutch War, and
ousted the king's chief minister.[63] The monarchy then attempted to rule
without Parliament, relying on loans from France, increased customs
revenues from a booming economy, and taxation of religious dissidents.[64]
It also embarked on a policy of influencing local elections, intimidating
intractable boroughs through litigational harassment, and pressuring JPs,
sheriffs, and the mayoralty of London. A new prerogative court was built
to enforce policy and punish opponents.[65] James II's attempt to rule without Parliament was a failure; opposition came from virtually every quarter, Whig and Tory alike. The last Stuart king was driven into exile, altogether rather easily, and a new dynasty was installed with the selection
of the House of Orange, a Dutch family enjoying few of the Tory loyalties
that had emboldened James. The final ouster of the Stuarts demonstrated
not only the strength of constitutional forces in England at this time, but
also the foolhardiness of attempting to build absolutism without the presence or imminence of war, which would serve to divide the estates and
provide the crown with the support, force, and rationale to deal with
domestic opposition.

After two bouts with the Stuarts, Parliament had become suspicious of
monarchal authority. It strengthened its hand by building oversight committees to work with the royal chancery on taxation, war policy, and
other matters of national import. Parliament met more often, and curtailed royal control over convening and dissolving sessions. This signaled
an initial fusion of legislature and executive, a central feature of modern
parliamentary government. Parliament was developing from an awkward
medieval estates only loosely integrated with the monarchal chancery,
and becoming an effective political body capable of assuming more state
functions.[66]

---

[63] J. R. Jones, *Country and Court: England, 1658–1714* (Cambridge, Mass.: Harvard
University Press, 1978), pp. 59–64, 184–85.

[64] Ibid., pp. 64–76.

[65] The extent of interference is illustrated by Jones's evidence that 200 localities (returning 400 of the 513 MPs) had been tampered with. J. R. Jones, *The Revolution of 1688 in
England* (London: Weidenfeld & Nicolson, 1972), p. 166. See also Jones, *Country and
Court*, pp. 237–42; and J. H. Plumb, *The Origins of Political Stability in England, 1675–
1725* (Boston: Houghton Mifflin, 1967), pp. 34–38.

[66] Jones, *Country and Court*, pp. 66–70, 267–78. Frequent Parliaments led to the development of party organizations ("the rage of parties") to assist in elections and better manage
affairs in session. This further strengthened Parliament and, as we shall see, facilitated
smoother crown-Parliament relations during the next few decades.

After this lengthy account, some recapitulation is due. England's constitutionalism traveled no simple, straightforward path. It was neither destroyed by war nor left untouched, but it did survive. The Thirty Years' War presented no challenge to the island nation and no military modernization came about. The Civil War saw no large modern armies on either side, but some state penetration, directed by Parliament, did take place. Local autonomy was treated roughly at times by Parliament, but it reasserted itself in the years leading up to and following the Restoration. No commanding bureaucracy or unlimited monarch ever emerged. James II's attempt to rule without Parliament led to his exile. Between 1600 and 1688, England was never exposed to heavy, protracted warfare requiring large, modern armies. It remained effectively removed from the continental wars; constitutional government prevailed. The decades following 1688 were quite different, though. England became involved on the continent to a much larger extent than during the Tudor and Stuart periods.

The Wars with France (1688–1713)

By the late seventeenth century, the geopolitical situation that had allowed England to remain largely uninvolved in continental wars was gone. The Habsburg attempt to control Europe originated from Europe's center, distant from England and its sea lanes, and was defeated by Sweden and France. But after its military and political revolutions of the mid-seventeenth century, France became the dominant military power, and now sought to establish hegemony. If successful, its designs on the wealth of the Dutch Republic would make it by far the most powerful nation, a state of affairs upon which the other states, particularly England, could not look with indifference, even from the perspective of across the Channel. The French threat (combined with the new king's Dutch heritage) led to the Nine Years' War (1688–1697) and the War of the Spanish Succession (1701–1713), and required the first sizable deployments of English armies on the continent since Tudor times. Owing to the number of allies, the relatively modest size of the English army, and newly developed instruments of war finance based on the country's expanding commercial wealth, domestic resource mobilization and strains on constitutional government were limited. Each of these factors was even more critical in Dutch war making, but they will be outlined here.

The wars against Louis XIV were fought by coalitions; England never confronted French might alone. It fought alongside Prussia, Spain, the Netherlands, and Austria, while Louis was allied only with smaller German principalities and Sweden, whose armies were preoccupied with Russia in the Great Northern War (1700–1721). England did not need to mobilize drastic amounts of its resources against Louis. The number of English soldiers in the War of the Spanish Succession reached seventy-five thousand at one point—still not a large army by the standards of the day, but one which could be decisive in giving advantage to a coalition.[67] Marlborough's army in the War of the Spanish Succession was not huge, but it was larger than previous armies and placed definite fiscal demands on the nation. Inasmuch as England (and the Dutch Republic) subsidized the armies of many of its allies, the financial burden cannot be dismissed. Various taxation measures (excises, hearth taxes) had been experimented with during the Restoration (1660–1688), but none was able to cover the expenses of two brief Anglo-Dutch wars. The tax-collection machinery was woefully inefficient; tax farming resulted in no greater yields, and was gradually abandoned. Public debt went up without adequate guarantees, and the government's inability to repay led to a financial crisis in 1672.[68] By the later years of the century, during the wars with France, the means of floating long-term national debt had developed, which led to the founding of the Bank of England, fiscal instrument par excellence of English war making.[69] The country could mobilize future revenue's and allocate them to the coalitional wars against Louis. England became, as the author of an excellent recent study put it, "a fiscal-military state."[70]

At this point, English public debt might seem to have magically res-

---

[67] Barnett, *Britain and Her Army*, p. 142. The size of the army was also determined by domestic difficulties in raising an army. The nation, still perturbed by the treatment of the New Model Army, was loath to allocate the money to assemble a sizable force that might attempt to force its will on Englishmen. A broad-based hostility to the army pervaded, and conscription had to be authorized by Parliament. Of the forty thousand soldiers in the English army of Flanders, fewer than half were British; the rest were mainly German and Danish mercenaries. See Barnett, *Britain and Her Army*, pp. 140–42; *The New Cambridge Modern History*, Volume 6, p. 411.

[68] C. D. Chandaman, *The English Public Revenue, 1660–1688* (Oxford: Clarendon Press, 1975), pp. 1–228; *The New Cambridge Modern History*, Volume 5, pp. 302–3; P.G.M. Dickson, *The Financial Revolution in England: A Study in the Development of Public Credit 1688–1756* (London: Macmillan, 1967), pp. 42–44.

[69] Ibid., pp. 42ff; *The New Cambridge Modern History*, Volume 6, pp. 285–88. For statistics on national debt and expenditures, see Dickson, *Financial Revolution*, p. 10.

[70] John Brewer, *The Sinews of Power: War, Money and the English State, 1688–1783* (London: Unwin Hyman, 1989). Brewer might underestimate the role of alliances in English military power during this period. England relied not only on foreign armies but also on foreign money: a sizable percentage of investments in the Bank of England came from Dutch merchants. See Dickson, *Financial Revolution*, pp. 249–330; C. R. Boxer, *The Dutch Seaborne Empire, 1600–1800* (London: Penguin, 1988), pp. 123–25. As late as 1777, the Dutch held forty percent of English national debt. See R. R. Palmer, *The Age of the Democratic Revolution*, Volume 1 (Princeton, N.J.: Princeton University Press, 1959), p. 324.

cued fair England from the perils of domestic resource extraction. It might be asked why this method of war finance was adopted by England (and the Dutch Republic), but not by the Great Elector or Richelieu, neither of whom was without resourcefulness and cunning. Part of the answer lies in the countries' respective levels of economic development. The advanced capital markets on which war finance depends are, quite obviously, found only in relatively developed countries such as the Dutch Republic and England, and the latter experienced a remarkable economic boom in the second half of the seventeenth century.[71] These maritime powers derived large amounts of wealth from control of shipping and commerce, and to a lesser extent the exploitation of colonies in the New World and elsewhere. This contrasts with the static, agrarian economies of Brandenburg and France. (The latter, though more developed than Brandenburg, did not become a major economic power until after the constitution had been undone and Colbert embarked on economic development programs.) Effective guarantees to bankers meant convoking the estates. In a largely static agrarian economy, estates will find financing a modern army exorbitant and intolerable (leading to the decisions of the Great Elector and Richelieu to rule without the estates), whereas estates in a dynamic, commercial economy will find the same level of military finance less onerous, perhaps markedly so.

In addition to commercial wealth, an institutional factor also accounts for the smoothness of English war making after 1688. Parliament had become more of a modern governing body. Traditional histories have made this point, but perhaps too baldly.[72] Parliament had by no means subordinated the monarchy in 1688, in 1714, or at any time in the eighteenth century, for that matter. Most of the Parliamentary safeguards enacted after the Glorious Revolution were never insisted upon: the Bill of Rights proscribed standing armies but Parliament regularly financed armies; triennial elections became tiresome and costly, leading to the Septennial Act (1716); oversight committees disappeared in 1714; and impeachment of royal ministers was a lengthy procedure rarely even pondered. William of Orange and George I may be numbered among the strongest of

---

[71] D. C. Coleman, *The Economy of England 1450–1750* (Oxford: Oxford University Press, 1978), pp. 131–50. The author suggests that these innovations in paying for war served to assist England's future economic development: "The economy whose entrepreneurs were the first to launch the industrial revolution did not do so on a basis of free trade and economic liberalism, but of protection created, in part at least, by the needs of war finance" (p. 195). See also Peter Padfield, *The Tide of Empires: Decisive Naval Campaigns in the Rise of the West*, Volume 2: *1654–1763* (London: Routledge & Kegan Paul, 1982), pp. 118–20.

[72] See Keir, *Constitutional History*, pp. 252–74.

English monarchs, and the monarchy remained a powerful institution throughout the eighteenth century.[73]

The key to Parliamentary development after 1688 lies not in the decline of the monarchy—the baleful seesaw metaphor often encountered in Tudor history might be trying to reassert itself here—but in the increased power of king *and* Parliament. To a certain extent, this development is attributable to the seventeenth-century constitutional struggles that led to some warfare but not to absolutism. Conflicts with the Stuarts led to heightened awareness of an internal constitutional danger and of national politics as a whole. When the Glorious Revolution ousted the internal danger in the person of James II, and he allied with Louis XIV, national and international matters merged, and defense of the constitution was inexorably linked to an external Jacobite-Bourbon threat. More importantly, however, was the development of political parties following the Restoration in 1660. Though we encounter the term in the 1640s with the "war party" and "peace party," these were really transient factions, without organizational backbone, without lasting significance.[74] It was not until after 1660 that Whigs and Tories began to coalesce on either side of the issue of monarchal strength, and, with the routinization of elections after 1688, rapidly so. Party organizations came into being to manage country elections and matters of government in London.[75] Parliament was no longer akin to the chaotic medieval estates that kings on the continent sometimes had to disband in order to defend the realm. It now had routine procedures and organizations that could build consensus and, in conjunction with the monarchy, more smoothly govern the country. War blended the two halves of constitutional government, as it had during the Hundred Years' War: "The pressure of business connected with the French Wars imposed a rhythm and routine down to 1712. Parliament met every year, with sessions beginning in the autumn. . . . The

[73] Clark, *Revolution and Rebellion*, pp. 70–80; J.C.D. Clark, *English Society 1688–1832: Ideology, Social Structure and Political Practice during the Ancien Regime* (Cambridge: Cambridge University Press, 1988). Perhaps the best check Parliament had on the monarchy was a rather dishonorable one: rampant venality of army commissions ensured that the army was no tool of the monarch. Of the 374 regimental colonels between 1714 and 1763, 152 of them had been in Commons, "a sign not of the militarization of government but of the permeation of the military by civilian politics." Brewer, *Sinews of Power*, p. 44.

[74] "[Parties in the 1640s] were at best loose, amorphous, and transient, with neither discipline nor organization; vaguely identifiable groups of men who happened for a time to think alike on one or more of the major issues of the day." Underdown, *Pride's Purge*, pp. 45–46.

[75] Jones, *Country and Court*, pp. 33, 267–68; W. A. Speck, *Tory and Whig: The Struggle in the Constituencies 1701–1715* (London: Macmillan, 1970). Both works are highly critical of Walcott's earlier work, which argued that parties had not yet emerged. See Robert Walcott, Jr., *English Politics in the Early Eighteenth Century* (Cambridge, Mass.: Harvard University Press, 1956).

primary business was to pass supply bills to finance the next year's campaign, so that a regular duration became conventional."[76]

The year 1688 ushered in new constitutional as well as geopolitical configurations. England became increasingly involved in continental wars against France, but none threatened the constitution. Domestic resource mobilization was attenuated by alliances—which in effect allocated Dutch, Spanish, and Austrian resources against Louis—and by the emergence of national debt to finance war.[77] Its economy booming, repayment was easier, future revenues were more confidently relied upon, and a smaller proportion of national wealth was mobilized for war, further decreasing potential internal conflicts. The monarchy did not defeat the estates as in Brandenburg-Prussia and France; neither had Parliament in any way subordinated the monarchy. At the outset of the eighteenth century, government in England was, as it had been at the outset of the seventeenth, composed of king and Parliament working within a consensual framework.

. . .

In order to examine England using the analytical framework of this study, it has been necessary to divide its history into three parts. In the first, from the Tudor period until the outbreak of the Civil War in 1642, the country endured no war comparable to the struggles in Germany. Tudor expeditions were small, and amateur forces disbanded as soon as the last shot had been fired. Participation in the Thirty Years' War was slight for the fortunate island nation. Second, the Civil War and ensuing conflicts led to a somewhat modernized but only medium-sized army, and to meddlesome, often authoritarian, but ultimately transient local penetration by the state, at whose head stood not an autocrat, but Cromwell and Parliament. A third period, that from 1689 to 1713, covered major wars with France, and required increases in military outlays, despite the ameliorating presence of powerful allies and the still far from large size of the army. Domestic extraction was also limited owing to the availability of

[76] Jones, *Country and Court*, p. 26. This routine, the author continues, served to further party organization.

[77] A third, rather minor, factor limiting domestic resource mobilization may be pointed out. The Duke of Marlborough eschewed conventional military wisdom and, like the Swedish army, relied on plunder to support his army in a decisive campaign. His system of supply, or lack thereof, might have seemed to augur poorly, but his magnificent Blenheim estate is evidence that mobile foraging could still be used successfully against more rationally supplied militaries. See Barnett, *Britain and Her Army*, pp. 144–45; Martin van Creveld, *Supplying War: Logistics from Wallenstein to Patton* (New York: Cambridge University Press, 1977), pp. 32–33; Fuller, *Military History*, Volume 2, pp. 127–55.

sufficient commercial wealth brought in from overseas, mediated through the Bank of England and a modernizing Parliament. It was upon this wealth and its institutionalization in the form of private banks that English power rested.

The ancient constitution was preserved. England entered the eighteenth century with the medieval legacy of Parliament, local autonomy, and personal freedoms quite healthy. We can in no sense, however, meaningfully derive the political trajectory following 1713 from the present analysis. Put another way, liberal democracy does not necessarily follow from the survival of medieval constitutional arrangements. It would take, inter alia, a dynamically expanding economy, political balance between parties leading to franchise extension, and several other factors, small and large, in order to achieve liberal democracy. None of these follows necessarily from our ending point in 1713, and, as such, they fall well outside the scope of this study. The issue at hand is the preservation of a constitutional basis for liberal democracy in the crucible of early modern military conflicts.

One of many problems in a comparative study is to avoid exaggerating the contrasts. This is all the more important when the categories are dictatorship and democracy, and comparisons can take on manichean qualities, contrasting the forces of good and evil. It is important not to draw the lines of difference between Prussia and England too simplistically. Neither England nor any other country of the time was a democracy or anything really like one, and comparisons between England and Prussia reveal important similarities. Foremost, in the eighteenth century, after absolutism had consolidated in Prussia and constitutionalism had in England, both were essentially monarchal-aristocratic countries in which nobles received extraordinary privileges in the form of exemptions, office, and access to the king's ear—for the most part to the detriment of state efficiency and honesty, and probably more so in England than in Prussia, where government was autocratic but less corrupt. Furthermore, state ownership of some forms of industry and commanding heights over others was not unheard of in seventeenth-century England, even after the dissolution of most royal monopolies in the 1640s. Shortages of timber and iron (critical for naval vessels) during wars with the Dutch led to state-owned enterprises. Shipbuilding contracts gave the English state considerable clout in the years before the Industrial Revolution.[78] But it is important to bear in mind that ownership of industry and clout were not wielded solely by a royal bureaucracy as in Prussia

[78] See G. Hammersley, "The State and the English Iron Industry in the Sixteenth and Seventeenth Centuries," as well as other essays in D. C. Coleman and A. H. John, eds., *Trade, Government and Economy in Pre-Industrial England: Essays Presented to F. J. Fisher* (London: Weidenfeld & Nicolson, 1976).

but, rather, by a monarchy in conjunction with Parliament, which eventually pressed for the privatization of iron and timber concerns, and whose Whigs and Tories later wrested control of contracts to build patronage networks.[79]

So state ownership of enterprise was not unknown, and neither was the abrogation of individual rights in the name of military necessity. The manpower requirements of the French wars were not met by appeals to the patriotic ardor of Englishmen. Attempts in 1707 to build an army of sixteen thousand for deployment in Flanders had a year later yielded fewer than a thousand soldiers from the nation, an embarrassing situation that led to reluctant passage of a conscription act. Accordingly, many an unfortunate lad had to be hoodwinked or overtly impressed into military service by unscrupulous recruiting sergeants. Without the necessary machinery for a national system of conscription, such measures were the only ones available. Though trickery and impressment were measures that challenge roseate views of the long-standing rights of Englishmen, comparison with the Prussian Kantonsystem is unwarranted. Impressments were by no means routine parts of life, the male populace was not tied to a local regiment, and impressment was authorized during times of war by act of Parliament, and hence reflected a sense of the country rather than a royal decree.[80] Legality might not have consoled the unfortunate lads who toasted the king's health with a recruiting sergeant, but it is important for constitutional questions.

The difficulties in meeting manpower requirements were part and parcel of a general cultural hostility to militarism, which predates the Civil War, but was greatly increased by the rough hands of the New Model Army. Parliament tried to prevent any such recurrence by keeping standing armies to a bare minimum, and, through the purchase of commissions, by ensuring that the officer corps remained the privileged vocation (one is tempted to say avocation) of the aristocracy, often MPs and their relatives.[81] If avoidance of another Colonel such as Pride came at the cost

---

[79] Hammersley, "The State and the English Iron Industry," pp. 178–79; Linda Colley, *In Defiance of Oligarchy: The Tory Party 1714–60* (Cambridge: Cambridge University Press, 1985), pp. 122–25.

[80] Barnett, *Britain and Her Army*, pp. 140–42. Distinctions between crude impressments and a more genteel conscription system, between trickery and modern recruitment advertisements, must be drawn cautiously.

[81] See Cecil Woodham-Smith, *The Reason Why* (New York: Atheneum, 1982), pp. 21–26; and Brewer, *Sinews of Power*, p. 44. Venality also reduced military expenditures: "[T]he purchase system offered the state and nation such solid financial advantages that it became a rooted institution. If officers could gain their main income privately out of rackets, there was no need to pay them economic salaries; and there was thus a marked saving on the cost of the army, to the great joy of a grudging tax-payer." Barnett, *Britain and Her Army*, p. 138. On general antipathy toward the military, see Schwoerer, *"No Standing Armies!"*

of too many like Blimp and Flashman . . . well, that was an agreeable trade-off. So one discernible consequence, or price, of the survival of constitutionalism was the quality of the English army, which remained in almost all respects inferior to the juggernauts of continental absolutisms. Without an organization to standardize promotion guidelines, research and development of new weapons and tactics, and professional codes, the army remained backward, venal, and barely competent. It would take the grim lessons of the Crimean War to force badly needed reforms. No country benefited more from alliances and the balance of power than recidivist Albion, but then no country's medieval constitutionalism has had a greater legacy.

CHAPTER EIGHT

Sweden

THE SWEDISH CASE illustrates that the linkage between engagement in warfare with modernized armies and the destruction of medieval constitutionalism is not a direct one. Domestic resource mobilization is the crucial intermediary between warfare and constitutional change. In order to finance modern warfare, Brandenburg-Prussia and France mobilized their own resources, to the detriment of constitutional patterns. Spared protracted large-scale war for most of the seventeenth century, England maintained a constitutional trajectory. Sweden was not spared by continental wars. It was as heavily involved as Spain and France, but the constitution endured. During the Thirty Years' War, Sweden availed itself of foreign resources in Germany, obviating pressures to dismantle constitutional government. Though there was substantial rationalization of the state, the constitutional impact of this otherwise cataclysmic war that so shaped the history of Europe was not proportionate to its military involvement.

Sweden's constitutional government encountered another threat: a curious form of absolutism mixing militarism and populism. A second period, that of Caroline absolutism, will be examined. Like Cromwell's rule in England, this period saw damage to constitutional practice, more than the Lord Protector's rule had inflicted, but it was by no means military-bureaucratic absolutism. Constitutional government was weakened, pushed to one side perhaps, but Caroline absolutism could not completely do away with constitutional institutions without losing its popular base, part of which was fused with the king's state. When Charles XII attempted to move toward firmer control, that is, in the direction of military-bureaucratic absolutism, the estates reasserted themselves at the expense of the monarchy and redirected the nation toward constitutionalism.

CONSTITUTIONAL GOVERNMENT IN SWEDEN

Swedish constitutionalism differed in important ways from that in most of Western Europe, but it was no less vigorous and no less significant for that country's political development. Indeed, in some respects, notably village government and peasant rights, Sweden was far ahead of its fellow

European countries, including England. Rough topography and remoteness from the medieval empires prevented the introduction of feudalism into Sweden, and, though slavery had been known during the days of the Viking raiders, it had disappeared by the fourteenth century.[1] Late medieval Sweden knew no repressed labor, and freeholds accounted for over fifty percent of the land distribution in 1523.[2]

The absence of feudal authority also resulted in the persistence of ancient forms of village government. Medieval Sweden had three levels of local institutionalization. The provinces forming the national union had representative assemblies (*landsting*), combining legislative and judicial functions. Presiding over the assembly was the popularly elected *lagman*, who acted as provincial magistrate, circuit judge, and administrative link to the villages and village hundreds.[3] It is here, at the level of the hundreds, that we find the core of local constitutionalism. The hundreds moot was an informal assembly where the yeomanry and free peasants openly debated and noisily decided local matters. The moot evolved into a popularly elected standing body, both court of law and executive, handling elections to the national parliament (riksdag), justice, public works, local taxes, and charities.[4] The vitality of the ting and other aspects of local government approaches that of a Tönniesian ideal:

> [It] was a robustly democratic body, in which every tax-paying peasant was entitled to take part. Meetings still often took place in the open air, procedures were rude though formalistic, and the voice of the commonalty could make itself heard with effect. And this primitive democracy was an essential characteristic of Swedish society. It appeared again in the village councils, which regulated petty local affairs, in the elected vestry men, who managed parochial business, and—perhaps most important of all—in the standing jury of the county, which, drawn as it was from peasants of local weight and reputation, provided a real safeguard for the poor man entangled in the antique complexities of the law.[5]

[1] Thomas Lindkvist, "Swedish Medieval Society: Previous Research and Recent Developments," *Scandinavian Journal of History* 4 (1979): 253–68; Michael Roberts, *The Early Vasas: A History of Sweden, 1523–1611* (Cambridge: Cambridge University Press, 1968), p. 28. My debt to the work of Professor Roberts is great. His discerning eye for the interplay between military organization and constitutional questions is such that it is only a small overstatement to say that the arguments of this chapter could be made by interposing several quotes from his writings. I hope it is a little more.

[2] Ibid., p. 38.

[3] Michael Roberts, *Gustavus Adolphus: A History of Sweden, 1611–1632*, Volume 1 (London: Longmans, Green, 1953), pp. 315–42; Roberts, *The Early Vasas*, pp. 39–40; Ingvar Andersson, *A History of Sweden* (Stockholm: Natur och Kultur, 1962), pp. 32–33; *The Cambridge Medieval History*, Volume 4, pp. 369–70. The hundred (*härad*), like its Anglo-Saxon namesake, was a community above the village level with a degree of political authority.

[4] Roberts, *Gustavus Adolphus*, Volume 1, pp. 325–26.

[5] Roberts, *The Early Vasas*, pp. 39–40. For the continued resilience of local government

Kingship, when it came to Sweden in the late medieval period, was superimposed on a congeries of well-entrenched local governments, more than equal to the task of thwarting attempts by a grasping crown or nobility to expand power at the expense of commoners.[6]

The vigor of the village may be contrasted with the weakness of the middle classes. As late as the early modern period, Sweden was an economically backward land, only slowly and reluctantly emerging from slash-and-burn agriculture. The economy was largely unmonetarized and peasants often paid taxes in kind. The thriving towns of Flanders and Germany had no counterparts to the north. Commerce existed, but more often than not under the tutelage of Dutch and German merchants.[7] In fact, Sweden was often at war to free itself of constraints placed on it by Hanse merchants. Swedish middle classes played only a minor role in their country's constitutional history.

A larger role was played by the two-tiered aristocracy (magnates and minor nobility), which exchanged military service (*Rusttjanst*) for privileges and immunities. Unlike typical Western feudalism, however, this system did not endow the noble with labor to work his estate; nor were his lands and privileges sufficient to make the average aristocrat especially wealthy. Poor nobles—an oxymoron perhaps, but not a rarity— sought supplementary employment in the small state bureaucracy.[8] Above the majority of the aristocracy was the magnate class (*Högadel*). A relatively small, tightly knit elite of great landowners, the magnates figured highly in their country's constitutional history. Their preeminence in state councils and the army, intermittent conflicts with the crown, and frequent antagonisms with much of the nation are recurrent themes.[9] It was they who, like the English baronage at Runnymede, forced a constitutional charter from the crown. The Land Law of 1350, as it is known, was a written constitution outlining fundamental principles governing relations among the crown, nobility, clerics, burghers, and peasants. It was invoked twice to depose kings (1439 and 1600) and to ensure magnate influence in the state. Its basic tenets were in the oath kings took at their coronations: the king himself was bound by law; land was recognized as property and could be seized only in accordance with specified procedures; policy had to be made in conjunction with the magnate council

in the eighteenth century, see Birgitta Ericsson, "Central Power and Local Right to Dispose over the Forest Common in Eighteenth-Century Sweden," *Scandinavian Journal of History* 5 (1980): 75–92.

[6] *The Cambridge Medieval History*, Volume 6, p. 363; Roberts, *Gustavus Adolphus: A History of Sweden, 1611–1632*, Volume 2 (London: Longmans, Green, 1958), pp. 150–51.

[7] Claude Nordmann, *Grandeur et liberté de la Suéde (1660–1792)* (Paris: Béatrice-Nauwelaerts, 1971), pp. 36–38; Roberts, *Gustavus Adolphus*, Volume 2, pp. 326–27.

[8] Ibid., pp. 49–53.

[9] Kurt Ågren, "Rise and Decline of an Aristocracy: The Swedish Social and Political Elite in the 17th Century," *Scandinavian Journal of History* 1 (1976): 55–80.

(*råd*); and matters of national interest, including taxes, war, and law, had to be approved by the riksdag.[10] The Land Law had enormous import for Sweden's political history:

> [I]t stood as a constitutional norm to which appeal could be made, and against which existing conditions could be measured. It was in itself a constitution; and its influence on the subsequent course of Swedish history is comparable with that of Magna Carta upon the history of England. And, as with Magna Carta, it was capable of being made the jumping-off ground for constitutional developments—and particularly for further restraints upon royal authority—not all of which were necessarily implicit in its text or consonant with its spirit.[11]

The national parliament or riksdag has rather obscure origins in the late fifteenth century, but its procedures and competences seem to have attained a measure of consistency during the sixteenth. King Gustav Vasa used the embryonic riksdag as an ally in his rivalry with the magnates, and in so doing inadvertently bestowed upon it unintended prestige and purviews.[12] By the outset of the seventeenth century, the riksdag was probably the most democratic parliament in all Europe. It contained a chamber for nobles, burghers, and clerics, as well as one for the peasantry. The majority of male peasants could vote; only tenants on noble lands were excluded.[13] Owing to the weakness of the burghers, the aristocracy was the main mover in the riksdag, but support from the peasant estate was often critical. In 1600 the lowest but largest estate was instrumental in the ouster of an unpopular monarch. The clergy was excluded from high office following the Reformation, but nonetheless retained representation in the riksdag, generally siding with the peasantry, although a minority supported the nobility owing to the latter's control of offices in the countryside and tendency to withhold tithes from intractable vicars.[14]

[10] Michael Roberts, *On Aristocratic Constitutionalism in Swedish History, 1520–1720* (London: Athlone, 1966); Stellan Dahlgren, "Charles X and the Constitution," in Michael Roberts, ed., *Sweden's Age of Greatness, 1632–1718* (New York: St. Martin's Press, 1973), p. 180. The råd was similar to the magnate council of medieval England but, whereas the latter had become a Tudor organ comprised mostly of members of the middle classes, the råd remained a strong baronial check on royal power.

[11] Roberts, *The Early Vasas*, p. 41.

[12] Ibid., pp 82–83, 189–94, 226, 433–36; *The Cambridge Medieval History*, Volume 8, p. 548. See also Erik Lönroth, "Representative Assemblies of Modern Sweden," *Studies Presented to the International Commission for the History of Representative and Parliamentary Institutions* 18 (1958): 123–32.

[13] Roberts, *Gustavus Adolphus*, Volume 1, p. 301. The author suggests that some pressure might have been exerted at elections owing to the presence of royal bailiffs, but this does not seem to have shaped constitutional patterns.

[14] Stellan Dahlgren, "Estates and Classes," in Roberts, *Age of Greatness*, pp. 115–16.

A national monarchy was established in 1523 with the accession of Gustav Vasa (r. 1523–1560), who united with the aristocracy to break free from confederation with Denmark. The monarchy was initially weak and remained elective until the end of the century.[15] The royal chancery was ill-defined and unbureaucratic. In an oblique comparison to the Tudor revolution in government, Roberts quips, "No dazzling revelation of the transcendant importance of the Wardrobe or the Chamber is ever likely to illumine the undifferentiated obscurity of the institutional history of mediaeval Sweden."[16] Penetration of the countryside by royal authority was light, and where it obtained, it cooperated harmoniously with local government. Throughout the fifteenth and sixteenth centuries, kings appointed provincial bailiffs to manage crown lands and to provide communication ties with the provinces. Although the network of bailiffs grew with the spoliation of ecclesiastical lands during the Reformation, and despite the construction of regional *ståthållare* to supervise the bailiffs, royal officials did not supplant local officials in the hundreds and provinces. But it was never the bailiff's mission to do so; his was mainly to collect rents and taxes approved by the riksdag. Perhaps the severest point of conflict between royal agent and moot lay in the former's disposition toward peculation, which itself suggests limits on royal control.[17]

Initially frail, the house of Vasa grew in strength during the sixteenth century for two reasons. Gustav Vasa and his successors, like early Tudors, rallied lower classes to their side in disputes with the magnates. Though the power of the king vis-à-vis the aristocracy increased, it was at the expense of introducing lower orders into the political process; one consequence of this step, the rise of the riksdag, has been mentioned.[18] Both monarchy and riksdag emerged strengthened. Second, the monarchy was successful in developing sources of revenue that reduced magnate influence, though not that of the riksdag. Revenues from customs and the land's mineral wealth gave the crown sufficient funds for household government.[19] This itself is hardly unusual and does not deviate from the pattern of medieval constitutionalism: monarchs throughout medieval Europe were expected, whenever possible, to finance government from their demesnes and routine revenues. But the Vasas of the

---

[15] Andersson, *History of Sweden*, pp. 41, 120–21; Roberts, *The Early Vasas.*

[16] Ibid., p. 122.

[17] Roberts, *Gustavus Adolphus*, Volume 1, pp. 315–19.

[18] Rallying lower-class support against the magnate is a recurrent theme in Swedish history. As shall be shown, it was the basis for the populist absolutism of Charles XII, as well as for the Age of Liberty that followed.

[19] Michael Roberts, *The Swedish Imperial Experience, 1560–1718* (Cambridge: Cambridge University Press, 1979), pp. 30–31, *The Early Vasas*, pp. 187–89, *Gustavus Adolphus*, Volume 2, pp. 88–104.

late sixteenth century were also able to wage small wars on the Baltic littoral with their revenues. War-making capacity independent of the riksdag suggests one characteristic of military-bureaucratic absolutism, and has encouraged many to describe these kings as absolute monarchs. The compatibility of this war-making capacity with constitutional government calls for discussion.

First, the riksdag and magnate råd did not cease to operate; in fact, they supported the wars, politically and financially. They remained parts of consensual government.[20] Second, the copper, iron, and silver mines from which the crown derived revenue were not state enterprises. They were owned by nobles and often commoners, who, like the medieval burghers on the continent, exchanged revenue for local autonomy and privileges, and hence the process contained a definite quid pro quo that advanced constitutionalism.[21] The most important aspect of this state of affairs is the nature of the Swedish army, which was neither feudal nor modern, but was highly supportive, indeed a part of constitutionalism. Gustav Vasa initially relied on German mercenaries to win independence from Denmark, but soon found them unreliable in suppressing an anti-Reformation rebellion (Dacke's Revolt of 1543), and also too burdensome on the treasury. His solution was a system of national conscription (*utskrivning*), able to field an army of modest size and armament, capable of acquitting itself well against the armies of Poland and pre-Petrine Russia.[22] Centralization at the expense of local government was limited by cooperation and codetermination of utskrivning with local officials, and by the extension of tax immunities to soldiers.[23] Meshing local and central authority actually solidified and further legitimated assemblies and customs in the localities. The Swedish army was a national one, predating by hundreds of years the armies of the French Revolution and the mass armies of the nineteenth century. It differed markedly from the instrument of royal power in Brandenburg-Prussia, and resembled in critical ways the soldier-citizen armies of Republican Rome, which were the basis of ancient democracy.[24]

[20] Roberts, *The Early Vasas*, pp. 181–89.

[21] Ibid., p. 32.

[22] Ibid., pp. 138–39; *Gustavus Adolphus*, Volume 2, pp. 190–215; Alf Åberg, "The Swedish Army, from Lützen to Narva," in Roberts, ed., *Age of Greatness*, pp. 265 87.

[23] Roberts, *Gustavus Adolphus*, Volume 2, pp. 207–9. On the interplay between center and periphery, one author has said, "[T]here was something like a system of conscription resting on free agreement between the provinces and the king." Åberg, "The Swedish Army," p. 265. One might point out the comparable arrangement between national and local government in the old American system of conscription.

[24] "[T]his was no ordinary army of mercenaries, bound to the sovereign by strong ties of self-interest, alien to the country in which it served, and indifferent to the constitutional and social implications of royal policies. The men lived too close to the soil, they were too

Thus far, four important differences between Sweden's medieval constitutionalism and that of the European pattern have been underlined: weak towns and middle classes, highly developed village government and personal rights, peasant representation in the national parliament, and a national army that itself strengthened constitutionalism. To this must be added the essentially volatile nature of Swedish politics. The power of the crown vis-à-vis the magnate stratum rises and falls throughout the sixteenth and seventeenth centuries with far more regularity than encountered elsewhere. During the confederation with Denmark, the magnates rallied the commonalty to its side; in the late sixteenth century, it was the crown that won lower-class support in its conflict with the magnates; in the seventeenth, magnate regencies were followed by populist movements that strengthened the monarchy.[25] These vicissitudes notwithstanding, lurches in power did not precipitate civil war, and constitutional government was never undermined. No Vasa king ruled without considerable support from the country. There was only temporary ascendency or decline of the crown or the high aristocracy, with neither able to establish autocracy or oligarchy. It is critical to note that these conflicts entailed garnering support from lower classes, often from the peasantry. Such appeals advanced the cause of constitutionalism by forcing elites to settle disputes by bringing other social groups into government and thereby further obstructing the possibility of autocracy or oligarchy.

WARFARE IN THE EARLY MODERN PERIOD

In the seventeenth century, Sweden reluctantly entered the great wars on the continent and became one of the principal combatants in the Thirty Years' War. It fielded huge armies that defeated or deadlocked the legions of the great military powers of the day, and did so without mobilizing its own resources. Instead, the Hammer of Europe, as Sweden was fearfully called, relied mainly on mobilizing the resources of foreign territories. Sweden also benefited from subsidies from common enemies of the Habsburgs, of which there were many. Though secondary to the revenue from German resources, French and Dutch subsidies came at critical times, buoying the army in times of dearth. Let us look at Swedish

---

intimately associated with their families and friends, for the spirit of the barracks to develop, or the professional soldiers contempt for civilian attitudes and sensibilities to take root. Between this sort of army and the civilian population the distance was too small, at times scarcely perceptible, and their interests and outlooks tended to be the same. It is hardly too much to say that the nature of Sweden's standing army, as Gustav Vasa founded it in 1544, was one of the most powerful negative factors in securing the survival of popular liberties, and in shoring up the concept of the rule of law." Roberts, *The Early Vasas*, p. 139.

[25] Ibid., pp. 5–6, 82–83, 327–93, 426–35.

military power prior to entry into the Thirty Years' War in 1630, the army and its means of support during the great war, and the impact on the state back home.

At the end of the sixteenth century and the outset of the seventeenth, Sweden was almost constantly at war. Denmark harbored plans to reestablish control over its erstwhile confederate, and the collapse of the Livonian Knights on the Baltic littoral presented a power vacuum that, if filled by the Muscovite principality (as popular legend had foretold), would endanger Swedish security.[26] Incursions into Livonia and Courland led to wars with Poland and Russia. Though not lacking in courage or cohesiveness, the armies of Charles IX and the youthful Gustavus Adolphus were greatly inferior to the modern ones rumbling distantly to the south, but Sweden was not yet facing them. The Swedish military was small and ill-equipped, all too often performing badly against Polish cavalry and Danish mercenaries, but nonetheless able to establish a defensive glacis across the Baltic. Transportation and supply of these trans-Baltic engagements were achieved by means of a small navy.[27] These forces, which never exceeded fifteen thousand men, were paid and outfitted mainly from ordinary royal revenues and routine parliamentary aids, but Sweden also began to use a method of covering war expenses that it would use extensively and successfully in the Thirty Years' War—mobilizing the economic resources of foreign countries in which it was fighting. Prior to entering the Thirty Years' War, Sweden built an empire and a reputation as a regional military power, but it did so without building a large modern army, at the expense of Poland and pre-Petrine Russia, neither of which had modernized its military systems.

The Thirty Years' War ended Sweden's enjoyment of supremacy in the minor leagues of northeastern Europe. Catholic armies under Tilly and Wallenstein had utterly destroyed the Bohemian rebels and the Danish-German coalition, and now seemed in position to annex northern Germany and threaten Sweden.[28] Aiming to repel Habsburg intrusions into

[26] Roberts, *The Swedish Imperial Experience*, pp. 1–42. Cf. the class-based explanations of Sweden's expansion (discussed by Roberts) in Perry Anderson, *Lineages of the Absolutist State* (London: Verso, 1974), pp. 15–42, 173–91; and Andreas Dorpalen, *German History in Marxist Perspective: The East German Approach* (Detroit, Mich.: Wayne State University Press, 1985), pp. 138–67.

[27] Roberts, *Gustavus Adolphus*, Volume 1, pp. 60–61, 202–5, Volume 2, pp. 192–225, *The Early Vasas*, pp. 257–58, 402–4; Roger Charles Anderson, *Naval Wars in the Baltic, 1522–1820* (London: Francis Edward, 1969).

[28] Geoffrey Parker, *The Thirty Years' War* (London: Routledge & Kegan Paul, 1987), pp. 1–120; C. V. Wedgwood, *The Thirty Years War* (Garden City, N.Y.: Anchor, 1961), pp. 11–258; Geoffrey Symcox, ed., *War, Diplomacy, and Imperialism, 1618–1763* (New York: Harper & Row, 1973), pp. 102–13. In point of fact, Wallenstein's Baltic campaign aimed

the region, Gustavus Adolphus (r. 1611–1632) landed in Germany in 1630 and in two years defeated Tilly at Breitenfeld and the Lech, and Wallenstein at Lützen. After that engagement with the legendary imperial commander (in which Gustavus Adolphus was slain), Swedish armies fought their Catholic opponents to a standstill, suffered a serious defeat at the hands of the Spanish at Nördlingen (1634), but recovered to fight the Habsburgs to a stalemate until, at length, peace came in 1648.[29]

Sweden fielded immense armies, comprising over 175,000 troops, which fought against the combined might of Austria, Spain, and the Catholic League. It also built a sizable navy to safeguard lines of communication between Stockholm and its armies in Germany. Yet domestic resource mobilization was not heavy. This cannot be attributed to extraordinary commercial revenues: Sweden was no commercial power; royal income from the copper trade declined as prices fell during the war; and as early as 1600 silver output had dwindled to negligible levels.[30] Nor did geographical advantages benefit the Swedes. Invading armies are often inhibited by mountains, marshes, rivers, and forests, thereby enhancing the efficacy of defenders. Centuries earlier, Sweden itself benefited from these geographic advantages, as invading Danes discovered to their sorrow.[31] But now the Swedish army was on the offensive, cutting a swath through central Europe, unable to benefit from defensive advantages of the land.

Coalitions did not aid Sweden, at least not in the critical early years of the war. Prior to landing in Germany, Gustavus Adolphus tried to build an anti-Habsburg coalition, but to no avail. Most rulers had been intimidated by the relentless onslaughts of Tilly and Wallenstein, or, facing

---

not at Sweden but at securing a port from which his Spanish backers could interdict Dutch commerce in the Baltic, the financial lifeline of the Dutch Revolt against Spain. See J. H. Elliott, *The Count-Duke of Olivares: The Statesman in an Age of Decline* (New Haven, Conn.: Yale University Press, 1986), pp. 352–61.

[29] On Sweden's remarkable military campaigns, see Wedgwood, *Thirty Years War*, pp. 259ff; Parker, *Thirty Years' War*, pp. 121ff; Günter Barudio, *Der Teutsche Krieg, 1618–1648* (Frankfurt: S. Fischer, 1985), pp. 356–415; Roberts, "Gustav Adolf and the Art of War," in his *Essays in Swedish History* (Minneapolis: University of Minnesota Press, 1967), pp. 56–81; Gunther E. Rothenberg, "Maurice of Nassau, Gustavus Adolphus, Raimondo Montecuccoli, and the 'Military Revolution' of the Seventeenth Century," in Peter Paret, ed., *Makers of Modern Strategy: From Machiavelli to the Nuclear Age* (Princeton, N.J.: Princeton University Press, 1986), pp. 38–63; Hans Delbrück, *History of the Art of War within the Framework of Political History*, Volume 4: *The Modern Era* (Westport, Conn.: Greenwood Press, 1985), pp. 173–84; J.F.C. Fuller, *A Military History of the Western World*, Volume 2: *From the Defeat of the Spanish Armada to the Battle of Waterloo* (New York: Da Capo, 1987), pp. 49–75; and H. G. Koenigsberger, *The Habsburgs and Europe 1516–1660* (Ithaca, N.Y.: Cornell University Press, 1971), pp. 245–52.

[30] Roberts, *Gustavus Adolphus*, Volume 2, pp. 34, 80–104.

[31] Ibid., p. 189.

determined opposition in the estates, were powerless to commit soldiers. Only France and to a lesser extent the Dutch Republic subsidized the Swedish army in Germany. Richelieu subsidized Sweden's Protestant forces throughout the war: 160,000 *riksdaler* in 1632 and annual remissions averaging over 400,000 riksdaler from 1637 until the end of the war. The Dutch delivered less than 100,000 riksdaler between 1631 and 1632, critical years of recruiting mercenaries to bolster the small Swedish army.[32] Although the French army intervened following a Swedish defeat in 1634, Gustavus Adolphus and his successors turned the tide of the great war with only the dubious aid of a Saxon contingent, whose unreliability was shown at Breitenfeld, where it showed its heels to Tilly's army.

Measures taken to increase revenue from domestic sources prior to 1630 came to nought. Experiments with tax farming proved inefficient and caused grumblings; monopolies on salt and the grain trade ended in failure; taxes were raised, but the cold, mountainous countryside could not support a large army. Sufficient resources for a large modern army were simply not there. The transfer of crown lands yielded only somewhat better results. The crown alienated a substantial amount of its land holdings, which, because of the seizure of church lands a century earlier, were extensive. Land was conditionally transferred, mainly to the magnates, in the hope that intensification of agricultural technique would increase output and therefore tax revenue.[33] Despite these innovations, revenues remained inadequate for a country at war. Gustavus Adolphus's first principle of war, born of an inhospitable clime and backward economy, was that it ought to pay for itself (*bellum se ipsum alit*). The Swedish military enterprise was based on availing itself of resources in foreign lands, chiefly Germany, which it used to bolster its small army with German mercenaries, beginning a cycle of extraction and army expansion until it could field over 175,000 men.

A major source of revenue came from Sweden's control of the Baltic ports, through which came grain exports to the West. A truce worked out between Sweden and Poland enabled Gustavus Adolphus to levy tolls on ships engaged in the lucrative Baltic trade. Swedish revenue officials in-

---

[32] On foreign subsidies, see Barudio, *Der Teutsche Krieg*, p. 358; Richard Bonney, *The King's Debts: Finance and Politics in France, 1589–1661* (Oxford: Clarendon Press, 1981), pp. 163–64; Klaus-Richard Böhme, "Geld für die Schwedische Armee nach 1640," *Scandia* 33 (1982): 54–95; Parker, *Thirty Years' War*, pp. 124–25; and Sven-Erik Åström, "The Swedish Economy and Sweden's Role as a Great Power, 1632–1697," in Roberts, *Age of Greatness*, p. 95. Surely, Åström's title is intentionally ironic.

[33] Ågren, "Rise and Decline of an Aristocracy," pp. 55–56; Roberts, *Gustavus Adolphus*, Volume 2, pp. 43–44. The importance of the alienations and the crown's "resumption" of them will be seen in the next section.

stalled themselves at the port offices of Thorn, Lübeck, Königsberg, and the jewel of the Baltic, Danzig. The income derived was formidable and collected virtually effortlessly. Between 1630 and 1635, Sweden extracted tolls on Baltic shipping averaging 580,000 riksdaler per annum, reaching 812,000 riksdaler in 1634.[34]

Germany would pay in other ways as well. Swedish quartermasters were highly skilled at determining the wealth of a region, then systematically organizing and appropriating it:

> The main source of supply was Germany itself. By enormous exactions in cash and kind from occupied allied or enemy territories, or from cities prepared to buy their safety, the needs of the army were handsomely provided for. In the good years after [1630] Germany contributed annually to the Swedish armies a sum . . . estimated at as much as ten or twelve times the amount of Sweden's ordinary budget. A carefully devised and equitably applied system of 'contributions' was graded according to ability to pay; and since contributions' were paid in cash, and the money was usually spent in the area from which it was extracted, the system inflicted less damage on the economic life of Germany than might have been expected: indeed, it depended for its success upon the preservation of a reasonable measure of local prosperity. The immediate impact of these procedures upon the Swedish Exchequer was startling: in 1630 the Swedish taxpayer had to find 2,800,000 silver daler for the German war; by 1633 the amount he had to contribute had dropped to 128,000.[35]

While taxes soared in France and Spain, they plummeted in Sweden. With a Swedish army at the walls, Nuremberg contributed 100,000 riksdaler in 1632, Augsburg agreed to 20,000 riksdaler a month, while the burghers of Munich and Leipzig saw the advantages of delivering 163,000 and 400,000 riksdaler, respectively (and respectfully), to the Swedes.[36] Ransom also figured in war finance. Seeing no advantage in keeping ex-

---

[34] On Baltic tolls, see Åström, "The Swedish Economy," p. 92; Roberts, *Gustavus Adolphus*, Volume 2, p. 84; and Böhme, "Geld für die Schwedische Armee," p. 57.

[35] Roberts, *The Swedish Imperial Experience*, pp. 53–54. Roberts's contention that these extractions were not as destructive of the local economies as is often thought is supported by Böhme, p. 81. See also Fritz Redlich, *The German Military Enterpriser and His Work Force: A Study in European Economic and Social History*, Volumes 1 and 2 (Wiesbaden: Franz Steiner, 1964); and "Contributions in the Thirty Years' War," *Economic History Review* 12 (1959): 247–54. On the mobilization of Ingrian and Finnish resources, see Pär E. Back, "Diets in Ingria in the Seventeenth Century," in Commission Internationale pour l'Histoire des Assemblées d'Etats, *Liber Memorialis George de Lagarde* (Paris: Béatrice-Nauwelaerts, 1969), pp. 223–36; and Sven-Erik Åström, "The Role of Finland in the Swedish National and War Economies during Sweden's Period as a Great Power," *Scandinavian Journal of History* 11 (1986): 135–47.

[36] See Böhme, "Geld für die Schwedische Armee," pp. 59–65; Parker, *Thirty Years' War*, p. 169; and Roberts, *Gustavus Adolphus*, Volume 2, pp. 654, 702, 710–11.

pensive prisoners, Field Marshal Torstensson returned the imperial general staff captured at the battle of Jankov (1645) in exchange for 120,000 riksdaler.[37] To a certain extent, strong local support facilitated extractions in Germany, at least in Protestant regions. There, the Swedish army was seen as a liberator, perhaps even as a savior, delivering the faithful from Counter-Reformation armies trying to extirpate Protestantism. (Gustavus Adolphus is revered to this day in Lutheran churches; the anniversary of his landing in Germany is a day of commemoration.) But the Swedes also exacted contributions from Catholic towns along the Rhine and Main rivers, the *Pfaffengasse* ("priest alley"), as it was known. Friendly or not, voluntary or coerced, Lutheran or Catholic, the revenue did not come from Sweden.

In early 1633, prime minister Oxenstierna could confidently, though doubtless with some exaggeration, inform Stockholm: "But that Sweden should be at any charges or further expense upon this business [i.e., the Thirty Years' War!] I hold for quite out of the question, saving only such moneys as may be expended on the coastline." A year and a half later, he wrote: "We have now, by the space of four years, sent as good as no money out of the kingdom to the German war."[38] The Peace of Westphalia mandated that the Holy Roman Empire and several German principalities compensate Sweden with over five million riksdaler, which it used to defray the considerable expense of demobilizing the army deployed throughout Germany.[39]

We may now well inquire how a country of only one and a third million souls and an economy newly introduced to monetarization could endure the mobilization of a force of sufficient magnitude to battle the armies of the great continental powers. Surely such mobilization would have required authoritarian measures in the provinces to impress reluctant peasants into military service on the bleak frontiers of the empire or deep in Germany. It will at this point surprise perhaps no one that Sweden relied no more on its human resources than on its economic ones. Of the 175,000 troops Gustavus Adolphus fielded in 1632, only eighteen percent were Swedes, and even that figure dwindled in the next sixteen years. The rest, that is, the overwhelming majority, were mercenaries, mostly from Saxony and other principalities fearful of a Habsburg *Anschluss*, but also from Scottish and English opponents of the Counter-Reformation.[40]

---

[37] Parker, *Thirty Years' War*, p. 203. The going rate for ransoming an enemy general was approximately 25,000 riksdaler. See also Redlich, *The German Military Enterpriser*, Volume 1, pp. 365–68, 378–83.

[38] Roberts, *Gustavus Adolphus*, Volume 2, p. 81.

[39] Åström, "The Swedish Economy," pp. 95–97.

[40] Roberts, *The Swedish Imperial Experience*, p. 44; Böhme, "Geld für die Schwedische Armee," p. 55; Åström, "The Role of Finland." Many of the military leaders of both sides

The fortunes of war provided opportunities for quick recruitments, as defeated mercenary regiments were often enrolled en masse into the army of the victor. This is not to say that the war left the population back home unaffected. Regiments were often based on provincial levies, and, should the enemy roll up a given regiment in battle, the home community might suffer egregious losses, leaving scars of many kinds for a generation or more.[41]

The impact of war on the Swedish constitution and state did not compare with the impact elsewhere, but the long military campaigns left some mark. Pressures there were, but they were not strong and they encountered opposition from constitutional organs. Prior to intervening in the Thirty Years' War, Gustavus Adolphus personally appeared in the riksdag and won approval of war policy. At times each estate appointed committees of its own members (Committee Meetings) to handle business, especially matters of war strategy that could not be divulged to too many. Matters of conscription and supply, however, required approval of the full riksdag. Truncation of the assembly into Committee Meetings was by no means curtailment or circumvention of constitutional practice. It was an altogether sensible response with clear parallels in twentieth-century democracies, in war and peace. But attempts by Oxenstierna to have Committee Meetings substitute more and more for the riksdag led nowhere.

The state apparatus wielded by Gustavus Adolphus at the outset of his reign in 1611 was anything but impressive; there had been little organizational innovation in the executive since Gustav Vasa in the 1540s. There were neither clear procedures nor differentiated ministries, only a "mass of unborn departments, incapable itself of generating the energy to keep its own business in plausible vibration."[42] The continental wars proved to be the midwife. At the time of the intervention in the Thirty Years' War, a *krigsrätt* (war council) was created, charged with recruiting and outfitting the military. It operated within the confines of the chancery and never attained institutional predominance there, nor did it become autonomous of the parliamentary committees. The krigsrätt, like the exchequer and other newly forming ministries, was staffed not from a military elite, but principally from the ranks of the nobility and clergy, whose close ties to the riksdag precluded militarization of state and society.[43]

---

of the English Civil War, including Rupert, Monro, Leslie, and Skippon, won their spurs in Swedish service.

[41] See Jan Lindegren, *Utskrivning och Utsugning: Produktion och Reproduktion i Bygdeå 1620–1640* (Uppsala: Almqvist & Wiksell, 1980). I thank Michael Roberts for this reference.

[42] Roberts, *Gustavus Adolphus*, Volume 1, p. 273.

[43] Roberts, *The Swedish Imperial Experience*, pp. 61–64, *Gustavus Adolphus*, Volume 1,

The war's most significant impact was in the localities, and even here, owing to the strength of popular government and the limited nature of domestic resource mobilization, it was not drastic. The weak bailiff system was overhauled and systematized, since national taxation and recruitment, such as they were, required greater efficiency in local administration.[44] New royal officials deployed in the countryside, but whereas French intendants and Prussian Kommissariats wrested local control from traditional systems and subordinated them, a strengthened modus vivendi developed between the crown's new officials and the hundreds moot. Tax assessments, exemptions, and various procedures were codetermined by center and locality, by the traditional and the modern. The real administrative acceleration took place not in Sweden but in Germany with the armies, where administrative, logistical, and command structures were needed, close to the fronts and resources. A chancery and exchequer were built in Mainz to manage the armies, and magazines were constructed throughout Germany. Like the rank and file of the troops, the staff of these offices was mainly German, and when peace finally came they, like their kin in the regiments, were demobilized. Neither could be afforded in Sweden, and neither was needed.[45]

With the death of Gustavus Adolphus (1632) and the accession of his minor daughter, military command shifted to the able hands of Banér, Horn, and other members of the magnate class and the råd. This transfer of power is not without significance for constitutional history. It ensured continuity of constitutional control over what had become perhaps the most powerful army in Europe. Of course, constitutional control over the military is essential in any period of history, and under any circumstances, but it is all the more important for an army that enjoys the independence of action afforded by the absence of logistical and financial ties to the home government. It was the combination of a small distant state and powerful autonomous armies that doomed Republican Rome and ushered in continuous military intervention in politics, and the same unfortunate combination led to grief between the Habsburgs and their generalissimo, Wallenstein. Magnate and råd control over the military, paralleled by their control over the regency government, prevented the assumption of power by a dangerous self-aggrandizer like Wallenstein. Like Gustavus Adolphus and his successors, Wallenstein relied for the most part on contributions for supporting his army. Effectively indepen-

---

pp. 276–78. This early linkage between the state civil service and the riksdag is critical to understanding the nature of Caroline absolutism and its swift collapse and transition to parliamentarism.

[44] Andersson, *History of Sweden*, p. 208.

[45] Roberts, *Gustavus Adolphus*, Volume 2, pp. 620–3. Cf. Jan Lindegren, "The Swedish 'Military' State, 1560–1720," *Scandinavian Journal of History* 10 (1985): 305–36.

dent of Habsburg finances,[46] Wallenstein often acted in his own interests, accumulated enormous personal wealth, and even initiated diplomatic overtures without consulting Vienna. His was an autonomous war machine, operating increasingly to the benefit of the generalissimo himself—a state of affairs that led to the Habsburg order to assassinate him.[47]

Swedish military power during the Thirty Years' War was based less on resource mobilization than on resourcefulness. Domestic dearth was overcome by the occupation and systematic mobilization of German resources, and to a lesser extent by foreign subsidies. The preservation of constitutionalism was not based on the fortuitousness of a state decision to use foreign resources and thereby protect the constitution. The king and his ministers simply saw no possibility of mobilizing sufficient amounts of domestic resources to field an army capable of repelling the threats from the south. This method of warfare is not open to all countries; it is predicated on the proximity of a defenseless yet economically viable area, from which resources can be extracted without immediate counterattack from nearby powers. In this respect, intervention in Germany had specific prerequisites but also elements of a gamble: seizing foreign resources with a small army and using them to build a more viable war machine to fight more powerful enemies.

As the next section will argue, resources were not entirely lacking, and, as the Swedish economy emerged from barter, domestic resources could be used to support an army. True, the army was smaller than the

[46] The Imperial Exchequer said, "With respect to the maintenance of the Wallenstein armada, not only was nothing known, but it was, as it were, ensured that without any remuneration on the part of His Imperial Majesty it was [Wallenstein's] intention to provide his armada with all its needs until such time as a state of peace might again be attained." Golo Mann, *Wallenstein: His Life Narrated*, Charles Kessler, trans. (New York: Holt Rinehart & Winston, 1976), p. 271. As Mann and others have noted, the minister's statement is not without exaggeration. The generalissimo received subsidies from the Habsburgs, but nonetheless relied mainly on his own extractive apparatus.

[47] Mann, *Wallenstein*; J. V. Polisensky, *The Thirty Years War*, Robert Evans, trans. (Berkeley and Los Angeles: University of California Press, 1971), p. 198; Redlich, *The German Military Enterpriser*, Volume 1, pp. 325–27, "Contributions in the Thirty Years' War"; Victor-L. Tapié, *France in the Age of Louis XIII and Richelieu*, D. McN. Lockie, trans. (Cambridge: Cambridge University Press, 1984), pp. 317–23. Austria's reliance on foreign resource mobilization declined toward the end of the Thirty Years' War. Henceforth, its armies became less dependent on mobile plunder, reducing the likelihood of another Wallenstein, but leading to the decline of the estates and the rise of absolutism—the culmination of political trends that had begun with the Turkish wars of the previous century. See Robert A. Kann, *A History of the Habsburg Empire, 1526–1918* (Berkeley and Los Angeles: University of California Press, 1974), pp. 125–33; and Eugen Heischmann, *Die Anfänge des stehenden Heeres in Österreich* (Vienna: Österreichischer Bundesverlag, 1925), pp. 181–224.

one of the Thirty Years' War, and it possessed critical deficiencies that distinguish it from the ideal modern army of the period; but it nonetheless routed a much larger, modern Russian army at Narva (1700), and earned Sweden the awe of all Europe. The construction of this army would, however, take a deviation from its constitutional trajectory, which entailed a mixture of absolutism and populism.

CAROLINE ABSOLUTISM

Sweden, like England, underwent partial dismantling of constitutionalism. England endured a decade of Cromwell's authority, and Sweden experienced the abrogation of parts of its constitution under the rule of Charles XI (r. 1672–1697) and Charles XII (r. 1697–1718). Haughty and militaristic it was, but Caroline absolutism never reached the stage of what in this study has been called military-bureaucratic absolutism. Essential components of the constitution remained intact, and the populism of the period distinguishes it from the systems of Brandenburg-Prussia and France. There are three keys to understanding this populist absolutism; all have their origins in the finances and domestic tensions of the mid-seventeenth century.

First, Sweden's withdrawal from Germany at the end of the Thirty Years' War deprived it of most of the financial base upon which its armies relied. Without the verdant resources of Germany or some other country, Sweden could not field a modern army. The Northern War (1655–1660) proved disastrous. Attempts to mulct the Vistula valley, as Gustavus Adolphus had the Rhine and Main, were unsuccessful, and the army had to withdraw when Brandenburg switched sides. At war's close, Sweden had nothing to show but a burdensome debt, pointing out the inadequacies of its military.[48] Second, the alienation of crown lands, which began with Gustavus Adolphus and continued during magnate regencies, started to cause social unrest. The rapid accumulation of land in magnate hands spread fear among the peasantry that the manorial reaction of Eastern Europe would soon overwhelm them. Third, the magnates also incurred the wrath of the lesser aristocracy, who felt that opportunities for advancement were stymied by the magnate's stranglehold on high offices in the state. The nation as a whole was hostile to the magnate class, who, it was widely believed, had misruled during regencies and foisted war debt onto lower estates.

Facing war with Denmark and Brandenburg without prospects of ade-

[48] Roberts, *The Swedish Imperial Experience*, pp. 54–55; Åström, "The Swedish Economy," p. 88.

quate finance, Charles XI took advantage of class tensions and forcibly resumed crown control of the alienated crown properties. The *reduktion*, as it was called (reduktion = resumption), was at least quasi-constitutional: the Land Law of 1350 forbade the sale of crown lands; thus the crown's resumption without compensation (other than the revenues the magnates had derived during their alienation) was not as arbitrary as it might initially seem. Most Swedes saw the reduktion as privileged elites' taking on a fairer share of the tax burden; peasants also saw it as preventing serfdom from spreading into their villages. The aristocracy, which in 1655 had controlled seventy-two percent of the farmland, possessed less than thirty-three percent by the end of the century. During the same period, the numbers of the yeomanry doubled.[49]

Resumed land became the basis of the *indelningsverk*, a semifeudal military system based on exchanging land for military service. Each soldier and officer was granted either a tract of land or a percentage of the revenue from one. What emerged was a network of yeoman militias that could field almost a hundred thousand troops, integrated into a meticulous national mobilization plan, and able to acquit itself well on the field of battle with only a small amount of centralized organization.[50] However, the combination of a fairly modern army with decentralized control had a critical flaw. It had no extensive supply system, only a small network of magazines that were all too soon exhausted after the outbreak of war. Nor did it have central tax-collection facilities to extract resources for supply in a protracted war. Long-range offensive campaigns could only be undertaken by lightning strokes or foreign resource mobilization, a stratagem that had worked magnificently in the past, but one that Peter the Great knew how to counter.[51]

Indelningsverket had little in the way of extractive machinery to mobilize domestic resources, no substantive central logistical command as Vauban had built in France. It was essentially a land-for-service system with mutual exchange, not authoritarian extraction or the cash nexus, at its heart. Why were there no comparable organizations in Brandenburg-

---

[49] Andersson, *History of Sweden*, p. 216; Roberts, *Essays in Swedish History*, p. 248; Nordmann, *Grandeur et liberté*, pp. 73–80.

[50] On Swedish military organization during this period, see Roberts, *The Swedish Imperial Experience*, pp. 140–46; Georg Tessin, *Die deutschen Regimenter der Krone Schweden*, Part 2: *Unter Karl XI. und Karl XII. (1660–1718)* (Cologne: Böhlau, 1967), pp. 122–27; Åberg, "The Swedish Army," pp. 273–77; R. M. Hatton, *Charles XII of Sweden* (London: Weidenfeld & Nicolson, 1968), pp. 113–14; Christian von Sarauw, *Die Feldzüge Karl's XII: Ein Quellenmässiger Beitrag zur Kriegsgeschichte und Kabinetspolitik Europa's im XVIII. Jahrhundert* (Leipzig: von Bernhard Schlicke, 1881), pp. 24–27. Indelningsverket remained the basis for Sweden's national defense until the early twentieth century.

[51] Roberts, *The Swedish Imperial Experience*, p. 46; Åberg, "The Swedish Army," pp. 274–75; Kurt Ågren, "The 'Reduktion,' " in Roberts, *Sweden's Age of Greatness*, p. 248.

Prussia and France? Why had the Great Elector and Richelieu not built similar militaries? A partial answer lies in the relative simplicity and desirability of a centralized standing army. Surely, at least from the crown's perspective, a rigidly centralized army was more desirable than a congeries of dispersed militias, whose ties to a distant sovereign were less certain than those of a modern standing army. Second, by the end of the Thirty Years' War, solid logistical support was considered paramount, and this required systematic exploitation of resources. Not even Charles's clever indelningsverket had discerned a way to build a reliable support system for modern war—that, at least without the benefit of foreign subsidies or commercial wealth, would have required forced domestic mobilization. Perhaps most importantly, however, indelningsverket was simply incompatible with a repressed peasantry. Arming and training peasants without placing them under the regimentation of a standing army and a widespread administrative apparatus was out of the question in lands such as Prussia, France, and Poland, where lord-peasant relations were highly exploitative. Such an organization could only exist in a land of free peasants; in any other, it would have undermined the social order upon which the crown and social elites rested.

Constitutional government suffered from arrogated authority and the absence of dialogue between king and estates over revenue grants. The reduktion gave the crown sufficient revenues to manage government without much financial support from the riksdag, while indelningsverket was a latter-day hoplite army that relied on little or no parliamentary subsidy.[52] Populism replaced parliamentary debate. But Caroline absolutism maintained popular support in and through the riksdag, and integrated parts of it into his state. Politics under Caroline absolutism bears only little resemblance to that under military-bureaucratic absolutism. The crown, it is true, rode roughshod over the riksdag: forcing loans, intimidating on other issues, and successfully invoking necessity over strict constitutional propriety.[53] In the later years of Caroline absolutism, Charles XII arrogated complete control over war and taxation, and was ruling without the riksdag as such, only through substantial parts of it that he had fused with the bureaucracy. Furthermore, royal influence over elections and administration of the towns and villages was on the rise.[54]

Local government, however, was never undermined or demolished. Provincial and village institutions persisted despite encroachments of the

[52] Andersson, *History of Sweden*, p. 218; Roberts, *Essays in Swedish History*, p. 146.

[53] Günter Barudio, *Absolutismus: Zerstörung der "Libertären Verfassung": Studien zur "Karolinischen Eingewalt" in Schweden zwischen 1680 und 1693* (Wiesbaden: Franz Steiner, 1976), pp. 121–60; Roberts, *The Swedish Imperial Experience*, pp. 79–82.

[54] Barudio, *Absolutismus*, pp. 95–96; Nordmann, *Grandeur et liberté*, pp. 96–97.

king. Nor were personal rights and the rule of law suspended. We find no systematic use of torture or arbitrary justice; it would have been unwise for a monarch relying on popular support to do so. In fact, the crown remained scrupulously respectful of the law.[55] The riksdag was initially strengthened by the antimagnate program of Charles XI; it was charged with conducting an inquiry into magnate misrule, and its purview was expanded to include national economic policy and increased judicial functions.[56] Though it was largely circumvented during the rule of Charles XII, the riksdag was not abolished, and it was not without substantial influence in the state bureaucracy.

The state itself was never particularly extensive, at least by the standards of the day.[57] But of more significance is the state's relation to society. The bureaucracy never attained any semblance of corporate identity, giving it a social identity distinct from that of the social classes; indeed it was closely attached to them. The civil service was drawn from the ranks of the lower aristocracy, who resented the magnate's monopoly of office. As part of his antimagnate agenda, Charles XI brought into the civil service members of the riksdag itself, thereby fusing the bureaucracy and the estates.[58] Participation of riksdag members in the bureaucracy provided the opportunity for civil society itself to have its voice heard in the corporatist ministries of the Caroline period, in what might today be called the upward articulation of interest.[59] And, as Charles XII would learn, it also provided an important obstacle to any movement away from populist-militarist absolutism in the direction of military-bureaucratic absolutism.

But what of the army? Might not that large, independently financed military give kings the upper hand in state affairs, and its deployment throughout the country serve as the tentacles of central government in the provinces? The Swedish army of the Caroline epoch was no Prussian Kantonsystem. The crown contracted with provincial governments to determine troop requirements, and we find no hulking apparatus in the provinces. Above all, it was, like earlier Vasa armies, a citizen army with ties to the provinces as well as to the riksdag, which could not be de-

---

[55] "The crown was the common man's refuge, his ally, his safeguard against injustice and oppression." Roberts, *Essays in Swedish History*, p. 37.

[56] Ibid., p. 255. This expansion of riksdag power proved to be an unintended movement in the direction of ministerial/parliamentary government. See Roberts, *The Age of Liberty: Sweden, 1719–1772* (Cambridge: Cambridge University Press, 1986), pp. 4–5.

[57] Nordmann, *Grandeur et liberté*, pp. 94–95.

[58] Roberts, *Essays in Swedish History*, pp. 249–51.

[59] Ibid., pp. 254–58; Werner Buchholz, *Staat und Ständegesellschaft in Schweden zur Zeit des Überganges vom Absolutismus zum Ständeparlamentarismus, 1718–1770* (Stockholm: Almqvist & Wiksell, 1979). This fusion, as shall be seen, greatly facilitated a swift transition to parliamentary government.

ployed against institutions in which many officers and soldiers themselves participated.[60]

Perhaps the most important difference between Caroline and military-bureaucratic absolutism lies in the popular base of the former. Its origin lay in popular mobilization, augmenting royal power, and allowing a measure of constitutional trespass: "A monarch who was really serious about a *reduktion* would always find enthusiastic allies in the lower three Estates. To strengthen his hand they would not hesitate to make constitutional sacrifices, and were willing enough to shut their eyes to political implications if they could realize their programme."[61] But the populace would not allow trespass to degenerate into a dismantling of constitutionalism. The king walked a thin line: he was given wide latitude on domestic and foreign matters, but his field of opportunity was always restricted by the necessity of maintaining rapport with the three lower orders. Doing away with the estates, sweeping away local assemblies and privileges, and open abuse of the law would have eroded the crown's basis of support. Popular support is a decidedly untrustworthy pillar upon which to build absolutism; a strong state and a powerful army are much better. Transient political fortunes and malaise from military defeat can erode popular support and lead to swift collapse.

COLLAPSE AND THE EMERGENCE OF THE AGE OF LIBERTY

Important parallels may be drawn between the collapse of French absolutism and the demise of Caroline absolutism. Military failure, fiscal crisis, and state paralysis all figure prominently in the collapse of absolutism in both countries, but we encounter no peasant revolution in Sweden, and this probably accounts for a smooth and relatively nonviolent return to full constitutional government. The overthrow of absolutism was a purely political revolution that spared Sweden, and its constitution, the trauma of a full social revolution such as France endured toward the end of the century.

A long line of Swedish military successes came to a catastrophic close in the Great Northern War (1700–1721), which matched Sweden against

[60] Indelningsverket "preserved Sweden from the possibility of anything resembling the Great Elector's Generalkriegskommissariat, with all the social and constitutional consequences that flowed from it." Roberts, *Essays in Swedish History*, p. 235. The exchange of land (and often citizenship rights) for military service is a recurrent theme in military history, but a state using land to build a nonnoble military organization seems to have a parallel only in the *stratiotai* of the seventh-century Byzantine Empire. See George Ostrogorsky, *History of the Byzantine State*, Joan Hussey, trans. (New Brunswick, N.J.: Rutgers University Press, 1969), pp. 95ff.

[61] Roberts, *Essays in Swedish History*, pp. 238–89.

virtually every power in the region, including Russia, whose army had in recent years been modernized by Peter.[62] Defeat came to Charles XII deep in the Ukraine as a result, at least in part, of a glaring weakness of indelningsverket: its lack of a rationalized system of supply. Inasmuch as the modernity of armies and their support systems are central questions in this study, it might not be too discursive to outline the causes of Sweden's defeat in Russia. Its relation to absolutism's demise and support for parliamentary rule will be apparent.

Early in the war, the Swedish army, as was its habit and as was necessary given the absence of centralized supply, relied on plundering Courland, Saxony, and Livonia for supply, just as it had Germany during the Thirty Years' War. Charles XII's adventure into the Ukraine has been attributed to rashness, but the prospects of replenishing his stores on the fertile steppes and seeking an alliance with an ongoing Cossack rebellion were certainly more important.[63] Aware of his enemy's logistical Achilles heel, Peter the Great used his cavalry to interdict Swedish foragers, conducted one of the first scorched-earth policies in military history, and aggravated Charles's supply worries by delaying decisive engagement.[64] Charles was forced into a hasty attack on the Russian supply center at Poltava (1709), where superior Russian numbers crushed the Swedes and forced an almost complete surrender shortly thereafter.[65] Only a handful of those who boldly marched into the Ukraine ever saw Sweden again; the king himself had to seek sanctuary in the Ottoman Empire before secreting across Europe back to Stockholm. Poltava placed Sweden in a new and dangerous situation: a new army had to be raised in order to face Russian and Danish forces now pressing into the homeland itself. Driven from the continent, for the first time Sweden had to attempt to mobilize high levels of domestic resources—a move entailing constitutional contention—or face almost certain conquest by Russia and Denmark. These demands were met with resistance from the peasantry, the bureaucracy, and the riksdag, all of whom at this point were weary of the war.

Peasant opposition manifested itself not in overt rebellion but in withdrawal of critical support for populist-militarist absolutism. The absence of a massive peasant revolt was not for want of the institutional basis at the village level. Peasant institutions were probably more coherent and

[62] For a sketch of the diplomatic situation in Central and Eastern Europe during this period, see Buchholz, *Staat und Ständegesellschaft*, pp. 34–35.

[63] On this logistical explanation, see Nordmann, *Grandeur et liberté*, pp. 153–70; Fuller, *Military History*, Volume 2, pp. 169–75; and Hatton, *Charles XII*, pp. 300–6.

[64] Andersson, *History of Sweden*, p. 232; Fuller, *Military History*, Volume 2, p. 172; Hatton, *Charles XII*, pp. 277–93.

[65] Ibid., pp. 300–6; Fuller, *Military History*, Volume 2, pp. 174–86; von Sarauw, *Feldzüge Karls XII*, pp. 266ff.

capable of strong opposition in Sweden than anywhere else in Europe, including France and Russia, where they were parts of momentous social revolutions. But the source of rebellion in France and Russia lay not in broad constitutional questions—such matters rarely concern those scratching out a living from the soil—it lay in the more practical ones of seigneurial abuse and land ownership, and here the Swedish peasantry had no complaint. They were perhaps the freest cultivating class in Europe—the reduktion had seen to that. When taxes were raised and new army levies called for, the result was not revolutionary upheaval, only widespread unrest and disapproval of interminable and burdensome wars.[66] Without *Herr Omnes* to call upon to counter opposition from other quarters, as his predecessors had in their conflicts with the nobility, the king faced increasingly unified and institutionally entrenched opposition in the estates and bureaucracy.

The debacle at Poltava was followed by another decade of inconclusive war that led to fiscal strain and disaffection in the riksdag, the state, and the officer corps—three groups with substantial overlap and close ties. By 1718 calls for new taxes and increased economic controls had precipitated open conflict between the crown and state ministries. The nation, they reasoned, had endured enough. The magnates reemerged from unpopularity and joined in a united front against Charles.[67] Disaffection spread and bordered on open revolt when pervasive national discontent combined with the exchequer's inability to meet the payroll of the civil service and military.[68] An overt coup for which the riksdag had been planning was obviated by the death (some say assassination) of Charles. Elements of the constitution that had been in the background throughout the absolutist period came to the fore and coalesced into a practical parliamentary government. The riksdag reasserted itself and, as Parliament had done in 1688 with William and Mary, invited a foreigner to become constitutional monarch. Linkages between the civil service and the riksdag, begun by Gustavus Adolphus, continued by Charles XI in his anti-magnate program, and expanded throughout his son's rule, proved, through some cunning passage of history, to be the foundation of parlia-

---

[66] Nordmann, *Grandeur et liberté*, pp. 179–81; *The New Cambridge Modern History*, Volume 7, pp. 350–51.

[67] Buchholz, *Staat und Ständegesellschaft*, pp. 38–88; Roberts, *The Age of Liberty*, p. 6; Nordmann, *Grandeur et liberté*, pp. 203–4.

[68] "It is no doubt true that everyone suffered during the emergency of the war years, but officers in the military and civil services suffered more than most, for their wages dried up, and were diverted to fill the deficits in the exchequer. The outcome of this development can be seen in that political revolt of the serving classes which . . . broke the Caroline absolutism, and replaced it by the rule of the Estates under the leadership of the Nobility, and so inaugurated the so-called 'Age of Liberty.' " Ågren, "The 'Reduktion,' " p. 248.

mentary/ministerial government.[69] The Caroline kings, through their populism, had unwittingly fathered a modernizing, corporatist parliament from a medieval estates: "Die bisherigen Funktionäre der Macht des absoluten Herrschers werden nun selbst Inhaber der Macht. . . . Inhaber der Macht sind sie in ihrer Eigenschaft als Deputierte des Reichstages, Funktionäre dieser Macht sind sie als leitende Beamte der zentralen Behörden des schwedischen Reiches."[70] The riksdag dismantled the array of Caroline economic controls and state agencies in the localities.[71] Factions in the riksdag developed into fairly coherent political parties, the Caps and Hats, which alternated political power throughout the eighteenth century.[72]

Let us now refocus the analysis from the keys to the collapse of Charles's frail form of absolutism, to the reasons why his bid to move in the direction of military-bureaucratic absolutism met with failure where the Great Elector and Richelieu had succeeded. What conditions favor the forces of constitutionalism in such pivotal moments? Parts of the answer have already been discussed. First, the Swedish state was too closely linked with the riksdag to be an effective instrument of the crown should its populism wane. Second, indelningsverket was far from a standard mercenary or professional army as found in even preabsolutist Brandenburg and France. It was a citizen army that could not be deployed against the nation, and in any case much of it had perished in the Ukraine. The timing of Charles's move might be the most critical factor in its failure. It came not at the outset of war, when there was a clear foreign danger and parts of the aristocracy and public could be won over to or acquiesce in constitutional change; it came only after more than a decade of inconclusive and seemingly interminable war had sapped the country's energies, squandered much of a generation in the Ukraine, and alienated the aristocracy, peasantry, civil service, and even much of the officer corps.

Contrasts with Brandenburg-Prussia and France are noteworthy. Prior

[69] Roberts, *The Age of Liberty*, pp. 75–82.

[70] "The former functionaries of absolutist monarchal power now themselves became holders of power. . . . They were holders of power in their capacity as riksdag deputies; they were functionaries of this power as leading civil servants of the central government of the Swedish nation." Buchholz, *Staat und Ständegesellschaft*, p. 121. Through the reduktion the Caroline kings, again unwittingly, cleared out the rural obstacles to democracy that Barrington Moore discusses.

[71] Ibid., pp. 123–69.

[72] Roberts, *The Age of Liberty*, pp. 111–75; Michael F. Metcalf, "The First 'Modern' Party System? Political Parties, Sweden's Age of Liberty and the Historians," *Scandinavian Journal of History* 2 (1977): 265–87, "Structuring Parliamentary Politics: Party Organization in Eighteenth-Century Sweden," *Parliaments, Estates and Representation* 1 (1981): 35–49; *The New Cambridge Modern History*, Volume 7, p. 362.

to the installation of military-bureaucratic absolutism in both countries, the heads of state had at their disposal small but essentially loyal bureaucracies, drawn from the nobility and middle classes, but not through the intermediaries of the countries' parliaments. Second, each country had moved away from feudal militias and levies in favor of small mercenary or standing forces beholden less to the nation or its constitution than to the paymaster in the royal service. Whether their pay came from parliamentary subsidy or from coerced taxation measures meant little to them. Finally, the Great Elector and Richelieu executed their moves against constitutionalism at the outset of wars, with Poland and France in the Prussian case, with a Habsburg coalition in the French. At this propitious juncture, they were able to take advantage of divisions in the estates and in society at large, and garner support by pleading necessity in time of peril.

But let us turn from these analytical points and return to the straitened nation. What of the Russian and Danish armies that were now raiding the Swedish coasts? They were not to be mollified by the constitutional changes in their longtime enemy; better to deliver a coup de grâce and rid themselves of the worry of a resurgent Sweden. Yet here the dynamics of the European state system worked out in Sweden's favor and prevented a Russian invasion. Though delivery from Russian armies must have seemed miraculous to the Swedes, changes in alliances are very much part of the state system's hydraulics: "In international politics, success leads to failure. The excessive accumulation of power by one state or coalition of states elicits the opposition of others."[73] Successes in the Great Northern War made Russia a major power in the European power struggle, but this alarmed both France and England, the latter fearing that critical naval supplies from Scandinavia might be jeopardized. Diplomatic pressure from these countries extricated Sweden from its plight, and foreign financial aid helped it through its fiscal difficulties.[74]

The army never again attained the heights of glory reached during the Age of Greatness. The soldiers of indelningsverket became more interested in their crops than in empire or domestic intrigue.[75] The army was called upon to fight in the great coalition against Prussia of the Seven Years' War, but the Caroline mobilization machinery had become rusty. Mobilization took several years, exhausting the military budget, and the army saw little action. The army later became practically a fifth estate, as

[73] Kenneth N. Waltz, "The Origins of War in Neorealist Theory," in Robert I. Rotberg and Theodore K. Rabb, eds., *The Origins and Prevention of Major Wars* (Cambridge: Cambridge University Press, 1989), p. 49.

[74] Roberts, *The Age of Liberty*, pp. 9–19.

[75] Roberts, *Essays in Swedish History*, pp. 234–45.

each regiment elected representatives to the riksdag.[76] Its trans-Baltic empire gone, Sweden enjoyed the good fortune of remaining for the most part outside the European struggles, secure in a niche between great power rivalries, its constitutional government strong.

. . .

The analytical framework presented in this study has been used to study two periods of Swedish history: the Thirty Years' War and Caroline absolutism. In the first period, the Swedes assembled an enormous army that fought the major powers to a draw without affecting their constitution. This was the result of the mobilization of foreign resources to support the army. Sweden fought eighteen years of large-scale warfare without mobilizing much of its own resources, the key to the destruction of constitutional government in the early modern period. Constitutional government was partially dismantled but in some ways strengthened by populist-militarist kings. Caroline absolutism differed from military-bureaucratic absolutism in important respects: there was no sprawling autonomous bureaucracy undermining parliament and local privileges; its military was a citizen army loyal to, and very much a part of, the constitution; and its base of support was in the general population and the riksdag. Caroline absolutism disintegrated when the army was annihilated at Poltava, and it attempted to evolve in the unpopular direction of military-bureaucratic absolutism. The riksdag and the bureaucracy, two organizations that had become fused and that remained loyal to the constitution, thwarted this move and led the country back in the direction of liberal democracy.

Sweden's constitutional arrangements emerged unchanged from the Thirty Years' War and essentially intact from the Caroline period. Largely removed from European power politics, Sweden entered the eighteenth century with its constitutionalism in good order, its medieval political system adapting to the challenges of a modernizing society.

[76] Roberts, *The Age of Liberty*, pp. 44–45, 71–72.

CHAPTER NINE

The Dutch Republic

THE DUTCH REPUBLIC falls into the same analytical category as Sweden: that of countries experiencing heavy, protracted warfare, without suffering the destruction of constitutional patterns. Sweden preserved its constitutional trajectory mainly by means of exploiting foreign resources. But, because its century and a half of war against Spain and France was fought in essentially defensive struggles on its own territory, such a strategy could not help the Dutch. Owing to numerous alliances, which brought foreign resources to bear against enemies and limited the enemy resources deployed against the Republic, and to the benefits of geography, which gave formidable advantages to the defenders, Dutch constitutionalism also did not face the destructiveness of domestic resource mobilization. Perhaps the most important factor in preserving constitutionalism was the Republic's fantastic wealth—far greater than that of the agrarian economies of other countries—which allowed substantial amounts of resources to be allocated to the war effort without triggering serious constitutional conflict. The public debt instruments of eighteenth-century England had Dutch antecedents almost two centuries earlier—such was the Dutch lead in economic development. Military-bureaucratic absolutism was not a serious threat; in fact, owing to the ouster of Spanish monarchal authority, it was never really on the agenda. Like England during the Civil War period, the Dutch faced the problem of forming a coherent wartime executive; but the problem was worse owing to the confederal nature of the Republic. Furthermore, the Dutch faced the problem of preventing a populist-militarist regime like that of Caroline absolutism.

CONSTITUTIONALISM IN THE NETHERLANDS AND THE REVOLT AGAINST SPAIN

Dutch constitutional government, like that of most European countries, emerged in the Middle Ages. But it differed from that in the rest of Europe by the overwhelming power of the many towns. Along the North Sea coast and the rivers of the northern provinces of the Low Countries, a series of powerful, wealthy trading centers developed. Despite the preeminence of towns, the relative weakness of the aristocracy, and the absence of meaningful integration with a larger territorial power, Dutch constitutionalism endured imperial, Burgundian, and Habsburg efforts to establish firm control. When the Spanish crown attempted to impose a military-bureaucratic form of government on its recently acquired possession, it triggered a popular revolt against Habsburg authority. The rebellious provinces sought no new form of state, only the preservation of medieval constitutionalism. The essentially backward-looking revolt developed into an eighty-year war against Spain.

Geography, as we shall have more than one occasion to observe, favored the Netherlands. An early blessing was dispensed to the northern provinces of the Low Countries by making them quite marshy, and therefore unsuitable for the estate agriculture upon which feudal military and social organization rested. In the northern half of what was to become the Dutch Republic, a free peasantry had enjoyed private, heritable property since the eighth century. Village governments arose there to handle local affairs and protect liberties.[1] To the south, feudal services had been replaced by cash payments, and personal freedom was the rule by 1300.[2] Strong village government was not unique to the Netherlands; indeed it was also found in the Swiss cantons, East Elbia, and Scandinavia. The region's low-lying topography necessitated extensive local maintenance of dikes, levies, and drainage ditches, which proved to be a central function and unifying factor of village government.[3]

The scions of aristocratic families figure highly in Dutch history. Orange, Egmont, and Hoorn were among the early leaders (and martyrs) of the Revolt against Spain, executed or assassinated on Spanish orders. The aristocracy was a small caste, comprising only twelve accredited noble families according to one study.[4] Nobles stood at the head of no expansive estates—marshy topography prevented that—and few estates exceeded a hundred hectares. Their control over woodlands and pastures was negligible. The aristocracy monopolized provincial governorships (stadhold-

[1] Petrus Johannes Blok, *History of the People of the Netherlands*, Part 1: *From the Earliest Times to the Beginning of the Fifteenth Century* (New York: G. P. Putnam's Sons, 1898), pp. 156–57; Jan de Vries, *The Dutch Rural Economy in the Golden Age, 1500–1700* (New Haven, Conn.: Yale University Press, 1978), p. 34.

[2] Blok, *People of the Netherlands*, Part 1, pp. 319–20.

[3] Bernard Hendrik Slicher van Bath, "The Economic Situation in the Dutch Republic during the Seventeenth Century," in Maurice Aymard, ed., *Dutch Capitalism and World Capitalism* (Cambridge: Cambridge University Press, 1982), p. 25; de Vries, *Dutch Rural Economy*, pp. 28–29; Simon Schama, *The Embarrassment of Riches: An Interpretation of Dutch Culture in the Golden Ages* (Berkeley and Los Angeles: University of California Press, 1988), p. 40.

[4] de Vries, *Dutch Rural Economy*, p. 35. See also J. Huizinga, *Holländische Kultur im Siebzehnten Jahrhundert: Eine Skizze* (Basel: Benno & Schwabe, 1961), pp. 22, 40.

erates), which had substantial but not preponderant influence over administration, elections to provincial assemblies (States), and patronage networks. But they did not dominate administration or judiciary. That had been undermined by the introduction of royal justice, and by the burghers' purchase of royal lands and even seigneurial rights, in order better to control vital food production and burgeoning cottage industries.[5] The Habsburgs used the small noble class as stadholders, a move that maintained their prestige, and gave them substantial power in naming magistrates; but stadholders were constrained by the opposing forces of imperial and later Spanish authority on the one hand, and wealthy burgesses on the other. Though serving the Habsburgs, the nobility remained loyal to local custom, which the Habsburgs remained respectful of until Spain's financial trouble of the late sixteenth century.[6]

The dozens of trading towns of the Netherlands obtained charters of independence in the twelfth century, from either local powerholders or the Holy Roman Empire. The power of outside authority was limited to specified judicial spheres and to command but not control of town militias. Aldermanic elections were secure from interference.[7] Power in the cities lay firmly in the hands of oligarchies, save for Utrecht, where guilds had won a share in town governments.[8] In Amsterdam, a comparative late-developer that emerged only in the late Middle Ages but nonetheless became the economic and political center of the Dutch Republic, the town council comprised thirty-six patricians, appointed for life, from among whom a rotating clique of four burgomasters was selected to assume the day-to-day responsibilities of government.[9]

Provincial parliaments called States emerged in the late medieval period in each part of the Netherlands. Like their counterparts elsewhere, they controlled laws, taxation, tax collection, and matters of war and peace.[10] Furthermore, in lieu of meaningful ducal or royal authority dur-

[5] de Vries, *Dutch Rural Economy*, pp. 37–56.

[6] Petrus Johannes Blok, *History of the People of the Netherlands*, Part 2: *From the Beginning of the Fifteenth Century to 1559* (New York: G. P. Putnam's Sons, 1899), pp. 268–69; *The New Cambridge Modern History*, Volume 4, pp. 364–65.

[7] James D. Tracy, *Holland under Habsburg Rule, 1506–1566: The Formation of a Body Politic* (Berkeley and Los Angeles: University of California Press, 1990), especially pp. 9–63; Blok, *People of the Netherlands*, Part 1, pp. 222–25, 308–9; Henri Pirenne, *Early Democracies in the Low Countries: Urban Society and Political Conflict in the Middle Ages and the Renaissance* (New York: Harper & Row, 1963).

[8] Slicher van Bath, "Economic Situation in the Dutch Republic," p. 25; Huizinga, *Holländische Kultur*, pp. 48–56.

[9] J. G. van Dillen, "Amsterdam's Rôle in Seventeenth-Century Dutch Politics and Its Economic Background," in J. S. Bromley and E. H. Kossmann, eds., *Britain and the Netherlands*, Volume 1 (London: Chatto & Windus, 1960), pp. 133–47.

[10] Geoffrey Parker, *The Dutch Revolt* (Ithaca, N.Y.: Cornell University Press, 1980), pp. 32–33.

ing most of the medieval and early modern period, each States built its own administrative apparatus, including chancellor, comptroller, and specialized secretaries.[11] Provincial States sent delegates to a States-General, much as the French provincial assemblies sent carefully instructed delegates to the Estates-General. Like the town councils, the States were highly oligarchic. The States of Holland, by the seventeenth century the most powerful Dutch assembly, and more powerful than all other States combined, contained no peasants, common townsmen, or even clerics. Even the aristocracy had only one representative. Was the Netherlands less constitutional than the rest of Western Europe because of its oligarchic nature? Undoubtedly so. But it is critical to note that representative government and broad personal freedoms nonetheless existed, and served as a basis for liberal democracy in following centuries, just as they did in England and Sweden.[12]

Provincial States and the States-General combined to thwart attempts by Burgundian Dukes and Habsburg kings alike to impose high taxes and outside power. Charles the Bold's requests for money to fight dynastic wars with France met with counterdemands from the States-General for clarification, confirmation, and expansion of urban freedoms—a classic invocation of "redress before supply," a quid pro quo between monarch and estates reminiscent of those in England during the Hundred Years' War and in the Petition of Right.[13] Habsburg efforts in the early sixteenth century to impose centralizing measures were deflected, as were attempts to circumvent the States and negotiate with and intimidate individual towns.[14] The Habsburgs received subsidies for military campaigns, but on the States' terms. The only lingering effect was the States' increasing reluctance to fund Habsburg quests for universal empire. Such adventures made little sense to the regents of the Netherlands.

In other countries, parliaments and other constitutional institutions coexisted with some form of central government, the household government of early Hohenzollerns or Yorkists, or the relatively articulated Bourbons. The provinces and towns of the Netherlands, however, were more independent of central authority than those in any other region,

[11] J. W. Smit, "The Netherlands Revolution," in Robert Forster and Jack P. Greene, eds., *Preconditions of Revolution in Early Modern Europe* (Baltimore, Md.: Johns Hopkins University Press, 1970), p. 34.

[12] Parker, *The Dutch Revolt*, p. 32. As shall be seen, the oligarchic nature of the States and the States-General enabled coherent decision making during the long wars with Spain and France, and also hindered the development of a caesarist threat from the commanders of the Republic's army, the Orangist stadholders.

[13] Blok, *People of the Netherlands*, Part 2, pp. 263–36.

[14] H. G. Koenigsberger, "The States General of the Netherlands," *Studies Presented to the International Commission for the History of Representative and Parliamentary Institutions* 18 (1958): 143–58.

excepting perhaps the Swiss cantons or Venice. The Netherlands existed successively under the nominal rule of the Holy Roman Empire, the Dukes of Burgundy, and the Habsburgs, without yielding meaningful authority to any of these distant suzerains. The States were supreme. Above them was only a weak Council of State, in which the local nobility managed affairs under the scrutiny of the States.[15]

The constitutional order saw the coming and going of great warrior overlords such as Charles the Bold and Charles V, but it was the latter's son, Philip II of Spain, who upset this state of affairs when he tried to extract new revenues for distant wars. Following the Peace of Cateau-Cambresis (1559), which ended long wars with France, Philip deployed his military against the Ottomans, but initial campaigns fared poorly. More revenue was needed and he naturally looked to the opulent Netherlands.[16] New taxes were insisted upon and imposing new state structures were set forth. New taxes would be collected by Spanish officials. The Spanish governor, the Duke of Alva, seized upon ensuing protests and riots and attempted to settle once and for all the issue of sovereignty in the Netherlands. Alva assembled four regiments of seasoned Spanish veterans and set about castilianizing the land: taxes were forced through the States; the States-General was dismantled; and opponents were arrested and summarily tried by Alva's Council of Blood. Over a thousand were executed. Alva quartered troops in the towns and villages and strengthened a system of bishoprics, tightening Spanish control. The Inquisition was let loose to extirpate Calvinism. Opposition seemed to be quickly squelched, but actually it was only exiled to northern Germany and Huguenot bastions in France. From these sanctuaries Dutch raiding parties, the legendary and colorful Sea Beggars, sallied forth to Dutch coastal towns, expanded their control, and established a frail regime in the northern seven provinces of the Low Countries.[17]

To put these events in terms of this study, the Dutch Revolt was a successful rebuff of a monarch's attempt to dissolve constitutional government and build military-bureaucratic absolutism. A comparativist must inquire why the forces of constitutionalism succeeded here and failed in Brandenburg and elsewhere. In the Netherlands the conflict between

[15] Tracy, *Holland under Habsburg Rule, 1506–1566*, pp. 9–63; Pieter Geyl, *The Revolt of the Netherlands, 1555–1609* (London: Ernest Benn, 1980), pp. 70–71; *The New Cambridge Modern History*, Volume 4, p. 362.

[16] J. H. Elliott, *Imperial Spain, 1469–1716* (New York: St. Martin's Press, 1964), pp. 224–27.

[17] For the initial stages of the Revolt, see Parker, *The Dutch Revolt*; Geyl, *The Revolt of the Netherlands*; John Lothrop Motley, *The Rise of the Dutch Republic: A History in Three Volumes*, Volume 1 (New York: Harper & Brothers, 1856); and H. G. Koenigsberger, *The Habsburgs and Europe 1516–1660* (Ithaca, N.Y.: Cornell University Press, 1971), pp. 117–217.

central power and the States took on the added dimension of the intrusion of a foreign power: the extension of military-bureaucratic absolutism from Castile. The destruction of indigenous parliamentary power was accompanied by a foreign authority's increased power, not by the expansion of the prerogatives of a long-standing domestic prince whose family history was entwined with that of the country. Doubtless this figured in the Revolt, but we must not make too much of it: there is considerable agreement that Dutch nationalism did not precede the Revolt; it was for the most part forged during the long wars against Spain. Philip's attempts at expanding his rule struck at far more than political institutions. New taxation measures threatened the vitality of the merchant centers, and the burghers were all too aware of the devastating effects the *alcabala* and *millones* were having on the Castilian economy. Similarly, the introduction of the Inquisition made itself felt throughout the region. Its horrendous and illegal methods endangered the personal freedoms of almost all members of society, Calvinist or not. The specific forms of the Spanish encroachments attacked Netherlanders not only on political and constitutional fronts, but also on religious, economic, and cultural ones, and powerful, multidimensional opposition resulted.

The Great Elector used the threat of war, what we might today call a national security argument, to build support in the estates and cajole from them the army he later used to disband them. Furthermore, he dealt with an estates already divided over class and regional differences. The Dutch could not be convinced of any serious danger. The Turks were no threat to them or to their trading empire, which covered much of the world but was centered in the Baltic. Though eastern grain was shipped to Italy, trade was not extensive in the eastern Mediterranean, and what little took place was in any case with the Turks.[18] Fissures that wracked Parliament during the Civil War were greatly limited in the provincial States and States-General by their oligarchic nature. Comparisons with another Habsburg possession are also instructive. Philip was more successful in squeezing out more money for his Turkish war from Spanish-controlled Italy, where revolts were either nonexistent or short-lived. But of course the Turkish threat was more apparent here than in the Low Countries. Turkish vessels plied the waters near Italy, interdicted trade with the merchant towns, and landed soldiers ominously closer. Second, Spanish taxation measures varied across Italy. According to a contemporary saying, "In Sicily the Spaniards nibble, in Naples they eat, and in Milan they devour." Varying taxation measures meant varying levels of grievance, and little opportunity for solidarity among the towns and

[18] Jonathan I. Israel, *Dutch Primacy in World Trade, 1585–1740* (Oxford: Clarendon Press, 1989), pp. 53–60.

regions. A single town in revolt might well share the same fate Ghent and Antwerp met with in the mid-sixteenth century.[19]

The Revolt succeeded in thwarting the imposition of Spanish absolutism and in establishing a fledgling republic. But Spain would not part easily with the provinces: it was a dangerous precedent for an empire to tolerate, and, more importantly, the seven provinces were vital sources of revenue, contributing more than the wealth of the New World did. The Dutch faced eighty years of intermittent Spanish efforts to reclaim the rebellious provinces, and, after that, another forty years of Louis XIV's attempts to annex more territory for his domain. The constitution had weathered one storm, but it now faced perhaps the most arduous period of protracted warfare any European country has ever experienced.

War in the Golden Age, 1558–1713

The Dutch successfully repulsed Spanish efforts to expand Castilian military-bureaucratic absolutism into the northern provinces of the Low Countries. The question remained, however, whether or not the Dutch themselves would have to adopt similar autocratic measures in the next century and a half of warfare against the largest military powers of the time. Would forcible extraction of war resources lead to the overthrow of the constitutional order by an indigenous, albeit well-intended figure?

Two factors other than those related to resource mobilization made this unlikely. First, the Revolt itself changed the Dutch structure of government to one inauspicious for military-bureaucratic absolutism. Such forms of government develop only in lands with a strong autocratic predisposition, as in Russia and Castile, or in countries with medieval constitutionalism at the heart of the political system: that is, a dualistic system comprising an independent monarchy of some sort and a parliament, which manages the country's affairs within a consensual framework. With the ouster of Spanish officials at the outset of the Revolt, an autocratic trajectory was simply not possible: there was no figure at the head of a modicum of state machinery from which to overwhelm the estates and move the country toward military-bureaucratic absolutism. Stadholders administered several provinces, but had no central institutional power comparable to that of preabsolutist Hohenzollerns or Bourbons. The question remained whether or not the States would be able to conduct

[19] See Koenigsberger, *The Habsburgs and Europe*, pp. 48–50. This gradation in the taxation of the Italian cities parallels the gradations in the peasantry that block the solidarity necessary for coherent opposition.

government effectively.[20] A second factor making an autocratic outcome unlikely was the extreme wariness of central authority in the States of the Republic. Following the ouster of the Spanish monarchy, like their counterparts and competitors across the Channel after the Glorious Revolution (though probably doubly so), Dutch burghers viewed central power and military commanders with extreme mistrust. Emergency powers in the face of even the gravest military danger would not be forthcoming from the wary burghers.

The Republic faced war with many of the major powers, and some pressure to adopt authoritarian government obtained. Three main factors, however, reduced the need to mobilize constitutionally debilitating amounts of resources: state-system dynamics and alliances, geographic obstacles to invaders, and the country's extraordinary level of economic development. From the Dutch Republic's earliest days, to its triumph over France in the War of the Spanish Succession, it benefited enormously from formal and informal, often short-lived, communities of interest in battling a common foe. The importance for resource mobilization is not long to seek: alliances bring foreign military and financial support, which means that fewer domestic resources will have to be mobilized.[21] In effect, other countries' resources are being brought to bear, though willingly, as opposed to unwillingly in the Swedish style of foreign resource mobilization.

Even in the earliest days of the Revolt, the Dutch benefited from alliances and common enemies. This should hardly be surprising given the bellicosity and dynastic ambition of the Spanish Habsburgs; common enemies were in no short supply. The Dutch made every effort to bring the English into the war of independence. Elizabeth was offered titular sovereignty over the rebellious provinces, a move she diplomatically refused. She did, however, send a small armed force (eight thousand men under the Earl of Leicester) and an annual subsidy. Perhaps most importantly, however, the queen authorized Drake and twenty privateers to interdict Spanish commerce. This fateful decision dragged England into the war, and led to Philip's launching of the ill-starred Armada (1588), whose defeat ended a promising Spanish offensive against the Dutch.[22]

[20] The question of the States' political coherence and decision-making capacity shall be addressed in a later section. Though military-bureaucratic absolutism was off the agenda, a caesarist possibility—that is, a military commander attacking constitutionalism with the support of the lower orders—remained.

[21] For an excellent sketch of the role of Dutch diplomacy in the war effort, see Geoffrey Parker, "The Dutch Revolt and the Polarization of International Politics," in his *Spain and the Netherlands, 1559–1659* (Short Hills, N.J.: Enslow, 1979), pp. 65–81.

[22] On Anglo-Dutch diplomacy during this period, see Parker, *The Dutch Revolt*, pp. 209–18; C. V. Wedgwood, *William the Silent: William of Nassau, Prince of Orange 1533–1584* (New Haven, Conn.: Yale University Press, 1944), pp. 169–72; R. B. Wernham, "English

Spain's attention was diverted from the Dutch Revolt by another revolt, this one from the remaining Moors in southern Spain. The Morisco Revolt, as it is called, was thought to signal a Turkish invasion. Though this was not forthcoming, the Porte being content with annexing Cyprus from Venice, the rebellion nonetheless altered strategy in Madrid, and resources had to be diverted at a critical period in the Dutch Revolt.[23] In 1574 the Turks (after, but not necessarily because of, Dutch encouragement) went over to the offensive in the Mediterranean, seizing Tunis and requiring a withdrawal of resources from the Army of Flanders. This strain on Spanish resources led to complete fiscal collapse and the securing of Dutch independence, at least for a while.[24] Parker summarizes the nightmare haunting Philip II: "Spain always fought in the Netherlands with only one hand; at the same time she sought to defend the Mediterranean (until 1578), conquer Portugal (1579–83), invade England (1587–8), set a Habsburg on the French throne (1589–98) or secure the duchy of Mantua for a Spanish claimant."[25]

The Twelve Years' Truce (1609–1621) ended the first chapter of Dutch military and diplomatic history. A second chapter began with the expiration of the Truce, after which the Dutch Republic found itself in the midst of the Thirty Years' War. Catholic armies (Spanish, imperial, and Bavarian) were triumphant everywhere; Bohemia, Denmark, and the Palatinate had all been defeated. A peripheral war with France in Italy, the Mantuan succession question, diverted Spanish attention for a few years in the late 1620s, but a bid for full reclamation of the Netherlands was imminent. At this point (1630), Sweden entered the war and rolled back the Catholic armies until dealt a crippling blow at Nördlingen (1634).[26]

Policy and the Revolt of the Netherlands," in Bromley and Kossmann, *Britain and the Netherlands*, Volume 1, pp. 29–40; and J. E. Neale, "Elizabeth and the Netherlands, 1586–7," *English Historical Review* 45 (1930): 373–96. The French also aided the Revolt with men and money until the St. Bartholomew's massacre (1572) and a Catholic monarchy prevailed. Religious differences were put aside in the early seventeenth century and subsidies returned. See Parker, *The Dutch Revolt*, p. 237; Mack P. Holt, *The Duke of Anjou and the Politique Struggle during the Wars of Religion* (Cambridge: Cambridge University Press, 1986), pp. 171–96; and James B. Collins, *Fiscal Limits of Absolutism: Direct Taxation in Early Seventeenth-Century France* (Cambridge: Cambridge University Press, 1988), pp. 70–71.

[23] See Elliott, *Imperial Spain*, pp. 228–34; and I.A.A. Thompson, *War and Government in Habsburg Spain, 1560–1620* (London: Athlone Press, 1976), pp. 20–26.

[24] See Parker, *The Dutch Revolt*, pp. 165–68.

[25] Geoffrey Parker, *The Army of Flanders and the Spanish Road, 1567–1659: The Logistics of Spanish Victory and Defeat in the Low Countries' Wars* (Cambridge: Cambridge University Press, 1972), p. 146.

[26] We have already had occasion to discuss Nördlingen in conjunction with the rise of military-bureaucratic absolutism in France, and we shall come to it again in discussing the

The Cardinal-Infante's army was now poised for a northern reconquista. Once again, state-system dynamics came into play. France viewed the victorious Spanish army as a threat, mobilized for war, and invaded Germany. A French army seized Lorraine, thereby cutting the Spanish Road, a critical supply source for the Army of Flanders.[27] By the last decade of the Thirty Years' War, the Dutch Republic benefited from revolts on the Iberian peninsula itself. First Catalonia, then Portugal, took up arms against the Castilian monarchy. Resources neared exhaustion, armies began to mutiny, and defeat loomed on every front. The importance of common enemies of Spain in securing the Republic's independence is stated well here: "These reverses were due not so much to Spain's weakness as to her inability to concentrate her not inconsiderable military power on any one sector at any one time. She was now seriously overcommitted, with too many major enemies and no major allies."[28]

The Thirty Years' War ended the second and last Habsburg bid for European hegemony, but Louis XIV was quick to pick up where Charles V and Philip IV had left off. The wealthy Netherlands was high on his list of territorial aspirations. With its money and his armies, he reasoned, the continent would be ruled from Versailles. Dutch alliances won the day against the Bourbons, as they had against the Habsburgs. In 1672 both England and France warred against the Dutch, but diplomacy and a stunning naval victory over the English combined to drive England out of the war, and Louis was repulsed with the help of Prussia and even an old nemesis, Spain. In the Nine Years' War (1689–1697) and the War of the Spanish Succession (1701–1713), the Dutch allied with England (where a stadholder, William of Orange, was now king), the Empire, Prussia, and Spain to defeat France.[29]

Considerable weight must be given to alliances in the Dutch Republic's war effort, from the Revolt to the close of the War of the Spanish Succession. Was there a key to such remarkable diplomatic acumen? One suspects that, at least during the early modern period, a close relationship existed between successful diplomacy and international commerce. A maritime country such as the Dutch Republic would perforce have a

---

decline of Spain. It was this Swedish defeat that necessitated a fuller mobilization of French domestic resources and the destruction of constitutionalism.

[27] Parker, *Army of Flanders*, pp. 76–77; Pieter Geyl, *The Netherlands in the Seventeenth Century*, Part 1: *1609–1648* (New York: Barnes & Noble, 1961), pp. 108–22. The seizure of Lorraine was, to say the least, not without consequences for diplomatic and military history.

[28] John Lynch, *Spain under the Habsburgs*, Volume 2: *Spain and America, 1598–1700* (New York: Oxford University Press, 1969), p. 102. By the close of the Thirty Years' War, the armies of the Holy Roman Empire and the Catholic League had to be subsidized by Spain.

[29] Geyl, *The Netherlands*, Part 1, pp. 254–69; Carl J. Ekberg, *The Failure of Louis XIV's Dutch War* (Chapel Hill: University of North Carolina Press, 1979).

large number of international contacts, in and out of government, and a strong measure of experience in subtly or forcefully exerting pressure and presenting points of view. When combined with ungentlemanly lying in the interest of one's country, one has the very essence of diplomacy. Furthermore, a merchant country is of great value to its trading partners, as well as to their sovereigns, who cannot look with equanimity on danger to a major source of commerce and revenue. Trading countries undoubtedly incur the wrath of other traders, hence the three Anglo-Dutch Wars in the seventeenth century; but the historical evidence of the Netherlands, England, and Venice suggests that the diplomatic assets outweigh the liabilities. England, as we have seen, was successful at diplomacy, as was another maritime power, Venice, which realized it could never match the resources of the Turks, and so adopted a diplomatic strategy to bring other countries' resources to play against the Porte. Similarly, Venice used France to thwart Spanish ambitions in Italy, and also played off the smaller Italian states against each other.[30]

The Dutch never faced the full brunt of Habsburg or Bourbon military might. The Dutch Republic benefited from enemies of its enemies, and shrewdly orchestrated other powers to make its fight theirs. Accordingly, the enemy armies that the Republic did face did not necessitate the mobilization of nearly as many domestic resources as would have been needed had it fought alone.

Geography, too, favored the Dutch in ways limiting domestic resource mobilization. Spain's lines of communication stretched hundreds of miles, from Italy to the southern provinces of the Low Countries still under Habsburg control. Sea routes were longer still, and were plied by hostile raiders of numerous flags. Second, the Republic had a unique weapon that could be used with devastating effect on invading armies: dikes could be broken to flood vast areas, thereby driving back an enemy and insulating the economic and political centers of the nation, Holland and Zeeland. This weapon was used to repel a Spanish offensive in 1572–1573, and also Louis XIV's invasion a century later. The Dutch people saw the floodings as miraculous deliveries from their enemies, as the hand of Providence aiding the elect. They seemed clearly part of the same design that punished Pharaoh's army in the Red Sea.[31]

[30] See William J. Bouwsma, *Venice and the Defense of Republican Liberty: Renaissance Values in the Age of the Counter Reformation* (Berkeley and Los Angeles: University of California Press, 1984), pp. 102–9, 246–51, 506–7; William H. McNeill, *Venice, the Hinge of Europe, 1081–1797* (Chicago: University of Chicago Press, 1974), pp. 89–90; and M. E. Mallett and J. R. Hale, *The Military Organization of a Renaissance State: Venice c. 1400–1617* (Cambridge: Cambridge University Press, 1984).

[31] Schama, *The Embarrassment of Riches*, pp. 276–78; *The New Cambridge Modern His-*

Another obstacle to invaders lay in the numerous topographical features of the countryside. Spanish and French armies found themselves obstructed or bogged down by marshes, dikes, and rivers, just as Allied armies had during the autumn of 1944. Fording one branch of the Scheldt confronted them with only more marshes and rivers. On this point, the author of a classic study of the Revolt states: "In the trial of strength between Spain, based on the wide perimeter of the Netherlands . . . and the revolt, based on the maritime provinces of Holland and Zealand, the geographical configuration of the country, in particular the inestimable strategic importance of the great rivers, was the determining factor."[32] Operational problems were aggravated by scores of town bastions along the banks of these rivers.[33] We can now perhaps understand the irony that, in this land so close to Waterloo, there were no decisive open-field battles. Instead, most land battles were protracted sieges of towns heavily fortified in the trace italienne manner. The siege of Naarden took eight months, Jülich five, and Breda ten. The siege of Bergen op Zoom lasted four months and cost the Spanish nine thousand soldiers to casualties and desertions.[34] The futility of most of these sieges, which even if successful only opened a path to another bastion, is conveyed in remarks on one siege in 1634: "Militarily, Breda was a dead end which left the way to Holland just as securely blocked by defences as before. Financially, the campaign finally exhausted the resources painstakingly accumulated by the crown . . . since 1621. . . . [T]here was now nothing left with which to pay the troops and no means of obtaining further credit. . . . [Local Spanish authorities] were instructed to keep the army strictly on the defensive."[35] There was nothing like Waterloo here, only intimations of the Marne, the Somme, and Verdun.

---

tory, Volume 3, pp. 274–75, Volume 5, pp. 292–93; Wedgwood, *William the Silent*, pp. 162–68. Here we see an example of the development of nationalism in the course of warfare.

[32] Geyl, *The Revolt of the Netherlands*, p. 179. See also Parker, *The Dutch Revolt*, p. 164. Swiss constitutionalism also benefited from geography and international alliances. Cantonal militias took advantage of woodlands and mountainous terrain to repel invaders. French reliance on Swiss infantry led to a measure of protection over the confederation. "Pas d'argent, pas de Suisses" was certainly true, but so was "pas de Suisse, pas de Suisses." A more contemporary illustration of the importance of geography on military operations may be seen in World War II, in which the spectacular advances across the plains of France contrasted with the agonizingly slow advances across the mountainous terrain of Italy.

[33] Parker views the bastions as more important than the rivers in blocking invasions. See *The Army of Flanders*, p. 17; and *The Dutch Revolt*, pp. 156–58.

[34] Jonathan I. Israel, *The Dutch Republic and the Hispanic World 1606–1661* (Oxford: Clarendon Press, 1986), pp. 98–109; Parker, *The Dutch Revolt*, pp. 159–64; Lynch, *Spain under the Habsburgs*, Volume 2, p. 72; R. Fruin, *The Siege and Relief of Leyden in 1574* (The Hague: Martinus Nijhoff, 1927).

[35] Israel, *The Dutch Republic*, p. 109.

Natural obstacles and man-made bastions give tremendous advantages to an army on the defensive, as were the Dutch, especially after the Twelve Years' Truce expired in 1621. Behind rivers, marshes, and bastions the Dutch army could successfully defend the nation against numerically superior invaders. Furthermore, the Dutch could use poorly trained town militias to tie down even the most seasoned Spanish forces. Defensive advantages meant that a Spanish army would have to be vastly larger than its opponent's, and also better supplied, to avoid desertions and mutinies in the course of long, miserable sieges. But, as we have already seen, Spain was hopelessly over-committed throughout Europe, and as shall be seen, its supply system was anything but sound.

Geography and international assistance served to keep down military expenses, but the domestic costs, at least in absolute terms, were still considerable. Despite coalitions and defensive advantages, the Netherlands had to field armies that, though perhaps small by continental standards (averaging about 50,000), were nonetheless modernized, and reached a peak of 129,000 in 1629.[36] The Republic also put to sea one of the largest and most feared navies of the period. By the mid- to late seventeenth century, the heyday of the privateer was coming to a close. The fleets of England, Spain, and the Netherlands comprised ships built by government contract for the sole purpose of war. In 1620 the Dutch navy consisted of twenty-nine capital ships; by the end of the century, it boasted a hundred first-raters and over twenty thousand hands.[37] Even if, as Hintze observed, ships cannot be used for internal repression, inasmuch as many of these leviathans carried ninety or more guns, required crews of over a hundred, and adopted increasingly sophisticated equipment, the costs of naval warfare were considerable, and this presents a problem for an argument positing the importance of domestic resource mobilization in the destruction of constitutional liberties and institutions. A third financial burden of the war stemmed from the construction of town fortifications and a network of fortresses along the eastern border. In 1591 3.2 million florins were spent on fortifications alone. In 1632 the figure had more than quadrupled to 13.4 million, and eight years later the costs were 18.8 million.[38]

The wars with Spain were not limited to the Low Countries. As Parker

[36] Ibid., pp. 42–177.

[37] Ibid., p. 110; C. R. Boxer, *The Dutch Seaborne Empire, 1600–1800* (London: Penguin, 1988), pp. 310–11.

[38] Parker, *The Army of Flanders*, pp. 16–17, "War and Economic Change: The Economic Costs of the Dutch Revolt," in his *Spain and the Netherlands*, p. 191, *The Dutch Revolt*, pp. 157–59. Many of the bastions predated the Revolt, though; some were begun by Charles V in the mid-sixteenth century.

observes, the Eighty Years' War was the first global war. Soldiers and sailors from the two countries clashed in the Caribbean, Brazil, the Philippines, and the East Indies. But the impact of most of these battles was not as significant for Dutch state expenditures as one might initially expect. Most forces on the high seas and in the colonies were not in the service of the States-General, but in that of the East India Company or West India Company. The private sector contributed mightily and directly to the war effort.[39] The invasion of Brazil (Portugal was under Spanish rule 1580–1668) and the interdiction of Spanish bullion fleets from the Americas were unfriendly takeovers, effected by the private militaries of the Dutch free enterprise system, not by the state. Nor did the state benefit directly from these adventures: captured Spanish bullion was a dividend to be distributed to shareholders, and the directors of the East India Company curtly told their government that, "The places and strongholds which they had captured in the East Indies should not be regarded as national conquests but as the property of private merchants. . . ."[40] These exploits did, however, divert Spanish resources to convoy duty and far-flung garrisons.[41] Private vice, public benefit.

There is still the question of how the Dutch Republic shouldered the costs of a large army, a first-rate navy, and numerous town fortifications without adopting authoritarian means of extraction. The defensive nature of the land war in the Low Countries precluded mobilizing foreign resources as the Swedes had done. (Cavalry raids into southern provinces still under Spanish control relied on mobile plunder, but did not constitute a significant part of the war effort.) Naval preeminence and the large number of towns provide clues. The number of towns suggests a great deal of commercial activity, and a large navy suggests the need to protect the sea lanes on which commerce depended. Thus far in the study, the countries that have modernized their armed forces have had what might be called agrarian economies, relatively undeveloped systems of production that are hard-pressed to support modern armies without causing internal crises. But a more highly developed economy can sustain a large war effort without precipitating conflicts with the estates.

The Dutch Republic's was by no means an agrarian economy. Its rural sector produced only simple foodstuffs for local consumption. The Republic was an immensely wealthy trading center that by 1600 had attained commercial ascendency over Venice and Antwerp, mainly from a virtual monopoly on Baltic shipping. Its burgeoning colonial empire

---

[39] Boxer, *The Dutch Seaborne Empire*, pp. 25–29, 89–93; Israel, *The Dutch Republic*, pp. 117–34, 197–204.

[40] Quoted in Boxer, *The Dutch Seaborne Empire*, p. 50.

[41] Lynch, *Spain under the Habsburgs*, Volume 2, pp. 173–84; Israel, *The Dutch Republic*, p. 294.

served to further the Dutch commercial lead over other European powers.[42] And this astounding wealth was channeled into the war effort without undermining the constitution. Sustained economic growth took place
even amidst war, but was especially dramatic during the Twelve Years'
Truce (1609–1621). Spain itself contributed to the boom in the Republic
by closing Amsterdam's main rival, Antwerp, an event that led to trade
and capital fleeing to the Republic, and by allowing Dutch vessels to continue trade with the peninsula.[43] As long as the Dutch navy maintained
mastery of the sea, the economy and war finance were secure.[44]

The wealth of the Netherlands translated into the war effort in two
ways. The high level of economic activity meant greater tax revenues for
the state, most of which came from the maritime provinces of Holland
and Zeeland. Excises on basic food products, a surcharge on exports, and
a tax on capital over a hundred florins brought in considerable revenue.[45]
But taxation led to grumblings and some rioting. This led to the fuller
employment of another instrument of power available to economically
advanced states: public debt—a mechanism that entails no corrupt, inefficient tax farming or bureaucratic collection organs extending throughout the country, and one that minimizes both popular opposition to war
costs, and the need for repressive organs to deal with opposition. It is
one of the many ironies of the Eighty Years' War that it was the Habsburgs who had earlier helped to build the capital markets that later channeled a seemingly inexhaustible supply of money into wars against them.
In the first half of the sixteenth century, Charles V negotiated loans with
provincial States and towns, in order to finance war with France. Such

[42] Israel, *Dutch Primacy in World Trade*; Boxer, *The Dutch Seaborne Empire*; Geyl, *The
Netherlands*, Part 1, pp. 158–208, Part 2, pp. 63–95, 174–88; Schama, *The Embarrassment
of Riches*; Immanuel Wallerstein, *The Modern World-System 2: Mercantilism and the Consolidation of the European World-Economy, 1600–1750* (New York: Academic Press, 1980),
pp. 37–71; Peter Kriedte, *Peasants, Landlords and Merchant Capitalists: Europe and the
World Economy, 1500–1800* (Cambridge: Cambridge University Press, 1983), pp. 78–91.
Paul Kennedy rightly notes that countries that eschewed or closed off foreign trade did so
at the cost of limiting the future power of the state. See *The Rise and Fall of the Great
Powers: Economic Change and Military Conflict from 1500 to 2000* (New York: Random
House, 1987), pp. 14–16.

[43] Israel, *The Dutch Republic*, pp. 60–65; Geyl, *The Revolt of the Netherlands*, pp. 233–
34; Parker, "War and Economic Change," in *Spain and the Netherlands*, pp. 197–98. Trade
with the Dutch was unavoidable during famine in Castile: Baltic grain, the transportation
of which was controlled by Holland, had to be imported no matter who transported it.

[44] Privateers operating out of Dunkirk took a heavy toll on Dutch merchantmen, but
commercial revenue still rose throughout most of the war period. See Israel, *The Dutch
Republic*, pp. 192–96. The high level of commerce and shipping gave the Dutch as early as
1588 over two thousand ships with some war-making capacity. See Boxer, *The Dutch Seaborne Empire*, pp. 76–77.

[45] Parker, *The Dutch Revolt*, pp. 149–51.

were the wealth and intricacies of the capital markets of the province of Holland that, as early as the 1530s, Amsterdam could raise huge amounts of money without much effort and without any coercion.[46] The capital markets Charles V helped to develop were used against his successors' armies with devastating effect, but without any parallel effect on Dutch constitutional government. The States remained sovereign, local privileges thrived, and the rule of law prevailed. Wealth also meant that the army could rely on mercenaries rather than on conscripts. Work levies seem to have been limited to coastal reconnaissance and breaking holes in the river ice to prevent crossings.[47]

SPANISH WAR FINANCE

An argument that uses finance to explain the Dutch war effort raises the comparative question of the financial resources of its chief antagonist. Spain most certainly availed itself of European debt instruments and had access to no small amount of commercial wealth from the New World. Government in Spain, or strictly speaking in its core province, Castile, does not follow the European pattern of medieval constitutionalism. Centuries of war against the Moors left the political imprint of a crown with formidable if not complete taxation powers independent of the estates (cortes), control over legislation, and a strong apparatus of local administration throughout Castile. Expansion to the south gave the crown lands that it used as a considerable revenue base and benefice reserve for a service nobility. A state gradually expanding and placing beholden knights on conditional benefices is far more reminiscent of Muscovy and its pomestie system than it is of contractual western feudalism, and this

---

[46] On Dutch capital markets, see James D. Tracy, *A Financial Revolution in the Habsburg Netherlands: Renten and Renteniers in the County of Holland, 1515–1565* (Berkeley and Los Angeles: University of California Press, 1985), *Holland under Habsburg Rule*, pp. 115–46; Smit, "The Netherlands Revolution," pp. 42–43; Parker, *The Dutch Revolt*, pp. 38–39, 145–57; and Herbert H. Rowen, *John de Witt, Grand Pensionary of Holland, 1625–1672* (Princeton, N.J.: Princeton University Press, 1978), pp. 170–90. Amsterdam continued as a major center of war finance for over a century. The Dutch port provided the sinews for the coalitional wars against Louis XIV. Napoleon invaded the Netherlands to deny his enemies access to the capital markets there. See Geyl, *The Netherlands*, Part 2, pp. 311–12; J. Aalbers, "Holland's Financial Problems (1713–1733) and the Wars against Louis XIV," in A. C. Duke and C. A. Tamse, eds., *Britain and the Netherlands*, Volume 6: *War and Society* (The Hague: Martinus Nijhoff, 1977), pp. 79–93; and M. G. Buist, "The Sinews of War: The Role of Dutch Finance in European Politics (c. 1750–1815)," in Duke and Tamse, pp. 124–40. It might also be remembered that Dutch capital was crucial to the rise of English war finance at the end of the seventeenth century and throughout the next.

[47] A. Th. van Deursen, "Holland's Experience of War during the Revolt of the Netherlands," in Duke and Tamse, *Britain and the Netherlands*, pp. 20–51.

is the key to early monarchal power and the weakness of constitutional-ism.[48]

The Castilian cortes had no legislative power; they met infrequently, and only at the monarch's bidding.[49] Its only substantive power lay in negotiating new taxes. In this endeavor the cortes were more often than not intimidated by a powerful monarch, or bribed by offers of honors and offices into approving new taxes that were fobbed off onto others any-way.[50] Independent taxation in Castile and the wealth of the New World gave the crown great latitude in war making and other matters of state. These sources also gave it the resources to threaten and bribe the cortes into ceding more and more extraordinary taxes.[51] But most of Habsburg authority did not extend outside Castile. Local rights and privileges re-mained intact in Aragon, Valencia, and Catalonia.[52] As long as finances could be managed with the considerable sources from Castile, the Amer-icas, and other overseas possessions, the king saw no need to castilianize the rest of the peninsula.

Spanish fiscal problems led to pressures that brought about the Dutch Revolt, which only aggravated those problems. Between 1570 and 1573, revenue from the Low Countries plummeted from 8.8 million florins to 1.8 million; during the same period, extractions from Castile had to be more than quadrupled. But the Spanish army fighting the Revolt—only one of Spain's fronts—cost more than the combined revenues extracted from Castile and the West Indies.[53] The result was bankruptcy and the

[48] Angus MacKay, *Spain in the Middle Ages: From Frontier to Empire, 1000–1500* (Lon-don: Macmillan, 1977), pp. 97–104.

[49] Elliott, *Imperial Spain*, pp. 80–81; Lynch, *Spain under the Habsburgs*, Volume 2, pp. 85–91; Miguel Angel Ladero Quesada, "De la *Reconquista* à la fiscalité d'état dans la cou-ronne de Castille 1268–1368," in J.-Ph. Genet and M. Le Mené, eds., *Genèse de l'état moderne: Prélèvement et redistribution* (Paris: Editions du Centre National de la Recherche Scientifique, 1987), pp. 35–51.

[50] Elliott, *Imperial Spain*, pp. 193–95; MacKay, *Spain in the Middle Ages*, pp. 103–4; Lynch, *Spain under the Habsburgs*, Volume 2, pp. 85–86. Recent scholarship has argued that the Castilian cortes was not quite as supine as once thought. From the late sixteenth century to the mid-seventeenth, the cortes exchanged new taxes for royal concessions— none of which, however, elevated its authority to anywhere near that of the other estates in this study. There is agreement that the cortes had effectively exited the political scene by the 1650s. See Charles Jago, "Habsburg Absolutism and the Cortes of Castile," *Ameri-can Historical Review* 86 (1981): 307–26, "Philip II and the Cortes of Castile: The Case of the Cortes of 1576," *Past and Present* 109 (1985): 24–43; and I.A.A. Thompson, "The End of the Cortes of Castile," *Parliaments, Estates and Representation* 4 (1984): 125–33.

[51] Here we see the importance of control of commercial wealth. In England, Venice, and the Dutch Republic the merchants themselves controlled it. The Spanish kings, by con-trast, controlled much of the New World production, which they used to further their in-dependence of action.

[52] Lynch, *Spain under the Habsburgs*, Volume 2, pp. 30–39.

[53] Parker, *The Dutch Revolt*, pp. 162–65.

inevitable consequence of ill-financed armies of the time, mutiny. Between 1573 and 1607, there were over forty mutinies in the Army of Flanders, the impact of which on the prosecution of the war was enormous. Spanish mutinies led to quick, almost effortless, Dutch advances that negated painstaking and costly Spanish gains. Mutineers were not above exchanging the towns they garrisoned for Dutch money, nor above settling their pay problems by pillaging a nearby town. In the Spanish Fury of 1574, the army temporarily dealt with pay problems by letting its soldiers plunder Antwerp, a town still under Spanish authority. Settling short-run pay problems came at the cost of alienating an ambivalent or sometimes even sympathetic population, and depriving Spain of an important source of loans, as capital fled to the more hospitable northern provinces, where soldiers were better paid and therefore better disciplined. Fiscal collapse and mutiny meant Spain could no longer prosecute the war. A report on state finances lamented: "Short of a miracle, the whole military machine will fall in ruins so rapidly that it is highly probable that I shall not have time to tell you about it."[54] With its finances in a shambles, Spain had no alternative but to agree to a truce in 1609.[55]

A second fiscal crunch came during the second half of the Thirty Years' War, with catastrophic effect, not only for the war effort, but this time for Spain as a great power. Swedish armies were rolling back Catholic armies that so recently had appeared on the verge of establishing universal empire, and Spanish subsidies to armies in Germany had to be increased. Revenue from American bullion began to decline from its peak in 1600. Whole treasure fleets were captured by the Dutch, and privateers attacked Spanish shipping the world over. Elation following the Spanish victory over the Swedes at Nördlingen quickly disappeared when it became apparent that war with France was imminent.[56] Castilian

[54] Quoted in Parker, *The Dutch Revolt*, p. 169.

[55] On the mutinies, see Geoffrey Parker, "Mutiny and Discontent in the Spanish Army of Flanders 1572–1607," *Past and Present* 58 (1973): 38–52, *The Dutch Revolt*, pp. 162–73, 222–40, *The Army of Flanders*, pp. 185–206; Koenigsberger, *The Habsburgs and Europe*, pp. 138–89; Geyl, *The Revolt of the Netherlands*, p. 145. Problems of mutiny and poor discipline were not innate to the troops themselves, as is sometimes thought by those distinguishing too sharply between northern and southern Europe. When properly paid and supplied, the Spanish army was among the finest in Europe. At Nördlingen they withstood the repeated onslaughts of the Swedes, and won the day. At Rocroi, faithful to Castile's laws, they fought to the last. In *The Army of Flanders*, Parker describes at length the rigors endured by the Spanish soldiers, whose pay was sometimes as many as six years in arrears. His is a rather sympathetic, almost Kiplingesque, treatment. In any case, brutal Dutch raids into the southern provinces alienated that population from the northern cause. See also Parker, *The Dutch Revolt*, pp. 234–35.

[56] J. H. Elliott, *The Count-Duke of Olivares: The Statesman in an Age of Decline* (New Haven, Conn.: Yale University Press, 1986), pp. 362–71, *The Revolt of the Catalans* (Cam-

resources had been exhausted; depopulation and economic decline were in evidence. Dwindling American revenues were mortgaged to rentiers for years to come, and experiments in debasing the currency only confirmed Gresham's Law.[57] It was time to make other provinces in Spain, especially Catalonia, contribute their proper share, and such a move would of course entail constitutional conflict: "The ministers in Madrid were now convinced that strict observance of every detail of the Catalonian constitutions was incompatible with the security of the Spanish Monarchy."[58] Conscription, new taxes, and the quartering of unruly troops exacerbated social tensions and erupted into revolt. The parallel is obvious: "Spain had another Holland on its hands."[59]

The longevity of the Catalonian Revolt (1640–1652) was due to French military assistance, and to the retrogade quality of the Spanish army on the peninsula. The best soldiers had already been deployed to Italy, Germany, and the Low Countries. Iberia had to be scoured for manpower, and the results were not good, militarily or politically: "Recruits unfortunate enough to be pressed into service resembled nothing so much as a feudal host, untrained, inexperienced, and led by amateurs."[60] The significance of this desperate levy is not limited to the duration of the revolt. Conscription in Portugal led to unrest and increased irritation over the Spanish suzerain's inability to do anything about the Dutch West India Company's invasion of Brazil. Portuguese merchants now threw in their lot with the nationalist cause led by the Duke of Brabanza, and opened yet another front against Spain. After twenty-eight years of war, Spain recognized Portugal's independence in 1668.[61] Revolts broke out among the Spanish holdings in Italy as well. Another parallel occurs: Two, three, many Hollands.

Regional autonomy in Spain, resulting in the revolts of the mid-seventeenth century and contributing significantly to the collapse of Spanish power, had no analogue in the other military-bureaucratic absolutisms

bridge: Cambridge University Press, 1963), pp. 263–72; C. V. Wedgwood, *The Thirty Years War* (Garden City, N.Y.: Anchor, 1961), pp. 414–44.

[57] Elliott, *Olivares*, pp. 514–19; Lynch, *Spain under the Habsburgs*, Volume 2, pp. 10, 34–35, 173–84; Parker, *Army of Flanders*, pp. 145–57; Jago, "Habsburg Absolutism," pp. 324–26.

[58] Elliott, *Revolt of the Catalans*, p. 356. See also Olivares's words cited on p. 75.

[59] Lynch, *Spain under the Habsburgs*, Volume 2, p. 105. See also Elliott, *Revolt of the Catalans* and *Imperial Spain*, pp. 103–7; and R. A. Stradling, *Philip IV and the Government of Spain, 1621–1665* (Cambridge: Cambridge University Press, 1988), pp. 172–88.

[60] Lynch, *Spain under the Habsburgs*, Volume 2, p. 116. See also Elliott, *Revolt of the Catalans*, pp. 454, 510–11.

[61] On the revolt in Portugal, see Elliott, *Revolt of the Catalans*, pp. 512–47, and *Imperial Spain*, pp. 342–44. The Dutch sent material to the rebels for obvious reasons. See Israel, *The Dutch Republic*, pp. 338–40.

considered in this study. Regional tensions certainly existed in France, but the Fronde (1648–1653) settled the issue in favor of absolutist power, and the problem did not recur until the Revolution. An explanation for regionalism might well lie in the Spanish monarchy's income from the Americas, which provided it with fluctuating but often dazzling revenue. As long as revenue from Castile, the New World, and elsewhere sufficed, it was best to let sleeping provincial estates and constitutions lie—a seemingly sensible policy, but one that left a volatile state of affairs to wait for the conjuncture of events that came in the last decade of the Thirty Years' War. Had the crown moved earlier and decisively against the provinces, that is, at a time when its best tercios had not been committed abroad, Spanish finances and war-making capacity would certainly have been sounder, and quite possibly the country would have been spared many of the regional conflicts that mark its history. In this respect, it is important to bear in mind that, as the "pacified" Scottish Highlanders and many other vanquished and silenced people would attest, the construction of nation-states is often carried out by equal measures of orchestrated sentiment and brutal repression.

Spanish resources, at least those that could be allocated to the Army of Flanders, could not match those of the Netherlands. The Thirty Years' War coincided with declining bullion revenue and the economic decline of Castile. New fiscal techniques conflicted with local constitutions at a time when too much of the state's military strength was deployed outside the peninsula. Revolts broke out and completely undermined Spanish finances and war-making capacity. By the close of the war in 1648, annual bullion revenue from America had been halved. Castile, by virtue of brutal taxation and conscription, was in decline, its young men thrown away in distant, often foolhardy wars.[62] The decline of Spain was brought on not by the defeat of the Armada—decades of military success followed 1588—and still less by the quality of its soldiers, but by the revolts and economic decline stemming from military overcommitment, from kings and ministers who lacked the courage not to use the military.

Executive Capacity and the Challenge of Caesarism

The Revolt ousted the foreign executive authority that Spain had sought to strengthen, leaving government in the many hands of provincial States. The Union of Utrecht (1579), the formal constitution of the Dutch

[62] On Spanish economic decline, see Lynch, *Spain under the Habsburgs*, Volume 2, pp. 126–59; Elliott, *Imperial Spain*, pp. 280–81; A. W. Lovett, *Early Habsburg Spain, 1517–1598* (Oxford: Oxford University Press, 1986), pp. 234–35; and Kennedy, *Rise and Fall of the Great Powers*, pp. 31–72.

Republic, reads more like a mutual defense pact, and a rather vague one at that, than it does a binding set of national principles of government. There is no substantive executive called for, nor even a provision for central finance; there is only the recognition of the ill-defined sovereignty of the seven provincial States, themselves tied to numerous town councils.[63] Given this confusing state of affairs, one might ask, "l'Etat c'est qui?" Rowen notes: "In a political structure such as that of the Dutch Republic, where there were so few paid officials and these were usually administrators rather than leaders, and where political power was distributed all up and down the scale and across the country, governance was more a matter of persuasion than of command."[64] How could such a congeries of provincial assemblies, even with the blessings of foreign alliances, spectacular wealth, and geographic barriers, govern during peace, let alone during war?[65]

One need not be any sort of economic determinist to admit that economic power as often as not leads to political power. In the Dutch Republic, economic and political power were concentrated in the province of Holland, to such an extent that, to this day, many confuse provincial part for national whole. Holland built political supremacy on its contribution of almost sixty percent of the country's budget, with half of that coming from the Amsterdam regents.[66] Executive power developed around the chief secretaries or pensioners of the States of Holland. Figures such as Oldenbarnevelt and de Witt labored to prevent centralization, in war and peace, and to continue Holland's supremacy over the other six provinces. When it was feared that the commander of the English expeditionary force (the Earl of Leicester) was seeking to arrogate a bit too much power, Oldenbarnevelt assumed executive authority from his position in the Holland States. The diplomacy upon which so much of the struggle depended was formulated not by the States-General, but mainly by the pensioner of Holland.[67]

[63] Herbert H. Rowen, *The Low Countries in Early Modern Times* (New York: Walker, 1972), pp. 67–74; Geyl, *Revolt of the Netherlands*, pp. 139–41, 186–87; *The New Cambridge Modern History*, Volume 4, pp. 361–62.

[64] Herbert H. Rowen, *The Princes of Orange: The Stadholders in the Dutch Republic* (Cambridge: Cambridge University Press, 1988), p. 98.

[65] The English queen evidently did not think they could. Elizabeth instructed the commander of the English expeditionary force, the Earl of Leicester, to press the Dutch on the matter of centralization. See Geyl, *Revolt of the Netherlands*, p. 203.

[66] Rowen, *Princes of Orange*, p. 84; Parker, "Why Did the Dutch Revolt Last So Long?" in his *Spain and the Netherlands*, p. 58.

[67] Jan den Tex, *Oldenbarnevelt*, Volume 1 (Cambridge: Cambridge University Press, 1973), pp. 40–151; Israel, *The Dutch Republic*, pp. 1–42; Rowen, *John de Witt*, pp. 238–56; F. G. Oosterhoff, *Leicester and the Netherlands 1586–1587* (Utrecht: H & S, 1988);

The contrast between an absolutist state and that of the Holland regents is clear: the former saw the state as the center of the country, something to be constantly expanded; the latter saw the state as a means, and a rather bothersome one at that, to sustain if not advance the main concern, commerce. There was no self-sustaining, self-expanding logic to Holland's political power. The absolute monarch's idée fixe of finding new methods of extracting resources contrasts with the Holland regents' concern with limiting the apparatus and cutting all possible expenses. The absolute monarch's control of finance and independent war-making capacity had no analogue in the Republic. Wars were defensive, and military leaders, as we shall see, were reined in. A deterrent to expanding its power, if any was needed, lay in recognition that too much power in Holland would lead to a coalition in the States-General against it. A moderate, unintrusive hegemony predicated on its contribution to the country's budget sufficed, both for Holland's interests and for the war effort.

Part of the logic of this study is that the cumbersome, particularist estates were serious obstacles to military modernization and the proper conduct of early modern warfare. Yet the States of Holland seems to have accomplished this, albeit with the aid of alliances, commercial wealth, and geography. Might the incompatibility between parliament and modern warfare have been a perceptual one, that is, the crown perceived parliament to be too slow and obsessed with constitutional pettifoggery for the dangerous times, and thus closed it with the army? Perhaps perceptions entered into play, but the Prussian and French estates were not forthcoming with revenue, and that concrete situation, not the perceptions and misperceptions of the prince, precipitated their dissolution. A vigorous economy made war finance easier, but how did the Dutch direct the wars? The record of parliaments ruling on their own, in war or peace, without a monarchy or some form of executive, is not good. The House of Commons tore itself apart during the Civil War period, alienated much of the population, and maintained representative government and executive capacity only after purges. The Parlement of Paris fell apart during the Fronde. The Polish diet was paralyzed by numbers and foreign intrigues, and the country was partitioned. The estates of Catalonia fared no better during the long revolt against Spain; French viceroys had to intervene and assume control of government.[68] It may be countered that each of these estates faced extraordinary circumstances that prevented effective rule: the House of Commons was divided over religious and political differences; the Polish gentry were more interested in their

Wallace T. MacCaffrey, *Queen Elizabeth and the Making of Policy, 1572–1588* (Princeton, N.J.: Princeton University Press, 1981), pp. 356–89.

[68] See Elliott, *Revolt of the Catalans*, pp. 533–41.

manors than in affairs of state, and were sprawled over an enormous territory from the Baltic to the Black Sea; and the Catalonian revolt coincided with, in fact was begun by, a peasant revolt aimed at the nobility and patriciate. Did the estates of these countries come to power at unfortunately difficult times, or was there something distinctive about the Dutch States that allowed them to function efficiently, even in dire straits?

The Netherlands was also divided along class, regional, and religious lines: antioligarchic sentiment smoldered, Hollanders were resented, and religious strife, though never degenerating into overt civil war as it did in Germany and France, was prevalent.[69] But at the level of political elites, especially within the States of Holland, there were few cleavages. Here, a merchant oligarchy, closely tied by maritime trade and based in a compact region, controlled government for the province, and, more often than not, for the entire Republic. It was a closed clique, a sort of mercantile cosa nostra, that deliberated and formed policy without the delays of convoking far-flung delegates and without the potentially paralyzing divisions of regionalism and class. Perhaps only in Holland and a few other commercial centers does Marx's observation about the state being a committee for the common affairs of the bourgeoisie really square with political realities. The political order in Venice seems to have been similar. After ousting a dynastic *doge* in the twelfth century, a patriciate-dominated Senate assumed control of the state, and placed effective control of day-to-day government in the hands of a compact *Signoria*.[70] Based on the scant evidence of two cases, the prescription for successful estate rule seems to be the ouster of monarchal authority prior to a significant level of political institutionalization, and the absence of deep social and regional divisions at the elite level. In essence, this means oligarchy, the barest minimum of constitutional government.[71]

Similarities there were between the two maritime powers, but two important differences stand out. First, the Netherlands was effectively governed by the oligarchy of a single province, but the regents of Holland had to deal with the other six provinces and the excluded lower classes

---

[69] See Benjamin Jacob Kaplan, "Calvinists and Libertines: The Reformation in Utrecht, 1578–1618," Doctoral Thesis, Department of History, Harvard University, 1989, pp. 149–214, 331ff.

[70] See Frederic C. Lane, *Venice: A Maritime Republic* (Baltimore, Md.: Johns Hopkins University Press, 1987); Bouwsma, *Venice and the Defense of Republican Liberty*, pp. 61–62; Mallett and Hale, *Military Organization of a Renaissance State*, pp. 160–62.

[71] The oligarchic nature of Dutch political power helped to preserve constitutionalism, but—and this points to another irony of democratic political development—it also made liberalization in ensuing centuries more difficult.

in their own—with those they might only hesitatingly and perhaps sarcastically call their countrymen. Second, another power center, the stadholderate, entered the political scene, and, in conjunction with the other provincial States and the disenfranchised lower classes, challenged the political power of Holland. Military-bureaucratic absolutism was not on the agenda after the ouster of Spanish authority, but some danger of populist-militarism or caesarism, like that of the Caroline monarchs in Sweden, was in evidence during the seventeenth-century wars. Prior to the Revolt, stadholders had been Habsburg officials, drawn from the local aristocracy, more loyal to the manner born than to foreign prince. Philip II's innovations in government aimed not at bolstering the stadholders, but at replacing them with more reliable Spanish officials. So it was that William the Silent, scion of the Nassau and Orange families, and stadholder of five of the Republic's provinces, became the leader of the Revolt. In so doing, he transformed the stadholderate from a Spanish governorship into the military leadership of the Dutch Republic, a position of substantial military and civilian authority, traditionally held by an Orange, that, though formally and in practice subordinated to the States, could nonetheless be used as a springboard by a commander desirous of greater power.[72] Caesarism was all the more likely in such a highly oligarchic society that excluded lower classes from most economic and political rewards.[73] The Dutch Republic had numerous parallels with the late Roman Republic, but was there an ambitious proconsul with loyal legions?

Stadholders built up authority in the States-General by means of their patronage powers, which included nominating magistrates and councillors, and by exploiting anti-Holland sentiment in other provincial States. They cultivated a popular following by playing upon antioligarchic and religious passions, and by taking advantage of mass exuberance following military success.[74] Stadholder power was limited in two ways significant

[72] Rowen, *Princes of Orange*, pp. 8–22.

[73] Parker, *The Dutch Revolt*, pp. 179–86. Venice avoided the potential of populist-militarism by employing only foreigners as its commanders. It was thought that only a Venetian could mobilize popular sentiments against the oligarchy. But after the successes and martyrdom of William the Silent, the use of foreign commanders for the Dutch army was not practical; the House of Orange had acquired considerable support from the States and public. After William of Orange became the English king (1689), however, the Duke of Marlborough commanded Dutch forces during the War of the Spanish Succession. On Venetian military commanders, see Lane, *Maritime Republic*, pp. 231–32; McNeill, *Venice*, p. 70.

[74] Jonathan I. Israel, "Frederick Henry and the Dutch Political Factions, 1625–1642," *English Historical Review* 98 (1983): 1–27, *The Dutch Republic*, pp. 223–49; Pieter Geyl, *Orange and Stuart 1641–72* (London: Weidenfeld & Nicolson, 1969), pp. 349–400, *The Netherlands*, Part 2, pp. 126–49. On the excluded lower orders, see Kaplan, "Calvinists and Libertines," pp. 107–48.

for constitutional questions. First, mobilization of upper-class support lay in politicking and building coalitions in the provincial States and town governments outside Holland. Direct appeal to the urban masses would have coalesced insurmountable opposition in all the States, and led to an immediate cutoff of money, dismissal, or, possibly, assassination. Politicking in the States to some extent invigorated the political system, and the oligarchy of Holland, itself a long-term obstacle to liberal democracy, was checked. Even when tensions between the Orangists and Holland ran high, as they did at least twice, to the brink of civil war, the stadholder was not acting on his own, but rather as an agent, with the full authority of the States-General.[75] Second, the impact of popular mobilization was attenuated by the specific issues that pitted Orange versus Holland, namely war and peace. The burghers of Holland successfully countered Orangist calls for continued war by convincing lower classes that war was detrimental to prosperity and therefore to their own material interests.[76]

Perhaps of most importance, the stadholder, unlike the virtually autonomous Roman proconsuls and legion commanders, never obtained independent sources of revenue. Nor did he acquire an overpowering amount of power in the States; there was always the counterpoise of Holland's political and economic power. A popular following and support in the States he had:

> All of which adds up to something less than monarchical status when certain other facts are considered. First, and of overwhelming importance for someone who saw himself as a great captain, [the stadholder] remained utterly dependent upon the resources made available to him by the authentic sovereigns in the Dutch Republic, the States. He commanded the army of the States, but he could not command the States of Holland, its principal paymaster, to provide the funds which enabled it to fight. . . . There is no indication that [the stadholder] ever contemplated trying to wrest from the States their control of the purse. All his military plans would have foundered in the civil wars or at least in the immense political turmoil that would have inevitably resulted.[77]

[75] Rowen, *Princes of Orange*, pp. 39–50, 84–94; Israel, *The Dutch Republic*, pp. 262–63.

[76] Popular support for the stadholder also waned due to a sudden peace, a conspicuous absence of shining military success, and the absence of meaningful rewards to the lower classes. Timely deaths and William III's ascendancy to the English throne in 1689 also limited stadholder power. See Geyl, *The Netherlands*, Part 2, pp. 160–61, 202–6. Owing to the reliance on mercenaries rather than conscripts, and to the perception that war ultimately hurt the economy and the common man, Dutch society and culture never acquired strong militaristic trappings. Indeed, the military was often depicted rather pejoratively in popular and other forms of culture. See Huizinga, *Holländische Kultur*, pp. 45–50; and Schama, *The Embarrassment of Riches*, pp. 252–53.

[77] Herbert H. Rowen and Andrew Lossky, *Political Ideas and Institutions in the Dutch*

In addition to finance, war policy remained outside Orange control, and largely under that of Holland. In 1631, in order to respond to a threat from another quarter, Holland compelled the stadholder Frederick Henry to break off a promising offensive in the Spanish Netherlands. Fourteen years later, Holland rejected Frederick Henry's strategy for a land offensive, in favor of a naval attack against Denmark, which was threatening the vital Baltic sea lanes. The same stadholder's efforts to continue the Thirty Years' War came to nought when Holland adamantly withheld money for the two years prior to the Peace of Westphalia.[78] No Dutch proconsul was going to conquer the Belgae or Gauls.

In addition to tight fiscal controls, Holland and the other States had several institutional checks on the military. After all, a highly corporate military, loyal to its commander, could all too easily overpower civilian paymasters. The command structure of the Dutch army, the "States army" as it was called, was anything but Weberian. Individual regiments were paid for by separate provinces and administered by a single province's States. Owing to Holland's share of the budget, this device served to maintain its control of most of the army. Troop movements could not be made without the appropriate provincial States's approval.[79] Officers were not simply appointed by a general staff, they had to be approved by the States-General. Furthermore, the States-General assigned field deputies to each unit, to monitor movements and plan tactics, just as the Venetian Senate assigned *provveditores* to its military enterprisers. Nor was the navy any more unitary: there were five admiralties to contend with in planning naval strategy.[80] Stadholders were not legion commanders with complete control over autonomously supplied forces. Had one cast his die and moved against constitutional government, a substantial part of the army would have refused to cross the Rubicon.

An effective wartime executive developed in the form of the oligarchs of Holland, whose hegemony over the other provinces approximated the decision-making capacity of a miltary-bureaucratic state. Indeed, if we

---

Republic (Los Angeles: William Andrews Clark Memorial Library, 1985), p. 15. In Geyl's words: "The numerous and wealthy town oligarchies of Holland could preserve their independence when the States of the other provinces were falling more and more under the Prince's control." See *The Netherlands*, Part 1, 135–36.

[78] Israel, *The Dutch Republic*, pp. 319–23; Rowen, *Princes of Orange*, p. 63.

[79] Such byzantine channels of authority were probably compatible with only a slow-paced, defensive war.

[80] Rowen, *Princes of Orange*, pp. 60–84; Parker, *The Dutch Revolt*, pp. 122–25; den Tex, *Oldenbarnevelt*, Volume 1, p. 245. On the Venetian provveditores, see Mallett and Hale, *Military Organization of a Renaissance State*, pp. 18, 170–72, 264–83; and Lane, *Maritime Republic*, pp. 231–32. This same fear of increased military prestige and power led to the Soviet Union's system of political commissars.

consider the cliques, intrigues, and venal machinery of the Bourbon and later Hohenzollern states, the oligarchs were probably even more effective. Holland's economic and political clout served as a counterpoise to the potential of a caesarist stadholder. Stadholders were kept well within the boundaries of the constitution and never attained the authority of caesarist figures such as Charles XII of Sweden. They cut colorful figures in Dutch history, and contributed more than their share to the art of war, but their institutional authority never rivaled that of Frederick the Great or Napoleon. They remained subordinate to Holland and the States-General, subordinate to the constitution.

. . .

The Dutch Republic withstood continuous warfare, against major military powers, without undermining the patterns of representative government and liberties handed down from the Middle Ages. Military assistance from other countries and geographic obstacles played major roles in reducing the level of domestic resource mobilization. But Dutch economic supremacy meant that, like England in the eighteenth century, the country had a vastly superior reservoir of resources to draw upon without bringing about political conflict. The same amount of resources could not have been extracted from static agrarian economies without causing serious trouble with the estates, the rule of law, local government, and individual freedoms. The oligarchic nature of government in the Netherlands made it somewhat less constitutional than other countries, but in the long and arduous wars oligarchy aided executive competence and served to preserve constitutional government—an ironic law of oligarchy. The States, legal principles, and personal liberties of the Netherlands emerged intact from a century and a half of war. Their vigor was such that even Marx believed that democracy, as he imagined it, could gradually evolve even in this most bourgeois of countries.

CHAPTER TEN

Conclusions

AFTER THIS VOYAGE through several centuries of European history, summary and discussion of the major arguments should be helpful. Three main propositions are set forth. First, by virtue of particular institutions and power relations that developed during the medieval period, much of Europe had an appreciable predisposition toward democratic government. Decentralized constitutional political structures in Europe had no counterparts in Muscovite Russia, China, Japan, or anywhere else. In this respect, it is important to avoid accounting for political outcomes in European history solely by reference to processes beginning with economic modernization. Parliament predates capitalism. Nor can European and non-European countries be used in a comparative study without making clear the importance of Europe's medieval past, representative assemblies, local government, and town charters. Second, warfare in parts of early modern Europe led to military modernization using domestic resources, and that was at least as important for authoritarian political outcomes as labor-repressive agricultural systems and a weak commercial impulse. In Brandenburg-Prussia it was war and not economic change that occasioned the destruction of the estates and the rise of autocracy, though, as we shall see, the introduction of export agriculture into the East Elbian plains also had adverse consequences for constitutionalism. Third, warfare was critical in the formation of states in early modern Europe. It was war and not domestic pressures that led to the rise of autocratic states in Prussia and France. The Junkers needed no elaborate state apparatus to market grain in the West or tie labor to the soil. The Prussian state that emerged from the household rule of the Hohenzollern electors was a machine geared toward war and preparation for it.

I have argued the case for a variation-finding model of political change brought on by military modernization, mainly in the seventeenth century. Countries faced with heavy protracted warfare that required substantial domestic resource mobilization suffered the destruction of medieval constitutionalism and the rise of a military-bureaucratic form of government. Second, where war was light, or where war needs could be met without mobilizing drastic proportions of national resources (through foreign resources, alliances, geographic advantages, or commercial wealth), conflict with the constitution was much lighter. Constitutional government endured and provided a basis for the development of democracy. Third, where war was heavy and protracted, where domestic politics prevented military modernization and political centralization, and where the benefits of foreign resources, alliances, geography, or economic superiority were not available, the country lost its sovereignty to strong expansionist states.

In Prussia military modernization required drastic mobilization of its resources, which destroyed the estates, local government, the rule of law, and personal rights. Military-centered absolutism replaced constitutional government. The Prussian state took on an increasingly managerial position vis-à-vis civil society, and held off liberalization for centuries. Similarly, French mobilization for the Thirty Years' War destroyed or at least circumvented many of that country's constitutional institutions, and the articulation of the Bourbon state paralleled that of the Hohenzollerns. But owing to fiscal crisis, peasant revolution, and elite disaffection—none of which obtained in Prussia—French absolutism collapsed in the late eighteenth century, and a violent social revolution offered a second chance for democracy, one made more arduous without the continuity of established constitutional institutions.

England, on the other hand, was fairly removed from the heavy warfare raging on the continent. The wars in which it did take part either were naval conflicts fought by small navies and privateers or did not require wholesale mobilization of resources. England never fought a major land power without numerous allies, two of which, Prussia and Spain, were themselves autocracies. The wars against France in the seventeenth and eighteenth centuries suggest that English constitutionalism was preserved, in part, by covenants with Prussian and Spanish military-bureaucratic absolutisms, whose military might came to bear against English enemies, reducing pressures to mobilize domestic resources. Wars, such as they were for England, were financed by ordinary Parliamentary subsidies, which kept that venerable assembly in the political process. Constitutional conflict during the Stuart periods stemmed less from war and military modernization than from internal political and religious issues, resulting in the Civil War and the Glorious Revolution. Finance remained in Parliament's hands, even under Cromwell, and the constitution was intact at the close of the seventeenth century. Indeed, owing to the elimination of numerous gray areas between royal prerogative and constitutional trespass, as well as to the development of party organization in the chaotic chambers of Parliament, constitutional government emerged strengthened. From a cumbersome medieval estates, Parliament evolved in the direction of a modern parliament.

Poland faced numerous powerful enemies but failed to modernize its army of gentry cavalry hosts. Because of the weakness of the elective monarchy and the political power of the gentry class, military modernization was impossible. There was no center of power to defeat the estates and initiate state reforms, and the parsimonious and factioned gentry itself refused to modernize the army. The price paid for a constitutional government defended by only a retrograde army was a fearful one. Poland was partitioned by Russia, Prussia, and Austria. Whereas Prussian and French constitutions fell to internal monarchal power, Poland's succumbed to foreign military-bureaucratic absolutisms.

Sweden and the Netherlands are perhaps the most theoretically informative cases. Although deeply involved in protracted wars, Sweden fought them on foreign soil, and relied on the resources extracted from enemy and neutral countries. Pressures on the constitution were thus slight. Constitutional government in the Dutch Republic was greatly aided in its long wars by alliances with major powers, geographic barriers to invaders, and the enormous wealth brought in by commerce. Merchant oligarchs served as an inexpensive, ersatz state.

All six countries entered the early modern period with forms of government that I have called medieval constitutionalism. That is, political power was not highly centralized in a bureaucratic monarchy. Power was spread out among the crown, the estates, town councils, and other regional governments. The rule of law prevailed and substantial numbers of the population enjoyed personal rights and liberties. The main arguments regarding military modernization's effect on medieval constitutionalism may be summarized in Table 2.

It is no overstatement to say that every page of this study was written with attention to Barrington Moore's classic study of the same questions.[1] Nor is it an overstatement to say that without *Social Origins* this study would have been impossible. A generation of social scientists has benefited from his map of the terrain, and future ones will continue to do so. *Si monumentum quaeris, circumspice*. Comparison of findings and discussion of compatibility are important. His model stressing the significance of the commercialization of agriculture and my own looking more to military and geopolitical variables are, at least in my view, generally compatible and complementary. Still, a few areas of disagreement must be pointed out.

A major argument of this work is that medieval Europe possessed several institutions that gave it a different starting point, a head start in the direction of liberal democracy; and, unlike Moore's, my case selection has been limited to those countries that had constitutional institutions.

---

[1] Barrington Moore, Jr., *Social Origins of Dictatorship and Democracy: Lord and Peasant in the Making of the Modern World* (Boston: Beacon Press, 1966).

TABLE 2
Warfare, Resource Mobilization, and Political Change

Country	Level of Warfare	Domestic Mobilization	Political Outcome
Brandenburg Prussia	High	High	Military-bureaucratic absolutism
France	High	High	Military-bureaucratic absolutism (collapses 1789)
Poland	High	Low (state paralysis)	Loss of sovereignty
England to 1648	Low	Low	Preservation of constitutionalism
England, 1688–1713	High	Medium (wealth, alliances, geography)	Preservation of constitutionalism
Sweden	High	Low (foreign resources)	Preservation of constitutionalism
Netherlands	High	Medium (wealth, alliances, geography)	Preservation of constitutionalism

Moore himself notes the importance of Europe's medieval history by observing the importance of a rough balance between crown and nobility, a balance between town and country, and the prevalence of feudal immunities and mutual contracts.[2] Nevertheless, he places central importance on the commercialization process; the importance of a medieval legacy remains unexplored. Furthermore, his argument, like those of the social historians upon whom he relied for historical evidence, remains at the level of social relations, which are not adequately integrated with existing political institutions. This is unfortunate because, by restricting the analysis to social relations, one can miss the institutional arenas in which conflicts are fought and domestic political alliances made. On this point there is substantial agreement on the existence of medieval constitutionalism, but possibly some difference on its relative importance.

My other major argument involves the role of warfare and military modernization in shaping political change. Comparisons to Moore will be

[2] Ibid., pp. 415–20.

made along the lines of the six cases presented here. Moore accounts for Prussia's nondemocratic political outcome by reference to the relative weakness of the landed upper class's impetus to commercialization, to Junker reliance on overt political repression to ensure labor supply, and to the absence of the capacity for a peasant revolution altering the country's authoritarian trajectory, as it did in France. These dynamics have political consequences: nobles need state help in order to repress labor. At a later point in history, when they need further state help to shore up declining world-market competitiveness, an authoritarian alliance—a "solid phalanx" of threatened nobles and weak bourgeoisie—sets the stage for state-directed industrial modernization, and preservation of a martial, aristocratic ethos hostile to personal freedom.

Some skepticism might greet his point regarding the different strengths of commercializing classes in Prussia and, say, England or the United States, but the anticonstitutional impact of Prussian commercialization is clear. First, the majority of the population was stripped of the independence it had enjoyed since the late medieval period. The peasantry was legally tied to the soil at a time when peasant freedoms were on the rise in Western Europe. Second, towns and their political independence suffered from the commercialization of agriculture, as shippers preferred to pick up grain at a few ports, bypassing costly Hanse towns. Tensions arose between the towns and the nobility over control of runaway peasants and the shouldering of excises. Battles erupted in the late fifteenth century, ending with the towns' defeat and loss of much political independence.[3] But the companion of these constitutional setbacks was the political rise of the Junkers, whose vitality in the estates made the East Elbian parliaments among the strongest in Europe. When faced with the need to build a modern army with domestic resources, the Great Elector abolished the estates and began the task of building a military-bureaucratic state.

Agrarian changes in the fifteenth and sixteenth centuries and heavy warfare in the seventeenth complemented each other, destroyed constitutionalism, and placed Prussia firmly on the track of autocracy. It must be pointed out, however, that fusion of nobles to the state took place quite early; fusion began when relatively poor Junkers supplemented their incomes by serving in the state and army. The preservation of a martial ethos into modern times makes better sense within the context of a highly militarized society. And Bismarck's rapid industrialization, the great revolution from above, was nothing unique in German history. It was but the most dramatic example of state-directed economic develop-

[3] F. L. Carsten, *The Origins of Prussia* (Oxford: Clarendon Press, 1964), pp. 136–48.

ment begun by earlier Hohenzollerns to help finance the army. In general, though, military modernization and commercialization, by destroying the estates, local privileges, the rule of law, and peasant freedoms, delivered a double blow to German chances for democracy.

Similarly, France was placed on an unconstitutional trajectory by authoritarian lord-peasant relations and by the demands of modernizing the army for the Thirty Years' War. There is strong agreement on the role of the French Revolution in altering political trends there. But just what was destroyed? Moore asserts that it was the mechanisms of labor repression that were abolished, thereby freeing the peasantry and removing feudal obstacles to democratic development. My readings have suggested that village government was retained under absolutism; it continued to provide a measure of personal freedom, and labor repression did not compare with that in Prussia or other lands to the east. Still, aristocratic exploitation and controls were prevalent and often extreme. Perhaps more important than the destruction of seigneurial authority, however, was the elimination of a military-centered state, which had previously pushed aside provincial estates and other components of constitutionalism. A long-term political cost of this second chance for a liberal outcome is lucidly identified by Moore. The large peasant class became a popular basis for authoritarian politics from Louis Bonaparte to Poujad, a legacy that hindered, but did not ultimately prevent, a liberal outcome.

The English landed upper class was strong and independent, relying on market mechanisms for labor supply instead of overt political repression. Here, feudal chains and monarchal ambitions were done away with, promoting the possibility of a democratic outcome. Ironically—and this brings up Moore's subtheme of the violent beginnings of democracy—this destroyed the English peasantry by making them obsolete for sheep farming and other non-labor-intensive processes. Agrarian changes in the English countryside bolstered the forces of constitutionalism in several ways. The new wealth from wool and cereal production strengthened the landowners' hand in Parliament and in local government, without enserfment of the peasantry. Economic growth (but also even simple inflation) led to the enfranchisement of thousands whose property value met the forty-shilling freehold requirement. Parliament and local government thus were infused with new members, whose wealth, numbers, and energy aided constitutionalism in struggles with the Stuarts, though hardly in the one-sided, pro-Parliament way once thought.[4]

[4] The increase in the electorate had the effect of precipitating the beginnings of political campaigns and genuine contestations, as local elites vied for the votes of the newly enfranchised. See J. H. Plumb, "The Growth of the Electorate in England from 1600 to 1715," *Past and Present* 45 (1969): 92–95; and W. A. Speck, *Tory and Whig: The Struggle in the Constituencies 1701–1715* (London: Macmillan, 1970), pp. 12–32.

The rise of commercial agriculture did not coincide with the demise of the towns, as it had in Prussia. Whereas Hanse towns suffered from the loss of trade to the Dutch, and from the circumvention of the large ports by the grain ships, English towns throve on global commerce and on textile industries supplied by rural wool producers. The commercialization of English agriculture strengthened landowners as well as burghers, and gave them economic resources and common interests to defend. When combined with a relatively safe international environment (which Moore notes[5]), constitutional government in England entered the modern world in good order.

The cases of Sweden and the Netherlands present problems for Moore's agrarian change argument. We will not find a strong, independent impetus to commercialization of agriculture in either country. The impetus to the commercialization of Swedish agriculture stemmed from the state and not from a gentry or hardy yeoman class. It was the need for cash to fight wars that converted the barter economy into an increasingly monetarized and commoditized one: taxes had to be paid in cash and crown lands were alienated to raise revenue. The upshot of this was, at least in the short run, the concentration of land in the hands of the nobility, especially the magnates—a situation that, by expanding noble demesnes, undermining traditional peasant rights and liberties, and tying peasants to seigneurial authority, threatened to prussianize Swedish agriculture. This unpleasant scenario was done away with by the crown's resumption of alienated lands, a step that transferred huge tracts of alienated land back to the king, who then used them to institute the indelningsverk system of military benefices that, willy-nilly, preserved a solid yeomanry. Two principal restructurings of agriculture, which did away with rural obstacles to democracy, were initiated by the state, without discernible pressure from any social class, and without any apparent adverse consequence for democratic political development.[6] No bourgeois, yet democracy.

The Dutch agrarian sector recedes into virtual irrelevance in comparison to maritime commerce. Rural parts of the Netherlands were economic backwaters whose inability to assist in funding the war effort ensured the political dominance of the maritime provinces. The commercialization of agriculture was not decisive in the political outcome of the Dutch Republic; it neither strengthened constitutionalism as in England, nor weakened it as in Prussia. The political as well as economic contours of Dutch history were formed by forces centered in the mer-

[5] Moore, *Social Origins*, p. 31.

[6] See Timothy A. Tilton, "The Social Origins of Liberal Democracy: The Swedish Case," *American Political Science Review* 68 (1974): 561–71.

chant towns of Holland and Zeeland, not in the marshy hinterlands, where we find no great economic or political importance, but neither do we find any obstacles to democracy.

What then are we to make of these two nonconformists? We cannot dismiss them as smaller countries that depended economically and politically on more powerful ones that wrote their national destinies for them. Though many countries suffered this fate, it was not the case for the Dutch or Swedes. The Dutch Republic was the economic center of Europe, if not the world; and Batavia ruled the waves in the seventeenth century—singeing the beard of the King of England on more than one occasion. Sweden was a formidable, perhaps even the dominant, land power for much of the same century; its diplomats sat at Westphalia the equals of Spanish, French, and Austrian emmisaries. If not from commercializing rural classes, whence came the impetus to democratic forms in Sweden and the Netherlands? In the Dutch case, it might be argued that the impetus came from the urban centers, and this more than compensated for the dearth of rural dynamism. Doubtless so, but this argument shifts attention from the rural actors central to Moore's argument, refocuses attention on political institutions predating the time period he emphasizes, but still leaves us nowhere with Sweden. I argue that the impetus to democracy in Sweden, as well as in England and the Netherlands, came not from any single social class, but rather from several, and from the institutional momentum of the medieval estates, local governments, personal freedoms, and independent judiciaries—in short, from the momentum of medieval constitutionalism.

To summarize the comparisons, in Prussia and France labor-repressive commercialization combined with drastic military mobilization to block liberal political outcomes. The French Revolution, however, undermined those obstacles and offered the opportunity for a more fortuitous result. In England commercialization strengthened the legacy of medieval constitutionalism, while a relatively benign military situation offered the opportunity for sustained movement in the direction of liberal democracy. Neither Sweden nor the Netherlands seems smoothly to follow the model argued by Moore, but, inasmuch as we do not find his causes of dictatorship in their political histories, there is no sharp conflict either. In that we have no contradiction, we have compatibility.

Though it shifts attention to rural elites rather than simply urban ones, Moore's argument is a sophisticated elaboration of the "bourgeois revolution" line of thinking. This theory, briefly put, sees the forces of capitalism as undermining and overthrowing feudal or traditional authority, thereby bringing about a new form of government conducive to, if not culminating in, liberal democracy.[7] My readings have obviously suggested an earlier origin for liberal democracy: in the medieval period. What role then did ascending bourgeoisies have in the development of democracy? This question is one deserving of a book in itself, and should I ever be so unwise as to take on another multicase, macrohistorical study, this would be a tempting project. For now some sketchy remarks will have to suffice. We should begin with a look at textbook cases of the bourgeois revolution—the English Civil War, the French Revolution, and the Dutch Revolt—and attempt to determine precisely what changed with these upheavals.

If anything was overthrown in the English Civil War or the Glorious Revolution, it was not feudal authority; rather it was a modernizing central state, a creeping absolutism, that had endeavored to free itself of the reins of Parliament, the venerable Common Law, and the seemingly outmoded custom of respecting the views of local notables. In short, custom, tradition, and medieval institutions defeated Stuart efforts at innovation. Tradition triumphed over modernity. Where did the bourgeoisie and the leaders of commercialization stand during all this strife? The evidence of recent work on the Civil War suggests that their support was not overwhelmingly on one side or the other. London merchants sided with Parliament against the Stuarts, but this might have been due less to political sympathies than to the simple fact that Parliament controlled the region, while the crown's army rallied in the north.[8] The aristocracy and the gentry (even the more commercially oriented ones) divided their support fairly evenly between king and Parliament. Class does not seem to have been a significant factor in determining loyalties during the war.[9]

The bourgeois revolution interpretation of the Civil War can be rescued if one retreats to a functionalist position: in that the conflict abolished royal monopolies and autocratic government, it may be categorized as bourgeois, irrespective of the actual role played by the bourgeoisie.[10]

[7] For thoughtful critiques of the "bourgeois revolution" interpretation, see Jon Elster, *Making Sense of Marx* (Cambridge: Cambridge University Press, 1986), pp. 429–37; and Göran Therborn, "The Rule of Capital and the Rise of Democracy," *New Left Review* 103 (1977): 3–41.

[8] See Conrad Russell, *The Crisis of the Parliaments: English History 1509–1660* (Oxford: Oxford University Press, 1971), pp. 341–43; and Lawrence Stone, *The Causes of the English Revolution, 1529–1642* (New York: Harper & Row, 1972), pp. 55–56.

[9] Russell, *Crisis of the Parliaments*, pp. 341–43; Stone, *English Revolution*, pp. 47–58; Jack A. Goldstone, "Capitalist Origins of the English Revolution: Chasing a Chimera," *Theory and Society* 12 (1983): 143–80.

[10] See Christopher Hill, "A Bourgeois Revolution?" in J.G.A. Pocock, ed., *Three British Revolutions: 1641, 1688, 1776* (Princeton, N.J.: Princeton University Press, 1980), pp. 109–39; and Lawrence Stone, "The Bourgeois Revolution of the Seventeenth Century Revisited," *Past and Present* 109 (1985): 44–54.

A defensible position perhaps, but one quite different from the original, and one that avoids the twin matters of the continuity of medieval institutions and continued aristocratic political domination well into the nineteenth century. Furthermore, German capitalism developed at a remarkable pace within an autocratic and authoritarian framework, with monopolies and cartels leading the way, even overtaking England by the end of the nineteenth century. England's economic boom of the mid- to late seventeenth century did not necessarily follow from previous political events. The English Civil War, I contend, was not bourgeois in nature or origin, nor was it modernizing. Insofar as it preserved a political status quo worked out in previous centuries, it was, in a sense, reactionary. But in that it preserved the medieval basis for liberal democracy and prevented absolutism, this form of reaction might be called quite progressive.

Turning now to the French Revolution, it might be asked exactly what was overthrown in 1789.[11] The simple answer of feudal authority will not do; most of that was abolished by the Bourbon state in the previous century. Seigneurial authority survived in the countryside, but even here the relationship was less that of lord and serf than that of exploitive capitalist rentier and tenant.[12] The countryside at this point was at least as capitalist as it was feudal, probably more so. The aristocracy abounded in the prominent positions in the Bourbon state, but not as beneficed vassals or feudal councillors, rather as salaried officials, courtiers, and formally contracted tax farmers. It should be apparent that the term "feudalism" has been used by many (including de Tocqueville) in a less than precise manner. All too often, the term is used to signify a distant and ill-understood past, undesirable forms of government, or institutional and cultural obstacles to democracy or capitalism.[13] Hence, the antebellum

[11] The historiography of the French Revolution is almost as divided and vitriolic as that of the English Civil War. The wellspring of the Marxian interpretation is found in Georges Lefebvre, *The Coming of the French Revolution* (Princeton, N.J.: Princeton University Press, 1967). For useful summaries of debates, see William Doyle, *Origins of the French Revolution*, Second Edition (New York: Oxford University Press, 1988); and T.C.W. Blanning, *The French Revolution: Aristocrats versus Bourgeois?* (Atlantic Highlands, N.J.: Humanities Press, 1987).

[12] "In the French seventeenth century there were no longer medieval feudal domains, surviving as closed economies, based on servile labor. There was instead a peasantry which was legally free and often owning land, even though it was under the economic domination of the *seigneurs*." Hubert Méthivier, "A Century of Conflict: The Economic and Social Disorders of the Grand Siècle," in P. J. Coveney, ed., *France in Crisis, 1620–1675* (Totowa, N.J.: Rowman and Littlefield, 1977), p. 74. See also Barry Hindess and Paul Q. Hirst, *Pre-Capitalist Modes of Production* (London: Routledge & Kegan Paul, 1979), pp. 221–59.

[13] In this study I have followed Henri Pirenne's recommendation for the use of the term:

We are accustomed to give the name of "feudal" to the political system which prevailed in Europe after the disappearance of the Carolingian dynasty. This habit of ours goes back to the French Revo-

South, Islamic government, and pre-Revolution France are all casually classified by many as feudal regimes. If feudalism has any analytical, rather than purely polemical, meaning, it is a decentralized form of government by which a relatively weak monarch rules in conjunction with an independent, beneficed aristocracy that controls local administration and constitutes the basis of the military. The old regime, by contrast, was a powerful centralized state that had integrated much of the aristocracy at least partially into its bureaucracies, built an elaborate system of intendants throughout the country, and controlled a modern centrally-financed army.

The Revolution did not overthrow feudalism, only some rotten remnants that the Bourbons had not bothered or did not find time to sweep away. It was military-bureaucratic absolutism that fell: the military-centered state begun by Richelieu to fight the Thirty Years' War, not the feudal system of the Carolingians or Capetians. But if what was overthrown was not feudalism, did a bourgeoisie at least play a central role? If so, we would have support for a modified version of the bourgeois revolution thesis: no feudal chains, but a bourgeois impetus to democracy. My readings have suggested that the bourgeoisie got along with, indeed was fostered by, the absolutist state under Colbert. Eventual opposition from that quarter came only later, and stemmed not from any profound incompatibility between capitalism and absolutism, but simply from opposition to Bourbon war debt and remedial tax reforms. Middle-class opposition came less from manufacturers, merchants, bankers, or other components of the bourgeoisie than from professionals and lawyers, who differ markedly from the bourgeoisie in interests and socialization, and can be lumped together with the bourgeoisie into a single social class only at the cost of much confusion. In any case, the mortal blows to the state came from different quarters, from the aristocracy and the peasantry.

Neither the English nor the French case provides much support for the bourgeois revolution view of democratic development. The Dutch Republic might offer support; after all, it was here that capitalist merchants led the fight for independence. But there are three problems.

lution, which indiscriminately attributed to the feudal system all the rights, privileges, usages and traditions which were inconsistent with the constitution of the modern State and modern society. Yet if we accept the words in their exact sense, we ought to understand, by the terms "feudal" and "feudal system," only the juridical relations arising from the fief or the bond of vassalage, and it is an abuse of language to stretch the sense of these terms to include a whole political order, in which the feudal element was, after all, only of secondary importance, and, if we may say so, formal rather than substantial.

Pirenne, "The Feudality," in Reinhard Bendix et al., eds., *State and Society: A Reader in Comparative Political Sociology* (Berkeley and Los Angeles: University of California Press, 1973), p. 140.

First, the Revolt was not against feudalism or any indigenous form of government; it was against a foreign absolutism that sought to impose new political and religious authority. Second, we find no opposition between bourgeoisie and aristocracy. Burghers and nobles combined into a solid phalanx devoted to preserving the constitution against Spanish absolutism. Third, burgher political power in the Netherlands emerged far back in the Middle Ages with the rise of the towns in the twelfth century. It in no way emerged with the flourishing of capitalism in the early modern period. To return to one of the main arguments of this work, it rested mainly on medieval constitutional government. And in any regard, the Dutch bourgeoisie struggled to retain narrow oligarchy, not build democracy.

There remains the matter of bourgeois impact on political development in nineteenth-century Europe. It can be argued that it was this century that witnessed the middle classes' assumption of power. This question must go unaddressed here; the scope of the present project has been to establish the preconditions for liberal democracy and not to chart its full development. I will close, however, with some skeptical comments. By the beginning of the nineteenth century, parliamentary rule and property rights were already firmly established in the countries following the liberal trajectory; aristocratic political power persisted well into the century; and there is interesting research suggesting that the German bourgeoisie, supine poltroons in the bourgeois revolution school, actually accomplished more in the fields of law and politics than has been commonly thought, while their exalted English counterparts accomplished much less. The English industrial and commercial middle classes, far from being self-reliant opponents to a foundering aristocracy, came into a world in which property and personal rights as well as constitutional government had existed for centuries, and used their wealth to emulate, in the same manner as the vilified and allegedly "feudalized" German burghers, the lifestyles of the aristocracy, acquiring a country manor and if possible a peerage.[14]

My conclusions regarding the middle classes and democracy are tentative but skeptical. Bourgeois boasts of having built liberal democracy will find little support here. They seem closer to what one might call

[14] See David Blackbourn and Geoff Eley, *The Peculiarities of German History: Bourgeois Society and Politics in Nineteenth-Century Germany* (Oxford: Oxford University Press, 1984); Arno Mayer, *The Persistence of the Old Regime: Europe to the Great War* (New York: Pantheon, 1981); J.C.D. Clark, *Revolution and Rebellion: State and Society in England in the Seventeenth and Eighteenth Centuries* (Cambridge: Cambridge University Press, 1986); John Cannon, *Aristocratic Century: The Peerage of Eighteenth-Century England* (Cambridge: Cambridge University Press, 1984); and Martin J. Wiener, *English Culture and the Decline of the Industrial Spirit 1850–1980* (Cambridge: Cambridge University Press, 1982).

bourgeois ideology: begun by gentleman Whig historians of the nineteenth century, accepted uncritically by many later professional historians, and even embraced by Marxists, whose evolutionary schema make
political change an ineluctable consequence of economic change, and
whose main objection has only been to denigrate liberal democracy. Instead of locomotives of democratic development, the bourgeoisies encountered in this study are perhaps better seen as, in some countries,
coupling onto a train of constitutional development originating in the late
medieval period, but in other countries coupling onto absolutist trains
built for military power and opposed to democracy. Bourgeoisies have
traveled on and benefited from both, without trying to gain control. Put
another way, as middle classes of the industrial revolution entered the
scene in England, Sweden, and the Netherlands, they encountered an
existing constitutional polity, replete with property rights and liberties
dating back to the late medieval period, and worked within that framework to establish the rights and legal guarantees necessary for new forms
of increasingly complicated economic enterprises. In Prussia, however,
middle classes emerged within a military-bureaucratic framework and
worked within that system for the same goals, and achieved results not
entirely disparate.[15] Each bourgeoisie gained power in its respective political system; neither established a new political system. My point, however, is not to vilify the bourgeoisie, uncover its hypocrisies, and pro-
claim a truer form of democracy for the future. My point is only to
recover the past—the medieval past—and reveal its little-appreciated
virtues and significance for political development.

. . .

Medieval government and the military revolution have shaped the modern world in no small way. Their legacies are everywhere. As seen in the
histories of Prussia, France, and Russia, military-bureaucratic absolutisms are exceedingly difficult to do away with. Once gone, however, usually through social revolution or complete military defeat, military-bureaucratic absolutism leaves a legacy that continues to shape the state and

---

[15] "[E]conomic leadership . . . does not readily expand, like the medieval lord's military
leadership, into the leadership of nations. On the contrary, the ledger and the cost calcu-
lation absorb and confine. I have called the bourgeois rationalistic and unheroic. He can
only use rationalistic and unheroic means to defend his position or to bend a nation to his
will. He can impress by what people may expect from his economic performance, he can
argue his case, he can promise to pay out money or threaten to withhold it, he can hire the
treacherous services of a *condottiere* or politician or journalist. But that is all and all that is
greatly overrated as to its political value." Joseph A. Schumpeter, *Capitalism, Socialism
and Democracy* (New York: Harper & Row, 1975), pp. 137–38.

hinder democratic development. History gives no clean slates. The collapse of the state entails the unfortunate and disastrous conjuncture of the disintegration of political institutions and a marked increase in previously repressed popular unrest, demands, and mobilizations. Political institutions are no longer intact to deflect or repress popular demands, nor are rapidly assembled democratic institutions sufficiently developed to accommodate them. The result is what has been called a "praetorian society,"[16] an unstable state of affairs such as we find in nineteenth-century France, and in Germany and Russia at the end of World War I. Such a situation is likely to result in military intervention, the construction of new or the resurrection of old repressive apparatuses, and continued mistrust between state and population—hindrances all to democratization. A second legacy of military-bureaucratic absolutism persists in the nation's popular culture. The past is remembered by many as a golden age of national greatness, an era of shining military success and national unity, a halcyon epoch prior to the emergence of divisive politics and its discontents, and a refuge from the uncertainty that the freedom of the new regime brings. A vague and selective memory of the past provides a vast cultural reservoir of mythic imagery that can be cleverly exploited by leaders of dark, backward-looking movements.

This account of the rise and development of military-bureaucratic absolutism might combine with contemporary analyses of third-world armies overthrowing democratically elected officials to leave an impression of the military as the great villain in the story of democracy. Although most of this study has discussed military modernization in the sixteenth and seventeenth centuries, other forms of military organization have also been touched upon. Military service and citizenship were intertwined in antiquity. Medieval militaries were conducive to, indeed formed an actual part of, medieval constitutionalism. Knight service was contractual: the knight exchanged forty days of military service for liberties and privileges. This decentralized military and political arrangement was part of the rough balance between center and periphery from which sprang parliaments, formal charters, and defense of legal guarantees. Towns exchanged the service of militias in royal armies for charters and political autonomy. Peasant militias established and preserved fundamental citizenship rights for those who bore arms in the name of their king or canton.

Most of this type of military organization disappeared with the coming of the military revolution and the rise of large standing armies comprising

---

[16] Samuel P. Huntington, *Political Order in Changing Societies* (New Haven, Conn.: Yale University Press, 1968). Of course, Huntington focuses mainly on the developing world, but the argument seems applicable to a post-absolutist politics as well.

conscripts and mercenaries. In many countries, the costs of these new armies could not be met within the framework of constitutional government, and powerful coercive states replaced consensual government from the medieval period. This work has concentrated on the consequences and dynamics of this second form of military organization, but, beginning with the French Revolution, or more correctly with the Swedish indelningsverk, a new military emerged: the national army. During the Revolution, the huge number of soldiers could not be drilled and trained in the traditional methods set by Maurice of Nassau and Martinet. Instead, political indoctrination instilled a sense of patriotism that motivated soldiers to fight not for pay, but for their nation. The public, too, was involved in the immense war effort and became citizens rather than subjects. Peace could lead to the demobilization of the bulk of the army, but not of the citizens. New political systems had to be built to deal with the now politically aware and demanding—one might say militant—population.

Military service became part of the process of liberalization and franchise extension. English soldiers returning from World War I won the right to vote and even welfare benefits in "a land fit for heroes." In Sweden, working-class soldiers demanded the vote under the slogan, "one man, one gun, one vote." As late as the 1960s, the franchise was extended to Americans eighteen years of age who, it was compellingly argued, were "old enough to carry a gun, but not to vote." If we broaden our conception of democracy a bit, we see that war has led to fundamental changes in social structure, and that senses of injustice born of national service have encouraged previously second-class citizens to question basic inequities and to demand full citizenship. Furthermore, the military has provided an important means of upward social mobility for less privileged strata in society. And perhaps when Frederick the Great gave veterans preference for state employment, and when Louis XIV built invalid hospitals, they laid the foundations of the welfare state.

Yet it is impossible to deny an essential tension between twentieth-century warfare and democracy.[17] In our own time, war or the perceived approach of war has caused conflict between guardians of the nation's security and the by now deeply rooted democratic institutional legacies of medieval constitutionalism. But the humbling of monarchs to quaint national symbols or their outright abolition has made a modern variant of military-bureaucratic absolutism highly unlikely. The blunt methods of the Great Elector are no longer possible in the age of developed Western economies and mass democracy in which the state is entirely in the hands

---

[17] For a classic but hardly dated treatment of this tension, see Edward S. Corwin, *Total War and the Constitution* (New York: Alfred A. Knopf, 1947).

of constitutionally elected officials, and political parties and economies are sufficiently developed to allow substantial resource mobilization without destroying the constitutional order. Should modern constitutional democracies be threatened from within during times of war, I suspect that the danger is far more likely to come from the dynamic here called populist-militarism. There remains in the hearts of many at least an ambivalence toward, if not a longing for, the romantic imagery and power prestige of war.

The broad theoretic message here is that military organization has had immensely important consequences for state and society. Class-based arguments on the origins of dictatorship and democracy need to be complemented by ones recognizing the importance of military organization, geopolitics, and resource mobilization. Weber knew well the importance of both economic and military structures:

> Whether the military organization is based on the principle of self-equipment or that of equipment by a military warlord who furnishes horses, arms and provisions, is a distinction quite as fundamental for social history as is the question whether the means of economic production are the property of the worker or of a capitalistic entrepreneur. [18]

But it is, of course, not my aim to substitute for a one-sided materialistic an equally one-sided military causal interpretation of history. Recognition of the importance of both, as well as openness to the possibility of others, should be parts of one's ordinary working equipment.

[18] Max Weber, *General Economic History*, Frank H. Knight, trans. (New Brunswick, N.J.: Transaction Books, 1982), p. 320.

Selected Bibliography

SOCIAL SCIENCE

Almond, Gabriel. Review of Barrington Moore, Jr.'s *Social Origins of Dictatorship and Democracy*. *American Political Science Review* 61 (1967): 768–70.

Almond, Gabriel, and James S. Coleman, eds. *The Politics of the Developing Areas*. Princeton, N.J.: Princeton University Press, 1960.

Almond, Gabriel, and Sidney Verba. *The Civic Culture*. Princeton, N.J.: Princeton University Press, 1963.

———, eds. *The Civic Culture Revisited*. Boston, Mass.: Little, Brown, 1980.

Alter, Peter. *Nationalism*. Translated by Stuart McKinnon-Evans. London: Edward Arnold, 1989.

Anderson, Benedict. *Imagined Communities: Reflections on the Origin and Spread of Nationalism*. London: Verso, 1989.

Anderson, Perry. *Lineages of the Absolutist State*. London: Verso, 1974.

———. *Passages from Antiquity to Feudalism*. London: Verso, 1974.

Andreski, Stanislav. *Military Organization and Society*. Berkeley and Los Angeles: University of California Press, 1971.

Baechler, Jean, John A. Hall, and Michael Mann, eds. *Europe and the Rise of Capitalism*. Oxford: Basil Blackwell, 1989.

Barry, Brian. *Sociologists, Economists and Democracy*. Chicago: University of Chicago Press, 1978.

Beetham, David. *Max Weber and the Theory of Modern Politics*. London: George Allen & Unwin, 1974.

Bendix, Reinhard. "Tradition and Modernity Reconsidered." *Comparative Studies in Society and History* 9 (1967): 292–346.

———. *Nation-Building and Citizenship: Studies of Our Changing Social Order*. Second Edition. Berkeley and Los Angeles: University of California Press, 1977.

———. *Kings or People: Power and the Mandate to Rule*. Berkeley and Los Angeles: University of California Press, 1978.

———, et al., eds. *State and Society: A Reader in Comparative Political Sociology*. Berkeley and Los Angeles: University of California Press, 1973.

Berghahn, V. R. *Militarism: The History of an International Debate 1861–1979*. Cambridge: Cambridge University Press, 1984.

Binder, Leonard, James S. Coleman, Joseph LaPalombara, Lucien W. Pye, Sidney Verba, and Myron Weiner. *Crises and Sequences in Political Development*. Princeton, N.J.: Princeton University Press, 1971.

Bonnell, Victoria. "The Uses of Theory, Concepts and Comparisons in Historical Sociology." *Comparative Studies in Society and History* 22 (1980): 156–73.

Breisach, Ernst. *Historiography: Ancient, Medieval, and Modern*. Chicago: University of Chicago Press, 1983.

Brunt, P. A. *Social Conflicts in the Roman Republic*. New York: W. W. Norton, 1971.

Butterfield, Herbert. *The Whig Interpretation of History*. New York: W. W. Norton, 1965.

Casanova, José. "Legitimacy and the Sociology of Modernization." In Arthur J. Vidich, ed., *Conflict and Control: Challenges to Legitimacy of Modern Government*. Beverly Hills, Calif.: Sage, 1979.

Chirot, Daniel. "The Rise of the West." *American Sociological Review* 50 (1985): 181–95.

———, ed. *The Origins of Backwardness in Eastern Europe: Economics and Politics from the Middle Ages until the Early Twentieth Century*. Berkeley and Los Angeles: University of California Press, 1989.

Collins, Randall. *Conflict Sociology*. New York: Academic Press, 1975.

———. *Weberian Sociological Theory*. New York: Cambridge University Press, 1986.

Corwin, Edward S. *Total War and the Constitution*. New York: Alfred A. Knopf, 1947.

Dahl, Robert A. *Polyarchy: Participation and Opposition*. New Haven, Conn.: Yale University Press, 1971.

Deutsch, Karl. "Social Mobilization and Political Development." *American Political Science Review* 55 (1961): 493–514.

Downs, Anthony. *An Economic Theory of Democracy*. New York: Harper & Row, 1957.

Duncan, Graeme, ed. *Democracy and the Capitalist State*. Cambridge: Cambridge University Press, 1989.

Eisenstadt, S. N. *The Political Systems of Empires*. New York: Free Press, 1963.

———. "Breakdowns of Modernization." *Economic Development and Cultural Change* 12 (1964): 345–67.

Elster, Jon. *Making Sense of Marx*. Cambridge: Cambridge University Press, 1986.

Emerson, Rupert. *From Empire to Nation: The Rise to Self-Assertion of Asian and African Peoples*. Cambridge, Mass.: Harvard University Press, 1962.

Evans, Peter B., Dietrich Rueschemeyer, and Theda Skocpol, eds. *Bringing the State Back In*. Cambridge: Cambridge University Press, 1985.

Friedrich, Carl J. *Constitutional Government and Democracy: Theory and Practice in Europe and America*. New York: Blaisdell, 1964.

Gellner, Ernest. *Nations and Nationalism*. Ithaca, N.Y.: Cornell University Press, 1987.

Genet, J.-Ph., and M. Le Mené, eds. *Genèse de l'état moderne: Prélèvement et redistribution*. Paris: Editions du Centre National de la Recherche Scientifique, 1987.

Gerth, H. H., and C. Wright Mills, eds. *From Max Weber: Essays in Sociology*. New York: Oxford University Press, 1976.

Giddens, Anthony. *The Nation-State and Violence*. Berkeley and Los Angeles: University of California Press, 1985.

Gilbert, Felix, ed. *The Historical Essays of Otto Hintze*. New York: Oxford University Press, 1975.

Goldstone, Jack A. "Capitalist Origins of the English Revolution: Chasing a Chimera." *Theory and Society* 12 (1983): 143–80.

―――. "Reinterpreting the French Revolution." *Theory and Society* 13 (1984): 697–713.

Gould, Mark. *Revolution in the Development of Capitalism: The Coming of the English Revolution*. Berkeley and Los Angeles: University of California Press, 1987.

Grew, Raymond, ed. *Crises of Political Development in Europe and the United States*. Princeton, N.J.: Princeton University Press, 1978.

Hall, John H. *Powers and Liberties: The Causes and Consequences of the Rise of the West*. Berkeley and Los Angeles: University of California Press, 1986.

Hechter, Michael, and William Brustein. "Regional Modes of Production and Patterns of State Formation in Western Europe." *American Journal of Sociology* 85 (1980): 1061–94.

Hindess, Barry, and Paul Q. Hirst. *Pre-Capitalist Modes of Production*. London: Routledge & Kegan Paul, 1979.

Huntington, Samuel P. *Political Order in Changing Societies*. New Haven, Conn.: Yale University Press, 1968.

―――. *The Soldier and the State: The Theory and Politics of Civil-Military Relations*. Cambridge, Mass.: Harvard University Press, 1981.

Huntington, Samuel P., and Joan Nelson. *No Easy Choice: Political Participation in Developing Countries*. Cambridge, Mass.: Harvard University Press, 1976.

Kesselman, Mark. "Order or Movement? The Literature of Political Development as Ideology." *World Politics* 22 (1973): 139–54.

Kronman, Anthony T. *Max Weber*. London: Edward Arnold, 1983.

LaPalombara, Joseph, ed. *Bureaucracy and Political Development*. Princeton, N.J.: Princeton University Press, 1963.

LaPalombara, Joseph, and Myron Weiner, eds. *Political Parties and Political Development*. Princeton, N.J.: Princeton University Press, 1966.

Lasswell, H. D. "The Garrison State and the Specialists on Violence." *American Journal of Sociology* 47 (1941): 455–68.

Lerner, Daniel. *The Passing of Traditional Society: Modernizing the Middle East*. New York: Free Press, 1958.

Levi, Margaret. *Of Rule and Revenue*. Berkeley and Los Angeles: University of California Press, 1988.

Linz, Juan J., and Alfred Stepan, eds. *The Breakdown of Democratic Regimes*. Four volumes. Baltimore, Md.: Johns Hopkins University Press, 1978.

Lipset, Seymour Martin. "Some Social Requisites of Democracy." *American Political Science Review* 53 (1959): 69–105.

―――. *Political Man: The Social Bases of Politics*. Baltimore, Md.: Johns Hopkins University Press, 1981.

Lloyd, Christopher. *Explanation in Social History*. Oxford: Basil Blackwell, 1986.

Mann, Michael. *The Sources of Social Power*, Volume 1: *A History of Power from the Beginning to A.D. 1760*. New York: Cambridge University Press, 1986.

Mann, Michael. *States, War, and Capitalism: Studies in Political Sociology*. Oxford: Basil Blackwell, 1988.

Marx, Karl, and Frederick Engels. *Collected Works*, Volume 3. London: International Publishers, 1975.

———. *Collected Works*, Volume 5. London: International Publishers, 1976.

Mommsen, Wolfgang J. *The Age of Bureaucracy: Perspectives on the Political Sociology of Max Weber*. New York: Harper & Row, 1977.

———. *Theories of Imperialism*. Translated by P. S. Falla. New York: Random House, 1977.

———. *Max Weber and German Politics 1890–1920*. Translated by Michael S. Steinberg. Chicago: University of Chicago Press, 1985.

Montesquieu. *The Spirit of the Laws*. Cincinnati, Ohio: Robert Clarke, 1873.

Moore, Barrington, Jr. *Political Power and Social Theory*. Cambridge: Harvard University Press, 1958.

———. *Social Origins of Dictatorship and Democracy: Lord and Peasant in the Making of the Modern World*. Boston, Mass.: Beacon Press, 1966.

———. *Injustice: The Social Bases of Obedience and Revolt*. Armonk, N.Y.: M. E. Sharpe, 1978.

———. *Privacy: Studies in Social and Cultural History*. Armonk, N.Y.: M. E. Sharpe, 1984.

Neumann, Franz L. *The Rule of Law: Political Theory and the Legal System in Modern Society*. Leamington Spa, U.K.: Berg, 1986.

Neumann, Sigmund, ed. *Modern Political Parties: Approaches to Comparative Politics*. Chicago: University of Chicago Press, 1956.

Nicolet, Claude. *The World of the Citizen in Republican Rome*. Translated by P. S. Falla. Berkeley and Los Angeles: University of California Press, 1988.

Nisbet, Robert. *Twilight of Authority*. New York: Oxford University Press, 1975.

———. *History of the Idea of Progress*. New York: Basic Books, 1980.

Nordlinger, Eric A. *On the Autonomy of the Democratic State*. Cambridge, Mass.: Harvard University Press, 1981.

O'Donnell, Guillermo, and Philippe C. Schmitter. *Transitions from Authoritarian Rule: Tentative Conclusions about Uncertain Democracies*. Baltimore, Md.: Johns Hopkins University Press, 1986.

Parsons, Talcott. "Evolutionary Universals in Society." *American Sociological Review* 29 (1964): 339–57.

Perlmutter, Amos, and Valerie Plave Bennett, eds. *The Political Influence of the Military*. New Haven, Conn.: Yale University Press, 1980.

Poggi, Gianfranco. *The Development of the Modern State: A Sociological Introduction*. Stanford, Calif.: Stanford University Press, 1978.

Pollard, A. E. *Factors in Modern History*. Boston: Beacon Press, 1960.

Prosterman, Roy, and Jeffrey M. Riedinger. *Land Reform and Democratic Development*. Baltimore, Md.: Johns Hopkins University Press, 1987.

Przeworski, Adam, and Henry Teune. *The Logic of Comparative Social Inquiry*. New York: Wiley, 1970.

Pye, Lucian W. *Aspects of Political Development*. Boston: Little, Brown, 1966.

Pye, Lucian W., and Sidney Verba, eds. *Political Culture and Political Development*. Princeton, N.J.: Princeton University Press, 1965.

Ragin, Charles C. *The Comparative Method: Moving beyond Qualitative and Quantitative Strategies*. Berkeley and Los Angeles: University of California Press, 1987.

Rasler, Karen, and William R. Thompson. "War and the Economic Growth of Major Powers." *American Journal of Political Science* 29 (1985): 513–38.

———. *War and State Making: The Shaping of the Global Powers*. Boston: Unwin Hyman, 1989.

Reddy, William M. *Money and Liberty in Modern Europe: A Critique of Historical Understanding*. Cambridge: Cambridge University Press, 1987.

Rotberg, Robert I., and Theodore K. Rabb, eds. *The Origins and Prevention of Major Wars*. Cambridge: Cambridge University Press, 1989.

Rudolph, Lloyd I., and Susanne Hoeber Rudolph. *The Modernity of Tradition: Political Development in India*. Chicago: University of Chicago Press, 1967.

Rustow, Dankwart. "Transitions to Democracy: Towards a Dynamic Model." *Comparative Politics* 22 (1970): 337–63.

Schumpeter, Joseph A. *Imperialism and the Social Classes*. Translated by Heinz Norden. New York: Augustus M. Kelley, 1951.

———. *Capitalism, Socialism and Democracy*. New York: Harper & Row, 1975.

de Schweinetz, Karl. *Industrialization and Democracy: Economic Necessities and Political Possibilities*. New York: Free Press, 1964.

Scott, James C. *The Moral Economy of the Peasant: Rebellion and Subsistence in Southeast Asia*. New Haven, Conn.: Yale University Press, 1976.

———. *Weapons of the Weak: Everyday Forms of Peasant Resistance*. New Haven, Conn.: Yale University Press, 1986.

Sherwin-White, A. N. *The Roman Citizenship*. Second Edition. Oxford: Clarendon Press, 1987.

Shils, Edward, *Political Development in the New States*. The Hague: Mouton, 1965.

Shonfeld, Andrew. *Modern Capitalism: The Changing Balance of Public and Private Power*. New York: Oxford University Press, 1980.

Skocpol, Theda R. "A Critical Review of Barrington Moore's *Social Origins of Dictatorship and Democracy*." *Politics and Society* 4 (1973): 1–34.

———. *States and Social Revolution: A Comparative Analysis of France, Russia and China*. New York: Cambridge University Press, 1979.

———, ed. *Vision and Method in Historical Sociology*. New York: Cambridge University Press, 1984.

Skocpol, Theda, and Margaret Somers. "The Uses of Comparative History in Macrosocial Inquiry." *Comparative Studies in Society and History* 22 (1980): 174–97.

Smith, Dennis. *Barrington Moore, Jr.: A Critical Assessment*. Armonk, N.Y.: M. E. Sharpe, 1983.

Sombart, Werner. *Krieg und Kapitalismus*. Berlin: Duncker & Humblot, 1913.

Stinchcombe, Arthur. *Theoretical Methods in Social History*. New York: Academic Press, 1978.

Stinchcombe, Arthur. *Constructing Social Theories*. Chicago: University of Chicago Press, 1987.

Therborn, Göran. "The Rule of Capital and the Rise of Democracy." *New Left Review* 103 (1977): 3–41.

Tilly, Charles, ed. *The Formation of the National States in Western Europe*. Princeton, N.J.: Princeton University Press, 1975.

————. *From Mobilization to Revolution*. Reading, Mass.: Addison-Wesley, 1978.

————. *Big Structures, Large Processes, Huge Comparisons*. New York: Russell Sage, 1984.

————. "Cities and States in Europe, 1000–1800." *Theory and Society* 18 (1989): 563–84.

————. *Coercion, Capital, and European States, A.D. 990–1990*. Oxford: Basil Blackwell, 1990.

Trimberger, Ellen Kay. *Revolution from Above: Military Bureaucrats and Development in Japan, Turkey, Egypt and Peru*. New Brunswick, N.J.: Transaction, 1978.

Trubek, David. "Max Weber on Law and the Rise of Capitalism." *Wisconsin Law Review* 3 (1972): 720–53.

Vallier, Ivan, ed. *Comparative Methods in Sociology*. Berkeley and Los Angeles: University of California Press, 1971.

Wallerstein, Immanuel. *The Modern World-System*. Three volumes. New York: Academic Press, 1974–1989.

Weber, Max. *The Methodology of the Social Sciences*. Translated by Edward A. Shils and Henry A. Finch. New York: Free Press, 1949.

————. *Economy and Society*. Two volumes. Guenther Roth and Claus Wittich, eds. Berkeley and Los Angeles: University of California Press, 1978.

————. *General Economic History*. Translated by Frank H. Knight. New Brunswick, N.J.: Transaction Books, 1982.

————. *The Agrarian Sociology of Ancient Civilizations*. Translated by R. I. Frank. London: Verso, 1988.

Zolberg, Aristide. "Strategic Interactions and the Formation of Modern States: France and England." *International Social Science Journal* 32 (1980): 687–716.

MEDIEVAL EUROPEAN HISTORY

Berman, Harold J. *Law and Revolution: The Rise of the Western Legal Tradition*. Cambridge, Mass.: Harvard University Press, 1983.

Bisson, Thomas N. "The Military Origins of Medieval Representation." *American Historical Review* 71 (1966): 1199–1218.

————. "The Problem of Feudal Monarchy." *Speculum* 53 (1978): 460–78.

Bloch, Marc. *Feudal Society*. Two volumes. Chicago: University of Chicago Press, 1961.

Blockmans, W. P. "A Typology of Representative Institutions in Late Medieval Europe." *Journal of Medieval History* 4 (1978): 189–215.

————. "Voracious States and Obstructing Cities: An Aspect of State Formation in Preindustrial Europe." *Theory and Society* 18 (1989): 733–55.

Jerome Blum. "The Internal Structure and Polity of the European Village Community from the Fifteenth to the Nineteenth Centuries." *Journal of Modern History* 43 (1971): 541–76.

Bowsky, W. M. "Medieval Citizenship: The Individual and the State in the Commune of Siena, 1287–1355." *Studies in Medieval and Renaissance History* 4 (1967): 193–243.

Bury, J. B., ed. *The Cambridge Medieval History*. Eight volumes. New York: Macmillan, 1911–1936.

Cheyette, F. L. "Custom, Case-Law, and Medieval 'Constitutionalism': A Reexamination." *Political Science Quarterly* 78 (1963): 362–90.

Colman, R. V. "Reason and Unreason in Early Medieval Law." *Journal of Interdisciplinary History* 4 (1973): 671–96.

Davies, Wendy, and Paul Fouracre, eds. *The Settlement of Disputes in Early Medieval Europe*. Cambridge: Cambridge University Press, 1986.

Duby, Georges. *The Chivalrous Society*. Berkeley and Los Angeles: University of California Press, 1980.

Estey, F. H. "The Scabini and Local Courts." *Speculum* 26 (1951): 119–29.

Fasoli, Gina. "Gouvernés et gouvernants dans les communes Italiennes du XIe au XIIIe siècle." *Gouvernés et Gouvernants* 4 (1984): 47–86.

Fichtenau, Heinrich. *The Carolingian Empire*. Toronto: University of Toronto Press, 1982.

Ganshof, François Louis. *Frankish Institutions under Charlemagne*. Providence, R.I.: Brown University Press, 1968.

————. *The Carolingians and the Frankish Monarchy: Studies in Carolingian History*. Ithaca, N.Y.: Cornell University Press, 1971.

Górski, Karol. "Les débuts de la representation de la *Communitas Nobilium* dans les assemblés d'Etats de l'est européen." *Standen en Landen* 47 (1968): 37–55.

Grant, Michael. *History of Rome*. New York: Scribner's, 1978.

Guenée, Bernard. *States and Rulers in Later Medieval Europe*. Oxford: Basil Blackwell, 1985.

Hibbert, A. B. "The Origins of the Medieval Town Patriciate." *Past and Present* 37 (1953): 15–27.

Hilton, Rodney, ed. *The Transition from Feudalism to Capitalism*. London: New Left Books, 1978.

Holton, R. J. *Cities, Capitalism and Civilization*. London: Allen & Unwin, 1986.

Immink, P.W.A. "Gouvernés et gouvernants dans la societé Germanique." *Gouvernés et Gouvernants* 2 (1968): 331–93.

International Commission for the History of Representative and Parliamentary Institutions. *Liber Memorialis Georges de Lagarde*. Paris: Béatrice-Nauwelaerts, 1970.

Kaeuper, Richard W. *War, Justice and Public Order: England and France in the Later Middle Ages*. Oxford: Clarendon Press, 1988.

Kahan, Arcadius. "Notes on Serfdom in Western and Eastern Europe." *Journal of Economic History* 33 (1973): 86–105.

Kantorowicz, Ernst H. *The King's Two Bodies: A Study in Mediaeval Political Theology*. Princeton, N.J.: Princeton University Press, 1957.

Kern, Fritz. *Kingship and Law in the Middle Ages*. Oxford: Basil Blackwell, 1939.

Lopez, Robert S. *The Commercial Revolution of the Middle Ages, 900–1350*. Cambridge: Cambridge University Press, 1976.

Lousse, Emile. "Parliamentisme ou corporatisme: Les origines des assemblées d'états." *Revue Historique du Droit Franc* 14 (1935): 683–706.

Lyon, B. "Medieval Constitutionalism: A Balance of Power." *Studies Presented to the International Commission for the History of Representative and Parliamentary Institutions* 24 (1961): 155–83.

McCormick, Michael. *Eternal Victory: Triumphal Rulership in Late Antiquity, Byzantium, and the Early Medieval West*. Cambridge: Cambridge University Press, 1986.

Marongiu, Antonio. *Medieval Parliaments: A Comparative Study*. Translated by S. J. Woolf. London: Eyre & Spottiswoode, 1968.

Myers, A. R. "The English Parliament and the French Estates-General in the Middle Ages." *Studies Presented to the International Commission for the History of Representative and Parliamentary Institutions* 24 (1961): 139–53.

Naef, Werner. "Frühformen des modernen Staates im Spätmittelalter." *Historische Zeitschrift* 171 (1959): 225–43.

Oakley, Francis. "Legitimation by Consent: The Question of the Medieval Roots." *Viator* 14 (1983): 303–35.

Ostrogorsky, George. *History of the Byzantine State*. Translated by Joan Hussey. New Brunswick, N.J.: Rutgers University Press, 1969.

Painter, Sidney. *The Rise of the Feudal Monarchies*. Ithaca, N.Y.: Cornell University Press, 1975.

Pirenne, Henri. *Early Democracies in the Low Countries: Urban Society and Political Conflict in the Middle Ages and the Renaissance*. New York: Harper & Row, 1963.

———. *Medieval Cities: Their Origins and the Revival of Trade*. Princeton, N.J.: Princeton University Press, 1974.

Reynolds, Susan. *Kingdoms and Communities in Western Europe, 900–1300*. Oxford: Clarendon Press, 1986.

Rörig, Fritz. *The Medieval Town*. Berkeley and Los Angeles: University of California Press, 1967.

Soule, Claude. "Les fondements historiques de l'élection du parlement européen." *Parliaments, Estates and Representation* 33 (1983): 135–39.

Southern, R. W. *Western Society and the Church in the Middle Ages*. Harmondsworth, U.K.: Penguin, 1983.

Spufford, P. "Assemblies of Estates, Taxation and Control of Coinage in Medieval Europe." *Studies Presented to the International Commission for the History of Representative and Parliamentary Institutions* 31 (1964): 113–30.

Stephenson, Carl. "The Origins and Significance of Feudalism." *American Historical Review* 46 (1941): 788–812.

Strayer, Joseph R. *Western Europe in the Middle Ages*. New York: Appleton-Century-Crofts, 1955.

———. *On the Medieval Origins of the Modern State*. Princeton, N.J.: Princeton University Press, 1970.

Tierney, Brian. *The Crisis of Church and State 1050–1300*. Toronto: University of Toronto Press, 1988.

Tierney, Brian, and Brian Linehan, eds. *Authority and Power: Studies on Medieval Law and Government Presented to Walter Ullman on His Seventieth Birthday*. Cambridge: Cambridge University Press, 1981.

Vinogradoff, Sir Paul. *Roman Law in Medieval Europe*. Oxford: Clarendon Press, 1929.

Wallace-Hadrill, John Michael. *Early Germanic Kingship in England and on the Continent*. Oxford: Clarendon Press, 1971.

White, Lynn, Jr. *Medieval Technology and Social Change*. Oxford: Oxford University Press, 1968.

Wickham, Chris. "The Other Transition: From the Ancient World to Feudalism." *Past and Present* 103 (1984): 3–36.

Wolff, Hans Julius. *Roman Law: An Historical Introduction*. Norman: University of Oklahoma Press, 1978.

MODERN EUROPEAN HISTORY

Aston, Trevor, ed. *Crisis in Europe, 1560–1660*. London: Routledge & Kegan Paul, 1980.

Aston, T. H., and C.H.E. Philpin, eds. *The Brenner Debate: Agrarian Class Structure and Economic Development in Pre-Industrial Europe*. Cambridge: Cambridge University Press, 1985.

Bean, Richard. "War and the Birth of the Nation State." *Journal of Economic History* 33 (1973): 203–21.

Davis, Ralph. *The Rise of the Atlantic Economies*. Ithaca, N.Y.: Cornell University Press, 1973.

Dehio, Ludwig. *The Precarious Balance: Four Centuries of the European Power Struggle*. New York: Vintage, 1962.

Dorn, Walter L. *Competition for Empire, 1740–1763*. New York: Harper & Row, 1963.

Forster, Robert, and Jack P. Greene, eds. *Preconditions of Revolution in Early Modern Europe*. Baltimore, Md.: Johns Hopkins University Press, 1970.

Fulbrook, Mary. *Piety and Politics: Religion and the Rise of Absolutism in England, Württemberg and Prussia*. Cambridge: Cambridge University Press, 1983.

Gerhard, Dietrich, ed. *Ständische Vertretungen in Europa im 17. und 18. Jahrhundert*. Göttingen: Vandenhoek und Ruprecht, 1968.

Griffiths, Gordon. *Representative Government in Western Europe in the Sixteenth Century*. Oxford: Oxford University Press, 1968.

Gutmann, Myron P. "The Origins of the Thirty Years' War." *Journal of Interdisciplinary History* 18 (1988): 749–70.

Hamerow, Theodore. *The Birth of a New Europe: State and Society in the Nineteenth Century*. Chapel Hill: University of North Carolina Press, 1983.

Hartung, Fritz. "Der Aufgeklärte Absolutismus." *Studies Presented to the International Commission for the History of Representative and Parliamentary Institutions* 54 (1974): 54–76.

Hayes, Carlton J. H. *The Historical Evolution of Early Nationalism*. New York: Richard R. Smith, 1931.

Hexter, J. H. *On Historians: Reappraisals of Some of the Masters of Modern History*. Cambridge, Mass.: Harvard University Press, 1979.

———. *Reappraisals in History: New Views on History and Society in Early Modern Europe*. Second Edition. Chicago: University of Chicago Press, 1979.

Iggers, Georg G. *New Directions in European Historiography*. Middletown, Conn.: Wesleyan University Press, 1984.

Jones, E. L. *The European Miracle: Environments, Economies and Geopolitics in the History of Europe and Asia*. Cambridge: Cambridge University Press, 1981.

Kautsky, John H. *The Politics of Aristocratic Empires*. Chapel Hill: University of North Carolina Press, 1982.

Koenigsberger, H. G. *Estates and Revolutions: Essays in Early Modern European History*. Ithaca, N.Y.: Cornell University Press, 1971.

———. *The Habsburgs and Europe 1516–1660*. Ithaca, N.Y.: Cornell University Press, 1971.

———. "Monarchies and Parliaments in Early Modern Europe." *Theory and Society* 5 (1978): 191–217.

Kohn, Hans. *Prelude to Nation-States: The French and German Experience, 1789–1815*. Princeton, N.J.: D. Van Nostrand, 1967.

Langbein, John H. *Torture and the Law of Proof: Europe and England in the Ancien Régime*. Chicago: University of Chicago Press, 1977.

Lefebvre, Georges. "Der Aufgeklärte Absolutismus." *Studies Presented to the International Commission for the History of Representative and Parliamentary Institutions* 54 (1974): 77–88.

McCracken, W. D. *The Rise of the Swiss Republic: A History*. New York: AMS Press, 1970.

Maravall, José Antonio. "The Origins of the Modern State." *Journal of World History* 6 (1961): 188–208.

Mayer, Arno. *The Persistence of the Old Regime: Europe to the Great War*. New York: Pantheon, 1981.

Mosse, George L. *Fallen Soldiers: Reshaping the Memory of the World Wars*. New York: Oxford University Press, 1990.

Mousnier, Roland. *Peasant Uprisings in Seventeenth-Century France, Russia, and China*. Translated by Brian Pearce. New York: Harper & Row, 1970.

North, Douglass C., and Robert Paul Thomas. *The Rise of the Western World: A New Economic History*. Cambridge: Cambridge University Press, 1973.

Oestreich, Gerhard. *Strukturprobleme der frühen Neuzeit: Ausgewählte Aufsätze*. Berlin: Duncker & Humblot, 1980.

Palmer, R. R. *The Age of the Democratic Revolution*. Two volumes. Princeton, N.J.: Princeton University Press, 1959.

Parker, Geoffrey. "The Emergence of Modern Finance in Europe, 1500–1730." In Carlo M. Cipolla, ed., *The Fontana Economic History of Europe*, Volume 2: *The Sixteenth and Seventeenth Centuries*. Glasgow: Collins, 1974.

————. *Europe in Crisis 1598–1648*. Ithaca, N.Y.: Cornell University Press, 1980.

Parker, Geoffrey, and Lesley M. Smith, eds. *The General Crisis of the Seventeenth Century*. London: Routledge & Kegan Paul, 1985.

Pirenne, Henri. *Early Democracies in the Low Countries*. New York: Harper & Row, 1963.

Potter, G. R., et al., eds. *The New Cambridge Modern History*. Seven volumes. Cambridge: Cambridge University Press, 1957–1970.

Prestwich, Menna, ed., *International Calvinism 1541–1715*. Oxford: Clarendon Press, 1986.

Rabb, Theodore K. *The Struggle for Stability in Early Modern Europe*. New York: Oxford University Press, 1975.

Rudé, George. *Europe in the Eighteenth Century: Aristocracy and the Bourgeois Challenge*. Cambridge, Mass.: Harvard University Press, 1972.

Russell, Conrad S. R. "Monarchies, Wars, and Estates in England, France, and Spain, c. 1580–c. 1640." *Legislative Studies Quarterly* 7 (1982): 205–20.

Slicher van Bath, B. H. *The Agrarian History of Western Europe A.D. 500–1850*. London: Edward Arnold, 1966.

Spring, David, ed. *European Landed Elites in the Nineteenth Century*. Baltimore, Md.: Johns Hopkins University Press, 1977.

Symcox, Geoffrey, ed. *War, Diplomacy, and Imperialism, 1618–1763*. New York: Harper & Row, 1973.

————. *Victor Amadeus II: Absolutism in the Savoyard State 1675–1730*. Berkeley and Los Angeles: University of California Press, 1983.

Taylor, A.J.P. *The Struggle for Mastery in Europe 1848–1918*. Oxford: Clarendon Press, 1954.

Urfus, Valentin. "Die Steuergewalt des böhmischen Landtags und der Absolutismus." *Studies Presented to the International Commission for the History of Representative and Parliamentary Institutions* 31 (1964): 179–87.

Zagorin, Perez. *Rebels and Rulers 1500–1660*. Two volumes. Cambridge: Cambridge University Press, 1984.

MILITARY HISTORY

Bak, János M., and Béla K. Király, eds. *War and Society in Eastern Central Europe*, Volume 3: *From Hunyadi to Rákóczi, War and Society in Late Medieval and Early Modern Hungary*. New York: Brooklyn College Press, 1982.

Bar-Kochva, Bezalel. *The Seleucid Army: Organization and Tactics in the Great Campaign*. Cambridge: Cambridge University Press, 1976.

Barudio, Günter. *Der Teutsche Krieg, 1618–1648*. Frankfurt: S. Fischer, 1985.

Beeler, John. *Warfare in Feudal Europe*. Ithaca, N.Y.: Cornell University Press, 1984.

Best, Geoffrey. *War and Society in Revolutionary Europe, 1770–1870*. New York: Oxford University Press, 1982.

Bond, Brian. *War and Society in Europe, 1870–1970*. New York: St. Martin's Press, 1983.

Brunt, P. A. *Italian Manpower 225 B.C.–A.D. 14*. Oxford: Clarendon Press, 1987.

Chandler, David. *The Art of Warfare in the Age of Marlborough*. New York: Hippocrene, 1976.

Clark, G. N. *War and Society in the Seventeenth Century*. Cambridge: Cambridge University Press, 1958.

Contamine, Philippe. *War in the Middle Ages*. Translated by Michael Jones. Oxford: Basil Blackwell, 1986.

Corvisier, André. *Armies and Societies in Europe, 1494–1789*. Translated by Abigail T. Siddall. Bloomington: Indiana University Press, 1979.

Creveld, Martin van. *Supplying War: Logistics from Wallenstein to Patton*. New York: Cambridge University Press, 1977.

———. *Command in War*. Cambridge, Mass.: Harvard University Press, 1985.

Delbrück, Hans. *History of the Art of War within the Framework of Political History*, Volumes 1–4. Westport, Conn.: Greenwood Press, 1975–1985.

Duffy, M., ed. *The Military Revolution and the State*. Exeter: University of Exeter Press, 1980.

Forrest, W. G. *A History of Sparta 950–192 B.C.* New York: W. W. Norton, 1968.

Fowler, Kenneth Alan, ed. *The Hundred Years War*. London: Macmillan, 1971.

Fuller, J.F.C. *A Military History of the Western World*, Volume 2: *From the Defeat of the Spanish Armada to the Battle of Waterloo*. New York: Da Capo, 1987.

Gaier, C. "La cavalrie lourde en Europe Occidentale du XIIe au XVe siècle." *Revue Internationale d'Histoire Militaire* 31 (1971): 385–96.

Gillingham, John, and J. C. Holt, eds. *War and Government in the Middle Ages: Essays in Honour of J. O. Prestwich*. Totowa, N.J.: Barnes & Noble, 1984.

Gutmann, Myron P. "The Origins of the Thirty Years' War." *Journal of Interdisciplinary History* 18 (1988): 749–70.

Hale, J. R. *War and Society in Renaissance Europe, 1450–1620*. Baltimore, Md.: Johns Hopkins University Press, 1985.

Hanson, Victor Davis. *The Western Way of War: Infantry Battle in Classical Greece*. New York: Alfred A. Knopf, 1989.

Harris, William V. *War and Imperialism in Republican Rome 327–70 B.C.* Oxford: Clarendon Press, 1989.

Howard, Michael. *War in European History*. New York: Oxford University Press, 1976.

Jespersen, Knud J. V. "Social Change and Military Revolution in Early Modern Europe: Some Danish Evidence." *Historical Journal* 26 (1983): 1–13.

Kamen, Howard. "The Economic and Social Consequences of the Thirty Years' War." *Past and Present* 39 (1968): 44–61.

Keegan, John. *The Face of Battle: A Study of Agincourt, Waterloo and the Somme*. Harmondsworth, U.K.: Penguin, 1988.

———. *The Price of Admiralty: The Evolution of Naval Warfare*. New York: Viking, 1988.

Kennedy, Paul M. *The Rise and Fall of British Naval Mastery*. London: Ashfield Press, 1987.

———. *The Rise and Fall of the Great Powers: Economic Change and Military Conflict from 1500 to 2000*. New York: Random House, 1987.

McNeill, William H. *The Pursuit of Power: Technology, Armed Force, and Society since A.D. 1000*. Chicago: University of Chicago Press, 1982.

Modelski, George, and William R. Thompson. *Seapower in Global Politics, 1494–1993*. Seattle: University of Washington Press, 1988.

Nef, John U. *War and Human Progress: An Essay on the Rise of Industrial Civilization*. Cambridge, Mass.: Harvard University Press, 1950.

Oman, Sir Charles. *A History of the Art of War: The Middle Ages from the Fourth to the Fourteenth Century*. London: Methuen, 1898.

———. *A History of the Art of War in the Sixteenth Century*. New York: E. P. Dutton, 1937.

Padfield, Peter, *The Tide of Empires: Decisive Naval Campaigns in the Rise of the West*, Volume 2: *1654–1763*. London: Routledge & Kegan Paul, 1982.

Paret, Peter, ed. *Makers of Modern Strategy: From Machiavelli to the Nuclear Age*. Princeton, N.J.: Princeton University Press, 1986.

Parker, Geoffrey. "The 'Military Revolution,' 1550–1660—A Myth?" *Journal of Modern History* 48 (1976): 195–214.

———. *The Thirty Years' War*. London: Routledge & Kegan Paul, 1987.

———. *The Military Revolution: Military Innovation and the Rise of the West, 1500–1800*. Cambridge: Cambridge University Press, 1988.

Polisensky, J. V. "The Thirty Years' War and the Crises and Revolutions of Seventeenth-Century Europe." *Past and Present* 39 (1968): 34–43.

———. *The Thirty Years War*. Translated by Robert Evans. Berkeley and Los Angeles: University of California Press, 1971.

———. *War and Society in Europe, 1618–1648*. Cambridge: Cambridge University Press, 1978.

Postan, M. M. "Some Consequences of the Hundred Years' War." *Economic History Review* 12 (1942): 1–12.

Ralston, David B. *Importing the European Army: The Introduction of European Military Techniques and Institutions into the Extra-European World, 1600–1914*. Chicago: University of Chicago Press, 1990.

Redlich, Fritz. "Contributions in the Thirty Years' War." *Economic History Review* 12 (1959): 247–54.

———. *The German Military Enterpriser and His Work Force: A Study in European Economic and Social History*. Two volumes. Wiesbaden: Franz Steiner, 1964.

Rothenberg, Gunther E. *The Art of Warfare in the Age of Napoleon*. Bloomington: Indiana University Press, 1980.

Semmel, Bernard, ed. *Marxism and the Science of War*. Oxford: Oxford University Press, 1981.

Seward, Desmond. *The Hundred Years War: The English in France, 1337–1453*. New York: Atheneum, 1982.

Shaw, Martin, ed. *War, State and Society*. London: Macmillan, 1984.

Strachan, Hew. *European Armies and the Conduct of War*. London: George Allen & Unwin, 1983.

Watson, G. R. *The Roman Soldier*. Ithaca, N.Y.: Cornell University Press, 1987.

Wedgwood, C. V. *The Thirty Years War*. Garden City, N.Y.: Anchor, 1961.

Winter, J. M., ed. *War and Economic Development: Essays in Memory of David Joslin*. New York: Cambridge University Press, 1975.

AUSTRIA

Barker, Thomas M. *Army, Aristocracy, Monarchy: Essays on War, Society and Government in Austria, 1618–1780*. New York: Columbia University Press, 1982.

Bernard, Paul P. *The Limits of Enlightenment: Joseph II and the Law*. Urbana: University of Illinois Press, 1979.

Good, David F. *The Economic Rise of the Habsburg Empire, 1750–1914*. Berkeley and Los Angeles: University of California Press, 1984.

Heischmann, Eugen. *Die Anfänge des stehenden Heeres in Österreich*. Vienna: Österreichischer Bundesverlag, 1925.

Kann, Robert A. *A History of the Habsburg Empire, 1526–1918*. Berkeley and Los Angeles: University of California Press, 1974.

Melton, James Van Horn. *Absolutism and the Eighteenth-Century Origins of Compulsory Schooling in Prussia and Austria*. Cambridge: Cambridge University Press, 1988.

Schulze, Winfried. *Landesdefension und Staatsbildung: Studien zum Kriegswesen des innerösterreichischen Territorialstaates (1564–1619)*. Vienna: Hermann Böhlaus, 1973.

CHINA

Balazs, Etienne. *Chinese Civilization and Bureaucracy: Variations on a Theme*. New Haven: Yale University Press, 1972.

Bergère, Marie-Claire. "On the Historical Origins of Chinese Underdevelopment." *Theory and Society* 13 (1984): 327–37.

Bodde, Derek, and Clarence Morris. *Law in Imperial China: Exemplified by 190 Ch'ing Dynasty Cases*. Philadelphia: University of Pennsylvania Press, 1967.

Chang, Kwang-chih. *Shang Civilization*. New Haven, Conn.: Yale University Press, 1980.

Ch'en Wen-shih. "The Creation of the Manchu *Niru*." *Chinese Studies in History* 14 (1981): 11–46.

Creel, Herrlee G. *The Origins of Statecraft in China*, Volume 1: *The Western Chou Empire* Chicago: University of Chicago Press, 1970.

Dreyer, Edward L. *Early Ming China: A Political History 1355–1435*. Stanford, Calif.: Stanford University Press, 1982.

Eberhard, Wolfram. *A History of China*. London: Routledge & Kegan Paul, 1977.

Feuerwerker, Albert. "The State and the Economy in Late Imperial China." *Theory and Society* 13 (1984): 297–326.

Huang, Pei. *Autocracy at Work: A Study of the Yung-cheng Period, 1723–1735*. Bloomington: Indiana University Press, 1974.

Kierman, Frank A., Jr., and John K. Fairbank, eds. *Chinese Ways in Warfare*. Cambridge, Mass.: Harvard University Press, 1974.

Kuhn, Philip A. *Rebellion and Its Enemies in Late Imperial China: Mobilization and Social Structure, 1796–1864*. Cambridge, Mass.: Harvard University Press, 1980.

Liu Chia-chü. "The Creation of the Banners in the Early Ch'ing." *Chinese Studies in History* 14 (1981): 47–75.

Loewe, Michael. *Imperial China: The Historical Background to the Modern Age*. New York: Praeger, 1966.

Michael, Franz. *The Taiping Rebellion: History and Documents*, Volume 1. Seattle: University of Washington Press, 1966.

Mi Chu Wiens. "Lord and Peasant: The Sixteenth to the Eighteenth Century." *Modern China* 6 (1980): 3–39.

Nee, Victor, and David Mozingo, eds. *State and Society in Contemporary China*. Ithaca, N.Y.: Cornell University Press, 1983.

Pao Chia Hsieh. *The Government of China 1644–1911*. New York: Octagon, 1966.

Perry, Elizabeth J. *Rebels and Revolutionaries in North China, 1845–1945*. Stanford, Calif.: Stanford University Press, 1980.

Schwartz, Benjamin I. *The World of Thought in Ancient China*. Cambridge, Mass.: Harvard University Press, 1985.

Spence, Jonathan D., and John E. Wills, Jr. *From Ming to Ch'ing: Conquest, Region, and Continuity in Seventeenth-Century China*. New Haven, Conn.: Yale University Press, 1979.

T'ung-tsu Chü. *Local Government in China under the Ch'ing*. Cambridge, Mass.: Harvard University Press, 1988.

Wittfogel, Karl A. *Oriental Despotism: A Comparative Study of Total Power*. New York: Vintage, 1981.

ENGLAND

Allan, D.G.C. "The Rising in the West, 1628–31." *Economic Historical Review* Second Series 5 (1952): 76–85.

Allmand, C. T. *Society at War: The Experience of England and France during the Hundred Years' War*. Edinburgh: University of Edinburgh Press, 1973.

———. *The Hundred Years War: England and France at War c. 1300–c. 1450*. Cambridge: Cambridge University Press, 1988.

Andrews, Kenneth R. *Elizabethan Privateering: English Privateering during the Spanish War, 1585–1603*. Cambridge: Cambridge University Press, 1964.

———. *Trade Plunder and Settlement: Maritime Enterprise and the Genesis of the British Empire, 1480–1630*. Cambridge: Cambridge University Press, 1984.

Ashton, Robert. *The English Civil War: Conservatism and Revolution, 1603–1649*. New York: W. W. Norton, 1978.

Aston, T. H., ed. *Landlords, Peasants and Politics in Medieval England*. Cambridge: Cambridge University Press, 1988.

Aylmer, G. E. *The King's Servants: The Civil Service of Charles I*. New York: Columbia University Press, 1961.

———. *The State's Servants: The Civil Service of the English Republic 1649–1660*. London: Routledge & Kegan Paul, 1973.

Aylmer, G. E. *Rebellion or Revolution? England, 1640–1660*. New York: Oxford University Press, 1986.

Barnett, Corelli, *Britain and Her Army 1509–1970: A Military, Political and Social Survey*. London: Allen Lane, 1970.

Baron, Frederic S. "The Social Process of Historical Interpretation: A Study of the Gentry Controversy." Masters thesis, Division of the Social Sciences, University of Chicago, 1988.

Beckett, J. V. *The Aristocracy in England 1660–1914*. Oxford: Basil Blackwell, 1986.

Boynton, Lindsay. *The Elizabethan Militia, 1558–1658*. Toronto: University of Toronto Press, 1967.

Brailsford, H. N. *The Levellers and the English Revolution*. Stanford, Calif.: Stanford University Press, 1961.

Brenner, Robert. "The Civil War Politics of London's Merchant Community." *Past and Present* 58 (1973): 53–107.

Brewer, John. *The Sinews of Power: War, Money and the English State, 1688–1783*. London: Unwin Hyman, 1989.

Burton, I. F. " 'The Committee of Council at the War-Office': An Experiment in Cabinet Government under Anne." *Historical Journal* 6 (1961): 78–103.

Butterfield, Herbert. *George III and the Historians*. London: Cassell, 1988.

Cannon, John. *Aristocratic Century: The Peerage of Eighteenth-Century England*. Cambridge: Cambridge University Press, 1984.

Capp, Bernard. *Cromwell's Navy: The Fleet and the English Revolution 1648–1660*. Oxford: Clarendon Press, 1989.

Chandaman, C. D. *The English Public Revenue, 1660–1688*. Oxford: Clarendon Press, 1975.

Childs, John. "The Army and the Oxford Parliament of 1681." *English Historical Review* 94 (1979): 580–87.

————. *The Army, James II, and the Glorious Revolution*. New York: St. Martin's Press, 1980.

————. "The British Brigade in France, 1672–1678." *History* 69 (1984): 384–97.

Chrimes, S. B. *An Introduction to the Administrative History of Medieval England*. Oxford: Basil Blackwell, 1959.

Clark, J.C.D. *Revolution and Rebellion: State and Society in England in the Seventeenth and Eighteenth Centuries*. Cambridge: Cambridge University Press, 1986.

————. *English Society 1688–1832: Ideology, Social Structure and Political Practice during the Ancien Regime*. Cambridge: Cambridge University Press, 1988.

Coleman, Christopher, and David Starkey, eds. *Revolution Reassessed: Revisions in the History of Tudor Administration and Government*. Oxford: Oxford University Press, 1986.

Coleman, D. C. *The Economy of England 1450–1750*. Oxford: Oxford University Press, 1978.

Coleman, D. C., and A. H. John, eds. *Trade, Government and Economy in Pre-Industrial England: Essays Presented to F. J. Fisher*. London: Weidenfeld & Nicolson, 1976.

Colley, Linda. *In Defiance of Oligarchy: The Tory Party 1714–1760*. Cambridge: Cambridge University Press, 1985.

Colvin, H. M. "Castles and Government in Tudor England." *English Historical Review* 83 (1968): 225–34.

Cooper, J. P. "A Revolution in Tudor History." *Past and Present* 26 (1963): 110–12.

Croom, David. "The Later Eyres." *English Historical Review* 97 (1982): 241–68.

Cust, Richard. *The Forced Loan and English Politics 1626–1628*. Oxford: Oxford University Press, 1987.

Davies, R. G., and J. H. Denton, eds. *The English Parliament in the Middle Ages*. Manchester: University of Manchester Press, 1981.

Dickson, P.G.M. *The Financial Revolution in England: A Study in the Development of Public Credit 1688–1756*. London: Macmillan, 1967.

Dietz, Frederick C. *English Public Finance, 1558–1641*. New York: Barnes & Noble, 1964.

Elton, G. R. *Studies in Tudor and Stuart Politics and Government*. Cambridge: Cambridge University Press, 1974.

———. "Taxation for War and Peace in Early Tudor England." In J. M. Winter, ed., *War and Economic Development: Essays in Memory of David Joslin*. New York: Cambridge University Press, 1975.

———. *Reform and Revolution: England 1509–1558*. London: Edward Arnold, 1977.

———. "Parliament in the Sixteenth Century: Function and Foundations." *Historical Journal* 22 (1979): 255–78.

———. *The Tudor Revolution in Government: Administrative Change in the Age of Henry VIII*. Cambridge: Cambridge University Press, 1979.

———. *F. W. Maitland*. New Haven, Conn.: Yale University Press, 1985.

———. *Policy and Police: The Enforcement of the Reformation in the Age of Thomas Cromwell*. Cambridge: Cambridge University Press, 1985.

———. *The Parliament of England 1559–1581*. Cambridge: Cambridge University Press, 1986.

Fletcher, Anthony. *The Outbreak of the English Civil War*. London: Edward Arnold, 1981.

———. *Reform in the Provinces: The Government of Stuart England*. New Haven, Conn.: Yale University Press, 1986.

Gleason, J. H. *The Justices of the Peace in England 1558 to 1640: A Later Eirenarcha*. Oxford: Clarendon Press, 1969.

Gooch, G. P. *English Democratic Ideas in the Seventeenth Century*. New York: Harper & Row, 1959.

Guy, J. A. *The Cardinal's Court: The Impact of Thomas Wolsey in Star Chamber*. Hassocks, U.K.: Harvester Press, 1977.

———. "Henry VIII and the 'Praemunire' Manoeuvres of 1530–1531." *English Historical Review* 97 (1982): 481–503.

———. "The Origins of the Petition of Right Reconsidered." *Historical Journal* 25 (1982): 289–312.

Hale, John. "War and Public Opinion in the Fifteenth and Sixteenth Centuries." *Past and Present* 22 (1962): 18–35.

Harriss, G. L. "Medieval Government and Statecraft." *Past and Present* 25 (1963): 8–39.

————. "Parliament and Taxation: The Middle Ages." *Studies Presented to the International Commission for the History of Representative and Parliamentary Institutions* 31 (1964): 1–6.

————. *King, Parliament, and Public Finance in Medieval England to 1369*. Oxford: Clarendon Press, 1975.

————. "War and the Emergence of the English Parliament." *Journal of Medieval History* 2 (1976): 35–56.

————. "Parliamentary Taxation and the Origins of Appropriation of Supply in England, 1207–1340." *Gouvernés et Gouvernants* 3 (1984): 165–79.

Harvey, P.D.A. *The Peasant Land Market in Medieval England*. Oxford: Clarendon Press, 1984.

Haskins, George L. "Executive Justice and the Rule of Law." *Speculum* 30 (1955): 529–38.

————. *The Growth of English Representative Government*. New York: A. S. Barnes, 1960.

Hexter, J. H. *The Reign of King Pym*. Cambridge, Mass.: Harvard University Press, 1941.

Hill, Christopher. *Economic Problems of the Church: From Archbishop Whitgift to the Long Parliament*. Oxford: Clarendon Press, 1956.

————. *The Century of Revolution, 1603–1714*. New York: W. W. Norton, 1961.

————. *Puritanism and Revolution: Studies in Interpretation of the English Revolution of the Seventeenth Century*. New York: Schocken, 1964.

————. *God's Englishman: Oliver Cromwell and the English Revolution*. New York: Harper & Row, 1972.

————. *The World Turned Upside Down. Radical Ideas in the English Revolution*. Harmondsworth, U.K.: Penguin, 1972.

Hilton, Rodney. *Bond Men Made Free: Medieval Peasant Movements and the English Rising of 1381*. London: Temple Smith, 1973.

————, ed. *Peasants, Knights and Heretics: Studies in Medieval English Social History*. Cambridge: Cambridge University Press, 1981.

Hirst, Derek. *Authority and Conflict: England, 1603–1658*. Cambridge, Mass.: Harvard University Press, 1986.

Hogue, Arthur R. *Origins of the Common Law*. Indianapolis, Ind.: Liberty Press, 1985.

Hollister, C. Warren. "The Norman Conquest and the Genesis of English Feudalism." *American Historical Review* 66 (1961): 641–63.

————. *Anglo-Saxon Military Organizations on the Eve of the Norman Invasions*. Oxford: Clarendon Press, 1962.

Hooker, James R. "Notes on the Organization and Supply of the Tudor Military under Henry VII." *Huntington Library Quarterly* 23 (1959–1960): 19–31.

Horwitz, Henry. *Parliaments, Policy and Politics in the Reign of William III*. Manchester: Manchester University Press, 1977.

Hughes, Ann. *Politics, Society and Civil War in Warwickshire, 1620–1660*. Cambridge: Cambridge University Press, 1987.

Hunt, William. *The Puritan Movement: The Coming of Revolution in an English County*. Cambridge, Mass.: Harvard University Press, 1983.

Hutton, Ronald. *The Royalist War Effort 1642–1646*. London: Longman, 1982.

———. *The Restoration: A Political and Religious History of England and Wales 1658–1667*. Oxford: Clarendon Press, 1985.

Hyams, P. R. *King, Lords and Peasants in Medieval England*. Oxford: Oxford University Press, 1980.

Jewell, H. M. *English Local Administration in the Middle Ages*. Newton Abbot: David & Charles, 1972.

John, A. H. "Wars and the British Economy, 1700–1763." *Economic History Review* Second Series 7 (1955): 329–44.

Jolliffe, J.E.A. *The Constitutional History of England from the English Settlement to 1485*. London: A. and C. Black, 1939.

Jones, D. W. *War and Economy in the Age of William III and Marlborough*. Oxford: Basil Blackwell, 1988.

Jones, J. R. *The Revolution of 1688 in England*. London: Weidenfeld & Nicolson, 1972.

———. *Country and Court: England, 1658–1714*. Cambridge, Mass.: Harvard University Press, 1978.

Kearney, Hugh. *Strafford in Ireland 1633–41: A Study of Absolutism*. Cambridge: Cambridge University Press, 1989.

Keir, Sir David Lindsay. *The Constitutional History of Modern Britain since 1485*. Ninth Edition. New York: W. W. Norton, 1969.

Kenyon, J. P. *The Civil Wars of England*. New York: Knopf, 1988.

Kishlansky, Mark. *The Rise of the New Model Army*. Cambridge: Cambridge University Press, 1983.

———. *Parliamentary Selection: Social and Political Choice in Early Modern England*. Cambridge: Cambridge University Press, 1986.

Lachmann, Richard. *From Manor to Market: Structural Change in England, 1536–1640*. Madison: University of Wisconsin Press, 1987.

Lehmberg, Stanford F. *The Later Parliaments of Henry VIII, 1536–1547*. Cambridge: Cambridge University Press, 1977.

Lenman, Bruce. *The Jacobite Risings in Britain 1689–1746*. London: Eyre Methuen, 1980.

Levy, F. J. "How Information Spread Among the Gentry, 1550–1640." *Journal of British Studies* 21 (1982): 11–34.

Lloyd, T. O. *The British Empire 1558–1983*. Oxford: Oxford University Press, 1985.

MacCaffrey, Wallace T. *Queen Elizabeth and the Making of Policy, 1572–1588*. Princeton, N.J.: Princeton University Press, 1981.

MacCormack, John P. *Revolutionary Politics in the Long Parliament*. Cambridge, Mass.: Harvard University Press, 1973.

Macfarlane, Alan. *The Origins of English Individualism: The Family, Property and Social Transition*. New York: Cambridge University Press, 1979.

McFarlane, K. B. "England and the Hundred Years War." *Past and Present* 22 (1962): 3–17.

———. *The Nobility of Later Medieval England*. Oxford: Clarendon Press, 1973.

McInnes, Angus. "When Was the English Revolution?" *History* 67 (1982): 377–92.

McIntosh, A. W. "The Numbers of the English Regicides." *History* 67 (1982): 195–216.

Maddicott, J. R. "Magna Carta and the Local Community 1215–1259." *Past and Present* 102 (1984): 25–65.

Maitland, Frederic William. *Domesday Book and Beyond: Three Essays in the Early History of England*. Cambridge: Cambridge University Press, 1987 [1897].

———. *The Constitutional History of England*. Cambridge: Cambridge University Press, 1950 [1908].

———. *Selected Historical Essays*. Helen M. Cam, ed. Boston: Beacon Press, 1957.

Manning, Brian. "The Nobles, the People, and the Constitution." *Past and Present* 56 (1972): 42–64.

———. *The English People and the English Revolution 1640–1649*. London: Heinemann, 1976.

Mathias, Peter, and Patrick O'Brien. "Taxation in Britain and France, 1715–1810: A Comparison of the Social and Economic Incidence of Taxes Collected for the Central Governments." *Journal of European Economic History* 5 (1976): 601–50.

Millar, Gilbert John. *Tudor Mercenaries and Auxiliaries 1485–1547*. Charlottesville: University of Virginia Press, 1980.

Miller, Edward. "War, Taxation and the English Economy in the Late Thirteenth and Early Fourteenth Centuries." In J. M. Winter, ed., *War and Economic Development: Essays in Memory of David Joslin*. New York: Cambridge University Press, 1975.

Miller, Helen. *Henry VIII and the English Nobility*. Oxford: Basil Blackwell, 1986.

Miller, John. "Charles II and His Parliaments." *Transactions of the Royal Historical Society* 32 (1982): 1–32.

———. "The Glorious Revolution: 'Contract' and 'Abdication' Reconsidered." *Historical Journal* 25 (1982): 541–55.

———. "The Potential for 'Absolutism' in Later Stuart England." *History* 69 (1984): 187–207.

———. "The Crown and the Borough Charters in the Reign of Charles II." *English Historical Review* 100 (1985): 53–84.

Morrill, J. S. "Mutiny and Discontent in English Provincial Armies, 1645–1647." *Past and Present* 56 (1972): 49–74.

———. "The Army Revolt of 1647." In A. C. Duke and C. A. Tamse, eds., *Britain and the Netherlands*, Volume 6: *War and Society*. The Hague: Martinus Nijhoff, 1977.

————. *The Revolt of the Provinces: Conservatives and Radicals in the English Civil War, 1603–1650*. London: Longmans, 1980.

Omond, J. S. *Parliament and the Army, 1642–1904*. Cambridge: Cambridge University Press, 1933.

Painter, Sidney. *Studies in the History of the English Feudal Barony*. Baltimore: Md.: Johns Hopkins University Press, 1943.

Palmer, Robert C. *The County Courts of Medieval England 1150–1350*. Princeton, N.J.: Princeton University Press, 1982.

Pearce, Brian. "Elizabethan Food Policy and the Armed Forces." *Economic History Review* 12 (1942): 39–46.

Pennington, D. "Parliament and Taxation: 1485–1660." *Studies Presented to the International Commission for the History of Representative and Parliamentary Institutions* 31 (1964): 7–12.

Plucknett, Theodore F. T. *A Concise History of the Common Law*. Fifth Edition. London: Butterworth, 1956.

Plumb, J. H. "The Organization of the Cabinet in the Reign of Queen Anne." *Transactions of the Royal Historical Society* Fifth Series 7 (1957): 137–57.

————. *The Origins of Political Stability in England, 1675–1725*. Boston: Houghton Mifflin, 1967.

————. "The Growth of the Electorate in England from 1600 to 1700." *Past and Present* 45 (1969): 90–116.

Pocock, J.G.A., ed. *Three British Revolutions: 1641, 1688, 1776*. Princeton, N.J.: Princeton University Press, 1980.

Postan, M. M. *The Medieval Economy and Society: An Economic History of Britain in the Middle Ages*. Harmondsworth, U.K.: Penguin, 1984.

Powicke, Michael. *Military Obligation in Medieval England: A Study in Liberty and Duty*. Oxford: Clarendon Press, 1967.

Prestwich, J. O. "Anglo-Norman Feudalism and the Problem of Continuity." *Past and Present* 26 (1963): 39–57.

Pulman, Michael Barraclough. *The Elizabethan Privy Council in the Fifteen-Seventies*. Berkeley and Los Angeles: University of California Press, 1971.

Reynolds, Susan. *Introduction to the Study of English Medieval Towns*. Oxford: Clarendon Press, 1977.

Richardson, H. G., and G. O. Sayles. "Parliaments and Great Councils in Medieval England." *Law Quarterly Review* 77 (1961): 213–36.

Robbins, C. "Why the English Parliament Survived the Age of Absolutism and Some Explanations Offered by Writers of the Seventeenth and Eighteenth Centuries." *Studies Presented to the International Commission for the History of Representative and Parliamentary Institutions* 18 (1945): 199–215.

Rogers, P. G. *The Fifth Monarchy Men*. London: Oxford University Press, 1966.

Rowney, Ian. "Arbitration in Gentry Disputes of the Later Middle Ages." *History* 67 (1982): 367–76.

Russell, Conrad. *The Crisis of the Parliaments: English History 1509–1660*. Oxford: Oxford University Press, 1971.

————, ed. *The Origins of the English Civil War*. London: Macmillan, 1978.

Russell, Conrad. *Parliaments and English Politics 1621–1629*. Oxford: Clarendon Press, 1983.

———. "Why Did Charles I Call the Long Parliament?" *History* 69 (1984): 375–83.

Sacret, T. H. "The Restoration Government and Municipal Corporations." *English Historical Review* 45 (1930): 232–59.

Schwoerer, Lois. *"No Standing Armies!" The Anti-Army Ideology in Seventeenth-Century England*. Baltimore, Md.: Johns Hopkins University Press, 1974.

Slavin, Arthur J., ed. *Tudor Men and Institutions: Studies in English Law and Government*. Baton Rouge: Louisiana State University Press, 1972.

Speck, W. A. *Tory and Whig: The Struggle in the Constituencies 1701–1715*. London: Macmillan, 1970.

———. *Stability and Strife: England, 1714–1760*. Cambridge, Mass.: Harvard University Press, 1977.

Stone, Lawrence. "State Control in Sixteenth-Century England." *Economic History Review* 17 (1947): 103–20.

———. *The Crisis of the Aristocracy, 1558–1640*. Oxford: Oxford University Press, 1965.

———. *The Causes of the English Revolution, 1529–1642*. New York: Harper & Row, 1972.

———. "The Bourgeois Revolution of the Seventeenth Century Revisited." *Past and Present* 109 (1985): 44–54.

Tanner, J. R. *English Constitutional Conflicts of the Seventeenth Century, 1603–1689*. Cambridge: Cambridge University Press, 1928.

Tawney, R. H. "The Rise of the Gentry." *Economic History Review* 11 (1941): 1–38.

Trevor-Roper, Hugh R. "The Gentry 1540–1640." *Economic History Review* Supplement 1 (1953): 1–55.

Turner, Edward Raymond. *The Privy Council of England 1603–1788*. Baltimore, Md.: Johns Hopkins University Press, 1927.

Turner, R. V. "The Origin of the Medieval English Jury." *Journal of British Studies* 7 (1967–1968): 1–10.

Underdown, David. "Party Management in the Recruiter Elections, 1645–1648." *English Historical Review* 83 (1968): 235–64.

———. *Pride's Purge: Politics in the Puritan Revolution*. London: George Allen & Unwin, 1985.

———. *Revel, Riot, and Rebellion: Popular Politics and Culture in England 1603–1660*. Oxford: Oxford University Press, 1987.

Walcott, Robert, Jr. *English Politics in the Early Eighteenth Century*. Cambridge, Mass.: Harvard University Press, 1956.

Walton, Clifford. *History of the English Standing Army A.D. 1660–1700*. London: Harrison and Sons, 1894.

Wedgwood, C. V. *The Trial of Charles I*. Harmondsworth, U.K.: Penguin, 1983.

Weinzierl, Michael. "Parliament and the Army in England 1659: Constitutional Thought and the Struggle for Control." *Parliaments, Estates and Representation* 2 (1982): 47–55.

———. "John Reeves and the Controversy over the Constitutional Role of Parliament during the French Revolution." *Parliaments, Estates and Representation* 5 (1985): 71–77.

Wernham, R. B. *After the Armada: Elizabethan England and the Struggle for Western Europe 1588–1595*. Oxford: Clarendon Press, 1984.

Wiener, Martin J. *English Culture and the Decline of the Industrial Spirit 1850–1980*. Cambridge: Cambridge University Press, 1982.

Williams, Penry. "Dr. Elton's Interpretation of the Age." *Past and Present* 25 (1963): 3–8.

————. "The Tudor State." *Past and Present* 25 (1963): 39–58.

Wilson, Charles. *Profit and Power: A Study of England and the Dutch Wars*. The Hague: Martinus Nijhoff, 1978.

Wood, Charles T. *Joan of Arc and Richard III: Sex, Saints, and Government in the Middle Ages*. New York: Oxford University Press, 1988.

Woodham-Smith, Cecil. *The Reason Why*. New York: Atheneum, 1982.

Woodward, G.W.O. "The Rise of Parliament in the Henrician Reformation." *Studies Presented to the International Commission for the History of Representative and Parliamentary Institutions* 20 (1947): 15–24.

Woolrych, Austin. *Commonwealth to Protectorate*. Oxford: Clarendon Press, 1982.

————. *Soldiers and Statesmen: The General Council of the Army and Its Debates 1647–48*. Oxford: Oxford University Press, 1987.

Worden, Blair. *The Rump Parliament, 1648–1653*. Cambridge: Cambridge University Press, 1974.

Young, Peter. *The Cavalier Army: Its Organization and Everyday Life*. London: George Allen & Unwin, 1974.

Zagorin, Perez. *The Court and the Country: The Beginning of the English Revolution*. New York: Atheneum, 1971.

FRANCE

Agulhon, Maurice. *Marianne into Battle: Republican Imagery and Symbolism in France, 1789–1880*. Translated by Janet Lloyd. Cambridge: Cambridge University Press, 1979.

Asher, Eugene L. *The Resistance to the Maritime Classes: The Survival of Feudalism in the France of Colbert*. Berkeley and Los Angeles: University of California Press, 1960.

Baldwin, John W. *The Government of Philip Augustus: Foundations of French Royal Power in the Middle Ages*. Berkeley and Los Angeles: University of California Press, 1986.

Baxter, Douglas Clark. *Servants of the Sword: French Intendants of the Army 1630–70*. Urbana: University of Illinois Press, 1976.

Behrens, C.B.A. *Society, Government, and the Enlightenment: The Experiences of Eighteenth-Century France and Prussia*. New York: Harper & Row, 1985.

Beik, William. *Absolutism and Society in Seventeenth-Century France: State Power and Provincial Aristocracy in Languedoc*. Cambridge: Cambridge University Press, 1985.

Bertaud, Jean-Paul. *The Army of the French Revolution: From Citizen-Soldiers to Instruments of Power*. Translated by R. R. Palmer. Princeton, N.J.: Princeton University Press, 1988.

Bien, David D. "The Army in the French Enlightenment: Reform, Reaction and Revolution." *Past and Present* 85 (1979): 68–98.

Bitton, Davis. *The French Nobility in Crisis, 1560–1640*. Stanford, Calif.: Stanford University Press, 1969.

Blanning, T.C.W. *The French Revolution: Aristocrats versus Bourgeois?* Atlantic Highlands, N.J.: Humanities Press, 1987.

Bonney, Richard. "The French Civil War, 1649–53." *European Studies Review* 8 (1978): 71–100.

———. *Political Change in France under Richelieu and Mazarin 1624–1661*. Oxford: Oxford University Press, 1978.

———. "The English and French Civil Wars." *History* 65 (1980): 365–82.

———. *The King's Debts: Finance and Politics in France, 1589–1661*. Oxford: Clarendon Press, 1981.

Buisseret, D. "A Stage in the Development of the French *Intendants*: The Reign of Henry IV." *Historical Journal* 9 (1966): 27–38.

Carey, John A. *Judicial Reform in France before the Revolution of 1789*. Cambridge, Mass.: Harvard University Press, 1980.

Chaussinand-Nogaret, Guy. *The French Nobility in the Eighteenth Century: From Feudalism to Enlightenment*. Cambridge: Cambridge University Press, 1985.

Church, William F. *Constitutional Thought in Sixteenth-Century France*. Cambridge: Cambridge University Press, 1941.

———. *Richelieu and Reason of State*. Princeton, N.J.: Princeton University Press, 1972.

Cobb, Richard. *The People's Armies: The* Armées Révolutionnaires: *Instrument of the Terror in the Departments April 1793 to Floréal Year II*. Translated by Marianne Elliott. New Haven, Conn.: Yale University Press, 1987.

Cobban, Alfred. *A History of Modern France*. Three volumes. Harmondsworth, U.K.: Penguin, 1986.

Cole, Charles Woolsey. *Colbert and a Century of French Mercantilism*. Two volumes. Morningside Heights, N.Y.: Columbia University Press, 1939.

———. *French Mercantilism 1683–1706*. New York: Columbia University Press, 1943.

Collins, James B. *Fiscal Limits of Absolutism: Direct Taxation in Early Seventeenth-Century France*. Berkeley and Los Angeles: University of California Press, 1988.

Corvisier, André. *l'Armée Française de la fin du XVIIe siècle au ministère de Choiseul, Le Soldat*, Volume 1. Paris: Presses Universitaires de France, 1964.

Coveney, P. J., ed. *France in Crisis, 1620–1675*. Totowa, N.J.: Rowman and Littlefield, 1977.

Dawson, Philip. "The *Bourgeoisie de Robe* in 1789." *French Historical Studies* 4 (1965): 1–21.

Dent, Julian. *Crisis in Finance: Crown, Financiers, and Society in Seventeenth-Century France*. London: David and Charles, 1973.

Doolin, Paul Rice. *The Fronde*. Cambridge Mass.: Harvard University Press, 1935.

Doyle, William. *Origins of the French Revolution*. Second Edition. New York: Oxford University Press, 1988.

Dumont, F., and P. C. Timbal. "Gouvernés et gouvernants en France: Periodes du moyen âge et du XVIe siècle." *Gouvernés et Gouvernants* 3 (1966): 181–233.

Dunkley, Kenneth M. "Patronage and Power in Seventeenth-Century France: Richelieu's Clients and the Estates of Brittany." *Parliaments, Estates and Representation* 1 (1981): 1–12.

Ekberg, Carl J. *The Failure of Louis XIV's Dutch War*. Chapel Hill: University of North Carolina Press, 1979.

Ford, Franklin L. *Robe and Sword: The Regrouping of the French Aristocracy after Louis XIV*. New York: Harper & Row, 1965.

Forrest, Alan. *Soldiers of the French Revolution*. Durham, N. C.: Duke University Press, 1990.

Giesey, Ralph E. "State-Building in Early Modern France: The Role of Royal Officialdom." *Journal of Modern History* 55 (1983): 191–207.

Godechot, Jacques. *The Counter-Revolution: Doctrine and Action 1789–1804*. Translated by Salvator Attanasio. Princeton, N.J.: Princeton University Press, 1981.

Goubert, Pierre. *The French Peasantry in the Seventeenth Century*. Cambridge: Cambridge University Press, 1987.

Hamscher, Albert N. *The Parlement of Paris after the Fronde 1653–1673*. Pittsburgh, Pa.: University of Pittsburgh Press, 1976.

Hanley, Sarah. *The* Lit de Justice *of the Kings of France: Constitutional Ideology in Legend, Ritual, and Discourse*. Princeton, N.J.: Princeton University Press, 1983.

Harding, Robert R. *Anatomy of a Power Elite: The Provincial Governors of Early Modern France*. New Haven, Conn.: Yale University Press, 1976.

Hatton, Ragnhild, ed. *Louis XIV and Absolutism*. Columbus: Ohio University Press, 1976.

———, ed. *Louis XIV and Europe*. Columbus: Ohio University Press, 1976.

Hayden, J. Michael. *France and the Estates General of 1614*. Cambridge: Cambridge University Press, 1974.

Henneman, J. B. *Royal Taxation in Fourteenth Century France: The Development of War Financing 1322–1356*. Princeton, N.J.: Princeton University Press, 1971.

———. "Royal Taxation in Fourteenth Century France: The Captivity and Ransom of John II, 1356–1370." *Memoirs of the American Philosophical Society* 116 (1976): 1–338.

Holt, Mack P. *The Duke of Anjou and the Politique Struggle during the Wars of Religion*. Cambridge: Cambridge University Press, 1986.

Hunt, Lynn. *Politics, Culture, and Class in the French Revolution*. Berkeley and Los Angeles: University of California Press, 1984.

Hurt, John J. "The Parlement of Brittany and the Crown: 1665–1675." *French Historical Studies* 4 (1966): 411–33.

Jones, P. M. *The Peasantry in the French Revolution*. Cambridge: Cambridge University Press, 1988.

Kettering, Sharon. *Judicial Politics and Urban Revolt in Seventeenth-Century France: The Parlement of Aix, 1629–1659*. Princeton, N.J.: Princeton University Press, 1978.

————. "Patronage and Politics during the Fronde." *French Historical Studies* 14 (1986): 409–41.

Kierstead, Raymond F., ed. *State and Society in Sixteenth-Century France*. New York: New Viewpoints, 1975.

Kitchens, J. H. "Judicial Commissions and the Parlement of Paris." *French Historical Studies* 12 (1982): 323–50.

Kossmann, Ernst H. *La Fronde*. Leiden: Universitaire Pers Leiden, 1954.

Ladurie, Emmanuel Le Roy. *The Peasants of Languedoc*. Translated by John Day. Urbana: University of Illinois Press, 1976.

————. *Carnival in Romans*. Translated by Mary Feeney. New York: George Braziller, 1979.

Lassaigne, Jean-Dominique. "Les revendications de la noblesse pendant la Fronde." *Studies Presented to the International Commission for the History of Representative and Parliamentary Institutions* 23 (1960): 269–75.

Lefebvre, Georges. *The Coming of the French Revolution*. Princeton, N.J.: Princeton University Press, 1967.

LeGoff, T.J.A., and D.M.G. Sutherland. "The Social Origins of Counter-Revolution in Western France." *Past and Present* 99 (1983): 65–87.

Lewis, P. S. "The Failure of the French Medieval Estates." *Past and Present* 23 (1962): 3–24.

Lloyd, Howell. *The State, France, and the Sixteenth Century*. London: George Allen & Unwin, 1982.

Lublinskaya, A. D. "Les Assemblées d'Etats en France au XVIIe siècle. Les Assemblées des Notables de 1617 et de 1626." *Studies Presented to the International Commission for the History of Representative and Parliamentary Institutions* 31 (1964): 163–78.

————. *French Absolutism: The Crucial Phase, 1620–29*. New York: Cambridge University Press, 1968.

Lynn, John A. "The Growth of the French Army during the Seventeenth Century." *Armed Forces and Society* 6 (1980): 568–85.

————. *Bayonets of the Republic: Motivation and Tactics in the Army of Revolutionary France, 1791–94*. Urbana: University of Illinois Press, 1984.

————. "Tactical Evolution in the French Army." *French Historical Studies* 14 (1985): 176–91.

Major, J. Russell. *Representative Institutions of Renaissance France, 1421–1556*. Madison: University of Wisconsin Press, 1960.

————. "The Loss of Royal Initiative and the Decay of the Estates General in

France, 1421–1615." *Studies Presented to the International Commission for the History of Representative and Parliamentary Institutions* 24 (1961): 245–59.

———. "Henry IV and Guyenne: A Study Concerning the Origins of Royal Absolutism." *French Historical Studies* 4 (1966): 363–83.

———. *Representative Government in Early Modern France*. New Haven, Conn.: Yale University Press, 1980.

Mettam, Roger. *Power and Faction in Louis XIV's France*. London: Basil Blackwell, 1988.

Michaud, Claude. "Finances et guerres de religion en France." *Revue d'Histoire Moderne et Contemporaire* 28 (1981): 572–96.

Moote, A. Lloyd. "The Parliamentary Fronde and Seventeenth-Century Robe Solidarity." *French Historical Studies* 2 (1962): 330–54.

———. "The French Crown Versus its Judicial and Financial Officers, 1615–1683." *Journal of Modern History* 34 (1964): 146–60.

———. *The Revolt of the Judges: The Parlement of Paris and the Fronde 1643–1652*. Princeton, N.J.: Princeton University Press, 1971.

Mousnier, Roland. *Etat et société sous François 1ᵉʳ et pendant le gouvernment personnel de Louis XIV*. Paris: Centre de Documentation Universitaire, 1966.

———. *La vénalité des offices sous Henri IV et Louis XIII*. Second Edition. Paris: Presses Universitaires de France, 1971.

———. *The Institutions of France under the Absolute Monarchy 1598–1789*. Two volumes. Chicago: University of Chicago Press, 1979.

———. "Pourquoi Etats-Généraux et Etats-provinciaux ont-ils joué un si faible rôle pendant la Fronde?" *Parliaments, Estates and Representation* 1 (1981): 139–45.

———. *La monarchie absolue en Europe du Vᵉ siècle à nos jours*. Paris: Presses Universitaires de France, 1982.

———. "La participation des gouvernés à l'activité des gouvernants dans la France du XVIIe et du XVIIIe siècles." *Gouvernés et Gouvernants* 3 (1984): 235–97.

Orlea, Manfred. *La Noblesse aux Etats Generaux de 1576 et de 1588*. Paris: Presses Universitaires de France, 1980.

Parker, David. "The Social Foundations of French Absolutism, 1610–1630." *Past and Present* 53 (1971): 67–89.

———. *The Making of French Absolutism*. New York: St. Martin's Press, 1983.

Péronnet, Michel. "Une example d'opposition legale: Les assemblées du Clergé de France au dix-huitième siècle." *Parliaments, Estates and Representation* 6 (1986): 33–42.

Phillpotts, Christopher. "The French Plan of Battle during the Agincourt Campaign." *English Historical Review* 99 (1984): 59–66.

Porch, Douglas. *Army and Revolution: France, 1815–1848*. London: Routledge & Kegan Paul, 1974.

Ranum, Orest. "Courtesy, Absolutism and the Rise of the French State, 1630–1660." *Journal of Modern History* 52 (1980): 426–51.

Riley, James C. *The Seven Years War and the Old Regime in France: The Economic and Financial Toll*. Princeton, N.J.: Princeton University Press, 1986.

Rogister, John. "Parlementaires, Sovereignty, and Legal Opposition under Louis XIV: An Introduction." *Parliaments, Estates and Representation* 6 (1986): 25–32.

Root, Hilton R. *Peasants and King in Burgundy: Agrarian Foundations of French Absolutism*. Berkeley and Los Angeles: University of California Press, 1987.

Ross, Steven T. "The Development of the Combat Division in Eighteenth-Century French Armies." *French Historical Studies* 4 (1965): 84–94.

Rowen, Herbert H. "*L'Etat c'est moi:* Louis XIV and the State." *French Historical Studies* 2 (1961): 83–98.

———. *The King's State: Proprietary Dynasticism in Early Modern France*. New Brunswick, N.J.: Rutgers University Press, 1980.

Rubenstein, James M. *The French New Towns*. Baltimore, Md.: Johns Hopkins University Press, 1978.

Rule, John C., ed. *Louis XIV and the Craft of Kingship*. Columbus: Ohio State University Press, 1969.

Salmon, J.H.M. *Society in Crisis: France in the Sixteenth Century*. London: Ernest Benn, 1975.

Schaeper, Thomas J. *The French Council of Commerce 1700–1715: A Study of Mercantilism after Colbert*. Columbus: Ohio State University Press, 1983.

Schama, Simon. *Citizens: A Chronicle of the French Revolution*. New York: Alfred A. Knopf, 1989.

Shennan, J. H. *The Parlement of Paris*. Ithaca, N.Y.: Cornell University Press, 1968.

Soboul, Albert. "The French Rural Community in the Eighteenth and Nineteenth Centuries." *Past and Present* 10 (1956): 78–95.

Sonnino, Paul. *Louis XIV and the Origins of the Dutch War*. Cambridge: Cambridge University Press, 1988.

Soule, Claude. "Les pouvoirs des députés aux Etats Généraux de France." *Studies Presented to the International Commission for the History of Representative and Parliamentary Institutions* 27 (1963): 61–82.

Stone, Bailey. *The Parlement of Paris, 1774–1789*. Chapel Hill: University of North Carolina Press, 1981.

———. *The French Parlements and the Crisis of the Old Regime*. Chapel Hill: University of North Carolina Press, 1986.

Strayer, Joseph R., and Charles H. Taylor. *Studies in Early French Taxation*. Cambridge, Mass.: Harvard University Press, 1939.

Suleiman, Ezra N. *Politics, Power, and Bureaucracy in France: The Administrative Elite*. Princeton, N.J.: Princeton University Press, 1974.

Symcox, Geoffrey. *The Crisis of French Seapower 1688–1697: From the* Guerre d'Escadre *to the* Guerre de Course. The Hague: Martinus Nijhoff, 1974.

Tapié, Victor-L. *France in the Age of Louis XIII and Richelieu*. Translated by D. McN. Lockie. Cambridge: Cambridge University Press, 1984.

Taylor, C. H. "The Composition of Baronial Assemblies in France, 1315–1320." *Speculum* 29 (1954): 433–58.

Taylor, George V. "Types of Capitalism in Eighteenth-Century France." *English Historical Review* 79 (1964): 478–97.

———. "Noncapitalist Wealth and the Origins of the French Revolution." *American Historical Review* 72 (1967): 469–96.

Tilly, Charles. *The Vendée*. Cambridge, Mass.: Harvard University Press, 1964.

Tocqueville, Alexis de. *The Old Régime and the French Revolution*. Garden City, N.Y.: Doubleday Anchor, 1955.

Villers, Robert. "Réflexions sur les premiers Etats Generaux de France au début du XIVe siècle." *Parliaments, Estates and Representation* 4 (1984): 93–97.

Wolfe, M. *The Fiscal System of Renaissance France*. New Haven, Conn.: Yale University Press, 1972.

Wood, Charles T. *Joan of Arc and Richard III: Sex, Saints, and Government in the Middle Ages*. New York: Oxford University Press, 1988.

Wood, James B. *The Nobility of the* Election *of Bayeux, 1463–1666: Continuity through Change*. Princeton, N.J.: Princeton University Press, 1980.

JAPAN

Barnhart, Michael A. *Japan Prepares for Total War: The Search for Economic Security, 1919–1941*. Ithaca, N.Y.: Cornell University Press, 1987.

Bellah, Robert. *Tokugawa Religion: The Cultural Roots of Modern Japan*. New York: Free Press, 1985.

Berry, Mary Elizabeth. *Hideyoshi*. Cambridge, Mass.: Harvard University Press, 1989.

Bix, Herbert P. *Peasant Protest in Japan, 1590–1884*. New Haven, Conn.: Yale University Press, 1986.

Dower, John W., ed. *Origins of the Modern Japanese State: Selected Writings of E. H. Norman*. New York: Pantheon, 1975.

Hall, John Whitney. *Government and Local Power in Japan, 500–1700: A Study Based on Bizen Province*. Princeton, N.J.: Princeton University Press, 1966.

Hall, John W., and Marius B. Jansen, eds. *Studies in the Institutional History of Early Modern Japan*. Princeton, N.J.: Princeton University Press, 1968.

Henderson, Dan Fenno. *Conciliation and Japanese Law, Tokugawa and Modern*. Two volumes. Seattle: University of Washington Press, 1965.

Jansen, Marius B., and Gilbert Rozman, eds. *Japan in Transition: From Tokugawa to Meiji*. Princeton, N.J.: Princeton University Press, 1986.

Sansom, Sir George. *A History of Japan*. Three volumes. Stanford, Calif.: Stanford University Press, 1961–1963.

Smethurst, Richard J. *A Social Basis for Prewar Japanese Militarism: The Army and the Rural Community*. Berkeley and Los Angeles: University of California Press, 1974.

Smith, Thomas C. *The Agrarian Origins of Modern Japan*. New York: Atheneum, 1966.

Totman, Conrad T. *Politics in the Tokugawa Bakufu, 1600–1843*. Cambridge, Mass.: Harvard University Press, 1967.

Tsukahira, Toshio G. *Feudal Control in Tokugawa Japan: The Sankin Kotai System*. Cambridge, Mass.: Harvard East Asian Monographs, 1966.

Vlastos, Stephen. *Peasant Protests and Uprisings in Tokugawa Japan*. Berkeley and Los Angeles: University of California Press, 1986.

THE NETHERLANDS

Aymard, Maurice, ed. *Dutch Capitalism and World Capitalism*. Cambridge: Cambridge University Press, 1982.

Barbour, V. *Capitalism in Amsterdam in the Seventeenth Century*. Baltimore, Md.: Johns Hopkins University Press, 1950.

Blok, Petrus Johannes. *History of the People of the Netherlands*. Two volumes. New York: G. P. Putnam's Sons, 1898–1899.

Boxer, C. R. *The Dutch Seaborne Empire, 1600–1800*. London: Penguin, 1988.

Bromley, J. S., and E. H. Kossmann, eds. *Britain and the Netherlands*, Volume 1. London: Chatto & Windus, 1960.

Den Tex, Jan. *Oldenbarnevelt*. Two volumes. Cambridge: Cambridge University Press, 1973.

De Vries, Jan. "On the Modernity of the Dutch Republic." *Journal of Economic History* 33 (1973): 191–202.

———. *The Dutch Rural Economy in the Golden Age, 1500–1700*. New Haven, Conn.: Yale University Press, 1978.

Duke, A. C., and C. A. Tamse, eds. *Britain and the Netherlands*, Volume 6: *War and Society*. The Hague: Martinus Nijhoff, 1977.

Ekberg, Carl J. *The Failure of Louis XIV's Dutch War*. Chapel Hill: University of North Carolina Press, 1979.

Feld, M. D. "Middle-Class Society and the Rise of Military Professionalism: The Dutch Army 1589–1609." *Armed Forces and Society* 1 (1975): 419–42.

Fruin, R. *The Siege and Relief of Leyden in 1574*. The Hague: Martinus Nijhoff, 1927.

Geyl, Pieter. *The Netherlands in the Seventeenth Century*. Two volumes. New York: Barnes & Noble, 1961.

———. *Orange and Stuart 1641–72*. London: Weidenfeld & Nicolson, 1969.

———. *The Revolt of the Netherlands, 1555–1609*. London: Ernest Benn, 1980.

Gilissen, J. "Les etats Généraux des pays par deça, 1464–1632." *Anciens Pays et Assemblées d'Etats* 33 (1965): 261–321.

Grever, John H. "Committees and Deputations in the Assemblies of the Dutch Republic, 1660–1668." *Parliaments, Estates and Representation* 1 (1981): 13–33.

———. "The Structure of Decision-Making in the States General of the Dutch Republic, 1660–1668." *Parliaments, Estates and Representation* 2 (1982): 125–53.

———. "The French Invasion of the Spanish Netherlands and the Provincial Aseemblies of the Dutch Republic, 1667–1668." *Parliaments, Estates and Representation* 4 (1984): 25–35.

Griffiths, G. "The Revolutionary Character of the Revolt of the Netherlands." *Comparative Studies in Society and History* 11 (1959–1960): 452–72.

Gutmann, Myron P. *War and Rural Life in the Early Modern Low Countries*. Princeton, N.J.: Princeton University Press, 1980.

t'Hart, Marjolein. "Cities and Statemaking in the Dutch Republic, 1580–1680." *Theory and Society* 18 (1989): 663–88.

Huizinga, J. *Holländische Kultur im Siebzehnten Jahrhundert: Eine Skizze*. Basel: Benno & Schwabe, 1961.

Israel, Jonathan I. "A Conflict of Empires: Spain and the Netherlands 1618–1648." *Past and Present* 76 (1977): 34–74.

———. "The Decline of Spain: A Historical Myth?" *Past and Present* 91 (1981): 170–80.

———. "Frederick Henry and the Dutch Political Factions, 1625–1642." *English Historical Review* 98 (1983): 1–27.

———. *The Dutch Republic and the Hispanic World 1606–1661*. Oxford: Clarendon Press, 1986.

———. *Dutch Primacy in World Trade, 1585–1740*. Oxford: Clarendon Press, 1989.

Kaplan, Benjamin Jacob. "Calvinists and Libertines: The Reformation in Utrecht, 1578–1618." Doctoral thesis, Department of History, Harvard University, 1989.

Koenigsberger, H. G. "The Origin of Revolutionary Politics in France and the Netherlands during the Sixteenth Century." *Journal of Modern History* 27 (1955): 335–51.

———. "The States General of the Netherlands." *Studies Presented to the International Commission for the History of Representative and Parliamentary Institutions* 18 (1958): 143–58.

———. "Why Did the States General of the Netherlands Become Revolutionary in the Sixteenth Century?" *Parliaments, Estates and Representation* 2 (1982): 103–11.

Kriedte, Peter. *Peasants, Landlords and Merchant Capitalists: Europe and the World Economy, 1500–1800*. Cambridge: Cambridge University Press, 1983.

Marshall, Sherrin D. *The Dutch Gentry, 1500–1650: Family, Faith, and Fortune*. Westport, Conn.: Greenwood Press, 1987.

Motley, John Lothrop. *The Rise of the Dutch Republic: A History in Three Volumes*. New York: Harper & Brothers, 1856.

Neale, J. E. "Elizabeth and the Netherlands, 1586–7." *English Historical Review* 45 (1930): 373–96.

Oosterhoff, F. G. *Leicester and the Netherlands 1586-1587*. Utrecht: H & S, 1988.

Parker, Geoffrey. "Spain, Her Enemies and the Revolt of the Netherlands 1559–1648." *Past and Present* 49 (1970): 72–95.

———. *The Army of Flanders and the Spanish Road, 1567–1659: The Logistics of Spanish Victory and Defeat in the Low Countries' Wars*. Cambridge: Cambridge University Press, 1972.

———. "The Costs of the Dutch Revolt." In J. M. Winter, ed. *War and Economic Development: Essays in Memory of David Joslin*. New York: Cambridge University Press, 1975.

———. *Spain and the Netherlands, 1559–1659*. Short Hills, N.J.: Enslow, 1979.

———. *The Dutch Revolt*. Ithaca, N.Y.: Cornell University Press, 1980.

Pirenne, Henri. *Early Democracies in the Low Countries: Urban Society and Political Conflict in the Middle Ages and the Renaissance*. New York: Harper & Row, 1963.

Rowen, Herbert H. *The Low Countries in Early Modern Times*. New York: Walker, 1972.

Rowen, Herbert H. *John de Witt, Grand Pensionary of Holland, 1625–1672*. Princeton, N.J.: Princeton University Press, 1978.

———. "John de Witt: The Makeshift Executive in a *Ständestaat*." *Gouvernés et Gouvernants* 3 (1984): 439–51.

———. *John de Witt: Statesman of the "True Freedom"*. Cambridge: Cambridge University Press, 1986.

———. *The Princes of Orange: The Stadholders in the Dutch Republic*. Cambridge: Cambridge University Press, 1988.

Rowen, Herbert H., and Andrew Lossky. *Political Ideas and Institutions in the Dutch Republic*. Los Angeles: William Andrews Clark Memorial Library, 1985.

Schama, Simon. "The Exigencies of War and the Politics of Taxation in the Netherlands 1795–1810." In J. M. Winter, ed. *War and Economic Development: Essays in Memory of David Joslin*. New York: Cambridge University Press, 1975.

———. *The Embarrassment of Riches: An Interpretation of Dutch Culture in the Golden Ages*. Berkeley and Los Angeles: University of California Press, 1988.

Schöffer, Ivo. "Did Holland's Golden Age Coincide with a Period of Crisis?" *Acta Historiae Neerlandica* 1 (1966): 82–107.

Sonnino, Paul. *Louis XIV and the Origins of the Dutch War*. Cambridge: Cambridge University Press, 1988.

Tracy, James D. *A Financial Revolution in the Habsburg Netherlands: Renten and Renteniers in the County of Holland, 1515–1565*. Berkeley and Los Angeles: University of California Press, 1985.

———. *Holland under Habsburg Rule, 1506–1566: The Formation of a Body Politic*. Berkeley and Los Angeles: University of California Press, 1990.

Van Der Wee, H. *The Growth of the Antwerp Market and the European Economy, 14th to 16th Centuries*. The Hague: Martinus Nijhoff, 1963.

Vaughan, Richard. *Charles the Bold: The Last Valois Duke of Burgundy*. London: Longmans, 1973.

Wedgwood, C. V. *William the Silent: William of Nassau, Prince of Orange 1533–1584*. New Haven, Conn.: Yale University Press, 1944.

Wilson, Charles. *Anglo-Dutch Commerce and Finance in the Eighteenth Century*. Cambridge: Cambridge University Press, 1966.

———. *Profit and Power: A Study of England and the Dutch Wars*. The Hague: Martinus Nijhoff, 1978.

POLAND

Bardach, Juliusz. "Gouvernants et gouvernés en Pologne au moyen âge et aux temps modernes." *Gouvernés et Gouvernants* 4 (1965): 255–85.

———. "l'Election des députés à l'ancienne Diète polonaise, fin des XVe-XVIIIe siècles." *Parliaments, Estates and Representation* 5 (1985): 45–58.

Bieganski, Witold, Piotr Stawecki, and Janusz Wojtasik, eds. *Histoire militaire de Pologne: Problèmes choisis*. Warsaw: Edition du Ministère de la Défense Nationale, 1970.

Davies, Norman. *God's Playground: A History of Poland in Two Volumes*. New York: Columbia University Press, 1982.

Ekdahl, Sven. *Die Schlacht bei Tannenberg 1410: Quellenkritische Untersuchungen*, Volume 1: *Einführung und Quellenlage*. Berlin: Duncker & Humblot, 1982.

Fedorowicz, J. K. *A Republic of Nobles: Studies in Polish History to 1864*. Cambridge: Cambridge University Press, 1982.

Gasiorowski, Zygmunt J. "The Conquest Theory of the Genesis of the Polish State." *Speculum* 30 (1955): 550–60.

Górski, Karol. "Die Anfänge der Repräsentation der *Communitas Nobilium* in Polen, im Ordensstaat Preussen und in Ungarn im Mittelalter." *Studies Presented to the International Commission for the History of Representative and Parliamentary Institutions* 36 (1966): 19–24.

————. "Les chartes de la noblesse en Pologne aux XIVe et XVe siècles." *Studies Presented to the International Commission for the History of Representative and Parliamentary Institutions* 56 (1979): 247–72.

Grzybowski, Konstanty. "Gouvernés et gouvernants en Pologne aux XIXe et XXe siècles." *Gouvernés et Gouvernants* 6 (1965): 119–41.

Herbst, Stanislaw. "l'Armée polonaise et l'art militaire au XVIIIe siècle." *Acta Poloniae Historica* 3 (1960): 33–48.

Kaplan, Herbert H. *The First Partition of Poland*. New York: Columbia University Press, 1962.

Kieniewicz, Stefan. "Les récentes études historiques sur la Pologne au temps des partages." *Acta Poloniae Historica* 1 (1958): 59–74.

Knoll, Paul W. *The Rise of the Polish Monarchy: Piast Poland in East Central Europe, 1320–1370*. Chicago: University of Chicago Press, 1972.

Kowecki, Jerzy. "Les transformations de la structure sociale en Pologne au XVIIIᵉ siècle: La noblesse et la bourgeoisie." *Acta Poloniae Historica* 26 (1972): 5–30.

Leach, Catherine S., ed. *Memoirs of the Polish Baroque: The Writings of Jan Chryzostom Pasek, A Squire of the Commonwealth of Poland and Lithuania*. Berkeley and Los Angeles: University of California Press, 1976.

Lukowski, Jerzy T. "Towards Partition: Polish Magnates and Russian Intervention in Poland during the Early Reign of Stanislaw August Poniotowski." *Historical Journal* 28 (1985): 557–74.

Malowist, Marian. "The Economic and Social Development of the Baltic Countries from the Fifteenth to the Seventeenth Centuries." *Economic History Review* Second Series 12 (1959): 177–89.

Manteuffel, Tadeusz. *The Formation of the Polish State: The Period of Ducal Rule, 963–1194*. Detroit, Mich.: Wayne State University Press, 1982.

Miller, James. "The Polish Nobility and the Renaissance Monarchy: The 'Execution of the Laws' Movement, Part One." *Parliaments, Estates and Representation* 3 (1983): 65–87.

————. "The Polish Nobility and the Renaissance Monarchy: The 'Execution of the Laws' Movement, Part Two." *Parliaments, Estates and Representation* 4 (1984): 1–24.

Müller, Michael G. *Polen zwischen Preussen und Russland: Souveränitätskrise und Reformpolitik 1736–1752*. Berlin: Colloquium Verlag, 1983.

Opalinski, Edward, "Great Poland's Power Elite under Sigismund III, 1587–1632: Defining the Elite." *Acta Poloniae Historica* 42 (1980): 41–66.

Reddaway, W. F., J. H. Penson, O. Halecki, and R. Dyboski, eds. *The Cambridge History of Poland*. Two volumes. Cambridge: Cambridge University Press, 1950–1951.

Roos, H. "Standwesen und parlamentische Verfassung in Polen 1505–1772." *Studies Presented to the International Commission for the History of Representative and Parliamentary Institutions* 37 (1969): 310–67.

Russocki, Stanislaw. "*Consilium baronum* en Pologne médiévale." *Acta Poloniae Historica* 35 (1977): 5–20.

———. "The Origins of Estate Consciousness of the Nobility of Central Europe." *Acta Poloniae Historica* 46 (1982): 31–46.

———. "De l'accord commun au vote unanime: Les activités de la Diète nobilaire de Pologne, XVIIIème siècle." *Parliaments, Estates and Representation* 3 (1983): 7–21.

Schramm, Gottfried. *Der polnische Adel und die Reformation 1548–1607*. Wiesbaden: Franz Steiner, 1965.

Stone, Daniel. *Polish Politics and National Reform 1775–1788*. New York: Eastern European Quarterly, 1976.

Topolski, Jerzy. "Reflections on the First Partition of Poland." *Acta Poloniae Historica* 27 (1973): 89–104.

———. "The Development of the Absolutist Prussian State and Prussia's Role in the Partition of Poland." *Polish Western Affairs* 22 (1981): 24–39.

Wimmer, Jan. "l'Infanterie dans l'armée polonaise aux XV-XVIIIe siècles." In Witold Bieganski, Piotr Stawecki, and Janusz Wojtasik, eds., *Histoire militaire de Pologne: Problèmes choisis*. Warsaw: Edition du Ministère de la Défense Nationale, 1970.

Wyrobisz, Andrzej. "Power and Towns in the Polish Gentry Commonwealth: The Polish-Lithuanian State in the Sixteenth and Seventeenth Centuries." *Theory and Society* 18 (1989): 611–30.

PRUSSIA AND GERMANY

Behrens, C.B.A. *Society, Government, and the Enlightenment: The Experiences of Eighteenth-Century France and Prussia*. New York: Harper & Row, 1985.

Berdahl, Robert M. "The *Stände* and the Origins of Conservatism in Prussia." *Eighteenth Century Studies* 6 (1973): 298–321.

———. *The Politics of the Prussian Nobility: The Development of a Conservative Ideology 1770–1848*. Princeton, N.J.: Princeton University Press, 1988.

Biskrup, Marian. "The Secularization of the State of the Teutonic Order in Prussia, 1525: Its Genesis and Significance." *Polish Western Affairs* 22 (1981): 3–23.

Blackbourn, David, and Geoff Eley. *The Peculiarities of German History: Bourgeois Society and Politics in Nineteenth-Century Germany*. Oxford: Oxford University Press, 1984.

Blasius, Dirk, ed. *Preussen in der deutschen Geschichte*. Königstein: Verlagsgruppe Athenäum-Hain-Scriptor-Hanstein, 1980.

Born, Karl Erich. "Regierte und Regierung in der deutschen Geschichte des 19. Jahrhunderts." *Gouvernés et Gouvernants* 5 (1965): 167–212.

Bosl, Karl. "Zu einer Geschichte der bäuerlichen Repräsentation in der deutschen Landgemeinde." *Studies Presented to the International Commission for the History of Representation and Parliamentary Institutions* 26 (1963): 1–7.

Brady, Robert A. *The Rationalization Movement in German Industry*. Berkeley and Los Angeles: University of California Press, 1933.

Brady, Thomas A. *Turning Swiss: Cities and Empire, 1450–1550*. New York: Cambridge University Press, 1985.

Buchda, Gerhard. "Reichsstände und Landstände in Deutschland im 16. und 17. Jahrhundert." *Gouvernés et Gouvernants* 4 (1984): 193–226.

Burleigh, Michael. *Prussian Society and the German Order: An Aristocratic Order in Crisis, c. 1410–1466*. Cambridge: Cambridge University Press, 1984.

Büsch, Otto. *Militärsystem und Sozialleben im alten Preussen, 1713–1807: Die Anfänge der sozialen Militarisierung der preußisch-deutschen Gesellschaft*. Berlin: Walter de Gruyter, 1962.

Büsch, Otto, and Wolfgang Neugebauer, eds. *Moderne preußische Geschichte, 1648–1947: Eine Anthologie*. Three volumes. Berlin: Walter de Gruyter, 1981.

Calleo, David. *The German Problem Reconsidered: Germany and the World Order, 1870 to the Present*. Cambridge: Cambridge University Press, 1978.

Carsten, F. L. "Medieval Democracy in the Brandenburg Towns and Its Defeat in the Fifteenth Century." *Transactions of the Royal Historical Society* Fourth Series 25 (1943): 73–91.

———. "The Great Elector and the Foundation of the Hohenzollern Despotism." *English Historical Review* 65 (1950): 175–203.

———. "Prussian Despotism at Its Height." *History* 40 (1955): 42–67.

———. *Princes and Parliaments in Germany: From the Fifteenth to the Eighteenth Century*. Oxford: Clarendon Press, 1959.

———. "The Causes of the Decline of the German Estates." *Studies Presented to the International Commission for the History of Representative and Parliamentary Institutions* 24 (1961): 287–96.

———. *The Origins of Prussia*. Oxford: Clarendon Press, 1964.

———. "The German Estates in the Eighteenth Century." *Gouvernés et Gouvernants* 4 (1984): 227–38.

Craig, Gordon. *The Politics of the Prussian Army, 1660–1945*. London: Oxford University Press, 1979.

Dahrendorf, Ralf. *Society and Democracy in Germany*. New York: W. W. Norton, 1967.

Diefendorf, Jeffry M. *Businessmen and Politics in the Rhineland, 1789–1834*. Princeton, N.J.: Princeton University Press, 1980.

Dietrich, Richard. *Forschungen zu Staat und Verfassung: Festgabe für Fritz Hartung*. Berlin: Duncker & Humblot, 1958.

Dollinger, Philippe. *The German Hansa*. Translated by D. S. Ault and S. H. Steinberg. Stanford, Calif.: Stanford University Press, 1970.

Dorn, Walter L. "The Prussian Bureaucracy in the Eighteenth Century, I–III." *Political Science Quarterly* 46–47 (1931–1932): 403–23, 75–83, 83–94.

Dorpalen, Andreas. *German History in Marxist Perspective: The East German Approach*. Detroit, Mich.: Wayne State University Press, 1985.

Dorwart, Reinhold August. *The Administrative Reforms of Frederick William I of Prussia*. Cambridge, Mass.: Harvard University Press, 1953.

———. *The Prussian Welfare State before 1740*. Cambridge, Mass.: Harvard University Press, 1971.

Duffy, Christopher. *Frederick the Great: A Military Life*. London: Routledge, 1988.

Eley, Geoff. *From Unification to Nazism: Reinterpreting the German Past*. Boston: Allen & Unwin, 1986.

Epstein, Klaus. *The Genesis of German Conservatism*. Princeton, N.J.: Princeton University Press, 1975.

Fay, Sidney Bradshaw. "The Hohenzollern Household and Administration in the Sixteenth Century." *Smith College Studies in History* 2 (1916): 1–64.

Fay, Sidney B., and Klaus Epstein. *The Rise of Brandenburg-Prussia to 1786*. New York: Holt Rinehart & Winston, 1964.

Feldman, Gerald D. *Army, Industry, and Labor in Germany 1914–1918*. Princeton, N.J.: Princeton University Press, 1966.

Fischer, Fritz. *From Kaiserreich to Third Reich: Elements of Continuity in German History 1871–1945*. Translated by Roger Fletcher. London: Allen & Unwin, 1986.

Folz, R. "Les assemblés d'états dans les principautés allemandes fin XIIIe–début XVIe siècle." *Gouvernés et Gouvernants* 4 (1965): 163–91.

Frederick the Great. *Anti-Machiavel*. Athens: Ohio University Press, 1981.

Gerschenkron, Alexander. *Bread and Democracy in Germany*. Ithaca, N.Y.: Cornell University Press, 1989.

Gillis, John R. *The Prussian Bureaucracy in Crisis, 1840–1860: Origins of an Administrative Ethos*. Stanford, Calif.: Stanford University Press, 1971.

Gooch, G. P. *Frederick the Great: The Ruler, the Writer, the Man*. New York: Alfred A. Knopf, 1947.

Górski, Karol. "La Ligue des Etats et les origines du régime representatif en Prusse." *Studies Presented to the International Commission for the History of Representative and Parliamentary Institutions* 23 (1960): 177–85.

———. "Die Anfänge der Repräsentation der *Communitas Nobilium* in Polen, im Ordensstaat Preussen und in Ungarn im Mittelalter." *Studies Presented to the International Commission for the History of Representative and Parliamentary Institutions* 36 (1966): 19–24.

Gray, Marion B. "Prussia in Transition: Society and Politics under the Stein Reform Ministry of 1808." *Transactions of the American Philosophical Society* 76, part 1 (1986): 19–21.

Grünthal, Günther. "Crown and Parliament in Prussia 1848–1866." *Parliaments, Estates and Representation* 5 (1985): 165–74.

Hagen, William W. "How Mighty the Junkers? Peasant Rents and Seigneurial Profits in Sixteenth-Century Brandenburg." *Past and Present* 108 (1985): 80–116.

Hamerow, Theodore S. *Restoration, Revolution, Reaction: Economics and Politics in Germany 1815–1871*. Princeton, N.J.: Princeton University Press, 1967.

Hartung, Fritz. *Deutsche Verfassungsgeschichte vom 15. Jahrhundert bis zur Gegenwart*. Eighth edition. Stuttgart: K. F. Koehler, 1950.

———. *Staatsbildende Kräfte der Neuzeit: Gesammelte Aufsätze*. Berlin: Duncker & Humblot, 1961.

———. "Der Aufgeklärte Absolutismus." *Studies Presented to the International Commission for the History of Representative and Parliamentary Institutions* 54 (1974): 54–76.

Helbig, Herbert. *Gesellschaft und Wirtschaft der Mark Brandenburg im Mittelalter*. Berlin: Walter de Gruyter, 1973.

Henderson, W. O. *Studies in the Economic Policy of Frederick the Great*. London: Frank Cass, 1963.

———. *The State and the Industrial Revolution in Prussia, 1740–1870*. Liverpool: Liverpool University Press, 1967.

Hintze, Otto. *Staat und Verfassung: Gesammelte Abhandlungen zur allgemeinen Verfassungsgeschichte*. Fritz Hartung, ed. Leipzig: Koehler & Amelang, 1941.

———. *Regierung und Verwaltung: Gesammelte Abhandlungen zur Staats-, Rechts-, und Sozialgeschichte Preussens*. Gerhard Oestreich, ed. Göttingen: Vandenhoeck & Ruprecht, 1967.

Hoffman, Wolfgang. "Prussian Town Councils in the 19th Century as Representative Institutions." In Commission Internationale pour l'Histoire des Assemblées d'Etats, *Liber Memorialis George de Lagarde*. Paris: Béatrice-Nauwelaerts, 1969.

Holborn, Hajo. *History of Germany*. Three volumes. Princeton, N.J.: Princeton University Press, 1982.

Horn, Norbert, and Jürgen Kocha, eds. *Recht und Entwicklung der Grossunternehmen im 19. und früh 20. Jahrhundert: Wirtschafts-, sozial- und rechtshistorische Untersuchungen zur Industrialisierung in Deutschland, Frankreich, England und den USA*. Göttingen: Vandenhoeck & Ruprecht, 1979.

Hubatsch, Walther. *Frederick the Great of Prussia: Absolutism and Administration*. London: Thames and Hudson, 1973.

Hughes, Michael. "Die Strafpreussen: Mecklenburg und der Bund der deutschen absolutistischen Fürsten, 1648–1719." *Parliaments, Estates and Representation* 3 (1983): 101–13.

———. *Nationalism and Society: Germany 1800–1945*. London: Edward Arnold, 1988.

Iggers, Georg. *The German Conception of History: The National Tradition of Historical Thought from Herder to the Present*. Middletown, Conn.: Wesleyan University Press, 1983.

———. *The Social History of Politics: Critical Perspectives in West German Historical Writing since 1945*. Leamington Spa, U.K.: Berg, 1985.

Ingrao, Charles W. *The Hessian Mercenary State: Ideas, Institutions, and Reform under Frederick II, 1760–1785*. Cambridge: Cambridge University Press, 1987.

Johnson, Hubert C. *Frederick the Great and His Officials*. New Haven, Conn.: Yale University Press, 1975.

Kehr, Eckart. *Battleship Building and Party Politics in Germany, 1894–1901*. Translated by Pauline R. Anderson and Eugene N. Anderson. Chicago: University of Chicago Press, 1975.

———. *Economic Interest, Militarism, and Foreign Policy: Essays on German History*. Berkeley and Los Angeles: University of California Press, 1977.

Kitchen, Martin A. *Military History of Germany from the Eighteenth Century to the Present*. Bloomington: Indiana University Press, 1975.

Koselleck, Reinhart. *Preußen zwischen Reform und Revolution: Allgemeines Landrecht, Verwaltung und soziale Bewegung von 1791 bis 1848*. Stuttgart: Ernst Klett, 1967.

Krieger, Leonard. *The German Idea of Freedom: History of a Political Tradition*. Chicago: University of Chicago Press, 1957.

Lidtke, Vernon L. *The Alternative Culture: Socialist Labor in Imperial Germany*. New York: Oxford University Press, 1985.

Maier, Charles S. *The Unmasterable Past: History, Holocaust, and German National Identity*. Cambridge, Mass.: Harvard University Press, 1988.

Mann, Golo. *Wallenstein: His Life Narrated*. Translated by Charles Kessler. New York: Holt Rinehart & Winston, 1976.

Meinecke, Friedrich. *The German Catastrophe: The Social and Historical Influences Which Led to the Rise and Ruin of Hitler and Germany*. Translated by Sidney B. Fay. Boston: Beacon Press, 1963.

Melton, James Van Horn. *Absolutism and the Eighteenth-Century Origins of Compulsory Schooling in Prussia and Austria*. Cambridge: Cambridge University Press, 1988.

Mitchell, Allan. "Bonapartism as a Model for Bismarckian Politics." *Journal of Modern History* 49 (1977): 181–95.

Moraw, Peter. "Cities and Citizenry as Factors of State Formation in the Roman-German Empire of the Late Middle Ages." *Theory and Society* 18 (1989): 631–62.

Mosse, George L. *The Crisis of German Ideology: Intellectual Origins of the Third Reich*. New York: Universal, 1964.

———. *The Nationalization of the Masses: Political Symbolism and Mass Movements in Germany from the Napoleonic Wars through the Third Reich*. New York: Meridian, 1977.

Oer, Rudolfine Freiin von. "*Quod omnes tangit* as Legal and Political Argument: Germany, Late Sixteenth Century." *Parliaments, Estates and Representation* 31 (1983): 1–6.

Oestreich, Gerhard. *Friedrich Wilhelm I.: Preußischer Absolutismus, Merkantilismus, Militarismus*. Göttingen: Musterschmidt, 1977.

Orlow, Dietrich. *Weimar Prussia 1918–1925: The Unlikely Rock of Democracy*. Pittsburgh, Pa.: University of Pittsburgh Press, 1986.

Paret, Peter. *Yorck and the Era of Prussian Reform 1807–15*. Princeton, N.J.: Princeton University Press, 1966.

———. *Clausewitz and the State: The Man, His Theories, and His Times*. Princeton, N.J.: Princeton University Press, 1985.

Pflanze, Otto. *Bismarck and the Development of Germany: The Period of Unification, 1815–1871*. Princeton, N.J.: Princeton University Press, 1973.

Puhle, Hans-Jürgen. *Von der Agrarkrise zum Präfaschismus: Thesen zum Stellenwert der agrarischen Interessenverbände in der deutschen Politik am Ende des 19. Jahrhunderts*. Wiesbaden: Franz Steiner, 1972.

———. *Agrarische Interessenpolitik und preußischer Konservatismus im wilhelminischen Reich (1893–1914): Ein Beitrag zur Analyse des Nationalismus in Deutschland am Beispiel des Bundes der Landwirte und der Deutsch-Konservativen Partei*. Bonn: Neue Gesellschaft, 1975.

Rabb, T. K. "The Effects of the Thirty Years' War on the German Economy." *Journal of Modern History* 35 (1962): 40–51.

Ritter, Gerhard. *Frederick the Great*. Berkeley and Los Angeles: University of California Press, 1968.

———. *The Sword and the Scepter: The Problem of Militarism in Germany*, Volume 1: *The Prussian Tradition, 1740–1890*. Miami, Fla.: University of Miami Press, 1969.

Rosenberg, Hans. "The Rise of the Junkers in Brandenburg-Prussia." *American Historical Review* 49 (1943): 1–22.

———. *Bureaucracy, Aristocracy and Autocracy: The Prussian Experience, 1660–1815*. Boston: Beacon Press, 1966.

Roth, Gunther. *The Social Democrats in Imperial Germany: A Study in Working-Class Isolation and National Integration*. Totowa, N.J.: Bedminster Press, 1963.

Schevill, Ferdinand. *The Great Elector*. Chicago: University of Chicago Press, 1947.

Schmidt, Eberhardt. *Rechtsentwicklung in Preussen*. Darmstadt: Wissenschaftliche Buchgesellschaft, 1961.

Schorske, Carl. *German Social Democracy, 1905–1917*. New York: Russell & Russell, 1970.

Sheehan, James J., ed. *Imperial Germany*. New York: New Viewpoints, 1976.

Simon, W. M. "Variations in Nationalism during the Great Reform Period in Prussia." *American Historical Review* 59 (1953–1954): 305–21.

———. *The Failure of the Prussian Reform Movement 1807–19*. Ithaca, N.Y.: Cornell University Press, 1955.

Stern, Fritz. *Politics of Cultural Despair: A Study in the Rise of the Germanic Ideology*. Berkeley and Los Angeles: University of California Press, 1961.

———. *Gold and Iron: Bismarck, Bleichröder, and the Building of the German Empire*. New York: Knopf, 1977.

Strauss, Gerald. *Law, Resistance, and the State: The Opposition to Roman Law in Reformation Germany*. Princeton, N.J.: Princeton University Press, 1986.

Topolski, Jerzy. "The Development of the Absolutist Prussian State and Prussia's Role in the Partition of Poland." *Polish Western Affairs* 22 (1981): 24–39.

Tümpel, Ludwig. *Die Entstehung des brandenburgisch-preussischen Einheitsstaates im Zeitalter des Absolutismus 1609–1806*. Breslau: M. u. H. Marcus, 1915.

Tuttle, Herbert. *History of Prussia to the Accession of Frederic the Great, 1134–1740*. Boston: Houghton Mifflin, 1884.

Vann, James A., and Steven W. Rowan, eds. *The Old Reich: Essays on German Political Institutions, 1495–1806*. Brussels: Les Editions de la Librarie Encyclopédique, 1974.

Veblen, Thorstein. *Imperial Germany and the Industrial Revolution*. Ann Arbor: University of Michigan Press, 1966.

Walker, Mack. *German Home Towns: Community, State, and General Estate 1648–1871*. Ithaca, N.Y.: Cornell University Press, 1971.

Wegert, Karl H. "Patrimonial Rule, Popular Self Interest, and Jacobinism in Germany, 1763–1800." *Journal of Modern History* 53 (1981): 440–67.

Wehler, Hans-Ulrich. *Bismarck und der Imperialismus*. Franfurt: Suhrkamp, 1985.

———. *Das deutsche Kaiserreich 1871–1918*. Göttingen: Vandenhoeck & Ruprecht, 1988.

Willems, Emilio. *A Way of Life and Death: Three Centuries of Prussian-German Militarism—An Anthropological Approach*. Nashville, Tenn.: Vanderbilt University Press, 1986.

RUSSIA

Billington, James H. *The Icon and the Axe: An Interpretive History of Russian Culture*. New York: Vintage, 1970.

Blackwell, William L., ed. *Russian Economic Development from Peter the Great to Stalin*. New York: New Viewpoints, 1974.

Blum, Jerome. "The Rise of Serfdom in Eastern Europe" *American Historical Review* 62 (1957): 807–36.

———. *Lord and Peasant in Russia: From the Ninth to the Nineteenth Century*. Princeton, N.J.: Princeton University Press, 1972.

Bushkovitch, Paul. *The Merchants of Moscow 1580–1660*. Cambridge: Cambridge University Press, 1980.

Carstensen, Fred V., and Gregory Guroff, eds. *Entrepreneurship in Imperial Russia and the Soviet Union*. Princeton, N.J.: Princeton University Press, 1983.

Crummey, R. O. "Russian Absolutism and the Nobility." *Journal of Modern History* 49 (1977): 456–67.

———. *Aristocrats and Servitors: The Boyar Elite in Russia, 1613–1689*. Princeton, N.J.: Princeton University Press, 1983.

Esper, Thomas. "Military Self Sufficiency and Weapons Technology in Muscovite Russia." *Slavic Review* 28 (1969): 185–208.

Fuhrmann, Joseph T. *Origins of Capitalism in Russia: Industry and Progress in the Sixteenth and Seventeenth Centuries*. Chicago: Quadrangle Books, 1972.

Geyer, Dietrich. *Russian Imperialism*. New Haven, Conn.: Yale University Press, 1977.

Halperin, Charles J. *Russia and the Golden Horde: The Mongol Impact on Medieval Russian History*. Bloomington: Indiana University Press, 1987.

Hellie, Richard. *Enserfment and Military Change in Muscovy.* Chicago: University of Chicago Press, 1971.

Hittle, J. Michael. *The Service City: State and Townsmen in Russia 1660–1800.* Cambridge, Mass.: Harvard University Press, 1979.

Hulbert, Ellerd. "Sixteenth-Century Russian Assemblies of the Land: Their Composition, Organization, and Competence." Doctoral thesis, Department of History, University of Chicago, 1970.

Jones, Robert E. *The Emancipation of the Russian Nobility, 1762–1785.* Princeton, N.J.: Princeton University Press, 1973.

Keep, J.L.H. "The Decline of the Zemsky Sobor." *The Slavic and East Europe Review* 36 (1957): 100–22.

———. *Soldiers of the Tsar: Army and Society in Russia 1462–1874.* Oxford: Clarendon Press, 1985.

Kluchevsky, V. O. *A History of Russia.* Five volumes. Translated by C. J. Hogarth. New York: Russell & Russell, 1960.

———. [Vasili Klyuchevsky]. *Peter the Great.* Translated by Liliana Archibald. Boston: Beacon Press, 1984.

LeDonne, John. *Ruling Russia: Politics and Administration in the Age of Absolutism, 1762–1796.* Princeton, N.J.: Princeton University Press, 1984.

McClelland, James C. *Autocracy and Academics: Education, Culture and Society in Tsarist Russia.* Chicago: University of Chicago Press, 1979.

McDaniel, Tim. *Autocracy, Capitalism, and Revolution in Russia.* Berkeley and Los Angeles: University of California Press, 1988.

Miller, Forrestt A. *Dmitrii Miliutin and the Reform Era in Russia.* Nashville, Tenn.: Vanderbilt University Press, 1968.

Orlovsky, Daniel T. *Limits of Reform: The Ministry of Internal Affairs in Imperial Russia 1802–81.* Cambridge, Mass.: Harvard University Press, 1981.

Pinter, W. Mc., and D. K. Rowney, eds. *Russian Officialdom: The Bureaucratization of Russian Society from the Seventeeth to the Twentieth Century.* Chapel Hill: University of North Carolina Press, 1980.

Pipes, Richard. *Russia under the Old Regime.* London: Weidenfeld & Nicolson, 1974.

Presniakov, A. E. *The Formation of the Great Russian State: A Study of Russian History from the Thirteenth to the Fifteenth Centuries.* Translated by A. E. Moorhouse. Chicago: Quadrangle Books, 1970.

Raeff, Marc, ed. *Peter the Great Changes Russia.* Lexington, Mass.: D. C. Heath, 1972.

———. *The Well-Ordered Police State: Social and Institutional Change through Law in the Germanies and Russia 1600–1800.* New Haven, Conn.: Yale University Press, 1983.

Robinson, Geroid Tanquary. *Rural Russia under the Old Régime: A History of the Landlord-Peasant World and a Prologue to the Peasant Revolution of 1917.* Berkeley and Los Angeles: University of California Press, 1972.

Starr, S. Frederick. *Decentralization and Self-Government in Russia, 1830–1870.* Princeton, N.J.: Princeton University Press, 1972.

Szeftel, Marc. "La participation des assemblées populaires dans le gouvernement central de la Russie depuis l'époque Kiévienne jusqu'à la fin du XVIIIe siècle." *Gouvernés et Gouvernants* 4 (1984): 239–65.

Vernadsky, George. *The Mongols and Russia*. New Haven, Conn.: Yale University Press, 1959.

Von Hagen, Mark. *Soldiers in the Proletarian Dictatorship: The Red Army and the Soviet Socialist State, 1917–1930*. Ithaca, N.Y.: Cornell University Press, 1990.

Von Laue, Theodore H. *Sergei Witte and the Industrialization of Russia*. New York: Columbia University Press, 1963.

Vucinich, Wayne S., ed. *The Peasant in Nineteenth-Century Russia*. Stanford, Calif.: Stanford University Press, 1968.

Walicki, Andrzej. *A History of Russian Thought from the Enlightenment to Marxism*. Stanford, Calif.: Stanford University Press, 1979.

Wirtschafter, Elise Kimerling. *From Serf to Russian Soldier*. Princeton, N.J.: Princeton University Press, 1990.

Wortman, Richard S. *The Development of Russian Legal Consciousness*. Chicago: University of Chicago Press, 1976.

Yaney, George. *The Systematization of Russian Government*. Champaign: University of Illinois Press, 1973.

———. *The Urge to Mobilize: Agrarian Reform in Russia, 1861–1930*. Champaign: University of Illinois Press, 1982.

Yanov, Alexander. *The Origins of Autocracy: Ivan the Terrible in Russian History*. Berkeley and Los Angeles: University of California Press, 1981.

———. *The Russian Challenge and the Year 2000*. Oxford: Basil Blackwell, 1987.

Yarmolinsky, Avrahm. *Road to Revolution: A Century of Russian Radicalism*. Princeton, N.J.: Princeton University Press, 1986.

SPAIN

Collins, Roger. *Early Medieval Spain: Unity in Diversity, 400–1000*. London: Macmillan, 1988.

Elliott, J. H. *The Revolt of the Catalans*. Cambridge: Cambridge University Press, 1963.

———. *Imperial Spain, 1469–1716*. New York: St. Martin's Press, 1964.

———. *The Count-Duke of Olivares: The Statesman in an Age of Decline*. New Haven, Conn.: Yale University Press, 1986.

Fernández, Pablo Albaladejo. "Cities and the State in Spain." *Theory and Society* 18 (1989): 721–32.

Herr, Richard. *Rural Change and Royal Finances in Spain at the End of the Old Regime*. Berkeley and Los Angeles: University of California Press, 1988.

Jago, Charles. "Habsburg Absolutism and the Cortes of Castile." *American Historical Review* 86 (1981): 307–26.

———. "Philip II and the Cortes of Castile: The Case of the Cortes of 1576." *Past and Present* 109 (1985): 24–43.

Lomax, Derek W. *The Reconquest of Spain*. London: Longmans, 1978.

Lourie, Elena. "A Society Organized for War: Medieval Spain." *Past and Present* 35 (1966): 54–76.

Lovett, A. W. *Early Habsburg Spain, 1517–1598.* Oxford: Oxford University Press, 1986.

Lynch, John. *Spain under the Habsburgs*, Volume 2: *Spain and America 1598–1700.* New York: Oxford University Press, 1969.

MacKay, Angus. *Spain in the Middle Ages: From Frontier to Empire, 1000–1500.* London: Macmillan, 1977.

———. *Society, Economy and Religion in Late Medieval Castile.* London: Variorum, 1987.

Parker, Geoffrey. "Mutiny and Discontent in the Spanish Army of Flanders 1572–1607." *Past and Present* 58 (1973): 38–52.

———. *Philip II.* Boston: Little, Brown, 1978.

Powers, James F. *A Society Organized for War: The Iberian Municipal Militias in the Central Middle Ages, 1000–1284.* Berkeley and Los Angeles: University of California Press, 1988.

Stradling, R. A. "Spain's Military Failure and the Supply of Horses, 1600–1660." *History* 69 (1984): 208–221.

———. *Philip IV and the Government of Spain, 1621–1665.* Cambridge: Cambridge University Press, 1988.

Thompson, I.A.A. *War and Government in Habsburg Spain, 1560–1620.* London: Athlone Press, 1976.

———. "The End of the Cortes of Castile." *Parliaments, Estates and Representation* 4 (1984): 125–33.

SWEDEN

Ågren, Kurt. "Rise and Decline of an Aristocracy: The Swedish Social and Political Elite in the 17th Century." *Scandinavian Journal of History* 1 (1976): 55–80.

Anderson, Roger Charles. *Naval Wars in the Baltic, 1522–1820.* London: Francis Edward, 1969.

Andersson, Ingvar. *A History of Sweden.* Stockholm: Natur och Kultur, 1962.

Andrén, Anders. "States and Towns in the Middle Ages: The Scandinavian Experience." *Theory and Society* 18 (1989): 585–610.

Åström, Sven-Erik. "The Role of Finland in the Swedish National and War Economies during Sweden's Period as a Great Power." *Scandinavian Journal of History* 11 (1986): 135–47.

Back, Pär E. "Diets in Ingria in the Seventeenth Century." In Commission Internationale pour l'Histoire des Assemblées d'Etats, *Liber Memorialis George de Lagarde.* Paris: Béatrice-Nauwelaerts, 1969.

Barudio, Günter. *Absolutismus: Zerstörung der "Libertären Verfassung": Studien zur "Karolinischen Eingewalt" in Schweden zwischen 1680 und 1693.* Wiesbaden: Franz Steiner, 1976.

———. *Gustav Adolf der Große: Eine politische Biographie.* Frankfurt: S. Fischer, 1982.

Böhme, Klaus-Richard. "Geld für die Schwedische Armee nach 1640." *Scandia* 33 (1982): 54–95.

Buchholz, Werner. *Staat und Ständegesellschaft in Schweden zur Zeit des Überganges vom Absolutismus zum Ständeparlamentarismus, 1718–1770.* Stockholm: Almqvist & Wiksell, 1979.

Ericsson, Birgitta, "Central Power and Local Right to Dispose over the Forest Common in Eighteenth-Century Sweden." *Scandinavian Journal of History* 5 (1980): 75–92.

———. "Central Power and Local Community." *Scandinavian Journal of History* 7 (1982): 173–76.

Gaunt, David. *Utbildning till Statens Tjänst: En Kollektivbiografi av Stormaktsidens Hovrättsauskultanter.* Uppsala: Akademisk Avhandling, 1975.

Gissel, Svend. "Agrarian Decline in Scandinavia." *Scandinavian Journal of History* 1 (1976): 43–54.

Gohlin, P. "Entrepreneurial Activities of the Swedish Aristocracy." *Explorations in Entrepreneurial History* 6 (1953): 43–63.

Hatton, R. M. *Charles XII of Sweden.* London: Weidenfeld & Nicolson, 1968.

Lindegren, Jan. *Utskrivning och Utsugning: Produktion och Reproduktion i Bygdeå 1620–1640.* Uppsala: Almqvist & Wiksell, 1980.

———. "The Swedish 'Military' State, 1560–1720." *Scandinavian Journal of History* 10 (1985): 305–36.

Lindkvist, Thomas. "Swedish Medieval Society: Previous Research and Recent Developments." *Scandinavian Journal of History* 4 (1979): 253–68.

Lönroth, Erik. "Representative Assemblies of Modern Sweden." *Studies Presented to the International Commission for the History of Representative and Parliamentary Institutions* 18 (1958): 123–32.

———. "Government in Medieval Scandinavia." *Gouvernés et Gouvernants* 4 (1966): 453–60.

Lundquist, L. Cl. *Council, King and Estates in Sweden 1713–1714.* Stockholm: Almqvist och Wiksell, 1975.

Metcalf, Michael F. "The First 'Modern' Party System? Political Parties, Sweden's Age of Liberty and the Historians." *Scandinavian Journal of History* 2 (1977): 265–87.

———. *Russia, England and Swedish Party Politics, 1762–1766: The Interplay between the Great Power Diplomacy and Domestic Politics during Sweden's Age of Liberty.* Totowa, N.J.: Rowman and Littlefield, 1977.

———. "Structuring Parliamentary Politics: Party Organization in Eighteenth-Century Sweden." *Parliaments, Estates and Representation* 1 (1981): 35–49.

Musset, Lucien. "Gouvernés et gouvernants dans le monde Scandinave et dans le monde Normande des XIe–XII siècles." *Gouvernés et Gouvernants* 2 (1968): 439–68.

Nordmann, Claude. *Grandeur et liberté de la Suéde 1660–1792.* Paris: Editions Nauwelaerts, 1971.

———. "l'Armée suédoise au XVIIe siècle." *Revue du Nord* 54 (1972): 133–47.

Palme, Sven Ulric. "The Bureaucratic Type of Parliament: The Swedish Estates during the Age of Liberty, 1719–1792." In Commission Internationale pour l'Histoire des Assemblées d'Etats, *Liber Memorialis George de Lagarde*. Paris: Béatrice-Nauwelaerts, 1969.

―――. "Vom Absolutismus zum Parlamentismus in Schweden." *Studies Presented to the International Commission for the History of Representative and Parliamentary Institutions* 37 (1969): 368–97.

―――. "Le parliamentisme en Suéde au XVIIIe siècle à l'époque de la liberté." *Studies Presented to the International Commission for the History of Representative and Parliamentary Institutions* 52 (1972): 243–48.

―――. "l'Homme libre dans les anciennes lois suèdoise." *Studies Presented to the International Commission for the History of Representative and Parliamentary Institutions* 56 (1979): 17–28.

―――. "Stände und König in Schweden während der Freiheitszeit: Die Königsversicherung von 1751." *Studies Presented to the International Commission for the History of Representative and Parliamentary Institutions* 59 (1982): 235–80.

Roberts, Michael. "The Constitutional Development of Sweden in the Reign of Gustav Adolph." *History* 24 (1940): 328–41.

―――. *Gustavus Adolphus: A History of Sweden, 1611–1632*. Two volumes. London: Longmans, Green, 1953–1958.

―――. *On Aristocratic Constitutionalism in Swedish History, 1520–1720*. London: Athlone, 1966.

―――. *Essays in Swedish History*. Minneapolis: University of Minnesota Press, 1967.

―――. *The Swedish Imperial Experience, 1560–1718*. Cambridge: Cambridge University Press, 1979.

―――. "Oxenstierna in Germany, 1633–1636." *Scandia* 48 (1982): 61–105.

―――. *The Age of Liberty: Sweden, 1719–1772*. Cambridge: Cambridge University Press, 1986.

―――. *The Early Vasas: A History of Sweden, 1523–1611*. Cambridge: Cambridge University Press, 1986.

―――, ed. *Sweden as a Great Power, 1611–1697: Government, Society, Foreign Policy*. London: Edward Arnold, 1968.

―――, ed. *Sweden's Age of Greatness, 1632–1718*. New York: St. Martin's Press, 1973.

Samuelsson, Kurt. *From Great Power to Welfare State: 300 Years of Swedish Social Development*. London: George Allen & Unwin, 1968.

Sarauw, Christian von. *Die Feldzüge Karl's XII: Ein Quellenmässiger Beitrag zur Kriegsgeschichte und Kabinetspolitik Europa's im XVIII. Jahrhundert*. Leipzig: von Bernhard Schlicke, 1881.

Sawyer, P. H. *Kings and Vikings: Scandinavia and Europe A.D. 700–1100*. London: Methuen, 1982.

Schück, Herman, "Sweden as an Aristocratic Republic." *Scandinavian Journal of History* 9 (1984): 65–72.

Soom, Arnold. "Die merkantilistische Wirtschaftspolitik Schwedens und die Baltischen Städte im 17. Jahrhundert." *Jahrbücher für Geschichte Osteuropas* 11 (1963): 183–222.

Tessin, Georg. *Die deutschen Regimenter der Krone Schweden*, Part 2: *Unter Karl XI. und Karl XII. (1660–1718)*. Cologne: Böhlau, 1967.

Tilton, Timothy A. "The Social Origins of Liberal Democracy: The Swedish Case." *American Political Science Review* 68 (1974): 561–71.

Tønnesson, Kåre. "Tenancy, Freehold and Enclosure in Scandinavia from the Seventeenth to the Nineteenth Century." *Scandinavian Journal of History* 6 (1981): 191–206.

VENICE

Bouwsma, William J. *Venice and the Defense of Republican Liberty: Renaissance Values in the Age of the Counter Reformation*. Berkeley and Los Angeles: University of California Press, 1984.

Lane, Frederic C. *Venice: A Maritime Republic*. Baltimore, Md.: Johns Hopkins University Press, 1987.

McNeill, William H. *Venice, the Hinge of Europe, 1081–1797*. Chicago: University of Chicago Press, 1974.

Mallett, M. E., and J. R. Hale. *The Military Organization of a Renaissance State: Venice c. 1400–1617*. Cambridge: Cambridge University Press, 1984.

Martines, Lauro. *Power and Imagination: City-States in Renaissance Italy*. Baltimore, Md.: Johns Hopkins University Press, 1988.

Queller, Donald E. *The Venetian Patriciate: Reality versus Myth*. Urbana: University of Illinois Press, 1986.

Index